Before Imagination

Before Imagination

EMBODIED THOUGHT FROM
MONTAIGNE TO ROUSSEAU

John D. Lyons

STANFORD UNIVERSITY PRESS
STANFORD, CALIFORNIA
2005

Stanford University Press
Stanford, California

Printed in the United States of America on acid-free,
archival-quality paper.

Library of Congress Cataloging-in-Publication Data

Lyons, John D., 1946-
    Before imagination : embodied thought from Montaigne to
Rousseau / John D. Lyons
        p. cm.
    Includes bibliographical references and index.
    ISBN 0-8047-5110-2 (cloth : alk. paper)
1. French literature–16th century–History and criticism.
2. French literature–17th century–History and criticism.
3. French literature–18th century–History and criticism.
4. Imagination in literature. 5. Philosophy, French–16th
century. 6. Philosophy, French–17th century. 7. Philosophy,
French–18th century. 8. Imagination (Philosophy) I. Title.

PQ145.1.I45 L96 2005
840.9'384–dc22

2005003042

Typeset by TechBooks in 11/14 Adobe Garamond and Expert

Original Printing 2005

Last figure below indicates year of this printing:
14 13 12 11 10 09 08 07 06 05

Assistance for the publication of this title was provided by the
University of Virginia.

For Gwydeon

Contents

Preface

Virginia Woolf begins *To the Lighthouse* with the description of Mrs. Ramsay's son, looking forward to an outing to the lighthouse. "Since he belonged," says the narrator, "even at the age of six, to that great clan which cannot keep this feeling separate from that, but must let future prospects, with their joys and sorrows, cloud what is actually at hand, since to such people even in earliest childhood any turn in the wheel of sensation has the power to crystallize and transfix the moment upon which its gloom or radiance rests, James Ramsay, sitting on the floor cutting out pictures from the illustrated catalogue of the Army and Navy Stores, endowed the picture of a refrigerator, as his mother spoke, with heavenly bliss."[i] Little James Ramsay is not a philosopher, nor is he an artist. When he endows the illustrated refrigerator with the joy of a future trip to the shore, he does not do, in the storyteller's view, anything especially "creative." But he *is*, within a long tradition of European culture, using his imagination. He has fused one *image* with another and blended one day with the idea of the following day, thus losing control of the present time. As Woolf describes this small event within the mind of her character, she conveys disapproval of the "clan" of those who create such confusions. This disapproval is entirely consonant with Stoic warnings about misuse of the impressions that flow through our minds. James Ramsay, had he been a student of Epictetus, would have known better.

And he would have known better if had grown up in the great revival of imaginative practice that occurred, concurrently with a rediscovery of Stoic philosophy, in early-modern Europe. Instead of confusing the pleasure of the lighthouse with a refrigerator, he might have used the picture with more awareness. As did a young French woman (who would later become a nun at Port-Royal under the name Geneviève de l'Incarnation) one afternoon in 1629 when she stepped into the church of Saint Gervais in the Marais. There she had a series of thoughts that were part of her transformation from a lay person who pitied the cloistered nuns of Port-Royal de Paris to a postulant in that convent:

> I withdrew to a place apart, contrary to my routine, so that I would see no one and be seen by no one. From my retreat I looked at that church, which is a venerable Parisian edifice, and one of the largest and most beautiful sanctuaries that one can find. Its antiquity made me think of eternity. I pondered the idea that everything I was looking at was perishable, fragile, and ephemeral—which brought me extreme sorrow, because I very much loved this present life and these changes made me see that I was passing just as other things were.[ii]

What the young woman did in the church was not purely spontaneous but fits the pattern of a planned meditation of the kind set forth in contemporary manuals like *The Introduction to the Devout Life* by François de Sales. Meditations of this sort guided devout persons through a set of images and other purely mental sensory perceptions that supported and reinforced a pattern of reasoning and a set of values. As she pictured the "changes" that would occur in the future, as this ancient sanctuary crumbled over time, the young believer was making use of a faculty or a way of thinking that had recently been strongly promoted in religious and philosophical circles: imagination.

Now the importance of imagination in the early-modern period, and specifically between 1580 and 1680, may come as a surprise. "The Enlightenment created the idea of the imagination," correctly writes an important and informed scholar.[iii] Imagination as we know it, and as scores of books and hundreds of articles have described it, did not exist before the eighteenth century and would not have become a staple of the literary studies if Romanticism had not taken imagination as one of its crucial values. This, of course, is what we call today "the creative imagination"—a curious and even redundant expression, since imagination is often thought to be a synonym for creativity, and there would be lots of blank stares if one referred to something as "the uncreative imagination."[iv] Through imagination we are sometimes thought to reach the essence of art, the secret of poetry, the source of happiness, and the ultimate fusion with nature and the cosmos. And recent use of the term identifies imagination directly with metaphorical expression.[v]

Today, imagination is popularly considered to be a great endowment. People, and even institutions, are criticized for not having "enough" imagination or for not using their imagination.[vi] Mary Carruthers begins her influential *The Book of Memory*, "When we think of our highest creative power, we think invariably of the imagination. 'Great imagination, profound intuition,' we say: this is our highest accolade for intellectual achievement."[vii] According to a contemporary, "The greatness of Einstein lies in his tremendous imagination . . . ."[viii]

Our easy and enthusiastic acceptance of imagination is, however, a stumbling block when we attempt to understand writers of earlier periods because the word "imagination" was associated for centuries with a sharply different set of powers, achievements, and challenges. For us, the central quality of imagination is its creativity—Carruthers's reference to the "highest creative power" is eloquent—its capacity to innovate, to foresee, and to produce ideas rapidly and effortlessly. To say of someone "she is very imaginative" is the equivalent of saying that she is creative and does not lack for new ideas. In early-modern Europe, however, imagination was neither the highest and most prized intellectual gift nor was it, above all else, creative. René Descartes defined imagination very concisely, in 1637, as "a special way of thinking for material things" (*une façon de penser particulière pour les choses matérielles*).[xi] In other words, people would use their imagination when they needed to think about physical things, about things that they could see, smell, touch, hear, and taste. Sometimes, of course, these things might be new, or at least new combinations of things. But they might also be old things, things that we remember and for which imagination restores the sensory detail.

This book is a brief account of the importance of imagination before the Romantic promotion of this way of thinking as a kind of panacea and before critics of this faculty—anti-Romantic rationalists—had seized on imagination as the enemy, the eternal foe of reason and civilization. In a broader historical perspective, we can see the Enlightenment "creation" of imagination as the resurgence of polarized Platonic views of thought that gained renewed currency in the sixteenth century and achieved even wider influence in the eighteenth and nineteenth centuries. This study is devoted to the culture of imagination in a single century—there are already an immense number of studies that trace the theory of imagination from the pre-Socratics to the twentieth century—because the hundred years or so after the publication of Montaigne's *Essays* constitute an exceptional and neglected moment in the history of imagination.

It is worth repeating and stressing Descartes' definition of imagination: "a special way of thinking for material things." Most people, Descartes writes, do not raise their mind "beyond things of the senses" and thus think exclusively by using imagination. Of course this is only a partial description of imagination, but it is important to recognize Descartes's consistency in telling us that we *imagine*, strictly speaking, only when we think about *material* things, things that we perceive, seem to perceive, or could perceive with our senses. The very fact that we find it difficult to avoid the broader, more modern use of the verb "to imagine"—meaning to speculate or to contemplate alternative possibilities—may be a result of Descartes' own success in rehabilitating imagination. He writes in the second meditation that "imagining is nothing other than contemplating the figure or image of a bodily thing."[x] This statement follows the traditional view of the act of imagining, by which the mind registers and combines sense data, received from the senses through the "common sense" for processing by the faculties.

Associating imagination with the perception of the physical world, Descartes adheres to a broad view of imagination common to philosophical schools from the pre-Socratics up to the seventeenth century. Imagination, *phantasia*, is a type of thought that concerns sensation.[xi] The status of imagination, whether it is good or bad, has rested on more basic attitudes toward the nature of reality. If the material world is seen as bad or fallen, thought that is based on the perception of the material world is itself bad. In European thought through the centuries, the theory of imagination has usually been divided into Platonic and Aristotelian currents. The Platonic current rather dualistically sees imagination both as a dangerous faculty linked to the deceptive material world (following the *Sophist* and the *Theaetetus*) and, on the other hand (following the *Phaedrus*), as an almost numinous source of inspiration. The Aristotelian current takes a nonjudgmental, rather pragmatic approach toward imagination, seeing it as an inevitable part of most thought processes.[xii] Everything that we think of as material—whether remembered, perceived in the present, conceived as fictitious or hypothetical, expected, or dreamed—is thus, in the broad tradition of imagination (*phantasia*) the work of imagining. Conversely, thoughts that do not take the form of sense perception (or the simulation of sense perception) do not make use of imagination.[xiii]

The close association of imagination with the senses, and therefore with the body, has become so foreign to the post-Romantic world, that the early-modern way of using the mind to simulate bodily experience is often very strange. It might be best, then, to think of this study as a prehistory of imagination, for it describes a world of thought so radically different from the one we know that it is sometimes hard to hold together the contrasting things with the same word. Some readers may protest that the *word* "imagination" was simply used in the early-modern period for an entirely separate cultural practice. Others may complain that since reason and imagination are antithetical it makes no sense to write about the latter during the "age of reason," when imagination could only have been obscure and marginal.

Yet careful consideration of the culture of early-modern Europe helps us understand why imagination, as the form of thought that mediates between the body and the intellect, was central and crucial to themes that are widely recognized as typical of this period. We know that writers of the late Renaissance and the seventeenth century were often concerned with such themes as concealment, disguise, sociability, interiority, and mortality. For example, the development of an "inner" life of the mind, so often supposed to be a spiritual quest motivated by religious aims, is not really so distinct from the development of the tactical or strategic imagination necessary to the courtier.[xiv] In both cases, religious and worldly, the mind produces images and other sensory representations that are different from the world immediately present, and these images are frequently guarded carefully from the other people present. On reflection it seems unsurprising that both worldly and religious innerness is intensified during the same epoch since individual initiative in both religion and politics was "privatized" and partitioned in a way that made social interaction a skill of veiling, withholding, and mirroring.[xv] Not being able to take direct initiatives to control the world made it desirable to create inner alternatives to the outside world. So that the seventeenth century took for granted a general absent-mindedness—that is, the habit of supposing that people were always thinking something that they were not saying. People were in some important sense not *present* and engaged in their physical surroundings because they were expected, and even taught, to keep their minds on something else. It was this classical absent-mindedness that led to the Romantic revolt in favor of sincerity and spontaneity, a complete reversal of the seventeenth-century concept of civility. Such an absent-mindedness is recommended by religious authors (like François de Sales) as well as by secular ones (like Nicolas Faret and the Chevalier de Méré) and accompanies advice on developing the inner faculties, including imagination.[xvi]

As we consider contemporary seventeenth-century accounts of this inner life of the imaginative mind, we can discern the early stages of the movement toward the reconfiguration of thought that ends by setting up the opposition of reason and imagination and splitting the "creative" imagination, often assigned to an élite of prophetic and (or) asocial artists, from the practical imagination as experienced by a wide variety of people. Among the paradoxes that result from this glimpse of the early-modern period is the assertion that "classical" French culture is actually more egalitarian—more inclined to empower a broad cross-section of the population—in many respects than the Romantic culture with its disdain for the ordinary and the practical. Significantly, it is toward the end of the seventeenth century that imagination begins to appear in texts that include the term "genius" (*génie*) just before the eighteenth century assigns a quite different role to imagination than the one dominant before the Quarrel of the Ancients and the Moderns.

This study begins with the renewal of the third great source of ideas about imagination, alongside Platonic and Aristotelian doctrines, the Stoic philosophy that had such great impact on European writers like Michel de Montaigne in the late sixteenth century. Stoic thought, which survived in rhetorical as well as philosophical texts, was a major force when the *Essais* appeared (1580) because of its emphasis on individual practice and self-reformation. Even if Montaigne's early and enthusiastic adherence to Stoicism may have became nuanced and complicated as the writer matured, he gives vivid illustrations of the way imagination could form part of everyday life through the daily Stoic practice of imagining death. The practice that Montaigne developed under the influence of Stoicism may not seem to everyone to be an orthodox Stoicism, but this is a strand of thought that took root and flourished during the following century. This Stoic and secular practice blended with Christian influences in the work of François de Sales (as it had earlier in Ignatius of Loyola) in one of the true bestsellers of the French tradition, the *Introduction to the Devout Life*, which showed how thoughts based on intense sensory experience could be used for inner religious purposes.

After Montaigne and François de Sales imagination, as a deliberately cultivated part of daily life, never lost its association with death during the seventeenth century. Is this because the mind's relation to the body is, throughout that period, inevitably colored by religious admonitions about the soul's separation from its material frame? Is it because death is a unique challenge to thought? Is it because the verbal and visual representations of death were both central to the arts—in the forms of elegy, epic, and tragedy in literature, and paintings and statues of martyrdom and, above all, the Passion—and subject to practical and doctrinal limits? Although the imagination of death is not the focus of this study, it is a recurrent part of the account that we trace, alongside the imagination of love, of material inventions, of the cosmos, and of the minute processes of the body itself.

Montaigne's reflections on the role of imagination in our everyday life were not limited to his own use of imagination in meditative exercises. He also wrote insightfully about the centrality of sense-based thinking in the way human beings see themselves in society, in the social control exerted by institutions, and in the views that people adopt about the world, or cosmos, in the broadest sense. This aspect of Montaigne's thought is the basis for Blaise Pascal's ideas on how to put imagination to work in everyday life. His contrast between the analytic or geometric mindset and *finesse* is at least partly a distinction between abstract and concrete ways of thinking. In recommending *finesse* for most everyday situations—and most important, for persuading people of the truth of Pascal's own, Christian message—Pascal shows how important it is to develop the skill of making mental pictures of complex and realistic situations.

Another reader of Montaigne's *Essais*, Marie de Rabutin-Chantal, Marquise de Sévigné—who called François de Sales her grandfather—, is well known for her cultivation of the genre of the intimate letter and for her exemplary, even hyperbolic, performance of motherhood. Her preference for sense-based thinking appears in the descriptive detail of her letters, where her mind is always in at least two, and usually three, places at once: the scene of her act of writing, the incidents or places that she has recently witnessed or heard about and that she describes for her correspondent, and the situation of her correspondent. She urges her readers to "imagine" what she is writing about and she expresses her effort to imagine her correspondent, usually her daughter. Beyond this structure of the multiple scene of the letter exchange, common to many epistolary novels as to other collections of correspondence, however, Sévigné picks up Montaigne's Stoic invocation of the theme of change, loss, and death, seized in the concrete description of everyday life. A major subject of many of her letters is the death scene, particularly sudden death, described in exquisite sensory detail and explicitly presented as the subject for meditation.

Sévigné's letters indicate a taste for physical detail that might incline us to suppose that all her contemporaries shared her aesthetic preference for imagination over abstract conceptualization. Yet two of Sévigné's friends, Madeleine de Scudéry and Marie-Madeleine Pioche de La Vergne (Madame de Lafayette), wrote important novels based on radically conflicting views of the value of imagination. Scudéry guided her readers to imagine in detail the rich scenes she includes in her novels, as we can see in examples from *Clélie*. And Scudéry's characters use their imaginations in situations ranging from political intrigue to sexual relations at a distance. Lafayette does exactly the opposite in her *The Princess of Clèves*, where readers are given few clues as to the physical reality of the characters' world and where the characters, if they use their imagination, suffer as a consequence.

Lafayette's anti-imaginative aesthetic is one of the first intimations of the coming Quarrel of the Ancients and the Moderns, in which both sides of the Quarrel reject the view that using imagination is a good thing to do. The single most important text written during the Quarrel that makes abundant use of imagination, Fénelon's *The Adventures of Telemachus*, simply exemplifies its author's belief that imagination is for immature minds. Writing a pedagogical work addressed to a child, the young Duc de Bourgogne, Fénelon tactically stressed sensory detail because he believed that the brain of the young person was soft and impressionable, incapable of abstract reasoning. Several decades later, another educational reformer, Jean-Jacques Rousseau, wrote his *Emile, or on Education*, in which he definitively laid to rest the independent, active, inward-turning discipline of imagination in favor of a passive, and outward-turning receptive "sensibility."

Our investigation will draw mostly on already well-known books, texts that form part of the literary canon and the tradition of high culture. These works offer the advantage of their greater availability compared to other potential documents. By reading them with renewed attention to a specific practice, we can get a fresh look at works we may think we know quite well but that take on significantly different meaning when read with a view to the positive and concrete qualities of early-modern imagination. The use of imagination that they describe is not restricted to creative endeavors, nor does it suppose unusual mental gifts.

Finally, it is important to emphasize that this study is neither exhaustive nor encyclopedic. Many other texts could be brought forth to show how people used imagination in this period. The current of thought traced in this book is formed of *positive* views of imagination. It must be admitted that there are still, as there were for centuries before, negative portrayals of imagination as a pathology. Molière's comedy, for instance, vividly stages the experiences of its characters in the grip of an out of control imagination. *The Imaginary Invalid* still amuses theatre audiences, but it is only one of many plays, poems, and novels that show characters in the grip of a delusion. With a few exceptions, the chapters that follow unfold the less-known story of people who found imagination useful and valuable.

Acknowledgments

In the past few years, several important studies have broken with the tradition that looked at imagination either as a strictly negative phenomenon or as a highly specialized practice. Thomas Pavel's *L'Art de l'éloignement. Essai sur l'imagination classique* (1996) has explored the distance between the exterior world and the inner world of the cultured person and showed the way literary and dramatic works nourished this inner world. Marie-Hélène Huet's *Monstrous Imagination* (1993) explored beliefs concerning the impact of the mother's thought on the body of her child. Gérard Ferreyrolles's *Les Reines du monde* (1995) showed the huge role of imagination in Pascal's thought. These books provide the present study with specific insights and the encouragement to contribute to the lively renewal of our understanding of the culture that is variously described as classical, neoclassical, baroque, or early modern.

I owe much to colleagues who have generously shared their ideas with me and encouraged my project on imagination. Most of all I am indebted to Virginia Krause, George Hoffmann, John Campbell, Mary McKinley, Terence Cave, Thomas Pavel, Noel Peacock, Richard Goodkin, Tom Conley, Neil Kenny, Sara Melzer, Jean-Robert Armogathe, François Rigolot, Michèle Longino, and Daniel Russell. As I learned more about this topic, I discovered the research of other scholars working on similar projects. It has been very rewarding to learn from them and to exchange thoughts on our shared discoveries. I particularly wish to mention Rebecca Wilkin's dissertation at the University of Michigan, *Feminizing Imagination in France, 1563–1678*. Claudia Swan, director of the Program in the Study of Imagination at Northwestern University, has done much to provide an interdisciplinary forum for scholarship in this area. I owe much to The John Simon Guggenheim Memorial Foundation and the University of Virginia for their generosity in giving me the time to reflect and write during the final stages of the work.

Before Imagination

Introduction

When Descartes wrote that imagination is "a special way of thinking for material things" and that most people are limited in their pursuit of philosophical knowledge by their habit of relying exclusively on the imagination and thus do not go "beyond things of the senses," he was entirely within the traditional definition still prevalent in his day. There was a broad consensus since the time of Aristotle that imagination is a sense-oriented way of thinking that connects reason, on one hand, to sense perception on the other. As Gianfrancesco Pico wrote in the early sixteenth century, "phantasy has its starting-point in sense" and the Port-Royal *Logic*, in the late seventeenth century, declares vigorously that "it is . . . absurd to wish to imagine something that is not physical."[1]

The term *phantasia* seems to have made its first appearance in Plato's *Republic*, though without a definition.[2] According to Gerard Watson, *phantasia* in Plato's middle dialogues is "the combination of *doxa* and *aisthesis*" in thinking, in other words, it is not pure sensation but sensation combined with thought so that an account can be given of the sensation, thus distinguishing between sensation and perception and alerting the readers of the

Theatetus not to take the senses for granted.[3] In the *Sophist, phantasia* also appears as the term for thinking based on the appearances, coming from the senses, in the changing world (the world which is beneath the unchanging world available only to the intellect).[4] The infrequent and dispersed references to *phantasia* in Plato are followed by the much more substantial and consistent view presented in Aristotle, particularly in *On the Soul* (often called *De Anima*), where "Aristotle gave the first extended analytical description as a distinct faculty of the soul."[5] Thereafter virtually all writing on imagination included a commentary on Aristotle, or combined his ideas with Plato's earlier and less systematic comments on what Plato often calls *eikastike.* The Platonic influence on the theory of imagination, though congenial to Romantic views, was less important in the scholastic tradition that was the basis of Descartes's comment, a comment that is echoed in the less learned contexts of the earliest French dictionaries.[6] Through Aquinas and the Catholic tradition, the Aristotelian definition of imagination (*phantasia*) as a faculty concerned with sense was transmitted to Descartes and most French writers of the seventeenth century.[7]

Most of Aristotle's teachings on imagination, that is, *phantasia* (from *phainesthai*, appear, and ultimately from *phaos*, light) are in *De Anima* III, 3.[8] This short and confusing chapter has given commentators much to do over the centuries.[9] The basic elements of the psychic organization that Aristotle lays out are sensation, imagination, judgment, and memory, with another more fleetingly defined faculty—very important for the medieval tradition—called the common sense (*koinon aistheterion*) that coordinated the arriving sense data.[10] Sensation itself is generally considered to be "external" while the common sense, imagination, judgment, and memory are the "inner senses."[11] Imagination is apparently the form of thinking that corresponds to a sense perception, but imagination (in humans, at least) is not limited to the immediate, present stimulus. Imagination receives, arranges, retrieves, classifies, and combines the sense data, and if we did not have imagination, we would not know the color blue when we close our eyes. Wine tasting would be impossible, since as soon as we turned from a glass of merlot to a cabernet franc we would lose all knowledge of the first flavor and could never compare it to the next. And unless we had a thermometer handy, we would be unable to answer a question as simple as "Is it hot outside today?" If we see something, we imagine it, for sense perception arrives in the mind through imagination.[12] If we remember what something we saw looked like, we imagine it, since imagination is the presence in the mind of sense data from past experiences. And if we form the mental impression of something we have not seen, tasted, smelled, heard or touched, we also imagine it, by combining elements of what we are now or have in the past perceived. In this way we can imagine the result of accidentally using salt instead of sugar in making the filling of a fruit tart. In regard to the past, much of what we call simply "memory" is actually the work of imagination, though not all memories use imagination. For instance, if we recall that we have eaten rhubarb pie but do not remember the taste (and do not picture the occasion), then our memory is simply an intellectual conception and does not include the sensation that only imagination could contribute. These applications of "imagination" or *phantasia* would not have been at all surprising to Aristotle nor to centuries of his followers, yet to describe these everyday activities as "imaginative" would now appear unusual and rather quaint. It is tempting to say that the Aristotelian conception of imagination is actually broader and richer than our modern one, since we imagine—in Aristotelian terms—not only when we are producing hypothetical, unreal, or particularly novel ideas but almost constantly, whenever we are thinking in ways that are not abstract, that is, without a trace of any sensation. In fact, the difference between Aristotle's *phantasia* and what we usually mean by "imagination" in the nineteenth century and after is *so* great that we might be tempted to avoid using the term *imagination* in discussing Aristotle and his followers. Just the same, there is a stronger reason in favor of sticking with the term: the writers of the sixteenth and seventeenth centuries chose the words *fantasy* (or *fantaisie* in French) and imagination not only—in most cases—with knowledge of the tradition but also quite explicitly in order to convey the concept of thinking in concrete, physical, and sensory terms.[13]

Important aspects of Aristotle's *phantasia* are that it always contains sense perceptions, that it is a way of thinking (rather than entirely identical to the senses themselves), that it is something that we *can* do because we will to do so (though, in the case of dreams or sickness we lose this control over imagination as we do over other faculties), and that *phantasia* gives us freedom from constraints of time and place: we are not dependent on circumstance in order to think in sensory terms and in fact we are not dependent on the constraints of judgment itself:

> For imagination is different from either perceiving or discursive thinking, though it is not found without sensation, or judgment without it. That this activity is not the same kind of thinking as judgment is obvious. For imagining lies within our own power whenever we wish (e.g. we can call up a picture, as

in the practice of mnemonics by the use of mental images), but in forming opinions we are not free: we cannot escape the alternative of falsehood or truth.[14]

Aristotle says that sense is always present, but imagination is not always present. Sense is also always true, but imagination is "for the most part false" (428a17).[15] Imagination cannot be, for Aristotle, a blend of opinion and sensation, because "the content of the supposed opinion cannot be different from that of the sensation (I mean that imagination must be the blending of the perception of white with the opinion that it is white: it could scarcely be a blend of the opinion that it is good with the perception that it is white," 428a25). It seems, then, that imagination is not simply sensation but the consciousness that we are sensing something and the identification of what we are sensing (even if we misidentify it). Dorothea Frede suggests that one function of *phantasia* is, in Aristotle's view, to synthesize the sense perceptions in such a way that the fragmentary and momentary nature of each is overcome. In her example, "when I let my eyes glide over the different books on my bookshelves there is always just the piecemeal vision of this or that coloured object; the *overall impression* of all the different books (including those behind my back) would then be already a *phantasia*, a synthesis of what I perceive right now and what I have perceived a second ago."[16] This is a good example of how imagination can function in the present and in the presence of the object of perception, and not solely in the past or in speculative and composite sense data.

In distinguishing between imagination and discursive thinking, Aristotle gave imagination the in-between role that it continued to play in the work of subsequent thinkers, an in-between or mixed quality that later earns it praise from some and condemnation from others. Aristotle seems to have wanted to give the soul a certain freedom both with respect to the perceived world and to the judgments of truth and falsehood of discursive thinking.

The vast territory that Aristotle assigned to *phantasia*, while still recognized by philosophers for thousands of years, has gone unrecognized in ordinary usage, particularly in the past century. Aristotle's *phantasia* (like Descartes's *imagination*) was a broad faculty or function of the mind that included what we have now divided into immediate perception, memory, and "imagination." The latter being the specific ability to call to mind images (and other sensory details) of things that are absent, particularly when they are not considered memory images. The work of the early-modern writers studied later in this book is largely an effort to construct or reconstruct this broader understanding of imagination as a deliberate mental activity through which we experience the sensory details of the past, the present, and the possible.[17]

STOIC TRAINING OF THE IMAGINATION

For the Stoics *phantasia* was even more important than it had been for the Aristotelians, and this emphasis was extremely influential in the sixteenth and seventeenth centuries because of the vigorous renewal of Stoic thought, and the particular influence of the three great exponents of the Late Stoa: Seneca, Epictetus, and Marcus Aurelius. As A.A. Long writes, in Stoicism "*phantasia* has a centrality that it lacks in Plato and Aristotle."[18] And Dan Flory has described the Stoic doctrine of imagination in terms of a missing link between ancient and modern conceptions of imagination, the occluded doctrine that lies between Plato and Aristotle, on one hand, and Enlightenment and Romanticism on the other.[19] The Stoic description of the soul included the mind, or "governing principle" (*hegemonikon*), an undivided thinking power that included various functions, chiefly *phantasia*, impulse (*horme*), and assent (*synkatathesis*).[20] The latter allows us to control the impulses that we have upon the presence of certain *phantasiai*. For the Stoics, if we are thinking, we are having *phantasiai* or representations that are presented to our "governing principle" (the *hegemonikon*) for assent. This is a basic and inescapable fact of consciousness. Our task is to deal with this stream of representations or sense impressions.[21] In the following pages, let us consider the later Roman Stoics, who were much read and quoted by the Early Modern writers Montaigne, du Vair, and Lipsius. Moreover, although Seneca was the first of the three great Roman Stoic authors, in some ways his rather easily adapted and flexible approach brings him closer to later modern writers. We will therefore look first at Epictetus and Marcus Aurelius, who wrote in Greek and thus have a certain continuity in terminology with the Middle Stoa.

Epictetus was an important teacher of Stoic philosophy at the turn of the first century of the common era. His teachings survive in two texts: a synopsis known as the *Manual* or *Encheiridion* and a transcription by his disciple Arrian of some of his lessons, known as the *Discourses*. The first printed edition of the Greek text of these two works appeared in Venice in

1535, followed by Latin translations in 1554 and 1560.[22] The use of *phantasiai* was the core endeavor of the Stoic sage, in Epictetus's view:

> the gods have put under our control only the most excellent faculty of all and that which dominates the rest, namely, the power to make correct use of external impressions [*phantasiais*], but all the others they have not put under our control.[23]

The external impressions are not themselves the highest faculty, but managing them is the power on which depends our mental and our moral life. Reason itself is defined with reference to these external impressions:

> for what purpose have we received reason from nature? For the proper use of external impressions. What, then, is reason itself? Something composed out of a certain kind of external impressions. Thus it comes naturally to be also self-contemplation (1:134–35).

In describing these representations or external impressions, Epictetus mentions the margin of freedom that our mind has in relation to the material world that we perceive, for our representations are not necessarily *real* external things:

> The external impressions [*phantasiai*] come to us in four ways, for either things are, and seem so to be; or they are not, and do not seem to be, either; or they are, and do not seem to be; or they are not, and yet seem to be. Consequently, in all these cases it is the business of the educated man to hit the mark (1:168–69).

In dealing with these representations our aim is not simply to have accurate sensory data about what is present to us but to form habits in the way we perceive things and to become skilled in tactics to moderate the impact of certain dangerous sensory impressions and to amplify those that are useful. For Epictetus, then, *phantasia* is also *imagination* in the narrower, modern sense of mental representation of what is not immediately present to us in the physical world:

> To-day when I saw a handsome lad or a handsome woman I did not say to myself, "Would that a man might sleep with her," and "Her husband is a happy man," for the man who uses the expression "happy" of the husband means "Happy is the adulterer" also; I do not even picture to myself the next scene—the woman herself in my presence, disrobing and lying down

by my side. I pat myself on the head and say, Well done, Epictetus, you have solved a clever problem, one much more clever than the so-called "Master" (1:344–45).

Epictetus stresses that we have control over the pictures in our mind, even if the first one is simply given by the senses and comes to us without our choice. However, one image leads to another, and those other images, either from our repertory of memories or from a combination of those memories and the new sight that has just struck us, are ones we choose to have or not to have. The *phantasia* that sets off this struggle is best confronted with the active production of opposing images, the images of the wise men of the past. The best way to be prepared for the occasional tempting encounter as it appeals to our external senses is to develop an opposing internal repertory and habit of counterimages. Thus, in the occasion (and this can be a *phantasia* that awakens desire, as in Epictetus's example here, or one that provokes fear or sadness, as similar passages in Seneca show) one first combats the immediacy and vividness of the impression by examining it, and then one deals with the subsequent sequence of mental images by substituting alternatives:

> after that, do not suffer it to lead you on by picturing to you what will follow. Otherwise, it will take possession of you and go off with you wherever it will. But do you rather introduce and set over against it some fair and noble impression, and throw out this filthy one (1:346–47).

For Epictetus the mind develops itself for good not by shutting out sense impressions but by developing skill in confronting and appropriately recognizing them. This leads him to insist on practice or exercise in receiving the impressions of the outside world as an endeavor comparable to that of the athlete: "The man who exercises himself against such external impressions is the true athlete in training" (1:346–47). In a chapter entitled "How ought we to exercise ourselves to deal with the impressions of our senses?" (*phantasias gymnasteon*), Epictetus produces a list of events in which the experienced "athlete" of *phantasia* is not carried away by the image nor does he generate a dangerous set of associated images, as might the ordinary person.[24] Thus, "His ship is lost. What happened? His ship is lost. He was carried off to prison. What happened? He was carried off to prison" (2:60–61).[25] In another chapter on the force of habit in dealing with sense impressions, "On Training" (*Peri askeseos*), Epictetus recommends going beyond simple acceptance of sense impressions toward the active cultivation of sense impressions that we initially dislike.[26] One interesting aspect of Epictetus's technique of training is that, on one hand, it is familiar to us, and yet, on the other hand, we locate it in a very different domain from imagination. We would call some of this training "behavioral therapy" or "Pavlovian conditioning," because it is so centered on the body and, thus, on the external senses. Here is what Epictetus recommends for overcoming aversions:

> I am inclined to pleasure; I will betake myself to the opposite side of the rolling ship, and that beyond measure, so as to train myself. I am inclined to avoid hard work; I will strain and exercise my sense-impressions [*phantasias*] to this end, so that my aversion from everything of this kind shall cease (2:82–83).

For Epictetus, this kind of habit-formation is *not* purely external; it is not meant to produce some kind of reflex that does not involve the mind (it is not sure that Epictetus would have understood the idea of a subconscious reflex), but rather the build-up of an association in the mind between certain sensory impressions and certain patterns of assent. Epictetus says specifically that this training is *not* an outward but an inward exercise: "if you allow training to turn outwards, towards the things that are not in the realm of the moral purpose, you will have neither your desire successful in attaining what it would, nor your aversion successful in avoiding what it would" (2:82–83). This is *imaginative* training in that it concerns the way the sensations of the body are represented within the mind and presented to the "controlling faculty" for further action. Because the imagination is the bridge between judgment and sensation and is also a synthesizing faculty in its own right, it can produce sensations (within the mind) at will but it can also receive, sort, compare, and store sensations directly from the body. The imagination can thus be addressed or accessed in two ways: from the will or from the body. One can propose to oneself the idea of seasickness by drawing on past experience and calling the sensation, the *phantasia*, to mind or one can place oneself in a situation where the sensation will occur, as in the example of painful toil proposed above. Both approaches to imagination as mental apprehension of the physical world appear in Montaigne and Pascal, each deeply influenced by Epictetus.

   This counsel to train the mind to deal with sensory data—to "deprogram" selected aversions, desires, and fears that usually arise in the context of sights, smells, movements, and so forth—not only stresses the relation of the mind to the body through *phantasia*, but also suggests the temporal dimensions of this function of the mind. Epictetus's emphasis on habit in learning is particularly appropriate in light of imagination's independence from time, or, in other words, its ability to range across moments. Imagination can focus on a specific event or synthesize events. It can isolate a single experience from the past, remain within the stream of present sensations, or combine experiences to produce the thought of a new combination of sensations: a mental scene, an adventure, an object that has not yet been made in the external world. Epictetus's approach to training provides a stream of repeated sensations, and particularly extreme ones, so that the sensations while concrete are not limited to a single occurrence. They already have a nonspecific time quality that is congenial to imagination's roving ability to transfer or transpose the experience of one moment into another.

Marcus Aurelius Antoninus, emperor from 161 to 180 A.D., wrote a form of philosophical diary, *To Himself* (*Ta eis eauton*), that demonstrates the Stoic effort at constant self-improvement. In this unsystematic text, the author appears to jot down thoughts shaped by everyday experiences of frustration, discouragement, ambition, impatience, and so forth and exhorts himself according to the needs of the moment. Not a teacher of philosophy but a man with enormous responsibilities, actively engaged in the wars on the northern borders of the empire, Marcus stresses the retreat inward, the privacy of philosophical reflection, and even calls the mind "the inner fortress."[27] Given the role of imagination—*phantasia*, in the precise acceptation of sense-based thought—as a bridge between the world of the external senses and the inner activity of thought, it is not surprising that Marcus's view of imagination changes according to the situation to which he is reacting. There are frequent exclamations such as "Efface imagination!" (VII, 29, 176–77)[28] and "What then doest thou here, O Imagination?" (VII, 170–73). Yet there are also many injunctions to pay close attention to the thoughts that come from the senses: "Say no more to thyself than what the initial impressions (*phantasiai*) report" (VIII, 49, 223). In still other passages Marcus advises himself to make a productive use of *phantasia* to have a more complete view of reality: "Continually picture to thyself Time as a whole, and Substance as a whole, and every individual thing, in respect of substance, as but a fig-seed and, in respect to time, as but a twist of the drill" (X, 17, 274–77). These comments, scattered throughout Marcus's text, may seem at first to undercut our whole enterprise of studying a coherent concept, or family of concepts, linked across the ages under the terms *phantasia* and imagination.

Even with this single Stoic text the notion we call "imagination" seems to be breathtakingly broad and subject to radically opposed valuations. However, if we cling to the central idea that *phantasia*/imagination is thought that makes use of sensory data, we can understand why imagination preoccupies Marcus Aurelius even in the midst of his frequent exasperation with it.[29]

Like Epictetus, Marcus locates as the main challenge of imagination the tendency to lose focus and to slide, in thought, from what we have identified as the object of perception to associated and unjustified opinions. In order to understand this outlook, we need to bear in mind that *phantasia*, as Marcus calls it, and *imagination*, as Descartes calls it, concerns the idea of what is directly in front of our eyes or under our nose and not necessarily something that is false or absent. For Marcus, as for most philosophers in the Western tradition, it takes a real effort of mind simply to entertain the idea that corresponds to the input from our senses and thus to *see clearly* or to *hear clearly*.[30] Here is a passage that shows how deeply Marcus accepted Epictetus's teachings about the training of imagination as the awareness of what is:

> Say no more to thyself than what the initial impressions (*proegoumenai phantasiai*) report. This has been told thee, that so and so speaks ill of thee. This *has* been told thee, but it has not been told thee that thou art harmed. I see that my child is ailing. I see it, but I do not see that he is in danger. Keep then ever to first impressions and supplement them not on thy part from within, and nothing happens to thee (VIII, 49, 222–23).

Marcus is counseling himself against seeing what is *not there*. He follows that line of inquiry that, in a certain way, anticipates the phenomenological technique of "bracketing" an idea so that it can be examined in depth. The challenge is to avoid adding to the pure recognition of what we perceive. Seeing that his child is ailing, Marcus is tempted to add the worry that his child is in danger rather than to recognize simply what *is* and not to confuse that fact with various nonfacts that can be added. These nonfacts come from assumption or "reply" (*hypolepsis*, often translated as "opinion") that is the habitual course of the untrained mind.[31]

This analytical imagination, as we could call it, is one of Marcus's major contributions to the Stoic tradition of imagination. He did not invent it (e.g. Epictetus's teaching "His ship is lost. What happened? His ship is lost."), but he gives it a large place in his book and provides vivid examples not only of suppressing opinion and possible narrative developments (such as: "his ship is lost, therefore he will be a pauper") but of using imagination to see in detail and in decomposed or deconstructed form the object that we behold. The active phase of Marcus's analytic imagination goes beyond the immediate idea corresponding to the object of sense and summons the sensory representation of its elements, deliberately substituting the parts for the whole. Of the pleasant experience of the bath, reimagined, Marcus writes: "What bathing is when thou thinkest of it (*phainetai*)—oil, sweat, filth, greasy water, everything revolting" (VIII, 24, 208–09). The trained imagination can also decompose the sex act in order to see it differently: "of sexual intercourse, that it is merely internal attrition and the spasmodic excretion of mucus—such, I say, as are these impressions (*phantasiai*) that come to grips with the actual things and enter into the heart of them as they really are, thus should it be thy life through." (VI, 13, 134–35).

Aristotle had established imagination as a form of thought, distinct from the sense perceptions themselves on which that thought is based. Epictetus made the proper judgment and use of this sensory thought as the principal task of the Stoic philosopher. In Marcus we can see a particularly aggressive form of imaginative "objectivity." In recognizing the object of sense in his thought, he has to make himself see, feel, and smell what few people would actually register in their perceptions of everyday experience. Marcus's *phantasia* becomes what even today, with our much more limited concept, we would recognize as imagination. The initial perception is reworked to break the whole into ingredients, and often therefore to replace the object in its present-time form with the earlier or later states of its components. This is not the same thing as allowing "opinion" to take over nor is it replacing the sensory thought to be superseded by a more abstract, schematic, purely rational idea without sensory qualities. Instead Marcus proposes creating a bundle of alternative sensory items to supplement or replace the initial impression. He therefore directs his thought into a kind of hyperrealist or hypersensory mode that is the opposite of abstraction: "If a man's armpits are unpleasant, art thou angry with him? If he has foul breath? What would be the use? The man has such a mouth, he has such armpits" (V, 28, 122–23).

Frequently, the imaginative decomposition involves moving backward or forward in time:

> Unceasingly contemplate the generation of all things through change.... Even if [Reason's] closest associate, the poor body, be cut, be burnt, fester, gangrene, yet let the part which forms a judgment about these things hold its peace (IV, 37–39, 88–89).

This backward and forward movement is simply a voluntary composition of potential images. In going backward, Marcus rarely seems to be writing memories but creating intense sensory ideas about what some object must have been before it arrived at the stage he initially perceived prior to philosophical reimagining. Such reimagining might also be necessary, for some people, to see what they are seeing. For instance, if one has jaundice (this will be an important example for that thinker so similar to Marcus Aurelius, Michel de Montaigne), one needs to reconstruct the immediate sensory data in order to perceive the true taste of the very thing that one is eating.[32]

In addition to this analytic imagination, Marcus proposes a complementary form of synthetic imagination. Both approaches help the philosopher remember that all is in flux, that each existing thing will be transformed, and that things as we see them are infinitely small and ephemeral parts of the whole—"all substance is as a river in ceaseless flow . . . and ever beside us is this infinity of the past and yawning abyss of the future, wherein all things are disappearing" (V, 23, 120–21). The analytic imagination helps us demystify the present, in which things appear to be stable and solid, and to realize how we construct the present out of pieces that we normally do not allow ourselves to perceive. The synthetic imagination gives us a view of the onrushing mutation of things:

> Continually picture to thyself Time as a whole and Substance as a whole, and every individual thing, in respect of substance, as but a fig-seed and in respect of time, as but a twist of the drill (X, 17, 274–77).

Marcus does not give a detailed description of this *phantasia* of continuity, which seems to be a series of visualized metaphors intended to restore the dynamism to the objects that are picked out and decomposed in the mode of looking at the thing-in-itself (e.g. the bath as sweat and greasy water). These two movements of decomposition and recomposition are deeply rooted in Marcus's thought, and imagination—as much or more than theorizing—allows the thinker to grasp the flow of substance.[33] The choice of a longitudinal, future-oriented synthetic vision or the choice of an analytic present-centered vision depends on the emotional needs of the thinker as they fluctuate. Sometimes the view of life as a whole (*holou biou phantasia*) can be overwhelming, and it may then be preferable to cling fast to the present: "it is not the future nor the past but the present always that brings thee its burden. But this is reduced to insignificance if thou isolate it" (VIII, 36, 214–17).[34]

Although Lucius Annaeus Seneca died while Epictetus was still a youth (he was probably in his sixties when he committed suicide at Nero's command in

65 A.D.) and almost sixty years before Marcus was born, his writings show a less austere version of Stoic ideas than either of the two later men. Wealthy and well connected, Seneca exemplifies the theme that outward distinctions are of little importance and that philosophy can be practiced in all walks of life. His writings were a major source of Stoic doctrine for the Renaissance, and because Seneca was a prolific and talented writer, while Epictetus did not write at all, his vividness and eloquence won him a place of choice among later Humanists.[35] Seneca, like Epictetus, urged his readers—usually identified as younger Stoics being guided on the path to wisdom—to practice the discipline of the imagination, but Seneca couches his advice in terms that are much less technical than those employed by Epictetus. Seneca does not use the terms *imaginatio* or *phantasia*, probably for two reasons. The first is that Seneca has a fiercely Roman disdain for Greek terminology and even for certain Romanized transpositions of Greek concepts.[36] The second is that Seneca seems to take largely for granted a highly developed imagination and to assume that the skill of mental representation is part and parcel of the literary culture that he prized and shared with his correspondents.

Instead of writing *imaginare* or *imaginatio*, Seneca either says simply "to see" or uses some form of the expressions *ante oculos ponere*, to place before one's eyes or *proponere tibi*, place before yourself (in a purely mental sense). Here is some typical advice:

> We should therefore reflect upon all contingencies, and should fortify our minds against the evils which may possibly come. Exile, the torture of disease, wars, shipwreck,—we must think on these (*meditare*). Chance may tear you from your country or your country from you, or may banish you to the desert; this very place, where throngs are stifling, may become a desert. Let us place before our eyes in its entirety the nature of man's lot (*Tota ante oculos . . . ponatur*), and if we would not be overwhelmed, or even dazed, by those unwonted evils, as if they were novel, let us summon to our minds beforehand (*praesumamus animo*), not as great an evil as oftentimes happens, but the very greatest evil that possibly can happen. We must reflect upon fortune fully and completely.[37]

Seneca's advice to call events—past and potential—to mind is often, as here, accompanied by urgings to completeness and detail. He repeatedly makes it clear that he is not interested in abstraction and hair-splitting but in concreteness, forcefulness, and practicality. In deciding what intellectual talents to cultivate, he advises against the slippery verbal and theoretical distinctions called *sophismata*, that Seneca, true to his Roman heritage, prefers to call *cavillationes*. These are abstract and have no value for gaining wisdom.[38] Instead he encourages his readers to call experiences vividly to mind both in the grim cases of ultimate disaster and in the pleasanter instances of picturing the circumstances in which a letter is written.

An exchange of letters can be, writes Seneca, an experience of mental presence at a distant place with the author. It is not simply a question of understanding the writer's general ideas but rather shared experience and sensation. Therefore, the mental reproduction of sensation is, in the best of cases, included within the writing and reading of letters:

> I would therefore have you share your studies with me, your meals and your thoughts. I see you, my dear Lucilius, and at this very moment I hear you: I am with you to such an extent that I hesitate whether I should not begin to write you notes instead of letters.[39]

Seneca, in another, apparently subsequent, letter illustrates for Lucilius the exceptionally detailed and sense-oriented quality of the experience that a letter should occasion. Seneca describes his situation, at the moment he is writing in an apartment just above a gymnasium with a swimming pool and evokes a whole series of sounds: the grunting of a weight lifter, the smack of the masseur's hand on his client's back, the splash of a diver hitting the surface of the pool, the yelp of someone having body-hair removed, the cascade of water, street noises outside.[40] Not only does this description exemplify the inclusion of the nonvisual within imagination, but it also includes the crucial comment that the philosopher should be able to turn off the awareness of sensation as well as turn it on.

This description of sounds may, at first reading, appear to be a rather frivolous and bantering token of the older writer's friendship, the equivalent of a vacation postcard. However, on closer consideration, it is apparent that Seneca is giving his younger disciple Lucilius a virtuoso demonstration of how a senior Stoic handles the relationship between the inner life of the mind and the perception of the outer world. Consider this passage:

> Besides all those whose voices, if nothing else, are good, imagine the hair-plucker with his penetrating, shrill voice,—for purposes of advertisement,— continually giving it vent and never holding his tongue except when he is plucking the armpits and making his victim yell instead. Then the cake seller with his varied cries, the sausage man, the confectioner, and all the vendors of food hawking their wares, each with his own distinctive intonation.

So you say: "What iron nerves or deadened ears you must have, if your mind can hold out amid so many noises, so various and so discordant, when our friend Chrysippus is brought to his death by the continual good-morrows that greet him!" But I assure you that this racket means no more to me than the sound of waves or falling water . . .. (Epistle 56).[41]

Seneca here includes together the mental power of detailed perception and distinction, the power to summon to mind (*cogitare*) the characteristic sound of each tradesman's call, with the apparently opposite power to pay no attention to these sounds when they would be a distraction from more serious thought. Whether Seneca could actually neutralize ambient noise through the force of mental practice (later writers often charged the Stoics with boasting of their imperturbability) matters less than that he proposes this power of concentration as an ideal and that he does so in conjunction with such a display of exquisitely sensitive auditory perception. Both hearing and nonhearing manifest the philosopher's control over the way sense-perceptions are present to the mind.

This control is absolutely central to the Stoic goal of freedom, a goal that depends on a sharp distinction between the inside and the outside. In what at first appears to be a paradox, the Stoic holds that we should live according to nature and that we should locate what we value within ourselves, in what Epictetus calls the *prohairesis* and for which Seneca uses no technical term, preferring simply to write of the "I" (*ego, me*) or the soul or mind (*animum, mens*). All sorts of disturbances and distortions come about at the borderline between the inside and the outside, between the mind and the world of appearances, and these disturbances hinder our ability to live according to nature. The vacation letter to Lucilius simply puts in light form the very serious injunction to attain control of what perceptions are in the mind. The aim of freedom, together with the practical distinction, though often implicit, distinction between an "inside" and an "outside," appears throughout Seneca's writing, as when he describes the objective toward which the Stoic strives, the terms for which anticipate a modern colloquial expression, "having it together" (*esse compositum*): "You may therefore be sure that you are at peace with yourself, when no noise reaches you, when no word shakes you out of yourself . . .."[42]

Although Seneca does not have the term "imagination" (*imaginatio*) at his disposal, we can see from these passages that imagination is a key concept in his teachings. Imagination, as we have seen, is the form of thought that consists of the mental representation of sensation, whether that presence is due to an immediate stimulus, a memory, or some set of sensations that are neither present nor past but merely thinkable, as when we think about something that is going to happen in the future—when we worry about what is coming, writes Seneca, the mind *sibi falsas imagines fingit*, "makes for itself unreal images."[43] Imagination differs from brute perception by being in some way "processed," for example by being recognized. Thus Seneca, in his apartment above the gymnasium, receives (perceives) a set of grunts, yells, and water noises but then mentally connects this raw data to weight lifters, body-hair removal, and swimming. In order to be fully free, we must be able to entertain these mental representations when we choose and must be able to banish them when we choose. Real mental freedom—and for a Stoic this is all there is of freedom—requires both sides of this capacity. Separately, neither mere insensibility nor the ability to bring sensations to mind at will is an adequate control, according to Seneca's teachings.

A well-developed imaginative capacity, as we have described it, is not, of course, an aim in itself. There are many practical advantages to controlling mental representations: one's capacity for tolerating adverse conditions ranges from the fairly trivial ability to work in a noisy environment to the heroic acceptance (which even a millennium later we describe as "Stoic") of overwhelming misfortune. This acceptance, at the highest levels of virtue, permits the philosopher to be at one with the cosmic order, and this ability can be achieved only by daily practice, foresight, and a particularly active imagination. Let us consider these three interlocking themes in Seneca's writing.

Stoics in general taught that daily practice was indispensable to the achievement of wisdom. The view that wisdom was not simply knowledge but habit, or character (*habitus animi*),[44] had a great influence on later thinkers and facilitated the assimilation of Stoicism into forms of Christianity that also stressed daily, structured exercises, and it also was attractive to the military elite accustomed to drill and exercise. Seneca is typical of Stoics in strongly advising daily meditation (*cotidiana meditatio*)[45] as well as constant struggle in everyday situations to acquire good habits of thought and conduct.[46] Seneca describes his daily self-examination:

> All our senses ought to be trained to endurance. They are naturally long-suffering, if only the mind desists from weakening them. This [the mind] should be summoned to give an account of itself every day.... When the

light has been removed from sight, and my wife, long aware of my habit, has become silent, I scan the whole of my day and retrace all my deeds and words. I conceal nothing from myself, I omit nothing....[47]

In this one example, Seneca's comments on self-examination doubly concern imagination. First, his encouragement of self-examination comes in the context of the daily use of the senses, several of which he mentions in detail (hearing, sight, touch). Second, the review of his waking hours implies a recreation of them (an instant replay, we might say) that seems to require visualization, rehearing, etc. The spectacle that one contemplates, a single day, has a privileged, albeit partly arbitrary, status as a complete and closed unit. By preventing the mind from running forward and escaping into future possibilities, the daily examination keeps the seeker of wisdom from evading responsibility for what he has done and from useless worry:

> let us so order our minds as if we had come to the very end. Let us postpone nothing. Let us balance life's account every day. The greatest flaw in life is that it is always imperfect, and that a certain part of it is postponed. One who daily puts the finishing touches to his life is never in want of time.... But when I have paid my soul its due, when a soundly-balanced mind knows that a day differs not a whit from eternity... then the soul looks forth from lofty heights and laughs heartily to itself....[48]

Aiming at freedom, the forms of daily exercise have a long-term and consistent aim of canceling the difference between present and future. Taken out of context, it may seem contradictory for Seneca to urge his reader to take each day as a complete and closural unit—to think of each day as one's very last—and in other passages to encourage daily preparation for the ups and downs that life still has in store. However, these are simply two approaches to the same aspiration, making time and circumstance irrelevant to the philosopher's core of personal integrity. This is a theme that is deeply bound to imagination, since imagination functions freely within time, shifting easily from past to present, present to future. Imagination's capacity to transcend time and its unique ability to bring acute sensory realism to its representations makes it particularly precious as a tool to neutralize time and chance. Reason, or judgment, can work outside the bounds of time and can conceive values, rules of physics, and so forth that apply to the future as well as the past. But imagination has in addition the ability to involve the senses and thus to recall, focus upon, or simulate the actual experience of the thinker. The exercise of considering each day one's last—balancing life's account every day—is actually an exercise in imagination, one that completely reframes all our perceptions. It is one of many exercises that help us reframe the present and accept its contingent, fragile character. Seneca gives a comical example of this serious practice of pre-living one's own death:

> Pacuvius, who by long occupancy made Syria his own, used to hold a regular burial sacrifice in his own honour, with wine and the usual funeral feasting, and then would have himself carried from the dining-room to his chamber, while eunuchs applauded and sang in Greek to a musical accompaniment: 'He has lived his life, he has lived his life!' Thus Pacuvius had himself carried out to burial every day. Let us, however, do from a good motive what he used to do from a debased motive . . . .[49]

Pacuvius's funeral was one step beyond imagination. First, he had to picture what his burial celebration was going to be like—that is an act of imagination—and then he used that picture to organize an actual physical event, the mock funeral. Seneca is not recommending such enactments, of course, but instead endorses the imaginative act that is one step short, a detailed, realistic mental representation of one's death as if it were *right now*.

By rendering misfortune present one can practice accepting it. This is the training of the warrior:

> If a man can behold with unflinching eyes the flash of a sword, if he knows that it makes no difference to him whether his soul takes flight through his mouth or through a wound in his throat, you may call him happy; you may also call him happy if, when he is threatened with bodily torture . . . he . . . can say: . . . "Today it is you who threaten me with these terrors; but I have always threatened myself with them, and have prepared myself as a man to meet man's destiny."[50]

It is not enough, then, to accept the *idea* of death in the abstract. It is rather the ability to *act out* death with one's body and mind that the Stoic requires. This preparation is very much like the work of an actor preparing in minute detail every aspect of a role, except than in the case of the sage the repertory must be extremely large and be refreshed and restudied constantly in order to permit the philosopher to "act the part" that is appropriate for the particular form in which misfortune comes. One curious feature of the "part" in question, though, is that it is essentially unvarying and that the challenge is to maintain one's imperturbability in the face of a drastically changed situation. To know that sickness, sudden poverty, loss of station, military defeat, mutilation, and the death of one's family are *possible* is not enough for the Stoic as long as that knowledge is purely conceptual. What is necessary is to prepare the mind–body whole against surprise by practicing a whole range of events with that resource of the mind that specializes in the connection or boundary of mind and body (and let us recall that the Stoics were materialists, so that mind and body were both physical entities). That connective resource is, as we know, the imagination.

In the practice of imagination two sets of things are being fused together. On one hand, the mind and the body are being tuned or set so that difference is eliminated. The "inner" serenity of the mind is projected onto the "outer" serenity of the body so that the death of a Stoic sage is, in Stoic theory at least, a visible manifestation of wise conformity to the order of the universe. On the other hand, the present and the future are synchronized and thus time is actually eliminated. Thus, in the example above, the captured warrior who is threatened with torture has *already* been threatened with torture—the threat is nothing new.

As Seneca describes man's lot, the discrepancy among past, present, and future and our untrained imaginings of these different times are the major source of unhappiness. "We are," he writes, "plunged by our blind desires into ventures which will harm us, but certainly never satisfy us; for if we could be satisfied with anything, we should have been satisfied long ago."[51] We see images of a possible future and are tormented by what separates us from those images—time—while we cannot appreciate what is already present. To properly manage our desires we need to control our imaginings and abolish the sense of time difference that permeates the thoughts of the untrained mind when it uses its imagination. Seneca attaches such a strong negative valuation to this obsession with the future that it is not an exaggeration to say that *futurum* (what is going to be) is almost synonymous with "evil."[52]

Perhaps paradoxically, the way Seneca proposes to deal with the distraction and the torment of the future is to include such thoughts in philosophical practice so that the future becomes the present. Because we neither fear nor desire the present, but merely suffer or enjoy it, the reduction of the future to the present abolishes fear and desire. This is a task for imagination, and the better developed is the philosopher's imagination, the more truly he can say that he has already lived whatever comes his way and will not be taken by surprise, "for it is the unexpected that puts the heaviest load upon us. Strangeness adds to the weight of calamities, and every mortal feels the greater pain as a result of that which also brings surprise."[53]

The most striking illustration of the relation among time, disaster, and imaginative exercise is the letter to Lucilius about the total destruction of the Roman colony of Lyons (*Lugdunum*) in 64 A.D. Seneca and Lucilius's mutual friend Liberalis, who was from Lyons, was devastated by the news that his homeland had gone up in smoke in a single night. For Seneca, this is a demonstration of the need, even among accomplished Stoics, for still further development of their catastrophic imagination. Liberalis was distraught despite his training: "This incident has served to make him inquire about the strength of this own character, which he has trained, I suppose, just to meet situations that he thought would cause him fear."[54] In short, Liberalis suffered from a lack of imagination—here the ancient usage of the term and our own modern one converge—since this particular misfortune was not one that he possessed among his repertory of mentally pre-lived and accepted ones. Liberalis' disarray does not discredit the method of imaginative preparation, in Seneca's view, but simply exemplifies the need for more exercise:

> nothing ought to be unexpected by us. Our minds should be sent forward in advance to meet all problems, and we should consider, not what is wont to happen, but what can happen. For what is there in existence that Fortune, when she has so willed, does not drag down from the very height of its prosperity? . . . . No time is exempt . . . . We should therefore reflect upon all contingencies, and should fortify our minds against the evils which may possibly come. Exile, the torture of disease, wars, shipwreck,—we must think (*meditare*) on these. (76:432–433).

The concrete, sensory nature of this thinking is clear from Seneca's use of his main equivalent for the Greek *phantasia*, the expression "to place before one's eyes":

> Let us place before our eyes in its entirety the nature of man's lot, and if we would not be overwhelmed, or even dazed, by those unwonted evils, as if they were novel, let us summon to our minds beforehand, not as great an evil has oftentimes happens, but the very greatest evil that can possibly happen. (76:436–437)

He follows this general advice with a series of striking descriptions of cities collapsing, volcanoes erupting, and so forth, putting his imagination, and his reader's, to work in a kind of directed meditation.

The desired result of this intense practice of mentally converting the possible into the actual is mastery of the relation between oneself and

Fortune, gradually moving control from the latter to the former by eliminating chance and change, integrating everything into the mind's present, following the precept "Whatever can happen at any time can happen today."[55] Moreover, what can happen to one person can happen to all, and Stoic meditation makes of the sage a universal man by his mental experience of all that can befall any one of us. It is revealing to compare the kind of "universal subject" that Seneca thus theorizes to the subject that much later appears in Descartes. The French philosopher reaches universality in his transcendent "I" by eliminating differences, and, indeed, by locating his specificity in the most minimal thought that he cannot doubt. Seneca, while he resembles Descartes—and most philosophers in the Western tradition—in locating human specificity in reason, proposes a radically different philosophic experience by urging the imaginative living of all human situations. We can reach an experience of universal commonality when we can imagine and accept all hardships and conditions, even those we have clearly escaped, such as being born into poverty or deformed.[56] Not only should we experience the future as the present but we should also experience what befalls other people in order to posses a truly universal mental freedom from Fortune. Seneca makes it clear that this mental experience includes sensation; he illustrates the human lot by writing "Winter brings on cold weather; and we must shiver. Summer returns, with its heat; and we must sweat. Unseasonable weather upsets the health; and we must fall ill. In certain places we may meet with wild beasts . . .."(77:226–227).

Through imagination we can have inside our mind a world that is much richer than the world outside at any given moment, for we can create an infinite number of alternative and past realities. This pragmatic skill is much more precious than the intellectual games played by dialecticians and other teachers of abstract subtleties.[57] By making philosophy a daily, inward, personal practice and by basing it largely on the way of thinking that is most directly related to the replication of the distinctive traits of the outside world—sensation—Seneca, more than most earlier Stoics makes philosophy accessible to people in all walks of life, rather than a distinct calling that separates the philosopher from society. This social adaptability, based on the twin goals of inner self-development and service to society, renders the *inner* life crucial. By using imagination as laboratory for practical experience, one can live a conventional and highly adapted outward life while inwardly living in the utmost austerity. Despite the criticism of Seneca for what to some seemed his hypocrisy—he lived a life of immense wealth and political position, perhaps gained as a result of shameless opportunism—here seems to be a theoretical coherence to his view that the inner life could be as tangible and much more vast than the outer life if one has control over imagination in both its productive and its exclusionary operations. That is, the wise man can both exclude sensory perception and create it mentally.

The inner life permits both freedom through imagination (e.g., freedom from fear of the future) and the freedom to imagine, beyond the inquisitiveness and the control of those around us. This could hardly have been a small advantage for a philosopher living in Nero's household.[58] Seneca portrays the pursuit of his mental exercises as going on out of sight, concurrently with his busy life:

> As for me, Lucilius, my time is free; it is indeed free, and wherever I am, I am master of myself. For I do not surrender myself to my affairs, but loan myself to them, and I do not hunt out excuses for wasting my time. And wherever I am situated, I carry on my own meditations and ponder in my mind some wholesome thought. When I give myself to my friends, I do not withdraw from my own company....[59]

The value of the inner life is all based on the belief in becoming free from the constraints of the body, for the mind can have the benefit of the sensations without being controlled by them. Our mind should follow the senses that serve it and then withdraw back into itself to "be the master both of them and of itself."[60]

In short, the Stoics make managing *phantasia* a central activity of the life of the mind. The accomplished philosopher differs from the untrained person not by having more or less imagination but by directing and using imagination. After all, the mind is a stream of sense impressions, recollections of sense impressions, anticipations of things to come and visions of what might have been. In this respect, everyone is equal in regard to the *quantity* of imagination and imaginings but wise people are able to direct that stream in accordance with will and judgment.

RHETORIC AND THE TECHNICAL IMAGINATION

Roman theorists and teachers of rhetoric do not view *phantasia* in the same way as the Stoic philosophers. As it appears in Quintilian's rhetorical theory, imagination is a particular resource available to the trained orator on certain occasions. Like the Stoics, Quintilian emphasizes personal self-development, daily practice, and the strong distinction between the inner world of the mind and the outward world of public action. However, for Quintilian, *phantasia* does not permeate all of life but instead belongs to a distinct activity in which one can engage or not. In this respect, as in several others, Quintilian partly returns to an Aristotelian position in which *phantasia* is not central and partly anticipates a generally modern (Renaissance and after) view of imagination as a form of thought that we can choose or avoid, rather than as necessarily involved in all thinking. The shift in the status of imagination from central to human thought to separable instrument is tied to the controversy concerning the *professionalization* of speaking. The powerful, persuasive public speaker must have imagination, memory, inventiveness, voice, understanding of the matters debated, judgment and so forth. However, there were throughout Greek and Latin antiquity lively debates on the source of these attributes. Was the effective speaker simply born with these gifts? Or, if he needed to acquire them by study, should he turn to teachers of rhetoric or rather cultivate himself broadly by the study of philosophy, law, and so forth? Quintilian's position as head of the first state-sponsored school of rhetoric in Rome clearly gave him a reason to defend the view that rhetorical studies could supplement natural talents.[61] He therefore emphasized what the future orator could acquire as *technique*, rather than what the potential speaker might have as a spontaneous personal trait. Today, one of the best-known components of this professional rhetorical curriculum is *technical memory*, or the "art of memory," with which the speaker could learn a prepared speech by heart.[62] However, alongside technical memory and closely allied to it (in fact, required for memory development) is *technical imagination*, that is, the ability to turn sensory thought on and off according to what was needed by the professional situation.

At the same time as he professionalizes memory and gives it status as an art or technique (*tekhne*), Quintilian limits the meaning of *phantasia* in a way that anticipates the modern understanding of imagination as the mental representation of what is *not* immediately perceived by the senses. While for Aristotle and for the Stoics all things that we see, smell, taste, hear, and touch come to our mind in the form of *phantasiai*, for Quintilian, as for most thinkers in post-Enlightenment Europe, the conceptual network known as "fantasy" and "imagination" concerns exclusively what is absent from the thinker's here and now at the time she or he perceives it as a mental image.

These two transformations of imagination—from a constant mental activity to a somewhat marginalized skill and from the necessary gateway of all sensory perception to the evocation of a past or potential or even impossible experience—are closely intertwined in Quintilian's writing. To professionalize rhetoric, Quintilian needed to discard, or rather demote, immediately available experience. The sounds, sights, and smells of the street and forum are available to the untrained, to the nonprofessional, and therefore should be excluded from the *art* of the orator, or at least cast into the background as mere accessories. The orator, on the other hand, as the one who possesses to the highest degree possible, the *bene dicere sapientia*—the knowledge of how to speak well—will be able to do the seemingly impossible: see and show what is *not there*. This is why it is important for Quintilian to redefine imagination as a purely mental (interior) and verbal art, distinct from the activity of those who create a visual display.

With this defense of the professional status of the orator in mind, we can better understand why Quintilian takes some apparently far-fetched examples to illustrate a theoretical distinction that does not at first glance have much to do with imagination. Beginning with "The first question that confronts us . . . 'What is rhetoric?'," Quintilian points out that many have defined rhetoric as "persuasion or speaking in a persuasive manner."[63] This definition of rhetoric, supported by Aristotle's *Rhetoric*, is vigorously opposed by Quintilian, who rejects not only persuasion but even the study of the means of persuasion as the defining characteristics of rhetoric.[64] In its most plain and powerful statement, Quintilian's objection to this definition of rhetoric comes down to the role of the senses in persuasion. Besides discourse, he notes,

> many other things have the power of persuasion, such as money, influence, the authority and rank of the speaker, or *even some sight unsupported by language*, when for instance the place of words is supplied by the memory of some individual's great deeds, by his lamentable appearance or the beauty of his person. Thus when Antonius in the course of his defense of Manius Aquilius tore open his client's robe and revealed the honourable scars which he had acquired while facing his country's foes, *he relied no longer on the power of his eloquence, but appealed directly to the eyes of the Roman people* (book II, sec. 15; I, 303, emphasis added).

Quintilian does not dispute the great, indeed sometimes overwhelming, power of sight to persuade (*aspectus etiam ipse sine voce*), but distinguishes it sharply from the power of language, which is the core of rhetoric. Now, Quintilian does not remind us here—but those familiar with the tradition of *phantasia* will not need to be reminded—that the direct *sight* of some object, indeed all sensory experience that reaches our thought, is the domain of imagination. However, this sector of imagination, the mental recognition of *present* things, happens without art and can be used by persons without any training. Generally speaking, Quintilian denigrates the direct appeal to the senses and the bodily dimension in public speaking.[65]

When Quintilian explicitly introduces *phantasia* as a proper part of rhetoric, he limits it to the mental and verbal representation of *absent* things because it is this aspect of imagination that falls within his conception of the orator's profession, one requiring art and training.[66] Imagination, as we know it today, owes much to Quintilian's drive to separate present and immediate sensory perception from the perception of what is absent. In this latter form, Quintilian enthusiastically promotes *phantasia*:

> if we wish to give our words the appearance of sincerity, we must assimilate ourselves to the emotions of those who are genuinely so affected . . .. But how are we to generate these emotions in ourselves, since emotion is not in our own power? I will try to explain as best I may. There are certain experiences which the Greeks call *phantasiai*, and the Romans *visions* (*visiones*), whereby things absent are presented to our imagination (*imagines rerum absentium ita repraesentantur animo*) with such extreme vividness that they seem actually to be before our very eyes. It is the man who is really sensitive to such impressions who will have the greatest power over the emotions (book VI, sec. 2; vol. II, · p. 432–35).

Tellingly, the term "imagination" is itself absent from the text, and *phantasia* is described not as a faculty nor even as a skill but as a piece of the complex internal scene that the skilled rhetorician will use as an indirect aid to moving the audience. There seems to be no word available to Quintilian for a faculty or process that produces or manages the mental impression of sensory perception. The presumption that this activity is not a familiar one that his readers will take for granted is implicit in his prefatory statement that he will *try* to explain (*Temptabo etiam de hoc dicere*). Quintilian needs to use the Greek term and to provide a translation.[67] He stresses the way the things in the *phantasiai* appear to the thinker to be actually present, thus connecting *phantasia* with the senses themselves, and he gives an example of the vivid perception that the orator should have:

> I am complaining that a man has been murdered. Shall I not bring before my eyes all the circumstances which it is reasonable to imagine must have

occurred in such a connexion? Shall I not see the assassin burst suddenly from his hiding-place, the victim tremble, cry for help, beg for mercy, or turn to run? Shall I not see the fatal blow delivered and the stricken body fall? Will not the blood, the death-rattle, be indelibly impressed upon my mind? (book VI, sec. 2; vol. II, 434–35).

Although sight is the dominant sense here, sound is also important, and perhaps also touch (in regard to the blood). The speaker should be so plunged into the experience of this absent scene that the audience will see him in the grip of what may appear as an hallucination, for he appears "not so much to narrate as to exhibit the actual scene" (*quae non tam dicere videtur quam ostendere*), that is, he does not just *claim* to be seeing the scene but shows it. The people who have this power of vivid internal conception—again, Quintilian does not have the word "imagination"—are called by a Greek term for which no Latin equivalent is given:

> Some writers describe such a man as *euphantasiotos*, who is able to present (*finget*) to himself things, voices, and actions in their absence; a power that we can easily acquire for ourselves if we wish.[68]

We can develop this power, says Quintilian, stressing that it is a power internal to the orator, who makes things appear *to himself.*[69] So this is not simply vivid speaking or writing, but an experience within the mind of the orator. Only if he can first imagine the scene can he convincingly convey it to his audience.[70] The orator, then, seeks to be possessed or filled with a concrete *inner* reality which, however, does not correspond the *outward* reality:

> When the mind is unoccupied or is absorbed by these visions of which I am speaking to such an extent that we imagine that we are travelling abroad, crossing the sea, fighting, addressing the people, or enjoying the use of wealth that we do not actually possess, and seem to ourselves not to be thinking but doing (*nec cogitare sed facere*).[71]

Quintilian takes great care to emphasize the distinction between a general, intellectual thought about something, and the imaginative process that brings an experience to us as if we were living it with our body and not only our mind. Yet what makes this process interesting and valuable to Quintilian is that the mind has managed to *disconnect* from the body so that the *euphantasiotos*— the person who is good at imagining—can think that he is living elsewhere, at another time, and doing things that he is actually not doing. This internal skill on the speaker's part is—surprisingly, from our modern point of view—not primarily an advantage in the part of rhetoric that concerns writing the speech *inventio*, but with the performance (*elocutio*). Imagination is a power that helps the speaker control the way he is perceived by the people around him.

The Stoic Epictetus, teaching about *phantasia* at roughly the same time, certainly had a similar understanding about the ability to create vivid mental representations, but his emphasis was quite different. First of all, of course, Epictetus included the mind's perception of the *present* situation within the *phantasiai*. Yet even in regard to the mental simulation of experiences that were merely potential or foreseeable—the mental activity that converges with Quintilian's description of imagination—Epictetus does not stress the *absence* of these experiences as does Quintilian. For the rhetorician, the skill of the *euphantasiotos*, the imaginative man, is remarkable because it can make the absent seem present. This power of simulated perception is *in itself* a wonderful thing. For Epictetus, what matters is the relation between judgment and will (moral purpose) to sensory experience without respect to time. There is nothing especially admirable in the ability to have a vivid mental experience of, for instance, having one's hand burned off during interrogation by the enemy. What matters is the cultivated indifference to experience, past, present, and future. Pre-experience of such potential misfortunes is merely meant to neutralize them, to drain away the fear that they inspire. The fact that some of this practice takes place purely in thought and some takes place in actual physical life (restrictions in diet, extreme simplicity in one's lodging, strenuous physical exercise, etc.) is a distinction of only secondary interest to Epictetus. Hence, Quintilian can be said to be both more modern and more narrow in this conception of what we would call imagination, that is, the deliberate employment of *phantaisiai*.

For Quintilian, as we have said, cultivating the power to imagine things is inextricably tied to the *professionalization* of speaking. There is nothing artful about speaking passionately or even convincingly about the things that concern us and about injustices that we have actually suffered or witnessed. But the man who can speak of an injustice he has *not* actually witnessed is the trained orator:

> those vivid conceptions of which I spoke and which, as I remarked, are called *phantasiai*, together with everything that we intend to say, the persons and questions involved, and the hopes and fears to which they give rise, must

be kept clearly before our eyes and admitted to our hearts: for it is feeling
and the force of mind (*vis mentis*) that make us eloquent. It is for this reason
that even the uneducated have no difficulty in finding words to express their
meaning, if only they are stirred by some strong emotion.[72]

Even though a very large part of Quintilian's *Institutio Oratoria* is devoted
to questions of grammar, style, figures of speech, and so forth, the way the
orator develops his mind is a crucial component of proper rhetorical education. The distinction between the uneducated and the trained rhetorician is
most fundamentally, for Quintilian, the development of a certain relationship between the orator's interior and his outward appearance. Imagination
is one of the practices that permits the inner world of the orator to be usefully
independent of outer circumstance, for the orator does not depend on the
emotional stimulus of the speaking situation but supplies his own through a
simulated reality. As Terence Cave has shown, Quintilian, through a striking
paradox, bases the energy and the emotional impact of his delivery on the
skill of being, in a way, *absent* from the world of his audience. Not only
does the rhetorician acquire the ability to give himself the sensation of living
an experience—as if bodily—that he is in physical fact not living, but his
mind is constantly elsewhere, compartmentalized, in an effort to manage
the various moments of his oration. The result is, on one hand, "the total
active engagement of the speaker as the 'subject' of his utterance" and, on
the other, an "alienated voice" as the speaking continues while the orator's
thought is elsewhere.[73] It is the trained imagination, above all the other internal resources, that permits the orator to give the impression of speaking
naturally, as if possessed by his subject, and not as a technician of discourse
whose care and attention are fixed on language itself. The orator *is*, in an odd
sense, speaking naturally because he has induced what could be considered a
form of hallucination. That is, he is doing what the nonprofessional speaker
would do if confronted by an immediate danger or in the grip of real anger,
but the orator is doing this in response to a nonexistent situation that he is
living *in his mind*:

> For profound emotion and vivid imagination (*recentes rerum imagines*) sweep
> on with unbroken force, whereas, if retarded by the slowness of the pen, they
> are liable to grow cold . . . Above all, if we add to these obstacles an unhealthy
> tendency to quibble over the choice of words, and check our advances at each
> step, the vehemence of our onset loses its impetus . . . (book X, sec. 7; vol. 4,
> p. 140–41).

Imagination allows the orator to forget word choice, while improvising a speech, and to concentrate on the situation as a whole, since, after all, the speaker should to some extent become delusional. With imagination he can create smoother, more rapid, and more impassioned discourse, although paradoxically he has his mind directed toward an absent scene and not toward his words.

Being able, in the midst of the senate, to live an alternative existence, requires shutting out some sensory input while fabricating another. This dual power of exclusion and creation, recommended by Quintilian, resembles Seneca's advice and that of the Stoics generally:

> whether we be in a crowd, on a journey, or even at some festive gathering, our thoughts should always have some inner sanctuary of their own to which they may retire. Otherwise what shall we do when we are suddenly called upon to deliver a set speech in the midst of the forum, with lawsuits in progress on every side, and with the sound of quarrels and even casual outcries in our ears, if we need absolute privacy to discover the thoughts which we jot down upon our tablets? . . . It was for this reason that Demosthenes, the passionate lover of seclusion, used to study on the seashore amid the roar of the breakers that they might teach him not to be unnerved by the uproar of the public assembly. (book X, sec.3; vol. 4, p. 106–07).

Imagination is, for Quintilian as for everyone else who writes on the subject, inseparably connected with the development of a strong distinction between the "inside" of the mind and an "outside," a distinction that begins with the definition of *phantasia* itself as the mental trace, semblance, or recognition of a bodily, sensorial experience and that usually continues with the advice to cultivate the difference between inside and out. The ability to produce intense mental-sensorial experiences of an absent object is known to Quintilian as *enargeia* (Latin *evidentia*), and this ability has as its corollary the opposite ability to experience intensely, so to speak, the *absence* of sensory impressions. Both of these abilities manifest imagination's role as bridge— drawbridge, as it were—between the outside world and the inside world. The inner solitude of the speaker is a professional achievement that allows him to have at will the silence that is unavailable to the people around him.[74] This use of imagination to create an internal space in public runs against conceptions that we have, in a post-Enlightenment and post-Romantic world, to associate imagination exclusively with "creativity," conceived as the first step in story creation or content design.[75] To the extent that the speaker is creating, his creativity goes largely toward something that the public will never see—the inner world of the orator.

The inner world takes on a particularly strong positive, imaginative form, when it is placed at the service of artificial memory. Since artificial memory has been so well studied by Francis Yates, Mary Carruthers, and other scholars, little need be said here except, first, to emphasize that the correlated training of imagination and memory is tied to Quintilian's defense of rhetoric as a profession, and, second, to stress the layered or doubled function of imagination in most schemes of technical memory.

Memory is crucial to successful oratory, and "it is not without good reason that memory has been called the treasure-house of eloquence," says Quintilian (book XI, sec. 2; vol. 4, p. 212–13), yet, bizarrely, "even beasts, which seem to be devoid of reason, yet remember and recognize things" (p. 214–15). Just as the role of *phantasia* was to allow the orator to substitute an invisible world for the world of the merely visible, available to the untrained, so the art of memory is described in contrast to natural, spontaneous memory: "training enables us to do things which we cannot do before we have had any training or practice" (p. 216–17).

In describing the major form of artificial memory based on visualized places, Quintilian insists on the vivid sensory representation of the places and objects brought to mind. The speaker will select a place "such as a spacious house divided into rooms. Everything of note therein is carefully committed to the memory, in order that the thought may be enabled to run through all the details without let or hindrance" (p. 220–21). Symbolic objects are then placed in each room so that the orator, in giving his speech, can simply walk through the house, see each object, and remember in order the idea that is associated with the object. We just need the places to imagine: "Opus est ergo locis, quae vel finguntur vel sumuntur, et imaginibus vel simulacris, quae utique fingenda sunt" (p. 222–23). In this system, memory becomes dependent on internal vision, that is, on first recalling a known place or fashioning for oneself an unknown place, and then placing things within that imaginary—mentally perceived—place.

The Latin rhetorical tradition of *phantasiai* or *visiones* had an immense and productive influence in a culture that Quintilian could not have foreseen. In the following millennium of Christian culture, and far from courtrooms or deliberative assemblies, writers used the device of mental imaging to convey religious ideas. The story of imagination in the European Middle Ages has recently been told with brilliant erudition by Mary Carruthers in *The Craft of Thought*.[76] The practice of giving visual qualities (and even tactile or other sensory characteristics) to religious lessons inspired allegorical thinking, writing, and preaching, determined architectural form in church buildings, and enabled the truly devout to live in a different form of "reality" from that known to Christians of later centuries.

When the Latin rhetorical writings and Stoic philosophical and ethical doctrines became available in the sixteenth century in new editions and set off a wave of enthusiasm for self-cultivation, the ecclesiastical practices described by Carruthers were still alive for authors like Ignatius of Loyola and François de Sales. Other humanist writers, like Montaigne, seem to reach back over the medieval traditions to foster a sense of direct contact with the great minds of ancient Greece and Rome. The movement of imaginative practice that began in the sixteenth century was largely individualistic and adaptable. For some people private imaginative practices were a way of bringing the message of the Church into their homes. For others, it meant cultivating ethical, philosophical, or even erotic thought in vivid ways in the privacy of their minds. Both the rhetorical tradition and the Stoic ethical doctrines presented imagination as a skill available to any educated person for use, not simply in professional pursuits such as public speaking, painting, and writing, but in the everyday business of private life. A central figure in reviving and propagating this way of thinking was the learned Bordeaux landowner and jurist, Michel de Montaigne.

ONE

The Return of Stoic Imagination

"There is no desire more natural than the desire for knowledge," wrote Montaigne to begin "Of experience"(III, 13), the final chapter of his *Essays*. There is little doubt that Montaigne's combination of the drive to know and of corrosive doubt set in motion an important current of modern European philosophy.[1] Descartes and Pascal, careful readers of Montaigne, took up the challenge of his skepticism and, in attempting to confront and over-come radical doubt, laid the basis for several branches of modern thought.[2] Richard Rorty writes that "The 'epistemological turn' taken by Descartes might not have captured Europe's imagination had it not been for a crisis of confidence in established institutions, a crisis expressed paradigmatically in Montaigne."[3] Sketching the history of epistemology, Gilles Granger echoes the title of Montaigne's essay to designate a crucial problems of post-Cartesian epistemology, "The role assigned to experience—that is the starting point of the problems that lead to the development of this epistemology. Pascal's writings on physics are the most perfect example."[4] English and American scholars of literature have begun to write about Montaigne's epistemology.[5] From a modern perspective, nothing could be fitting; the "Apology for

Raymond Sebond" (*Essays* II, 12) is an important starting point for the critical study of perception and knowledge, and many other passages in the *Essays* bear on these issues.[6] Yet, in preferring the more scientific or technical term, we overlook two facts: first, that for Montaigne the study of knowledge—of our ability to know—was the study of imagination (the faculty through which all knowledge of the physical, external world must pass); second, that Montaigne sought to integrate reflection on knowledge into everyday situations and not to create a separate, specialized discipline.[7] For Montaigne, a critical awareness of how we know things is not separable from the constant exercise of managing our mental images of things.[8] An early chapter of the *Essays* presents this clearly:

> If what we call evil and torment is neither evil nor torment in itself, if it is merely our fantasy that gives it this quality, it is in us to change it. (I.14:50/33).

Although Montaigne sometimes uses *fantasie* in the broad sense of whimsy, here in "That the taste of good and evil depends in large part on the opinion we have of them" his allusion to the ancient Greek context connects *fantasie* to *phantasia*: "Men, says an old Greek maxim, are tormented by the opinions they have of things, not by the things themselves" (50/33).[9] Thus, very close to the outset of the *Essays*, imagination is presented as the bridge between the world of things outside us and our judgment within us. And he does not send his reader down the path that leads away from thinking in physical terms but rather points *toward* representation itself, the specialty of imagination, as a useful remedy to our ills. We should find out, he writes, if we can, when confronted with an ill, "give it a different savor and a different complexion; for all this comes to the same thing" (51/33). So the approach proposed is not simply an intellectual one involving our judgment but rather one that modifies the perception of the physical properties of things. We have an opportunity to change the way we sense it, the way we *taste* it. Ann Hartle has brilliantly noted that Montaigne's use of his imagination is the key to his ability to break out of unexamined, traditional patterns of thought: "The imagination is the faculty that is essential to Montaigne's openness."[10] In terms of Montaigne's relation to the tradition of philosophy, the claim that we need not be trapped in old perceptions and that we have the ability to reprogram our *phantasiai*—sense impressions as they are entertained in the mind—is a teaching that links Montaigne to the Stoics.

The revival of Stoic philosophy is one of the most important events of the sixteenth and the early seventeenth centuries. In the case of some writers, like Justus Lipsius and Guillaume du Vair, the systematic statement of Stoic thought became an almost exclusive focus of their work.[11] In France, in the wake of the Reformation and the wars of religion, selected elements of Stoicism blended variously with both Catholic and Protestant sensibilities while sometimes providing a common ground, particularly in ethics, for those on different sides of theological issues.[12] Calvin wrote a commentary on Seneca's *De Clementia*, Simon Goulart edited Seneca's moral writings, and the poet François de Malherbe (who was twenty-five years old when the *Essays* first appeared) translated Seneca's letters.[13] Although the sixteenth-century drew much of its view of Stoicism from Seneca and Cicero, there were numerous translations of Epictetus's *Manual* from Greek into Latin, beginning around 1453, and Montaigne owned Angelo Poliziano's 1498 translation.[14] Toward the end of the century, in 1591, Guillaume du Vair, who, after being a close advisor of King Henri IV was later to become a Catholic bishop, published still another translation of the *Manual* into French, along with other extensive writings on Stoicism.[15]

PRACTICING FOR DEATH

Montaigne's early chapter of the *Essays*, "That to philosophize is to learn to die" (I, 20), is often described as being one of the most deeply influenced by Stoicism, at least in the earliest, unrevised passages. Scholars have long been at odds over the depth of Montaigne's commitment to Stoicism, and Villey's view that Montaigne had only a brief infatuation with the movement has been very influential.[16] In Villey's perspective, Montaigne's career is described as an evolution away from Stoicism toward an acceptance of life, a less austere outlook, and a broader conception of philosophy, or at least of the life of the mind.[17] And it seems entirely right not to pigeonhole the extremely eclectic author of the *Essays* into any single philosophical school.[18] Montaigne's approach to death in this chapter does not simply express resignation to death or a rigid asceticism that ignores life, particularly the life of the senses, as we might think on the basis of a popular conception of a "Stoic" attitude. There is a very positive, though paradoxical, energy that Montaigne derives from perceiving death in its most vivid form, from willing to *imagine* death rather than simply accept it passively. If philosophizing is learning to die, then the philosopher is not so much one who formulates questions as one who repeatedly expands the repertory of vivid mental representations of death, not only historically (by acquiring a vast store of anecdotes, pictures, and first-hand glimpses of death) but also poetically, in the Aristotelian sense of creating representations of the way things *could* be, and not just the way they have been.[19] Just as one of Kafka's characters became an artist of hunger, Montaigne's philosopher becomes an artist of death: "At every moment let us picture it in our imagination in all its aspects. At the stumbling of a horse, the fall of a tile, the slightest pin prick, let us promptly chew on this: Well, what if it were death itself?" (86/60).[20]

Clearly Montaigne is not recommending that we think about the *idea* of death in an abstract sense, or about what death implies about the existence or nonexistence of the soul and other related traditional problems, but rather that we try to convert the abstraction of death into something that is concrete and present. The insistence on extreme specificity in this imagination of death, seizing on ordinary events and infusing their sounds and feelings with new significance, suggests that we should be cautious in accepting the many footnotes in editions of the *Essays* where "imagination" is glossed as "opinion" or "conception."[21] At times Montaigne uses the term so expansively that the terms seem like synonyms, but it might be more useful to move in the other direction and begin to think that the author means "imagination" when he wrote "opinion"—so strong is Montaigne's recurring theme that abstraction should be compelled to embodiment and should come to us as sights, sounds, and smells. "That to philosophize is to learn to die" is significantly located just before the chapter "Of the power of the imagination" (I, 21) and is the second chapter after "Of fear" (I, 18), both texts that strongly connect thoughts to their bodily manifestations and consequences.

Imagination is the bridge between the mind and the body, it is the faculty that gives the mind awareness of the physical world, not only in general terms but in terms of a specific perspective. Imagination is always a first-person sense, it always has a point of view, for it does not give us a general idea of smell or taste but rather the very precise knowledge "I am tasting . . ." or "I have tasted . . ." In order to convey an experience, imagination necessarily performs in the mind the act of perceiving that experience and must distinguish among stances toward experience. One can watch a battle as a distant spectator or one can see a battle as a participant. The idea of such events or conditions as sickness, pain, poverty, and death are no longer interesting as generalities but first become particularized (in the insistence on examples) and then experienced, either actually or hypothetically, in imagination. It is surely no accident that the raise in importance of imaginative practice in the Renaissance coincides historically with the establishment of optical perspective in drawing and painting, since both mental imagination and optical perspective require a unifying agent from whose real or hypothetical standpoint the physical world is perceived.[22] Yet in connecting the mind to the body, imagination—for Montaigne and other Renaissance thinkers influenced by the Stoics—asserts the superiority of mind over body, since in imagination we can make ourselves absent from the present world, try out the experience of incidents possible in the future, and bring back vividly a moment from the past. Angelo Poliziano, whose works Montaigne owned, was a particularly fervent promoter of practicing for the future. He recommended forethought as a form of exercise.[23] Poliziano, in his Latin translation of Epictetus's *Manual*, gave to the fourth chapter a title that stressed the active role of imagination, "Quo nos pacto in aspera quavis imaginatione gerere oporteat" (In what way we ought to bear any difficulties with imagination).[24]

If philosophies teach us to rise above suffering, poverty, and sickness then the highest problem is death, beyond "all our other woes. But as for death itself, it is inevitable" (83/57). So Montaigne approaches philosophy by its most élite topic and does so by the most élite method, disdaining the "common" habit of trying not to think about the problem at all: "The remedy of the common herd is not to think about it. But from what brutish stupidity can come so gross a blindness!" (84/57). While the unprepared will die surprised by mortality—"what torments, what cries, what frenzy, what despair overwhelms them! Did you ever see anything so dejected, so changed, so bewildered?" (86/59)—the philosopher, like a pilot today in a flight simulator, will try to preexperience his end: "let us take an entirely different way from the usual one. Let us rid it of its strangeness, come to know it, get used to it. Let us have nothing in our minds as often as death" (86/60).

Being able to imagine death voluntarily and concretely in this way (to translate, as it were, the most banal circumstance into the fictive experience of death) sets Montaigne apart from the people who need to have others organize reminders of death for them:

> Just as we plant our cemeteries next to churches, and in the most frequented parts of town, in order (says Lycurgus) to accustom the common people, women and children, not to grow panicky at the sight of a dead man . . . (89/62).

The philosophical élite possesses the most active, controlled imagination of death and does not require these external, institutional forms of *memento mori* because such thinkers understand and use imagination's power to overcome the limitations of time and place.

Imaginative predying makes philosophy a form of mental suicide. The example of Paulus Aemilius's reply to the captive King of Macedonia illustrates the aristocratic distinction of control over one's own death by suicide. Asked to spare him the humiliation of being led as prisoner in the triumph, Paulus Aemilius sent back the message that the King should make that request to himself (87), in other words, that the captive should retrieve his dignity through the free choice of death, an assertion of the Stoic principle that no material loss actually touches us because all that truly is ours, is our moral purpose.[25] If the thought of death is sufficiently concrete to remove from it any surprise and any experience of weakness, this mental experience liberates the philosopher from death by preempting death, provided that the imagination is strong enough and has managed to inventory and foresee all the possible surprises of death, so that the event becomes a nonevent.

Philosophical imagination parallels military planning, and the *Essays* describe it as an ambush that can be anticipated only by exhaustive simulation: "It is uncertain where death awaits us; let us await it everywhere" (87/60). The result of such a proliferation of scenarios of death is strange and, at first glance, contradictory insistence on the extreme concreteness of detail that enables foresight and prevents surprise, on one hand, and a universal leveling that abolishes meaningful distinction of times and places by bringing them all back to the thought that it does not matter when or where death occurs. The combination of extreme concreteness and extreme abstraction, which has often been noted as a characteristic of metaphysical or baroque poetry of meditation, is evident in Montaigne's Stoic-inspired practice.[26] This practice of remembering past experiences and projecting into the future various possible occurrences involve sensory experiences so that death ceases to be distant and purely conceptual but become associated with visceral and nervous reflexes—each of the cases Montaigne cites are likely to be the occasion for an involuntary, startled reaction of our body—and deeply interwoven into the fabric of daily life. At the same time the practice of imagination is framed within highly abstract philosophical puzzles about the relation between life and death:

All the time you live you steal from life; living is at life's expense. The constant work of your life is to build death. You are in death while you are in life; for you are after death when you are no longer in life. (93/65).[27]

The extreme formulation of the abolition of distinctions between times and places—since all can be the occasion of death and the threshold between time and eternity—states the identity of all moments:

> And if you have lived a day, you have seen everything. One day is equal to all days. There is no other light, no other night. This sun, this moon, these stars, the way they are arranged, all this is the very same your ancestors enjoyed and that will entertain your grandchildren. (93/65)

Imagination frees the thinker from the external imposition of sensation (and thus from the dominance of the present moment that imposes sensation) and gives him or her control over the images that pass through the mind. This control extends to the flow of time itself. Picturing death from a sudden fever or a fall removes the novelty from death when it actually comes, so that this "final" moment has already been lived mentally. Montaigne recalls an incident from his own life to illustrate this. One day, when he was a league from his house and perfectly healthy, he took a notebook and wrote down something that he wanted to have done after his death, just in case he did not make it home. Foreseeing the possibility of death when there was no likelihood of dying gave Montaigne mastery of death:

> Since I am constantly brooding over my thoughts and settling them within me, I am at all times about as well prepared as I can be. And the coming of death will teach me nothing new. (88/61).

There is nothing *new* about death just as there is nothing *new* in the sky for the imaginative philosopher who can picture the sky as it was for his great-grandfather (although he was not alive in those days) and can picture the sky as it will be many centuries after his death. This is not because the world is completely unchanging, for Montaigne frequently insists on change and instability in the physical world. This is not even because the most basic principles remain constant (though at a certain level of abstraction Montaigne would probably concede such a point). Instead, the thinker cancels out novelty and difference by picturing a multitude of configurations and then by locating what is constant and common to them all ("A thousand men, a thousand animals, and a thousand other creatures die at the very moment when you die" 95/67). In this way the controlled imagination, allied with will and judgment, can navigate through human experience and locate the philosopher's own identity in that vaster picture, even picturing and feeling something completely fictive and alternative to known reality, the intolerable detail of a life deprived of death. When Nature, personified, speaks toward the end of "That to philosophize is to learn to die," Montaigne shows the liberty that is achieved through the disconnection between the outer life and the inner life of the mind. As Nature says:

> The advantage of living is not measured by length, but by use; some men have lived long, and lived little; attend to it while you are in it . . . Imagine honestly how much less bearable and more painful to man would be an everlasting life than the life I have given him. (95–96/67).

If imagination is an important mental practice for the philosopher, this is because it helps overcome the paradox that is inherent in both knowing and "practicing" death. Practice—exercise, training—supposes repetition as a means to increase familiarity and to obtain mastery of something. But since we cannot die more than once, we apparently cannot learn to do it better. Montaigne deals with this objection at the beginning of his chapter "Of practice" (II, 6) when he mentions the efforts of men who have tried to study the experience of their own death. The problem is, of course, that they cannot share that knowledge, as Montaigne emphasizes with some humor by telling the story of one such attempt:

> Canius Julius, a Roman nobleman of singular virtue and firmness, after being condemned to death by the scoundrel Caligula, gave this among many prodigious proofs of his resoluteness. As he was on the point of being executed, a philosopher friend of his asked him: 'Well, Canius, how stands your soul at this moment? What is it doing? What are your thoughts?' 'I was thinking,' he replied, 'about holding myself ready and with all my powers intent to see whether in that instant of death, so short and brief, I shall be able to perceive any dislodgement of the soul, and whether it will have any feeling of its departure; so that, if I learn anything about it, I may return later, if I can, to give the information to my friends.' (II. 6:371/267).

In the absence of Canius's account of that experience, reasons Montaigne, we can only proceed on the basis of analogies. Here imagination is in its element because it is, first of all, the way of thinking that specializes in experience (all experience comes to us through the senses) and that extends experience on the basis of analogy. The way to tell people about a scent unknown to them is to compare scents that they have experienced and to guide them to combine and modify their mental representations accordingly.[28]

The incident that forms the core of "Of practice" gave Montaigne new material to expand what he, and we, can imagine. A near-death experience that Montaigne had after falling from his horse seems so similar to death that it offers a chance to learn what death is like from the point of view of the dying person and can thus be seen as an exceptional opportunity to "practice" dying.

Montaigne tells of going out riding on a small, easy-to-handle horse near his house during one of the civil wars of the 1570s. When his horse was struck by another, larger and more vigorous one, Montaigne was thrown and fell, apparently dead. Montaigne describes his thoughts and sensations both in the kind of coma that followed and lasted several hours and later when he had apparently revived and began talking, though he claims to have no recollection of speaking and even argues that his speech was a kind of reflex that did not come from "himself." This incident is a treasure-trove for Montaigne, because he thinks that it offers the inner experience similar to that of the moments that precede death, an experience that is unreachable even to those who watch carefully as someone else dies. However, while this experience of being close to death or perceived by bystanders as dead may circumvent the paradox of "practice" in regard to death—for Montaigne argues that the actual moment of expiring is so brief that it is unimportant and that the approaches of death, what we would call "dying," are what we really need to learn to endure—it raises another paradox that is related to imagination.

The author's near-death state can only be appreciated, in fact, can only be known, through some form or other of imagination. It can appear to Montaigne through imagination that faculty works in conjunction with memory, and it can appear to the reader to the extent that imagination is guided by the text, for here sound, bodily sensations of pain, sight, and more general sensations not easily fit into one of the specialized senses (such as "languor and extreme weakness") are described carefully.

"Of practice" is the essay that most clearly associates imagination and the body with an inside/outside opposition. "I can imagine no state so horrible and unbearable for me as to have my soul alive and afflicted, without means to express itself . . ." (375/270) writes Montaigne in describing what we call today "locked-in syndrome," the state of being alive and conscious and sensate, but being unable to communicate with the people around oneself, the people "outside." This state is the complement of the "locked-out syndrome" that philosophy encounters in trying to experience the death of other persons as they do. The only way to get inside the experience of dying is by imagining it, whether through the retrospective imagining of one's own happy fall, the disciplined premeditation of death, or by being guided in thought through the sensations claimed by another person.

When he was in the traumatic state that followed his fall, Montaigne experienced the gradual activation of three mental activities: sensation, thought (judgment), and imagination. At first he possessed a very unusual awareness of sensation, an awareness that was possible because it was detached from the usual anxieties and thoughts that either overwhelm the sensation or distract from it. This awareness is the pure *phantasia*, which the Stoics did so much to try to recognize *as such*, prior to the distorting effects of socially learned evaluations and associations. When he emerged from darkness and began to see "it was with a vision so blurred, weak and dead, that I still could distinguish nothing but the light" (374/269). In a kind of "bracketing" that a later phenomenologist might envy, Montaigne is able to perceive light itself rather than the myriad of things that emerge in sight because of light. He believes subsequently, when he begins to have something that he qualifies as a "thought" rather than a sensation, that he has been shot in the head. Thus, he is beginning to assemble cause–effect statements, and in this case starts with one that he later finds to be false. Then, he experiences what he describes as an act of *imagination*: "It seemed to me that my life was hanging only by the tip of my lips; I closed my eyes in order, it seemed to me, to help push it out, and took pleasure in growing languid and letting go. It was an imagination that was only floating on the surface of my soul, as delicate and feeble as all the rest . . ." (374/269).

This act of imagination is one that he identifies as such. He does not present himself as being possessed of the analytical consciousness that would be required for deliberate invocation of that faculty. Yet, unlike the two preceding stages of his awakening, sensation and "thought," this "imagination" is associated with will, the faculty that is central to our search for pleasure. Given that his life was on his lips, he chose to help push that life out and to help expiration along, mastering his own death by willing it. This is not the form of will often popularly associated with Stoicism—thought to be the harsh and almost violent coercion of the self to do something repugnant. But it is an act of will enabled by a corrected apprehension of sensory experience. Because Montaigne, at this point, has managed to perceive the simplicity of death, freed from the conventional trappings of horror that society has tied to it, his will can *choose* death freely.

As Montaigne makes use of imagination here, that faculty permits him and us to perceive what is not otherwise perceptible. This is one of the most interesting contributions of the *Essays*, and it is worth considering the additional paradox that emerges from the primary paradox of practicing the act of dying in "Of practice." Imagination, as we use the term here, is the mental representation of sensation. When we "perceive" things we use our senses to do so and the more general or abstract ideas of eternity or of friendship are not perceptible in terms of taste or smell. To say that imagination permits us to perceive what is not otherwise perceptible may seem to imply an abandonment of this fundamental definition. However, there are things that could be perceived, with the senses, if there were an occasion—a situation—in which those things were available to a perceiver. Incense, for instance, can be smelled, but incense sealed within the central chamber of an unopened pyramid is not smelled because there is no one alive in such a situation to perceive it.[29]

Dying—the experience of the approach of death—is, as Montaigne describes it, one of those boundary cases. Even though this passage of the *Essays* does not purport to be an account of actual death and a return to life to tell about the event, the encounter with the approach of death, this apparent coma, supposes an impossible person or at least an impossible vantage point. In order to appreciate the experience of the gradual return of mental faculties—sensation, judgment, imagination—the person must be able to put together, mentally, the knowledge of the complete spectrum of the faculties with the memory of the very limited sensation of light that he savored after his fall. These two things are mutually exclusive in "real" life—we cannot both be without full awareness and aware of our lack. Sensing light as pure light and knowing what is special and unusual about this sensation is an experience only available to us as a mental experiment. In a similar manner, to appreciate Montaigne's first experience of judgment, "the first thought that came to me," he (and the reader) must be both within the moment of the thought and beyond it, at a distance that permits a relativist weighing of its illusory quality. He was not hit by a musket shot, as he supposed, and the value of this statement in his account is metaphorical: his sensation was *like* that felt by people who have been hit by a musket shot (or what we suppose they feel).

If we were to be able to have a "pure" account of Montaigne's experience in the moments after his accident–something that becomes a widespread writerly device with the advent of stream-of-consciousness narration in the twentieth century–it would be either incomprehensible or false, or both at the same time. This account might tell us that he was shot in the head, that he had no idea where he was and no concern for himself or others, and that his body was intact and in good condition. By the time he wrote this passage he knew that his horse had been struck by another horse, that he had shown great concern for his wife's welfare, and that his body was all bruised. Neither one of these accounts is especially interesting, even though one is "true" (but distant and, very largely, second-hand) and the other one "false" (though based on a lived, first-person experience). It is the interplay between the two accounts that gives value to this description in "Of practice," for each account is incomplete without the other. Montaigne gives a first-person account that is split into the experience of the approach of death from the *inside*, as it was sensed, and from the *outside*, as it was seen by the normally aware bystanders.

Montaigne tries to overcome the dilemma posed by the horror of the "locked-in syndrome" that he evokes in his own commentary, while he confronts the "locked-out" syndrome that is the general problem of philosophy when it confronts death: how does it feel to die. By retaining the sensation of dying while deploying the full range of discursive and analytic power of the writer, Montaigne provides himself with a *new* experience, deeper and richer than the one that he would have had otherwise.

FREEDOM AND TIME

Death is the major instance and test-case for the seeker of practical wisdom because it concerns something that will happen *sooner* or *later* to everyone. The gap between now and then, during which we think about death, consists only of time, yet time is elusive in the *Essays*.[30] In his eclectic fusion of Stoic and Epicurean views of time, Montaigne, particularly in the first book of the *Essais*, attaches great importance to "*tranquillitas*, that is, being within the present": worries, regrets, and desires—all of which lead out of the present—should be avoided.[31] Finding a way to accepting our relationship to the moment bonds the subjective and the objective in harmony: *Jam fuerit, nec post unquam revocare licebit* ("Soon it will be past and never more can we bring the present back").[32] The apparently objective, external differences in times do not cause anxiety to the person who accepts the radical interior translation of those time differences into a different, stable measure. This is implied in Montaigne's comment, quoted above, about the difference between living *a long time* and living *little*, that is, with little intensity of purpose. Hence, "It lies in your will, not in the number of years, to assure that you have lived enough" (I.20:95/67).

Readers of the *Essays* who see a marked change in Montaigne's relation to Stoic philosophy in the courses of his life—and in the chronological layers of his book—sometimes contrast a supposedly rigid voluntarism of earlier passages to a more relaxed and accepting outlook in later ones. Françoise Joukovsky argues that Montaigne discovered that in contemplating death, "it is useless to tense and stiffen oneself in such a meditation."[33] There is a measure of truth in the idea that Montaigne modified his view of how to use the present moment, but this change is both subtle and consistent with the view that one of our major tasks as thinkers is to make proper use of imagination.

Montaigne formulated quite early the goal of removing the sting of the changes, including death, that will inevitably occur. Thus, imagining death and other hardships realistically removed the distinction between future and present, between present and past. If some hardship had been experienced many times in thought, that hardship was already old, it already seemed part of the past, when it came about. It then arrived in the present moment, not as strange, but as familiar. This particular use of imagination is a kind of hardening oneself, a stiffening (*se raidir*), and there are many examples of it in Montaigne's favorite Roman and Greek authors. However, this is not the only way to use imagination in order to protect the present moment by freeing it from fear, surprise, and pain. A certain detachment in the enjoyment of the present can also occur if one accepts the flow of appearances as they occur to the mind, without concern for their "reality" and thus their presentness. This is an approach vividly illustrated by "Of practice," where Montaigne did not have to make any particular effort to bring to his mind a representation of death; all he had to do was pay attention to what was passing through his mind in the form of sensations. This is without a doubt the passage in the *Essays* in which the ancient ideal of *tranquillitas* is most completely achieved, yet it is achieved by accepting the spontaneous productions of imagination, rather than by calling them into being according to a preconceived program. Accepting the instant as a succession of other moments with varying mental pictures permits us to view the world simply as a spectacle worth contemplating.[34] Ancient philosophers are often accused of showing off, even by Montaigne himself, and taken to task for "such Stoic sallies" by which they boast of their endurance for pain.[35] Yet Montaigne's exceptional and deep attention to the minute changes in his own body and to the physical detail of the things around him as they change over the years actually confirms the author's assimilation of basic Stoic concepts.[36] Things become interesting to observe when we are not afraid of them, and change is more clearly perceptible when we have a standpoint—a core stability of consciousness—from which to measure it.[37] Moreover, Montaigne's persistent fascination with constant change in the material world is compatible with his reading of ancient philosophers.[38] Imagination is an important part of how we relate to time, because it is the instrument that determines what we perceive, and therefore what portion of time we inhabit; it is the faculty that gives us a measure of control over the moment we choose to hold in our mind, whether it be the present, the past, or an anticipated future. If we do not realize that the choice is ours, we risk being stuck in the wrong moment. This is why effective action, and even truth, requires the use of imagination.

Let us consider the case of someone who is caught in the past. This is a not-infrequent imaginative mishap:

> Those who have been drubbed in some battle, and who are still all wounded and bloody—you can perfectly well bring them back to the charge the next day. But those who have conceived a healthy fear of the enemy—you would never get them to look him in the face. (I.18:76/53).

This conservative type of impression gives people an image of the past that they take for a permanent reality. When they are faced with a battle or even simply think about one, they do not perceive what is in front of them or what is simply possible but instead return to a fixed impression. This is not simply a "memory," for it is not recognized as an idea from the past, but rather a passive imagination. If the person can reconfigure his or her imagination and restore its flexibility, its openness to new "pictures" of the way things are, they will behave accordingly. Montaigne's chapter "Of the power of the imagination" is full of examples both of the immobilized imagination and appropriate reconfigurations of mental pictures that permit a sufferer to break out of a past moment. One telling example is that of the woman who believed that she swallowed a pin in her bread. She remains tormented by the feeling of the pin in her throat, even though no one can find a trace of this pin. The cure is effected by making her vomit and placing—when she is not looking—a pin into what she has disgorged, so that the new sight of the "dislodged" pin replaces her mental sensation of the one she believed she swallowed.

CHANGING THE WORLD WITH IMAGINATION

The cure of the woman who felt the pin in her throat is one of many examples of the impact of imagination on the body. In practical terms the distinction between "true" and "false" perceptions of the world is often canceled by imagination. Rather than accepting the world as it appears, we can intervene with our mental images to shape physical reality itself, according to a Latin adage quoted by Montaigne: *Fortis imaginatio generat casum* ("A strong imagination creates the case [the way things are]"[39]). In many ways Montaigne is a philosophical pragmatist who would be quite at home in Richard Rorty's intellectual world.[40] He does not make a rigorous and exclusive division between what is objectively true and what is simply false because he recognizes that such a division would not allow an active place for the perceiver. In real life the perceiver actually causes things to become what they are, sometimes simply by perceiving them. This fact is a traditional part of the philosophy of *phantasia* and justifies the Stoic attention to managing perceptions. This is not to say that Epictetus or Marcus Aurelius would endorse every application that Montaigne derives from their writings, but there is a recognizable kinship between the active use of imagination in the *Essays* and the Stoic teachings on taking charge of the perception of the world.

The difference between passive and active perception—which are simply two stances that one can take toward imagination—appears not only in "That to philosophize is to learn to die" but also, with astonishing examples, in "Of the power of the imagination." At first this chapter seems to be devoted to the consequences of purely passive imagination—imagination in the obsolete sense of how we perceive what is in front of us. Montaigne writes that he is so affected by the presence of sick people that he can become sick simply by seeing them: "The sight of other people's anguish causes very real anguish to me, and my feelings have often usurped the feelings of others. A continual cougher irritates my lungs and throat" (97/68). Conversely, for the author and for other people he has met, the presence of healthy, and especially young, people brings them health. This seems at first to put Montaigne at a disadvantage, as someone who simply suffers from imagination:

> I am one of those who are very much influenced by the imagination. Everyone feels its impact, but some are overthrown by it. Its impression on me is piercing. And my art is to escape it, not to resist it. (97/68).

Already, even in Montaigne's declaration that his "art" is to flee rather than to resist imagination, he is moving from a passive to an active stance. He accepts that his health is not simply a given, not simply an objective fact, but something that he can determine by changing the impressions that are in his mind.[41] However, these impressions do not necessarily come from *outside* the mind and therefore they do not depend on time and place. He mentions Ovid's story of Iphis, a girl disguised as a boy who married another girl and became male by the force of desire alone, "through his and his mother's vehement desire" (98–99/69). He also notes the astounding case of Gallus Vibius who

> strained his mind so hard to understand the essence and impulses of insanity that he dragged his judgment off its seat and never could get it back again; and he could boast of having become mad through wisdom. (98/68).

It seemed like a good idea at the time! Vibius did not become insane by suggestive contagion from the people around him, but rather, in Montaigne's account, because he willed himself into the mental outlook of the insane. He did not just imagine an insane person—this would be the equivalent of Montaigne picturing the death scene of such ancient philosophers as Epicurus and Cato rather than thinking his way into his own possible death—but Vibius instead made him see the world through the eyes of an insane man.[42] He did not picture himself acting insanely but entertained in his mind the images of the world, the complex of sensations, that he supposed went through the mind of troubled people. With the example of Vibius, Montaigne very explicitly conveys the idea that will can direct imagination, at least in certain circumstances (Vibius could not repeat his trick in order to return to the world of the sane, but perhaps he did not wish to come back). Since imagination can have physical results—can make people cough, have fevers, die, develop scars, be cured of scrofula, and even change sex—the will, in using imagination, gives itself an extremely powerful instrument. Montaigne may not have taken all of his examples at face value—he uses them "provided they are possible" (105/75)—, but he does give the first-hand example of a cure of impotence effected by a change in the affected man's imagination.[43]

Although Montaigne heaps up examples in "Of the power of the imagination" to show that imagination—and thus the mind—is more powerful than physical causes, along with the demonstration of that power runs the question of whose will is directing the imagination. Having established in "That to philosophize is to learn to die" that the philosopher is distinguished from "the common people" by his initiative in anticipating death with his imagination, Montaigne seems here in "Of the power of the imagination" to juxtapose examples of people who are affected by the decisions of other people and examples of people who seize the initiative themselves. For both categories, the way people perceive the world transforms the world. Changes in perception often lead to happy results. Montaigne stresses that imagination does not function randomly or unmanageably and that it can be directed to very precise ends. Power over imagination is *real* power, and Montaigne implies that it is better to know how to direct that way of thinking than to depend on others (such as physicians and priests) to do it.

Almost all of the cases treated here concern individual persons and the effect of their thoughts on their own bodies. In one case, however, Montaigne shows how imagination can be organized for broader social purposes to control a whole group of people. This collective imagination, which is a component of what we would call ideology,[44] is the major topic of the *Apology for Raymond Sebond* (as we will see shortly). The story of Marie Germain in "Of the power of the imagination" serves to prepare the way for the *Apology*. Here is her story:

> Passing through Vitry-le-François, I might have seen a man whom the bishop of Soissons had named Germain at confirmation, but whom all the inhabitants of that place had seen and known as a girl named Marie until the age of twenty-two. He was now heavily bearded, and old, and not married. Straining himself in some way in jumping, he says, his masculine organs came forth; and among the girls there a song is still current by which they warn each other not to take big strides for fear of becoming like Marie Germain. (99/69).

Now, the young woman Marie Germain—who is not given here a different name as a man—was not affected by her imagination but rather by a physical accident. Her story, or his story, strikes the imagination of other people and changes the way they see the material world. When the girls of the village think of jumping, their thought includes the possibility that jumping will make them males. So not only do they refrain from "big strides," but their actual feeling of their bodies is modified to the extent that vigorous movement is associated with the perception of a feared transformation. As each girl imagines herself jumping, she will concurrently imagine this modification of her body as if she were undergoing the experience of Marie Germain.[45] This song, with its didactic purpose, uses imagination to fashion the way young women move their bodies, feel their bodies, and relate those feelings to their thoughts.[46] It thus fits into Montaigne's series of examples of imagination modifying the body, but it goes beyond individual imagination to use of imagination by groups to inform and discipline members of the group.

One of the longest and most sustained early-modern writings on imagination (and a key text of the "epistemological turn" of modern thought) is Montaigne's "Apology for Raymond Sebond" (*Essays*, II, 12). In this long, complex, and even paradoxical attack on mankind's excessive confidence in its ability to attain knowledge of the world and specifically knowledge of God, the author repeatedly locates *imagination* and *fantaisie* at key points of his argument. While the "Apology" is generally described as Montaigne's engagement with the skeptical philosophy of Pyrrho and Sextus Empiricus, attention to the role of imagination in other chapters of the *Essays* makes it apparent that Montaigne's interest in how we use imagination transcends any allegiance on his part to one or the other of the ancient philosophical schools.[47] Stoic training in separating oneself from the input of the senses and in fabricating alternative mental representations can also serve as a basis of the social critique of imagination that unfolds in the "Apology." Early in the text Montaigne establishes the claim that imagination is the defining feature of the human race:

> Presumption is our natural and original malady. The most vulnerable and frail of all creatures is man, and at the same time the most arrogant. He feels and sees himself lodged here, amid the mire and dung of the world, nailed and riveted to the worst, the deadest, and the most stagnant part of the universe, on the lowest story of the house and the farthest from the vault of heaven, with the animals of the worst condition of the three; and in his imagination he goes planting himself above the circle of the moon, and bringing the sky down beneath his feet. It is by the vanity of this same imagination that he equals himself to God, attributes to himself divine characteristics, picks himself out and separates himself from the horde of other creatures, carves out their shares to his fellows and companions the animals, and distributes among them such portions of faculties and powers as he sees fit. How does he know, by the force of his intelligence, the secret internal stirrings of animals? By what comparison between them and us does he infer the stupidity that he attributes to them? (452/330–31).

While this passage obviously serves as a vigorous denigration of human claims to superiority through presumption, it also places imagination at the core of humanity's way of seeing the cosmos, locating human beings within the cosmos, and thus creating a human identity. If it were not for imagination—the faculty that sustains presumption—humanity would simply see itself as one kind of animal among others and would thus be animals. Imagination permits the founding, and foundational, gestures that draw the boundary between nature and culture, between human and animal. Through imagination mankind usurps divine attributes, not only descriptively but also performatively by actually forming the human race out of the indistinct biomass of creation. For Montaigne's cosmology, imagination has much of the force of the "big bang" in today's astronomical accounts of the origins of the universe, since without imagination there would be no humanity (as such) and no animality (no *bestise*) either. In this account imagination is an organizational or classifying activity that is indispensable to the construction of a self-identity for humanity as a whole, and this description clearly implies that subsequent individual self-descriptions are also the work of the same faculty.

The book of *Genesis* is not explicitly mentioned here, but by allocating to imagination such a power to create by dividing, Montaigne comes very close to the Vulgate's insistence on God's similar gestures: "Dixit quoque Deus: Fiat firmamentum in medio aquarum: et dividat aquas ab aquis. Et fecit Deus firmamentum, divisitque aquas, quae erant sub firmamento, ab his, quae erant super firmamentum" (1:6–7). By imagining the world through a series of divisions and rankings, mankind creates it, in Montaigne's cosmological departure from *Genesis*, and mankind here, in a sense, *precedes* the animals rather than following, as in the Bible, where the fish and birds are created on the fifth day, and the animals of the land are created on the sixth, apparently prior to the creation of male and female humans (1:20–27). In Montaigne's account, mankind created the distinction of human and animal out of a preexisting continuum of life, so that humanity and *bestise* appear either simultaneously or in rapid succession from the self-promoting vision of one part of creation. Yet in placing the presumption enabled by imagination at the beginning of mankind, as "our natural and original malady," Montaigne seems to accept the impossibility of separating mankind from this way of seeing things.[48] It is by the affliction of this sickness that mankind is true to its nature and its origin.

With this vigorous statement of the paradox that mankind is defined by a unique sickness and thus implying that the cure would eliminate mankind itself, Montaigne launches a series of arguments against mankind's claims to be distinctly different from the animals. It looks as if Montaigne is trying to undercut all these claims—to unique possession of reason, language, etc.— and thus to reestablish humans among the animals, but at the same time the elimination of the other rationales for human distinctiveness simply underscores with more force the proposition that mankind's particular use of imagination is the inherent and inseparable element in defining humanity. In one of the many iterations of the general sameness of humanity and the animals, Montaigne returns to the imagination as the sole (potential) differentiating feature:

> He is fettered and bound, he is subjected to the same obligation as the other creatures of his class, and in a very ordinary condition, without any real and essential prerogative or preeminence. That which he accords himself in his mind and in his fancy has neither body nor taste. And if it is true that he alone of all the animals has this freedom of imagination and this unruliness in thought that represents to him what is, what is not, what he wants, the false and the true, it is an advantage that is sold him very dear, and in which he has little cause to glory, for from it springs the principal source of the ills that oppress him: sin, disease, irresolution, confusion, despair. (459/336).

So mankind *is* different after all! Montaigne concedes this difference, rather obliquely, by listing all the ills that accrue to humanity from this peculiar freedom to represent things other than they *are*, a peculiar ability to depart from the objective ontological order. Despite the common constraints that weigh on animals and humanity, the latter has one possible way out: the capacity for mental representation of the nonexistent.

Humans are animals with imagination, and not, as is more often said, animals who reason. Animals communicate among themselves (453/331), have organized (or political) societies (455/332), possess judgment (455/333), have the capacity to imitate actions and to learn from experience (465/341), show gratitude, loyalty (477/350), and clemency (480/353), act prudently and with foresight (473/347), and so forth. Our superiority over the animals is in our imagination—in both senses of that expression: it is an illusion and it consists of our imagination. This is, of course, illogical or paradoxical, but that bizarre logic constitutes the human condition. If we were able to view our situation objectively, Montaigne seems to be saying, we would see that we have no superiority over the animals. On the other hand, if we were able to see things objectively, we would *be* animals. Since our unusual but characteristic way of thinking, as human beings, is to see things as they *are not* (but rather as they have been, might have been, will be, might be, etc.), we have a capacity that sets us apart from and (throughout tradition, as we define ourselves) above the animals. We have a "better" imagination than animals do. Despite Montaigne's own ambivalence in laying the basis for this reasoning, we can see in this thematic the source of Pascal's celebrated claim that humans are superior through thought, as "thinking reeds."[49]

Even the claim that humans are the imagining animals is hedged here with caveats and distinctions. Animals do imagine in a certain sense, because they are able to remember and so to represent sensory experience in their minds. Montaigne presents this position in an unusually difficult passage which at first seems to maintain that animals have the power to abstract from experience and thus to reach the world of pure ideas and to leave behind, when thinking of things, all their "accidents" of sense: size, weight, color, hardness, etc.[50] Montaigne, however, seems to mean simply that animals can, as we can, possess the sensory idea of a thing even in the absence of that thing. Animals can thus imagine in the sense of remembering and dreaming:

> so that the Rome and Paris that I have in my soul, the Paris that I imagine, I imagine and conceive it without size and without place, without stone, without plaster, and without wood—this same privilege, I say, seems very evidently to belong to the beasts. For a horse accustomed to trumpets, harquebus fire, and battles, whom we see tremble and quiver in his sleep, stretched out on his litter, as if he were in the fray: it is certain that in his soul he conceives a drum beat that has no sound, and an army that has no weapons or body. (481/354).

Montaigne clears up the ambiguity with which he starts this passage, for he makes explicit that the dreaming horse is not merely entertaining the "concept" of a battle but experiencing the mental recurrence of each of the senses through which he experienced battles in the past, hearing, for instance, a sound without noise.

Animals can remember, and this capacity for memory (involuntary during dreams and voluntarily while awake) permits them to imitate, to perform, what they have seen being done by another. Hence, a magpie that Plutarch describes as struck dumb by the sound of trumpets was thinking about the sound until she could reproduce it in her song. Although Montaigne does not use the term imagination in this anecdote, the magpie is plainly engaged in the kind of interior representation of sense experience that defines imagination elsewhere in Montaigne: "it was a profound study and a withdrawal within herself, while her mind was practicing and preparing her voice to represent the sound of these trumpets" (465/341). These are two cases of animal imagination, yet Montaigne does not seem to be troubled by his repeated insistence that human beings are uniquely defined (and deformed) by having imagination. In one of the cases Montaigne explicitly uses the term "to imagine" and in the other not, but both cases have in common the reproduction of a previous experience—in other words, an experience of memory. The magpie actually seems to *want* to remember the music in order to perform it, and while this may make the magpie seem almost human, the general trend of Montaigne's argument in the "Apology for Raymond Sebond" makes it plain that actual "mimetic" performance is not what he has in mind when he ascribes imagination to mankind. Certainly the magpie's achievement, like those of the dogs, cattle, lions, and other animals cited, undercuts many traditional foundations of mankind's claim of superiority, but it does finally return to real, external reality—to the bringing together of thought and action. This may be very noble, but it is not what is specifically human in Montaigne's account, for the existence, within thought, of a *gap* between what is and what might be, between what is and what is perceived to be, is the "sickness" that makes humans.

The need for this gap, constituted by mental replacement of the direct, sensory experience with an unreal picture, is part of man's uniqueness. Take the matter of nudity—one of Montaigne's favorite themes for knocking down claims of superiority by humans in general or Europeans in particular (in "Of cannibals" I. 31). Clothing isolates the body from the direct physical experience of the world, but Montaigne is more interested in the mental separation that clothing provides the mind:

> We are the only animal whose defectiveness offends our own fellows, and the only ones who have to hide, in our natural actions, from our own species. Truly it is also a fact worthy of consideration that the masters of the craft order as a remedy to amorous passions the entire and open sight of the body that we pursue; that to cool our love, we need only see freely what we love:
>   His loved one's private parts, bared to his sight,
>   Checked the man's passion in its headlong flight. (484/356–57).

Montaigne associates suggestively and with scant explanation the way nudity offends *only* humans, and the way clothing stimulates the desires *only* of humans. The explanation is not developed here, but we are alerted—by Montaigne's identification of this trait as distinctively human, alongside the "sickness" that is the freedom of imagination and the "unruliness in thought" (460/336)—to look to the human imagination for the cause of this peculiarity. While animals live entirely within being or factuality, humans live by replacing the seen with the unseen or even the obscene, the hidden, which is stimulus to imagine freely. This example of how humans think points toward a striking distinction between human beings and the apparently very human magpie. The magpie, like humans, has an "interior life," and within herself entertains a vivid mental representation of the concrete outside world. She even, like many humans, reduces the further solicitations of the senses in order to concentrate on her inner world by withdrawing into a profound retreat. However, the magpie's aim is to rejoin the outer world by replicating the original stimulus, the music. The matter is much less clear in the case of the human erotic imagination that Montaigne describes, for this is neither simply imitative nor is the interior picture ever divulged. The gap between "being" and "thinking," which is only temporary in the case of the magpie, seems to be a permanent characteristic in the case of human thought.

So in that part of human experience that some have considered to be most "animal," sexuality, Montaigne locates the distinctive human exercise of imagination. Yet, one might think, at least the highest domain of human activity, philosophy, must be relatively free from imagination, or must at least not *depend* on that faculty as a major resource. After all, sex and philosophy are radically different activities, are they not? In Montaigne's "Apology," apparently they are not so different. In both cases the elusiveness of the object is stimulating, and what we cannot see is somehow better and more energizing for the mind that what we can see:

> Why did not only Aristotle but most philosophers affect difficulty, if not to bring out the vanity of the subject, and keep the curiosity of our mind amused by giving it fodder in gnawing on this hollow and fleshless bone? [. . . .] Plato seems to me to have favored this form of philosophizing in dialogues deliberately, to put more fittingly into diverse mouths the diversity and variation of his own fantasies. (508–09/376–77).

Here, however, we are leaving what is specific to imagination—with its sensory qualities—since both sex and philosophy are activated by that protean and promiscuous trait of *curiosity* that was so often attacked by churchmen in Montaigne's day.

Montaigne does not view philosophy as an abstract discipline. He is neither Descartes nor Thomas Aquinas. Instead he links philosophical enquiry and philosophical systems to images of the world and its contents, at times in the modern sense of "worldview" and at times simply in the more partial meaning of a snapshot or sketch of something we see, hear, or taste. So when Montaigne writes that Plato places "his own fantasies" in the mouths of other participants in his dialogues, this noun is probably not merely a synonym for "ideas" or even for "strange ideas," but rather includes the implication that Plato is conveying a picture of the world that he composed mentally. If we look at several examples that come up in the continued discussion of the stimulating effect of obscurity and mystery in philosophy as in sex, we can see that ideas and sensory data are linked, sometimes spectacularly. Democritus, for instance, was determined to find an explanation for the honey-flavor of the figs he had eaten, even at the cost of ignoring the obvious explanation that the figs had been kept in a honey-coated bowl. However, he did manage, says Montaigne, to find such an explanation, in other words to provide an alternative story about the figs.

Other, more large-scale representations of the world are explicitly designed philosophical accounts that link abstractions to physical embodiments. This enterprise, that is explicitly assigned to imagination, is also tied to Plato, the philosopher of stimulating obscurity:

> He says quite shamelessly in his *Republic* that it is often necessary to trick men for their own good. It is easy to discern that some sects have rather followed truth, others utility; whereby the latter have gained credit. It is the bane of our condition that often what appears to our imagination as most true does not appear to it as most useful for our life. (512/379–80).

Here it is clear that imagination can be the repository of both true and false representations. While animals live in immediate contact with being, mankind apprehends being through imagination, at times truly and at times falsely. The latter can be more useful, so that the philosopher is not so much concerned with reducing the gap between being and mental representations of being as with exploiting that gap for social good. Imagination, or fantasy, is therefore not a synonym for falsehood but rather designates the usable capacity that mankind has for dissociating the image of the external world from its actual being. This view of imagination could not be further from the general Romantic concept of imagination to which we are accustomed in literary and intellectual history—the view (from Rousseau and Chateaubriand onward) that imagination permits us to reconnect with nature by overcoming the obstacles created by an excess of reasoning or by some other social constructs that have distanced us from the spontaneity of children, animals, or "primitive" peoples.[51] Instead, in the "Apology," Montaigne sees imagination as the very source of mankind's distance from nature and as the specific quality that distinguishes man from animals.[52]

Imagination is not only the quality that chiefly characterizes mankind, it is also a faculty that is put to use particularly by those who are most cultured or most thoughtful or perhaps simply the most pretentious—those, at any rate, who have represented the "high" culture that Montaigne both criticizes and practices. So suppressing the imagination, becoming more like the animals against which mankind defines itself, requires a "dumbing-down" of each individual from the exciting, if debilitating, exercise of the fancy.[53] Animals and ignorant people are most in touch with the present and the real and least likely to dwell on the past and on the multiple possibilities of the future.

Both truth and falsehood require imagination in order to function in real life. Hence, the highest of human ideas, the idea of God as "an incomprehensible power, origin and preserver of all things, all goodness, all perfection . . ." (513/380), requires imaginative embodiment in order to become available to human thought. Montaigne juxtaposes his approval of the necessary and logical impossibility of reducing such divinity to the finite limits of human minds with his recognition of the need to incorporate sensory components, imagination, in the representation of God. So, while Saint Paul found most excusable the ancient Greek cult of "a hidden and unknown Deity" (513/380) and while Montaigne protests as ludicrous theological attempts by which "our overweening arrogance would pass the deity through our sieve" (528/393), he acknowledges the craving for an embodiment through which humans can consider the idea of the divine. Thus in ancient Rome, king Numa was mistaken in attempting to have people grasp religious concepts without using the imagination:

> If Numa undertook to make the piety of his people conform to this plan, to attach it to a purely intellectual religion, without any predetermined object or any material admixture, he undertook something unusable. The human spirit cannot keep on floating in this infinity of formless ideas; they must be compiled for it into a definite picture after its own pattern. (513/381).

Imagination has the role of a bridge or of a transmission device by which the abstract (true) religious idea can become concrete (useful) institutional reality. Montaigne does not appeal to some specific requirement of coordinated social action in order to justify the sensory representation of ideas, but he rather points to the way *human minds work*. By using sensory elements ("material admixture") the mind organizes concepts and thus imposes form and scale when threatened by infinite size and connectedness within the network of thought. Imagination is not the truth but neither is it a vehicle of falsehood, since certain true concepts would remain ungraspable and therefore useless without the organizing and symbolic work that imagination performs. As a vehicle of truth, imagination can serve the ends of reason—indeed, Montaigne implies, we could not reason without it.

Once again we glimpse the in-between quality of imagination, its presence within a gap of some kind, between what *is* and what we *perceive* or *conceive*. Compared to the other animals, mankind dwells in imagination because it cannot limit itself to the direct life of the senses in the present (e.g., the fetishistic need for clothing and hence fantasy in sex), and thus imagination is what moves mankind *away* from the physical world into the mobile play of thought. But on the opposite end of the spectrum, where humanity tries to conceive and to understand ideas that are without material basis or far exceed human senses, imagination is what moves human thought *toward* the physical world by providing a structure for thought. Having chosen to found his cosmology on the gesture by which mankind separates itself imaginatively from the animals, Montaigne returns to this separation in presenting an image of the divine. If the animals were "created" in a sense by human imagination in its exercise of a presumptive superiority, they retain the mystery that nourishes imagination and thus provide a means to think about the relationship between man and God.

While Montaigne maintains his own distance, as usual, from particular imaginative constructions of God, he does not argue against their necessity. Instead, he shows that the most reputable of thinkers—Democritus, Plato, Parmenides, Aristotle, etc.—generated large numbers of such images, ranging from the circle to heat (515). However, there are distinctions in the usefulness of certain imaginative practices for religious purposes. Crucifixes, music, and ceremonies in churches are useful to entertain "that stirring of the senses" and "a religious passion" (514/381) while the ancient polytheistic representation of gods like humans with desires and faults is, on pragmatic grounds, less effective than setting the idea of divinity at greater distance, permitting the free-play of the imaginative gap, even, for example, by using animals as symbols: "I would even rather have followed those who worshiped the serpent, the dog, and the ox; inasmuch as their nature and being is less known to us, and we have more chance to imagine what we please about those animals and attribute extraordinary faculties to them" (516/383). What

is unknown—in philosophy, in religion, in sex, and in nature generally—
both requires and enables imagination.

In describing his imaginative practice in "That to philosophize is to learn to
die," Montaigne presents himself as capable of being mentally *elsewhere*. At a
dance, among a crowd of his friends, he wrote, he would be deep in thought,
thinking about how death might come upon him. This distinction between
what is happening in the mind and what is happening in the thinker's actual
physical situation is central to the traditional description of how imagination
works. As early as Aristotle's *De Anima* imagination is defined by its freedom,
its capacity to either accept the sensory stimulation coming from the body
or to reject or (mis)interpret that stimulation. The Stoics took this capacity
and recommended its active cultivation. Rather than being carried away by
the charms of the dance, then, Montaigne is asserting his freedom to think
about something else, creating for himself a mental retreat.

The view of mental practice that is the basis of "That to philosophize is
to learn to die" leads Montaigne to a critique of solitude that anticipates the
ideas of the following century. Essentially solitude is not a spatial concept in
the *Essays* but a concept or rather an achievement in the use of imagination.
In "Of solitude" (I.39) he writes that many people retire from society but
do not benefit at all from this apparent freedom because their mind (and
specifically, their imagination) is still filled with the unnecessary cares and
ambitions of the rat race:

> We take our chains along with us; our freedom is not complete; we still turn
> our eyes to what we have left behind, our fantasy is full of it. (240/176).

The insistence on *fantasie* in this case is easily understandable. Since
imagination is the way of thinking that pictures things and people (and
smells and touches them, etc.) the defect of the crowded solitude of the
unprepared thinker is not so much at the level of judgment as at that of sense
perception. Such an attempt at solitude fails to reach free use of judgment
and will because the individual's *view* is still overpowering the rest of the
mind. Because the mind is still filled with images of desired or feared objects
the mind is not in solitude even if the person's body is. Working on the mind,

preparing it for the supreme good, "how to belong to oneself" (242/178), should take precedence over any change of external living arrangements: "If a man does not first unburden his soul of the load that weighs upon it, movement will cause it to be crushed still more [. . .]. You do a sick man more harm than good by moving him" (I.39:239/176).

Montaigne wrote that we should only *lend* ourselves to others and *give* ourselves to ourselves ("My opinion is that we must lend ourselves to others and give ourselves only to ourselves").[54] True solitude does not depend on space, in the physical sense, but does create, metaphorically, a sense of place. The thinker capable of solitude has an internal "place" of retreat.[55] Montaigne calls this the "back shop": "We must reserve a back shop all our own, entirely free, in which to establish our real liberty and our principal retreat and solitude" (241/177). It is clear, from this expression, that not everyone has an *arriereboutique*, but only those who take steps to create such a resource. Montaigne's younger contemporary François de Sales seems to have agreed with him both in the need for sensory representation of religious beliefs in the desirability of having an interior place of retreat. François de Sales urged his readers to have an inner *cabinet*, and this interior place, under different names, was to become one of the major elements of French Baroque thought—Descartes proclaimed that he went around masked, Pascal emphasized the importance of a secret thought in the back of the head.[56]

Montaigne does not shrink from attacking some big names when he distinguishes between real solitude—mental solitude—and mere withdrawal. Pliny and Cicero recommend, he says, filling one's free time with ambitious scholarly projects that will guarantee future celebrity. One who thus goes off to write still has a mind full of the expected applause and admiring comments of future readers. People who follow Pliny and Cicero focus their desire, and thus their imagination, not only on what is absent but, laughably, on the society that they have supposedly left behind: "by a ridiculous contradiction they still aspire to reap the fruit of their plan from the world when they have left it." (245/180).

As an alternative use of imagination during physical, spatial retreat, Montaigne gives greater approval—though one detects that it is not Montaigne's own choice—to those who undertake religious meditation:

> The imagination of those who seek solitude for religious reasons, filling their hearts with the certainty of divine promises for the other life, is much more sane and consistent. They set before their eyes God, an object infinite both

in goodness and in power; in him the soul has the wherewithal to satisfy its desires abundantly in complete freedom [....] And he who can really and constantly kindle his soul with the flame of that living faith and hope, builds himself in solitude a life that is voluptuous and delightful beyond any other life. (245/180–81).

This passage, appearing for the first time in the 1595 edition, coincides strikingly with the imaginative project of François de Sales, whose *Introduction to the Devout Life* was published thirteen years later. Montaigne not only links imagination with devotion but writes of it in terms of its sensual qualities, as does de Sales.

However, Montaigne gives the place of emphasis in "Of solitude" to a synthesis of Stoic and Epicurean thought by making a combined paraphrase of advice from Epicurus and from Seneca, including the striking counsel, "Retire into yourself, but first prepare to receive yourself there..." (247/182). Montaigne attributes to these ancient writers the chapter's final and most concrete exercise of imagination that transcends time and place and makes the concept of good "solitude" depend on imagination:

> Always represent to yourself in imagination Cato, Phocion, and Aristides, in whose presence even fools would hide their faults; make them controllers of all your intentions; if these intentions get off the track, your reverence for those men will set them right again. (248/183).[57]

True mastery of imagination thus makes solitude possible in company but provides the best possible company in solitude. By giving oneself the resource of a "back room" and then by inviting as companions the great moral exemplars of antiquity, Montaigne shows how we can give ourselves mastery over time and place, and, above all, over ourselves.

TWO

Self-Cultivation and Religious Meditation

On January 13, 1547, in Trent, the Ecumenical Council approved the official statement of the Roman Catholic Church's doctrine on justification, that is, the way in which certain human beings were redeemed from sin and promised eternal happiness and others were condemned to eternal suffering. Central to the doctrine approved on that day is the freedom of the human will and the consequent responsibility of mankind to exert itself to cooperate with divine grace. In August 1608, François de Sales, bishop of Geneva (in absentia), completed the first edition of a bestseller of seventeenth-century French letters, the *Introduction to the Devout Life (L'Introduction à la vie dévote)*, a guide to spiritual self-improvement that calls upon the reader to develop her or his "inner life" through regular, structured use of imagination. Between the Church's strongly worded, even militant, emphasis on the *will* and François de Sales's promotion of the individual, private imagination, there is a direct relation, one that the Bishop of Geneva recalls frequently, especially in his second, more theoretical book, *Treatise on the Love of God (Le Traité de l'amour de Dieu*, 1616). We are called upon to augment our inner life, for the grace of the Holy Spirit will enter into us "only through the freely-given consent of our will . . . insofar as it pleases Him and according to our disposition and cooperation, as the holy Council declared."[1]

De Sales's insistence on disposition and cooperation furnishes the charter, so to speak, for his whole pastoral, and hence literary, project, and helps us to understand not only the simple fact that he and his Catholic contemporaries were avid practitioners of inner self-development but the particular form of that development, one that emphasized what could be called an active and imaginative form rather than a primarily hermeneutic or receptive one.[2] François de Sales's work was widely read and influential—there were at least twenty-four editions in the seventeenth century, and at least four hundred editions in French altogether.[3] Soon after the author's death in 1622 his tomb near Annecy became a place of pilgrimage, and he was canonized only forty-four years later in 1666. His call to develop the individual imagination may well have made subsequent use of this faculty or way of thinking easier even for those whose intentions were far from religious. Moreover, the practice of Salesian devotion goes hand in hand with the development of the absolutist compromise that made possible so much of what we know as French baroque and classical culture.[4] In this way, the use of imagination that is taught in the *Introduction to the Devout Life* has much importance for the development of politeness and civility in the nobility and upper middle classes.[5]

As we read François de Sales's guidance for developing imagination, we need to keep in mind that for the Bishop of Geneva and his contemporaries imagination concerned the way we use our minds to recognize, recall, and combine sense impressions. It is the way we think about things that are perceivable by the senses when we want to have that sensory impression present to our minds. For the authors of the Port-Royal *Logic*, for instance, following Descartes, there was a difference between thinking of a thing in a general or "spiritual" way and *imagining* it.[6] Imagination is the bridge between the "inner" world of the mind and the "outer" world of the body, and it gives the mind a way of dominating the physical world. With imagination the mind can have an idea not only of what is immediately present to the senses but also of what has been and could be perceived physically. Imagination also permits the mind to ignore, or at least distance itself from, immediate physical sensations. In this specific sense—a somewhat technical and archaic one for those of us living after the Enlightenment and Romantic revision of imagination—François de Sales repeatedly juxtaposes imagination with understanding and will, to form the trinity of internal faculties imagination, understanding, and will.

Here is a somewhat prosaic passage of the *Treatise of the Love of God* in which François de Sales reminds his readers of the traditional, Scholastic, structure of knowledge:

> When we look at something, even though that thing is present to us, it does not link itself to our eyes directly but rather it sends a certain representation or image of itself, that is called a sensible species, by means of which we can see; and when we contemplate or hear something, that which we hear does not link itself to our understanding except by means of another representation and image, a very delicate and spiritual one, that we call an intelligible species. Moreover, these species, do not they come to our understanding through many detours and modifications? They enter through the outward sense and from there pass to the inward sense, and then to the phantasy, and then to the active understanding, so that passing through so many filters they are purified and made more subtle and refined so that even though they start out as sensory, they end up being intellectual (*et que de sensibles elles soient rendues intelligibles, TAD*, 512–13).

Here we have the "outward sense," the "phantasy" (often called "imagination"), and then "understanding." François de Sales here mentions only two of the internal faculties, and shows the hierarchical scheme that goes from the most material to the most spiritual in a gradation that can also be expressed as the movement from outside to inside: sense, imagination, understanding, and will.[7]

It is not surprising that François de Sales's methodic guidance of his spiritual flock replicates this movement from imagination to will, for this insistence on will is the doctrinal touchstone that separates Protestants from Catholics, and thus, in the France of Henri IV, those who are tolerated from those who are empowered. *Introduction to the Devout Life* teaches the first steps—through the imagination—toward the perfection of a Catholic spiritual life and the *Treatise of the Love of God* guides its reader toward the ultimate, postimaginative union with God. To express the difference between the two books in Salesian terms, we can say that the *Introduction* is a book about the practice of "meditation," and the *Treatise* is about "contemplation." Despite the figurative and indirect way this distinction is drawn, we can see that contemplation, for François de Sales, is an unmediated contact of the soul with the divinity—it is at the highest level of the will—, while meditation is the preparation of a soul which is not yet ready for the highest and most direct spiritual experience. Both meditation and contemplation are mental disciplines of our *attention*, our will-directed consciousness: "the word 'meditation' is normally used for the attention that we give to divine things" (*TAD* 612). Attention can be directed toward ideas that are purely within the domain of understanding (*entendement*, or reason) or toward ideas that are sensory in origin and quality. In contemplation, attention is directed away from the sensory: "contemplation is nothing other than a loving, simple, and permanent attention given by the spirit to divine things." (*TAD* 616). In contemplation, "The soul . . . has no need . . . of memory, for her Lover is present; she has no need of imagination either, for one should one represent in an image, whether outward or inward, the person whose presence one enjoys?" (*TAD* 636). In contemplation, then, there is no *image*, and thus no need for the faculty that produces images, imagination.

If meditation uses imagination, while contemplation goes beyond and springs from understanding and will into a rapt attention, one might be tempted to think that for François de Sales the will comes later, after imagination. In fact, meditation depends on will also, for in the "cooperation" of the mind with grace—in the post-Tridentine system—the meditator uses will to spur the imagination to shape the will in a virtually endless spiral of aspiration. In fact, it takes a tremendous amount of work to get two rebellious faculties to work together since neither the will nor the imagination of the spiritual beginner is very reliable. This cyclical struggle may seem like mystical nonsense, but in practice it is something that we take perfectly for granted, even today: the appetizer, that is, any object or practice that produces or increases appetite (appetite being a manifestation of will) but that must be put into practice by the will itself—the will to will, the desire to desire, the wish to wish more strongly or more consistently. As Montaigne wrote of the will, when François de Sales was twenty-eighty years old, "Does it always want what we want it to want?"[8] Meditation is based on the individual's resolve to modify her—François de Sales's own preference was to address his reader by the feminine name "Philothée"—own desire, by following one of the "reasonable affections" (*affections raisonnables*)," by which "our will is incited to seek the peace of the heart, the moral virtues, true honor, and the philosophical contemplation of the eternal things" (*TAD* 366).[9] Unlike contemplation in its ultimate form, which is pure pleasure, meditation requires "suffering, effort, and language, since our spirit moves in meditation from one consideration to the next, looking in different places either for the Beloved whom the spirit loves or the love of the Beloved" (*TAD* 626). In short, meditation is something that one chooses to do to modify that manifestation of will known as *affection*: "for meditating and thinking repeatedly to incite the affections, these are simply the same thing" and "meditation tends to move us toward the affections, resolutions, and actions" (*TAD* 614).

The idea of meditating to move oneself to action is clearly in harmony with the Tridentine insistence on will and acts as necessary for justification, and it marks a boundary with the style of interiority against which François de Sales is proposing his alternative. The other form of interior life, in its most stark expression, is not based on the will of the human person but the will of God, "For all human faculties are corrupt, so that of themselves they can bear only evil fruit. In addition this grace is not given to all without distinction or generally, but only to those whom God wills."[10] Because no act of the human will can be of any significance, in the views of Luther, Calvin and many others of the Reform persuasion, the interior life of the Christian is entirely caused by God who directs the chosen "without respect for any merit at all, since in fact they can have no merit, either in their works or in their wills or even in their thoughts."[11] The insistence on the importance of the sole will of God did not prevent Protestants from developing forms of meditation very similar to those of their Catholic contemporaries—for instance, in England, the work of Joseph Hall[12]—but Catholic authorities were particularly wary of form of meditation or inner prayer that centers on receiving and interpreting marks of divine election.[13] Instead of deliberately fabricating certain visions or impressions, this receptive style of interiority considers authentic and useful only those perceptions that are involuntary on the part of the believer.[14] Otherwise, the belief could simply create an impression of salvation that depended simply on the human will, the wish to be saved and to be reassured about salvation.[15] Although the receptive or hermeneutic style of inner life is logically linked to an emphasis the will of God and on minimizing the human will and works, there were a number of Catholics who practiced this form of inner spirituality, even though it was a borderline practice that was often concealed. We are familiar with Pascal's "mémorial," that document sewn into his waistcoat to record the mystical experience of November 23, 1654 that gave him "Certainty, certainty, feeling, joy, peace" (*Certitude, certitude, sentiment, joie, paix*).[16] We may be less familiar with Ignatius of Loyola's spiritual diary, discreetly left unpublished until 1892 (and first published in its entirety only in 1934), in which the founder of the Jesuits recorded his sense of the movements taking place in his heart, movements certainly not directed by his will.[17] Ignatius, before becoming the paragon of Catholic militant orthodoxy that we know was imprisoned and interrogated by the Inquisition more than once, and his early followers were suspected of being *alumbrados*, seeking "spiritual perfection through internal illumination."[18] And one teaching in particular attracted the attention of the Inquisitors, that of "discernment of spirits" through which one uses "the movements in the soul of consolation and desolation [. . . .] in finding and following the will of God."[19] The voluntary inward experience of God as presented in François de Sales, though not without occasional anguish and moments of spiritual drought (*sécheresse*), is pointedly different from contemporary accounts of inwardness penned by writers less insistent on the active, will-centered doctrines of Trent.[20]

The Salesian active and optimistic approach to the interior life was not without rivals in seventeenth-century France—the Quietist controversy at the end of the century marked the culmination and the defeat of a form of passive mysticism that was finally condemned—it nonetheless marks the major and sometimes forgotten orthodoxy of the century.[21] Meanwhile, if the Catholic Church became increasing determined to favor an interior life based on "cooperation" with God's always-offered grace, that is, a spiritual life in which the believer makes deliberate efforts at self-improvement through the shaping of the affections, Protestant writers became increasingly explicit in their rejection of the idea that humans do anything to shape their desires and their behavior in any meaningful way.[22]

François de Sales's repeated linking of imagination to will is significant both for its starting point and its ending point: imagination is here established as a *practice*, as something that one deliberately does, and not as an affliction that one suffers.[23] And imagination is something that allows the practitioner to modify her will progressively and by herself, for herself.

THE METHOD OF SALESIAN MEDITATION

The general outline of Salesian meditation practice is well known and has much in common with the Ignatian *Spiritual Exercises* (ca. 1534), which have been spread by Jesuit education and have received more attention in the English-speaking world.[24] François de Sales was the student of the Jesuits both in Paris and Padua.[25] However, François de Sales's work differs by having been widely available *as a book* for the lay reader—the person we would call today the "end user"—rather than as a handbook for retreat directors who did not give the whole text to the persons undertaking the exercises.[26] Each reader could adapt Salesian devotion to her own needs and station in life, but she was urged to incorporate the devotional practices into the structure of her day.

In presenting an imagination-centered devotional approach, François de Sales makes two starts, first giving a series of scripted meditations, like those of the *Spiritual Exercises*, and then giving a more general set of guidelines for the persona embarked on the path of devotion. The fact that there seem to be two beginnings is an example of the spiraling or amplifying effect of the process of imagining, understanding, and willing, which again leads to the same process at a higher level. Ten prescribed meditations in book I of the *Introduction* follow an order that is both chronological and perspectival. The topics are, successively, the creation of the world, God's purpose in creating mankind, the graces (*bénéfices*) given by God to man, sins, death, the last judgment, hell, paradise, the individual believer's choice of paradise, and finally the believer's choice of the devout life.[27] By the end of this first cycle of meditation, the reader is expected to choose the devout life and imagine signing a contract (beginning "I the undersigned . . . ") before going on to the next round of exercises in which more individual initiative is required from the reader. In the themes of this set of ten meditations, there is an increasing "personalization" or subjectivity to the ideas. In the first, mankind as a whole had not been created; in the second, mankind is created for a specific purpose; in the third, the endowments that are given to mankind are reviewed with specific attention to the Philothée's own gifts; in the fourth, Philothée's individual sins are seen to violate the gratitude that she should feel in view of the gifts previously called to mind, and so forth.

Although, from a Romantic or post-Romantic perspective, we would be unlikely to choose the term "imaginative" to describe the work that is going on in this first phase of Salesian devotion, we can see that within the technical sense that is the author's, the reader of the *Introduction* is being asked to make use of the faculty that is the gateway from the senses to the mind. In fact, without giving a complex theoretical presentation of the higher faculties as he does in the *Treatise on the Love of God*, François de Sales subtly reminds his reader in the second meditation of the place of imagination among the faculties. Reviewing God's gifts to humanity, François de Sales recalls,

> He has given you understanding to know him, memory to remember Him, will to love Him, imagination to call to mind his gifts, eyes to see the marvels of His creation, language to praise Him, and likewise the other faculties. (*IVD* 49).

Understanding, memory, will—which is the faculty responsible for love—imagination, the exterior senses—exemplified here by sight—, and speech are mentioned here without further elaboration but in a way that is entirely consistent with the overall Salesian project. Imagination is a representative faculty, which is not collapsed into the exterior senses but juxtaposed with them in this list. Significantly, this mention of imagination occurs between a meditation that does not specifically call for a representation—visual or any other—a "consideration" of the world without us, an essentially negative imagination ("Consider that only a few years ago you were not in the world and that your being was a true nothing," *IVD* 47) and that the meditation that follows the list of the faculties begins with the body:

> Consider the bodily graces that God has given you: what a body, what opportunities to care for it, what health, what legitimate pleasures, what friends, what servants. But then compare your situation with that of so many other people who are really more worthy than you but who are deprived of these material advantages: some of them injured in their body, their health, their limbs . . . . (*IVD* 51).

François de Sales grounds the believer in her body in *detail*, not by making a checklist of all the parts of the body—an exercise that risks being relatively abstract and "objective"—but by instructing Philothée to think of the particular individual endowments that are hers. In other words, the meditation engages the reader's subjective view of her body as *she* (or *he*) sees it, appealing to what other Christian writers might consider her vanity, and thus creating an individual perspective on the world of bodies from within a specific, differentiated body, one with particularly beautiful hands, for instance. This is Philothée's body as she imagines it, that is, as she represents it to herself—this is not simply the body as a set of unmediated sensations but the body mentally created out of those sensations.

Having thus represented her persona, Philothée is ready, in the following meditation, to place that embodied individual within a scenario, the scenario of sin: "Think how long has been since you began to sin, and behold how the sins have proliferated in your heart since that first beginning . . . . Consider your evil inclinations and how often you have followed them . . . ." (*IVD* 53). The meditation urges the reader to remember instances of sin, both acted out and simply imagined. Of course, we know that memory (in the Aristotelian-Scholastic tradition), when it is not purely conceptual (memory of numbers, for instance), works in conjunction with imagination to present visual, auditory, or other sensory specifics of the moment remembered.[28] So the first phase of the meditation on sin is to recall the instances of sin, trying to cover the complete range of the senses—"that there is not a single one of my senses . . . that I have not spoiled, violated, and dirtied" (*IVD* 54), then to accumulate this evidence until the quantity of instances is overwhelming, before changing mental scenarios. Having taken the body constructed in the third meditation through its individual history of sin, the fourth meditation then moves from memory-based scenes to dramatic identification with an alternate self, taken from a stock of Biblical personae:

> Ask forgiveness, and throw yourself at the feet of the Lord like a prodigal child, like a Magdalene, like a woman who has fouled her marriage bed with all kinds of adulteries. O Lord, mercy on this sinner . . . . (*IVD* 54).

In the course of the meditations that follow, François de Sales leads the reader through situations in which the body, in all its fragility, is the point from which religious doctrine is understood. Whether it be death and the farewell to the body, "pale, pale, broken, hideous, and stinking" (*IVD* 56), hell, where bodies suffer "in all their senses and in all their members" and for which each sense must be imagined in turn, such as "the eyes, for their treacherous and evil glances, will suffer the horrible view of devils and of hell" (*IVD* 60), and the election of paradise. Without making explicit mention of the fact, François de Sales has trained the reader to represent herself to herself in situations that are increasingly foreign to her past experience, at least within her subjective view. She will have seen people dying but will not have died as she is expected to do in her imaginative cooperation with the author. By the time she reaches the meditation on the election of paradise, Philothée will be able to place her mental self in a transcendent scene:

> Imagine that you are in a barren landscape, all alone with your guardian Angel, just like the young Tobias going into Ragha, and imagine that your Angel shows you on high Paradise, opened up, with all the pleasures that you discovered in the meditation on Paradise that you have already performed . . . (*IVD* 63).

This skill will be important once the reader has committed herself to the program of self-cultivation that is set out in the four following sections of the *Introduction to the Devout Life* in which Philothée becomes responsible for directing her own inner life.

It is a little disconcerting to come upon the second chapter of part II, "A short method for meditation . . .," that seems to be a prologue, out of place when the reader has completed ten meditations. The difference is that now the reader is not given set topics but instead advice for exploiting the imaginative skills she acquired little by little in Part I. Since meditation is a form of inner or mental prayer (*oraison mentale*), Philothée is encouraged to develop the distinction between the inside and the outside of her self, essentially a difference between the mind, heart, or soul, on one hand, and the body on the other. This is where God and the human particularly reside, in a "*particulière résidence*"[29] François de Sales's insistence on the cultivation of interiority is important not because it is innovative but precisely because it popularizes for an audience that includes women in religious orders and lay persons of any gender, and station the inner self-cultivation that was such a prominent feature of Stoic practice.[30] Once devotional activity shifts from the outer life to the inner life, it can take place at any time, and in any place, and thanks to imagination, this interiorization does not require abstraction but can be (as if) physically present.[31]

The first preparatory phase of inner prayer is to obtain the sense of the presence of God, the "lively and attentive apprehension of the omnipresence of God," and this can be achieved in several ways, one of which is "simple imagination":

> representing to us the Savior in his sacred humanity as if he were right near us, just as we are used to imagining our friends and to say: I imagine that I see so-and-so who does this or that, and it is just as if he were in front of my eyes, or some such thing. (*IVD* 84).

Accompanied thus by the *physical* presence of Jesus—a physical presence due not to some unusual grace but through a vision willed by the meditator—Philothée will then guide herself through three stages of prayer that correspond to the three inner faculties—imagination, understanding, and will. The first of these, to be sure, is not appropriate for all meditations because there are some religious concepts that are entirely beyond the physical senses. In appropriate cases, however, one undertakes what

> some call this the "fabrication of the place" and others the "interior lesson." But it is nothing more than setting before one's imagination the physical aspect of the mystery that one wishes to meditate in one's presence. For example, if you wish to meditate on our Savior on the cross, you will imagine that you are on Mount Calvary and that you see all that was done there. (*IVD* 85).

This particular stage of meditation is well known, directly through the Ignatian *Spiritual Exercises*, through the poetry inspired by those exercises, and through the studies of Terence Cave, Louis Martz and others who have written about meditational poetry in the seventeenth century.[32] The composition of place is a particularly powerful example of the way imagination engages the reader/meditator in her subjective point of view. It takes a mystery of the Church or an event from the Bible and relates it to the meditator directly, physically, sensorily in a way that abolishes or attenuates hierarchy and removes restrictions of time and place. In aesthetic terms, it is the enemy of refinement and of that type of verisimilitude that will a few decades later be applied to drama, that is, the corrective "plausibility" that makes things the way they should be, ideally, and not the way they are or were.[33] Philothée has already worked to imagine her own death with its "stench" and is now advised, if she chooses to meditate on the death of Christ, to see it as if it were *really* happening. Most of all, Philothée sees this before her eyes, whether she places it in some distant place or in her own home: "you will imagine to yourself that in the very place where you are the crucifixion of Our Lord is taking place." (*IVD* 86).

There are limits to imagination, though, and the reader is given to understand right away that this faculty should be used only for mysteries "that concern visible and tangible things" (*où il s'agit de choses visibles et sensibles*, *IVD* 86) and not for more general themes such as the greatness of God, the excellence of virtues, and God's purpose in creating us, "which are invisible things." If imagination has opened the meditation, Philothée moves on to understanding (*entendement*) as a means of mobilizing her will, because meditation, at its core, "is nothing other than one or more considerations undertaken with the aim of moving our affections toward God and divine things." (*IDV* 87). Finally, the third part of meditation consists of the movement of the will itself (*la volonté ou partie affective de notre âme*) in the form of the love of God or neighbor, the desire for paradise, compassion, and other virtuous affections.

This overview of Salesian devotion reminds us that imagination is an important component of that practice, although it is never separated from the tightly woven structure of the faculties as a whole. It is likely that many of the readers of François de Sales's book had not systematically developed their imagination prior to undertaking devotion despite the advice from antiquity—from Epictetus, Seneca, and Quintilian, for instance—that imagination could and should be developed as a skill.

If we assume that Philothée took seriously the advice from François de Sales, we can sketch out a certain type of person, how she spent her day, and how she related to the outside world. The term "outside world" is itself tendentious, but it is thoroughly installed in the thought of François de Sales and his precursors in the tradition of imaginative practice. After all, imagination, as the faculty that permits the recreation of the sensory world, the world experienced by the body, within the mental world, is already, since antiquity, considered an "inner" sense.[34] Within that tradition, a commitment to developing imagination required a particular vigilance about the data from the senses that entered the mind and usually also supposed the intention to control the flow of appearances from the world of the body. Imagination, in the broad sense that comes to us from antiquity, deals with sense impressions from the things that are really, physically, present to the person at the time she perceives them as well as with sense impressions that come from past experience or are created, voluntarily or involuntarily, as purely mental. François de Sales invites his Philothée to form herself by using the full spectrum of the imaginative faculty, one that we can attempt to sort into two broad groups, imagination *in praesentia* and imagination *in absentia*, imagining the present and imagining the absent.

HOW TO SEE WHAT IS THERE AND WHAT IS NOT

Most of the imaginative exercises proposed in the introductory set of ten meditations consist of imagining the absent, that is, of shutting down awareness of the incoming perceptions from the body and of substituting another set of sensations that we choose. The vision of paradise in the eighth meditation is typical. François de Sales guides his reader in the composition of remembered perceptions into the vision of something never seen. First, Philothée is told, "Consider a beautiful, quiet night, and think how good it is to see the sky with that multitude and variety of stars." Then, as in a recipe book, she is told to add the next ingredient: "Now, join that beauty with that of a fine day, in such a way that the sun's light does not prevent you from seeing the stars and the moon" (*IVD* 61). In the third step, she is asked to embellish or intensify the resulting combination, since paradise must be even better than this set of combined memories. In calling to mind what is not there, wherever Philothée is meditating, she creates a three-dimensional alternative reality which she perceives through a set of inner senses no longer dependent on present external sensation, though drawing on a stock of such sensation as remembered. The fiction that Philothée creates is that she is *physically* present in the alternative space that she chooses to represent to herself. This mental transportation becomes ever more explicit in the course of the first part of the *Introduction*, so that the last two meditations both begin by asking the reader to place herself in a landscape—"Imagine that you are in a barren landscape . . . "—within which (in the tenth meditation) she first sees in great detail what is on her left side before turning to see what is on her right side.

An important technique of prayer is to perceive the *physical* presence of Jesus Christ. For de Sales, the belief in Christ's material presence is a doctrinal requirement that leads to some complications in his use of the verb "to imagine," but even the appearance of bread and wine after transubstantiation does not remove the possibility of an imaginative restoration of Christ's human form. Philothée, like Quintilian's orator, must make an effort of imagination to endow the spiritual Christ with his human body, seeing him as we do our friends, in "simple imagination." But Catholics in the presence of the Eucharist face the special problem that doctrine requires them to acknowledge that Christ *is* physically present:

> But if the very holy Sacrament of the altar were present, then that presence would be real and not purely imaginary. For the species and appearances of the bread would be like a tapestry, from behind which Our Lord is really present and sees us and watches us, even though we do not see him in his proper form. (*IVD* 84).

An imagined scene like this one seems to fit occasions when Philothée can go to some private space for quiet prayer. For those with enough wealth to have a study or *cabinet* of the kind, often next to a bedroom, that had become fashionable during the Renaissance, or even for a nun in a convent where private cells were available, this technique of inviting Jesus as a guest was a way to spur oneself one to the best use of privacy. François de Sales was also conscious of the theme of solitude or retreat that permeated French culture during his time and is represented in paintings, engravings, poems, novels, and letters. The inspirations for seclusion were sometimes religious—as we can see in the many images depicting the solitary meditation of such figures as Mary Magdalene or Saint Jerome—and sometimes secular.[35] However, François de Sales does not want his reader to be dependent on external contingencies of the sort, and he explicitly proclaimed that the devout life should be possible for people in all walks of life. A method of devotion that could be used only in the relative luxury of private space would not fulfill this purpose. In the later parts of the *Introduction*, Philothée learns to make for herself alternative interior places so that she can, several times a day, make "retreats in the solitude of her heart" (*IVD* 97). This interior imagined space is explicitly proposed as a form of liberation, giving her an alternative to the constraints of her external body when she wills to be elsewhere:

> while physically you are in the midst of conversations and business; and that mental solitude cannot be hindered by the crowd of people around you, because they are not around your heart but only around your body.

François de Sales gives both Biblical and historical models for this mental solitude, most of all Catherine of Siena who had a *cabinet intérieur* which she could use as a private oratory (*IVD* 97). This interior space gives Philothée a stage to produce and experience any place, event, and sensations from her own deathbed to the crucifixion, the stable in Bethlehem to the sky of the Ascension (*IVD* 98), from a vast landscape of mountains and plains to the microscopic fleshscape that is "the wound in the side of our sweet Jesus," where Blessed Elzéar, count of Arian in Provence claimed to dwell mentally (*IVD* 98). Constructing this inner space is an important task for Philothée's imagination:

> Just as birds have nests in trees so that they can take shelter there when they need to, and deer have thickets and protected places where they hide, enjoying the cool shade in the summer; even so, Philothée, our hearts should locate and choose some place each day, whether on Mount Calvary or in the wounds of Our Lord, or in some other place close to him, to make a retreat on all sorts of occasions, and there to unburden and refresh oneself amidst outward affairs and to be there as in a fort, in order to defend oneself from temptations. (*IVD* 96–97).

In this inner space, imagination can help not only move the will to the desired affections but can also allow a rehearsal of the good works that flow from the "resolution," one of the closing steps of any meditation. François de Sales urges his reader not simply to adhere to the *idea* of doing good but to practice mentally and in detail before and after the fact.[36] Philothée will therefore produce a new and amended version of her behavior, combining the image of familiar people and places with the newly resolved virtue, picturing herself in action as she thinks "I will no longer let myself be angered by the annoying words that so-and-so, my neighbor or my servant say about me" (*IVD* 88).

How to See What is There

When we imagine the present we either increase or decrease the filtering of the world as it is reported by our senses. We can pay more or less attention to it, we can discard the sensory impressions that come to us and substitute others, we can combine visions and other sensations from the past or from some other repertory with the stream of sense that flows around us. In fact, imagining the present and imagining the absent are not discrete and incompatible categories of mental action but are related as gradations of the will's intervention in submitting to the external world or excluding and correcting it. Imagination of the present and of the absent is also, simply, a way of expressing Philothée's subjective presence or absence from the world around her. She is more "absent" when she takes refuge in her internal *cabinet* and she is more "present" when she is giving her attention to the society and the material objects around her.

Often her attention to the world around her passes through an internal fiction deliberately constructed to modify her perception in ways she finds useful. We have already seen that Philothée can imagine that Jesus is physically present in the real location where she is praying. There are other examples of modification of the present. Catherine of Siena used this technique, which François de Sales recommends:

> she imagined that in preparing meals for her father she was serving at the table of Our Lord, like Saint Martha; and that her mother was in the place of Our Lady, and her brothers in the places of the Apostles, and in this way she motivated herself to serve in her spirit all the celestial court, performing all these menial tasks with a great sense of sweetness. (*IVD* 227).

This is an example of how imagination, in the most traditional (Aristotelian and Stoic) sense, differs from simple sense perception, for the information given by sight, sound, smell, and so forth is involuntary and is simply transmitted endlessly to the mind in a healthy, conscious organism. Imagination, however, intervenes to modify the way these sensations are accepted, excluded, or combined with other sensations stored in the mind's repertory. For Catherine Benincasa in her kitchen in Siena it must have been particularly easy to imagine the present in a particularly aggressive way because she had elaborated her internal imaginative repertory with frequent visions of Jesus and other Biblical figures. It therefore would be a simple matter to "correct" the image of her father into the physical image she had of Jesus or to imagine Jesus in the form of her father. In either case, it is important to recall that François de Sales refers to this process as an act of imagination and thus makes it clear that Catherine is not basing this active daily meditation ("the little and lowly meditation that she performed while doing menial and abject chores") on understanding or will. François de Sales in scores of passages in his two books makes very explicit distinctions among the three higher faculties and would not use the verb *imaginer* here if he meant merely that Catherine "understood" that her father is in some sense the equivalent of Christ in her life or that she merely "willed" to serve her family with the same energy she would give to serving the Holy Family. Instead, Catherine has willed to modify her perception of the people around her, thus leveraging her will power so that the whole vile and abject service no longer seems unpleasant. This step-by-step, spiral of the faculties (the will causes imagination to modify the perception, so that the understanding evaluates the experience as an agreeable and important one, so that the will is attracted to this service) is different from what we usually think of as doing something by "will-power," where we force ourselves to do something utterly repugnant without modifying our perception.[37]

Changing the affections by modifying perception is a major theme of François de Sales and this approach to, and through, the will explains why he promotes imagination with such vigor. The seventeenth century's forbidden fruit, the melon, serves as an example of this concept:

> In this way there are penitents who stop committing the sin but who never give up the sinful inclinations. That is, they plan not to sin again, but it's with a certain regret at the thought of depriving themselves . . . . They abstain from sin just as sick people abstain from melons, which they don't eat because the physician told them that they would die if they ate them. But they fret about not eating melons, and they talk about it and try to make some compromise, and at least they want to smell the fruit. (*IVD* 44).

The problem is that people cannot will to will, that the faculty of will does not control itself but rather controls the other faculties.[38] Imagination provides the instrument required to remove the desire for melons by control-ling the way melons taste and smell. A disciplined imagination is therefore useful not only for transporting the believer to some distant or physically nonexistent place but for making what is really, physically present take on the characteristics that reason—or the Church—have determined they should have.

INTERIORITY AND CIVILITY

Because Philothée has her internal *cabinet* at her disposal and retreats there several times a day, she is largely absent from the world around her even though her body is going through the motions required by her station in life and by all religious rules. In this way she is *honnête* (genuine or respectable) in one of the seventeenth-century senses of the term: she conforms to social expectations while concealing her core of desire and disagreement.[39] Although François de Sales did not invent *honnêteté* in this sense, his work appeared at a crucial time of transition that is associated with the formation of seventeenth-century concepts of politeness, civility, and refined love. His friendship with Henri IV, responsible for ending the turbulence of the civil wars, and with Honoré d'Urfé, author of the novel that gave the subsequent century its "social and literary mythology"[40] are not surprising given his commitment to the form of flexible personality that is required for a prosperous absolutist society.

In teaching his followers to cultivate this inward solitude, François de Sales certainly helped promote a model of the royal subject for a century of absolutism.[41] Although several decades ago Lucien Goldmann coined the striking phrase *le refus intramondain du monde* (refusing the world from within the world) to describe the Jansenism of Saint-Cyran,[42] it may well be that the *Introduction to the Devout Life* deserves precedence in the promotion of that concept, or of a similar, more nuanced one. By enabling the creation of an alternate world, the deliberate use of imagination to promote, on one hand interiority, and on the other hand, exterior conformity, the Bishop of Geneva made available to his readers freedom within social obligation and privacy while in public. In the absence of a real, physical solitude, the Salesian meditator could create an "inner solitude":

> But always, in addition to mental solitude to which you can withdraw in the midst of the most engrossing conversations [. . . .] you should also love real places of physical solitude, not so that you go to the wilderness, like Saint Mary the Egyptian, Saint Paul, Saint Anthony, Arsenius, and the other desert fathers, but so that you spend more time in your room, in your garden, and other places, where you can more freely turn inward in your heart and refresh your soul in good reflections and holy thoughts or in edifying reading . . . (*IVD* 201–02).

Making good use of private space—a major concern of upper-class Europeans in the seventeenth century—was thus part of the Salesian project, but more interesting and more empowering was the creation of an inner space of retreat. This skill of being in two "places" at once, an outward one and an inward one, became increasingly important with the growth in the size of both cities and the royal court over the course of the century—indeed, such a skill has continued to grow from de Sales' day to our own. As manuals of politeness proliferated, presence of mind in group situations and skill in conversation became a norm. The need to maintain an inscrutable exterior appearance and a corresponding ability to penetrate the mask-like surface of other courtiers became a staple of worldly literature.[43] What is most remarkable about the interior retreat of François de Sales's disciple "Philothée" is not that she has such an independent and secret place but that it is largely designed as a place to live, as a world that replaces the outside, physical world. It is true that meditations in the *Introduction* always conclude with resolutions to perform a set of good works in the material, social world, but the outer self of Philothée is largely automatized so that she can concentrate on the place in which she lives freely, according to her will, and in preparation for the spiritual delight that is fully developed in contemplation, as set forth in the *Treatise of the Love of God*. In a certain sense, Philothée is permanently elsewhere, even though she attends with ideal punctuality to all of the tasks of her station. De Sales's work gives a positive, happy view of this inner space, which we tend to conceive as a purely negative result of the repression of a courtly society. Other authors, either fairly close in time to de Sales, like Nicolas Faret, or many decades later, like La Rochefoucauld, present inwardness as deriving largely from social inhibition, as the repository of the desires, opinions, and secret factual knowledge that one cannot express without fearing reprisal or loss of face.[44] These writers teach their readers how to find discreet outlets for the intense, even unbearable, pressure of wanting to reveal what they are with difficulty holding inside. Freedom, in this case, consists of bursting out, and the turn toward the inner realm is a merely strategic expedient, but definitely an unpleasant one. La Rochefoucauld's depiction of sociability is exactly contrary to François de Sales's. The *Introduction to the Devout Life* describes Philothée as returning with pleasure to her inner cabinet or as never really leaving it. The more vividly she imagines this place inside her mind, the more completely it provides for her spiritual and emotional needs.

For one thing, in addition to the place of retreat, Philothée has at her disposal the "spiritual bouquet" that she carries forward from her morning meditation:

People who have enjoyed a stroll in a beautiful garden usually take with them four or five flowers to enjoy the scent throughout the day. Just so when our spirit has discoursed on some mystery in meditation, we should choose one or two or three points that we have found most to our taste and most suitable for our advancement to remember for the rest of the day and enjoy the spiritual scent. This choice is made in the very place where we have meditated, as we converse inwardly while walking alone there. (*IVD* 89).

Ideally, the meditation, with all its progression through the faculties, and including the resolutions for good works, should take place before leaving the bedroom in the morning. Whether or not this bouquet takes the form of an imagined representation—it consists of those points that we find most useful—it is part of a process of developing thoughts that can screen the outside world, in other words, thoughts that will attenuate, on one hand, the inrush of perceptions, and on the other, the memory and anticipation that can be activated by these perceptions.

The absentmindedness that the Bishop of Geneva recommends takes some fairly traditional forms, such as the advice not to pay attention to wealth. Philothée will be "poor in spirit":

A person is rich in spirit when he has his riches in his spirit . . . Your heart . . . should be . . . open only to heaven, and closed to wealth and decaying things: if you have wealth, keep your heart free from attachment to it. (*IVD* 170).

This general advice, it is true, does not directly address the matter of Philothée's imagination, but rather her will, her "affections." She may perceive her wealth but without attaching her desire to it, and this generally requires directing attention away from the very perception of the objects and circumstances that constitute that wealth. The *Introduction* sets the management of desire within the context of the self as a whole, since desire (the will to possess) is predicated on perception, and perception is the domain in which imagination works to accept and or modify the stream of the senses. The desire for wealth is like a fever, writes François de Sales, because those who have a fever are driven by their disordered body to drink water "with that kind of attention and glee that healthy people don't usually have" (*IVD* 172). All desire comes from the proper or improper management of this *attention*, and for that Philothée has developed the resources of her imagination, so that she can turn aside from worldly conversations to the presence of the Jesus Christ, whose feet she will kiss (*IVD* 269).

As the control of imagination of the absent and of the present progresses beyond meditation to contemplation—that is, progresses to a point at which the devout person loses consciousness of the surrounding physical world and of the body itself—the *spiritual* phenomenon that results is levitation. It is difficult to say with what literalness François de Sales intends us to understand the experience attributed to Mary Magdalene, the ideal contemplator. For thirty years, living in a grotto in Provence, she was swept into the air seven times every day, a rhythm corresponding to the seven canonical hours (*TAD* 697). In all probability this experience is an expression of the ultimate absentmindedness of the devout person, who first transfers her sensory perceptions from her body to her mind, then from her imagination to her understanding, and finally is fully occupied by desire for union with the divinity.

THE DARK SIDE OF IMAGINATION

The greatest challenge to managing the imagination is—this is no surprise—sex. Ever since antiquity, the sexual imagination has offered philosophers both their greatest challenge and their best examples of imagination at work. Closer to François de Sales is Montaigne's "Of the power of the imagination" (*Essais* I, 21), in which imagination and sexual performance are linked. In the *Introduction to the Devout Life*, sex provides the field for the most vivid descriptions of the control of imagination both of what is present and what is absent. In the midst of what François de Sales describes as the legitimate, and even required, sexual activity of marriage, the sensations—present, remembered, and anticipated—need to be filtered, and if possible, ignored. In Catholic marriage, the sexual act is a tolerated evil, as François de Sales describes it:

> It is not permissible to draw any shameless pleasure from our bodies in any manner whatsoever, except in legitimate marriage, whose holiness may, by a just compensation repair the harm that comes from enjoyment. And even in marriage one must preserve a purity of intention, so that if there is anything unseemly in the voluptuous act, there is still only purity in the will. (*IVD* 164).

Pleasure, *volupté*, comes from the imagination in its (now archaic) sense of awareness and recognition of sensation during an experience, and not merely before or after. For the married people reading the *Introduction*, there is a major difficulty: sexual intercourse is commanded but it must take place with the strict minimum of pleasure. The problem is not a physical one—the body simply goes through what it needs to go through—but rather the incidental sending of pleasure to the mind, the *déchet*, a decay or fall.[45] Philothée is warned not only against any sexual act, even permitted ones, if she can avoid it in marriage, but also against paying attention to pleasure: "just the same, one must never let the heart or the spirit pay heed to it" (*IVD* 164). Conjugal sexuality is a toxic thing. It is like a particularly extreme medication. Intended as a remedy against concupiscence, it is "violent, nonetheless, and consequently very dangerous if it is not used with discretion" (*IVD* 166). This violent, overwhelming deluge of sensation strains the capacity of imagination to exclude it or at least to make it vanish as soon as it has come. As the recipient and mediator of the outer senses, imagination is the faculty through which the mind must protect itself in both modes—in regard to the present, by excluding, modifying or accepting the information sent by the body and in regard to the absent by forming sexual representations that the will may subsequently use as a pattern for action:

> Chastity depends on the heart, as its place of origin, but it concerns the body as its substance; that's why chastity is lost through all the external senses of the body and by the speculations and desires of the heart. There is impurity when we view, hear, say, smell, or touch unclean things and when the heart lingers over them and takes pleasure. (*IVD* 168).

There is a certain ambiguity to this concept of lingering and taking pleasure. Is this the act of the will alone? Is it acceptable for the mind to recognize and to contain the impression of pleasure that comes from the five senses provided that the will never desires or accepts responsibility for this pleasure? Can the imagination itself be guilty during the unavoidable by-products of human reproduction? Without answering that question explicitly, François de Sales addresses it in an eloquent simile: "Not only do bees not wish to touch cadavers but flee and loath extremely all the stench that comes from them" (*IVD* 168). It seems as if, here as elsewhere, François de Sales is appealing to the ability of imagination to reconfigure the sensory data in order to offer the understanding, hence the will, a less difficult choice. If the sexual body is rethought as a rotting corpse, the imagination will have done its share of the work and thus lessened the pressure on the will. Philothée's approach to the nuptial bed can then be regulated on the model of a corporal act of mercy such as burying the dead rather than in response to the "brutal" senses.

The problem of thinking about sex is so important that the *Introduction* devotes several chapters to making the message clear. In the chapter entitled "On the cleanness of the nuptial bed" (part III, Chapter 39), François de Sales attempts to make his point by comparing sexual pleasure with a somewhat less violent sensory domain, eating. The desirability of writing about a less dangerous though similar sensory domain is clear: simply to mention sexual pleasure will bring a representation to the mind and this representation is sinful:

> There is a certain similarity between the shameful pleasures and those of eating, for both concern flesh, even though the former, because of their brutal vehemence, are simply called carnal. I will hence explain what I cannot say of these by speaking of the others. (*IVD* 240).

This indirection in François de Sales's writing gives us some indication of a possible compromise that imagination can use in dealing with thoughts of pleasure. Like Catherine of Siena serving meals to her family but imagining that she is serving Jesus and the apostles, the reader of the *Introduction* can think about food in order not to think about sex. Even though we understand or decode "food" as "sex" we will have blocked sexual imagery from the imagination by keeping it otherwise occupied, in effect participating in an allegorical system that leaves reason (*entendement*) free to absorb the intended message without risking the explosive rush of sensory representations that could overwhelm imagination and then drive reason and will into temptation.

The traditional theory of imagination to which François de Sales belongs assigns to this faculty sensory representation across the spectrum of time: past, present, and future—after, during, and before an experience. Conjugal sexuality fits into this view of imagination by accepting only the present representation (or reception) of sensory information.[46] The result is an odd discontinuity in Philothée's inner life, since there is not only a sharp distinction between her inner *cabinet* and the life of her body but also a required absence of memory and anticipation in regard to sexuality:

> It is truly the mark of a criminal, vile, abject, and infamous mind to think about victuals before meal time, and still more when afterwards one lingers over the pleasure that one had during the meal, thinking and talking about it, wallowing in one's mind in the memory of the delight one had in swallowing the pieces, like those who before dinner think about the roast and later about the dishes . . . (*IVD* 242).

There is, in other words, no preparation for sexual intercourse, not only no foreplay but no forethought. And there should be no memory—no detailed memory of bodily sensations, in any event—as François de Sales makes clear by using an anecdote of the animal most celebrated for its memory, the elephant.[47] To stress the need to forget about the sex act as soon as it is over, de Sales makes use of this symbol of remembering to illustrate the abolition of all sensory evidence of the experience. Just as refined people, when they have finished eating, "wash their hands and their mouths so that they no longer have the taste or the odor of what they ate," so the elephant, after mating, goes right to the river and washes its whole body before returning to the herd (*IVD* 243). In applying this example to human marriage, the *Introduction* stresses once again the supreme important of affection, that is, will, but the anecdote of the elephant makes it clear that the great danger for the will is the trace, the memory, of the sensory experience. The married couple should follow the example of the elephant which

> admonishes married people not to be attached to the sensuality and volup-
> tuousness which they undertook as required by their vocation, but rather,
> once these things have taken place, they will flush them out of their hearts
> and their desires. (*IVD* 243).

The memory and anticipation of sex, those mental activities closest to imagination in the modern sense with its emphasis on imagination *in absentia*, are the most dangerous. Conjugal love is hazardous because of the traces of pleasure it leaves in the mind, traces that powerfully drive the will by replicating themselves and projecting themselves forward into the possible future. If there is no memory of pleasure, there will be no anticipation of pleasure. If one does not notice any feelings during the conjugal act, one will not form a memory. This ideal control of sensation in the mind is, however, unlikely. And thus there is the problem of the widow, or as François de Sales would say, the *false widow*, the one who is only physically but not spiritually a widow. The widows who hope to remarry "are separated from men only in terms of the pleasure of the body, but they are already joined to men by the will of the heart" (*IVD* 244). Lacking the pleasure of the body, the carnal widows have the pleasure of the mind at their command and this pleasure in turn contaminates their will. The *Introduction* gives only one way to control the will in this situation, and that is to provide a counterpressure to the desire that comes from the sensual memory of the earlier marriage by instilling fear that comes from the image of damnation in the future. By taking a vow not to remarry, the widow loses all hope of paradise if she even thinks about sexual pleasure—"she will not even permit the slightest thought of marriage to linger in her heart for a single moment" (*IVD* 244).[48]

Although the deliberate, willed, direction of imagination generally uses purely mental means to leverage the will with the higher faculties alone (in the circle or spiral of will, imagination, understanding, will), one can address imagination indirectly by using the body in cases when the power of imagination alone is inadequate. The need to program imagination by using the body itself appears in extreme form in cases of sexual temptation, but there are a few less urgent situations. De Sales mentions such mild forms of bodily programming of the mind as when the devout person finds emotion, such as sadness, a distraction from meditation. In such cases physical work (*oeuvres extérieures*) are useful, as are corporal but symbolic actions, such as kissing the crucifix, praying out loud, and so forth (*IVD* 92, 275). At times, however, the mind needs stronger stuff. As François de Sales reminds us, an undesirable thought of some sensory object can be dislodged from imagination by causing an overwhelming surge of bodily sensation. As the "bridge" faculty between body and mind, imagination can be directed or programmed downward by understanding or upward by the sensations themselves. This is the role of ascetic practice generally, including the extreme or emergency discipline that saints use when they are strongly tempted. François de Sales briefly and allusively deals with situations in which imagination is not directly controllable by the will. In many situations, he explains, the devout person— indeed many saints—can remain sinless by steadfast refusal of the will to consent to forbidden pleasure:

> Let the enemies of our salvation put before us as much as they like those baits and lures, let them remain always outside the door of our heart ready to enter, let them make suggestive propositions to us as much as they want; just as long as we keep our resolve not to take pleasure in all that, it is not possible for us to offend God. (*IVD* 258).

In this insistence that mankind can only sin through will, François de Sales is making very explicit his loyalty to the Tridentine doctrine of justification through free will and acts, and sharply distinguishing himself from the reformers' doctrine of justification by grace independent of human choice. The problem that remains for Catholic devotion is a corrupt imagination, the situation that arises when the "enemy" has penetrated within the mind even though it has not gained the final citadel of the will. In these cases imagination is full of tempting representations of physical sensation and even takes pleasure in these thoughts: "it happens many times that the lower part [imagination] takes pleasure in temptation, without the consent, nay even against the will of the higher part" (*IVD* 259). Now, even if this involuntary physical pleasure is not sinful, it is a danger, because will and imagination are at war. What can one do about these dangerous imaginings?

One can, either methodically or on a single perilous occasion, fill the imagination with sensations so intense that the "bait" and "lures" are driven out. Saints are known for using this technique:

> great were ... the temptations that Saint Francis and Saint Benedict suffered, when one threw himself into the briars and the other onto the snow to temper them, and nonetheless they lost nothing of the grace of God in that way, but rather they much increased the grace they enjoyed ... (*IVD* 258).

The will can thus use the body to control imagination just as, in less acute circumstances, the will can use the imagination to modify the will itself.

This approach to imagination is so far from modern views of that faculty that we have difficulty recognizing ascetic discipline—such practices as fasting, hair shirts, and flagellation—as imaginative practices. Yet the information supplied by the body through the senses is the most direct and common way of filling the imagination, in the philosophic tradition to which François de Sales belonged. Many temptations come to the imagination from the senses. This is why dances are bad, "just as this exercise opens the pores of the body, so also does it open the pores of the heart ... and awakens in the soul a thousand kinds of bad inclinations [*affections*]" (*IVD* 223). Imagination is particularly sensitive to the presence of voluptuous objects (*IVD* 260). Ascetic discipline makes use of this possibility of "programming" imagination with unpleasant but edifying sensations to counteract the tempting representations that result from pleasant sensations.[49]

In regard to practices that program imagination by using the body, François de Sales is on the more "modern" side, preferring that the will work directly to guide imagination and thus to produce affections in the will itself.[50] The attraction of divine love, so emphasized in his vocabulary of *suavité*, *douceur*, and *débonnaireté* and in his almost obsessive return to the examples of bees visiting flowers and making honey, was to be a positive pole to replace the harsh discipline of the body. By expanding the imaginative capacity and by giving it practice to make it responsive and less likely to require the extreme measure of shock treatment with fire, snow, thorns or whips,

François de Sales could make the body a light, negligible, and uninteresting thing compared with what was happening on the inside. Philothée's automatized body, allowing her to carry on a conversation while her mind was elsewhere, is simply the first step toward the goal of total absorption of the mind in God and neglect of the body that de Sales represented by the levitating Mary Magdalene.[51]

Readers of the *Introduction to the Devout Life* are free to use what François de Sales gave them as they wish. The very form in which his teaching was disseminated—in a book rather than exclusively through retreats on the model of the Ignatian *Exercises*—permitted individual adaptation. Indeed, one of the defining characteristics of Salesian meditation is the initiative given to the reader for determining the details of her inner life. The author of the *Introduction* was aware that meditation could be used for purposes other than the edifying ones he recommends and particularly that the imaginative component of meditation could be exploited for worldly ends—"meditation . . . can be used for good and for evil"—but he explicitly limits his description of meditation to "the holy kind" (*TAD* 612). Meditation, we have seen, is the discipline of attention in regard to things perceptible through the senses. It is different from random thought and different even from attentive thought undertaken for the purpose of learning, insofar as meditation is directed toward moving the affections, that is, it is the way the will works on the will.[52] If will does not take action to remove from imagination dangerous or forbidden sensory thought, the believer sins, and if he or she deliberately brings to mind such thought, this is a serious sin.

Imagination, however, is generally in the control of the will, and one can will to imagine the wrong things, and if this happens, the acts follow: "why do you bother me with bad imaginings," says the body to the mind in one of François de Sales fictive examples, "Make good thoughts, and I will not make bad movements" (*IVD* 199). It is extremely easy, apparently, to activate imagination with regard to pleasant sensations. This is why the *Introduction* takes such a roundabout way to describe the direction of attention in regard to sex. This is why François de Sales talks about elephants and food to discuss the marriage of a man and a woman. He needs to reach the reader's understanding (*entendement*) without provoking her imagination. This is very difficult to do, given the topic in question, and leads to the author's revealing commentary on his own anti-imaginative rhetoric in the chapter on the nuptial bed: "I believe that I have said everything that I wanted to say, and allowed to be understood, without saying it, all that I was unwilling to say" (*IVD* 244). He needs to convey the idea of human sexuality without producing the image of human sexuality.

But suppose one wanted to produce the image of human sexuality? This is one of the things that the will does, when it directs the mind's attention. If the reader of the *Introduction to the Devout Life* systematically cultivates her ability to produce in her mind sensory experiences that are not present, if she creates for herself a *cabinet intérieur*—a room of her own, we might say—that is not subject to the control, the criticism, or the mockery of the people around her, and if she has understood that her will is free (her *franc arbitre*, *TAD* 444), she can decide what to do with her imagination. This is the point on which François de Sales's attempt to signify something without saying it is an exercise in futility, because the reader is free, not only in practice but in the very theological doctrine that he preaches. Read with a different will, the *Introduction* and the hagiographic and other devotional writings to which François de Sales refers become guides to, and repertories of, erotic imagination of the most intense sort. Here is an example of something that can be read in a different spirit from that of its author, who gives this anecdote to illustrate the control of attention and of action during an assault on imagination in the present:

> The young man described by Saint Jerome, who was tied to a soft bed with delicate silk scarves and was provoked by all kinds of vile touches and teasing by a shameless woman who was lying in bed with him for the very purpose of shaking his resolve—did he not feel strong sensations? Were not his senses overwhelmed with pleasure? And was not his imagination thoroughly occupied with the presence of voluptuous objects? (*IVD* 260).

The young man, unable to move any part of his body except his mouth, bites off his tongue and spits it out, manifesting, through this symbol of castration, the dominance of his will over his imagination. In another context, we might refer to this edifying anecdote as a bondage fantasy, no longer an example of how one can use one's imagination defensively. There are a number of passages in the *Introduction* that lend themselves to "adaptation" beyond the wishes of the author, such as the temptation of Catherine of Siena who was assaulted by "shameless suggestions" that arose in her imagination where the devil, "in the form of men and women [. . .], performed thousands of carnal and lascivious acts" (*IVD* 260).

Let us not forget that the central character of a well-known novel of the following century wrote of studying the moralists with an entirely different intent. Not relying on her direct observations of society, she says,

> I supplemented them with readings, but not of the kind you probably think. I studied manners in novels, beliefs in philosophers. I even sought in the most severe moralists what they demand of us. I thus assured myself of the appearance that I needed to present.[53]

Madame de Merteuil's libertine adaptation of edifying reading falls entirely within the scope of what François de Sales foresaw as the problem of the false widow, except that the "false widow" who has learned to discipline her attention so that the absent pleasures derived from memory can become inwardly present.

In an important article, "Sade's Discourse on Method: Rudiments for a Theory of Fantasy," Josué Harari explores the theory of erotic imagination in a number of passages in Sade's work and recalls that Roland Barthes "was the first to note [in Sade's *Juliette*] a kind of parody of Loyola's spiritual exercise."[54] François de Sales is probably closer to Sade than is Loyola because, for one thing, he has more to say about the temptations of sexuality, and for another, the progression François de Sales describes in such detail in his two major works parallels the development Harari locates in Sade's "method":

> 1) Our pleasure must not be grounded in the senses, over which we have no control. 2) We must identify our passions and explain them according to 'philosophical' principles in order to attain to the state of indifference to passion, the condition of ascetic wisdom achieved by the mastery of one's drives, which the Stoics call Apathy. 3) Apathy [...] constitutes [...] the condition of a superior eroticism, a particular method that guarantees the libertine's mastery over *jouissance*.[55]

With the difference that François de Sales aims at a *jouissance* so perfect that it is beyond eroticism but entirely motivated by desire for union with the object of desire, beyond any of the constraints of the body, and in fact, without any of the limitations of imagination itself, the comparison that Harari and Barthes make between Sade and the meditative imagination seems highly persuasive. Sade's erotic imagination is a plausible adaptation (perhaps parodic, and perhaps not) of François de Sales's work.

In both cases the mental dominates the physical, and not the inverse; there is a gradation in the intellectualization of desire; ordinary, natural desire must be left behind for a desire that in one case is philosophical and in the other theological; imagination itself, being useful only in thinking about physical, sensory objects, must finally be surpassed in favor of the understanding.[56] François de Sales's discipline of attention first takes Philothée as far as her imagination—as far as any imagination—can go, in order to move her from meditation to contemplation, from the senses to the understanding, and, always, higher and higher levels of the will. A major difference between Sade's theory of fantasy, as described by Harari, and Salesian contemplation, is that, perhaps contrary to what one might be tempted to think, François de Sales wishes to maintain his reader in a state of ever more intense desire and never wishes to lead her to apathy, a state that implies a transcendence of will:

> The good that is finite puts an end to desire when it gives pleasure and puts an end to pleasure when it gives desire, because such a good cannot be possessed and desired at the same time. But the infinite good fosters desire along with possession and gives possession in the midst of desire, because it has the power to satisfy desire by its holy presence and the power to maintain desire by the magnitude of its excellence, which nourishes in all those who possess it a desire that is always content and a contentment that is full of desire. (*TAD* 574).

FRANÇOIS DE SALES AND THE DEVILS OF LOUDUN

On November 11, 1638, François de Sales's approach to the inner life of devotion received one of its most sensational endorsements. On that day, sixteen years after the death of the author of the *Introduction to the Devout Life*, Mother Jeanne des Anges, an Ursuline nun whose diabolic possession and subsequent release through exorcism had fascinated people all over France, arrived at the future saint's tomb near Annecy to fulfill a vow she had made at the time of the deliverance from her devils. There had been seven of them who had possessed her for a number of years. Before the last of them, Béhémoth, left her, she had heard an inner voice telling her that he would depart only at the tomb of François de Sales.[57] Although she had not received permission to travel to Annecy from her convent in Loudun, in Poitou, prior to her deliverance, she had negotiated with Church authorities an agreement that she and her exorcist, the Jesuit Jean-Joseph Surin, would make a pilgrimage of thanksgiving after her complete recovery.[58] Her triumphal journey from Loudun to Annecy included many visits to important people, including King Louis XIII, Queen Anne of Austria, and Cardinal Richelieu, whom she showed the by-then famous "exit marks" (*signes de sortie*) that each devil had made on his departure. These were the marks—like temporary tattoos—on various parts of her body, but most importantly the names, said to be miraculously inscribed on the skin of her hand, of Jesus, Mary, Joseph, and François de Sales.[59] These names faded and then refreshed themselves periodically in a mysterious manner. The story of Jeanne des Anges has been the subject of many books, articles, and even films, but the important role she gives to the author of the *Introduction to the Devout Life* has not generally received its share of attention.[60] Yet Jeanne des Anges herself clearly placed François de Sales in a position of great prominence in her experience.

A controversial aspect of Jeanne des Anges's exorcism was the approach taken by her Jesuit exorcist, Jean-Joseph Surin, who himself became "obsessed" by the devils and was considered unorthodox and even eccentric by his Jesuit colleagues.[61] Although he occasionally performed the kind of vigorous public exorcisms that were expected at the time and that provided the religious equivalent of a circus freak show—intended to impress the Catholic faithful and to convert Protestants and freethinkers—Surin emphasized long-term, attentive pastoral counseling with the aim of renewing the interior spiritual life of the woman in his care. Even though the Jesuit tradition contained the spiritual exercises of Ignatius of Loyola, the work of François de Sales must have been an important influence as well, in view of the culminating pilgrimage to his tomb.[62]

Following the account written by Jeanne des Anges herself, the major change in the way she was treated by the exorcists occurred when Surin transferred responsibility for her state to the nun herself. Though there is no doubt that Surin was orthodox in his belief in the devils and their powers, he places the burden of responsibility on the sinner herself:

> I was thus, by the grace of Our Lord, firmly resolved to take responsibility for all my disorders, and *no longer to look on the devils as the authors of my troubles* [....] I soon recognized that *the evil came from me*, and that my enemies only used the materials that I provided them. (126, emphasis added).

Right from the beginning of his work with her, Surin told Jeanne des Anges, "Get a grip on yourself" (*Faites effort sur vous*), and gave her an active role in her cure. "If you unite your will to mine," he told her, "I assure you that you will get out of the state that you are in, with the help of grace . . . " (108). In a highly Salesian move, Surin prescribed for her the routine of a minimum of a half-hour of prayer each day. Jeanne henceforth had no difficulty in the exercise of mental prayer, which—in view of her highly disturbed state— Surin guided by whispering in her ear while she was strapped down to a bench to prevent the violent movements that the devils caused her to make (110–111).

The devils came to Jeanne des Anges through her imagination, that is, through her mental representation of the senses. Without any external stimulus perceptible to other people, Jeanne saw, touched, smelled, and heard the devils in a multiplicity of forms. To say that the devils were imaginary is not, strictly speaking, to say that they were nonexistent—it is not our purpose to examine that issue—but merely to describe how her mind apprehended them. She repeatedly notes that her possession took the form of a disorder in her imagination, "a continual upheaval in my imagination" (121). One devil in particular, Asmodée, who specialized in sexual appetite, is associated with "impressions of impurity in my imagination" (102). Gradually Jeanne began to accept the concept, so fundamental to François de Sales, that her imagination was in her control and that she needed to make positive use of it, rather than assume that it was in the control of outside forces. This is the Salesian message of the meditations through which Surin guided her while she was outwardly restrained:

> Although outwardly I was very agitated, inwardly I felt a calm and a brightness that were the effects of what the Father was saying to the demon, for although I do not understand Latin and the demon did what he could to distract my attention, I could not help formulating a number of thoughts on the misfortune of souls that are unfaithful to God and on the happiness of those that are faithful to Him. It seemed to me that something said in the depth of my heart that I could choose one of these two states, and that choice depended on me . . . (113).

She learned to discipline her *attention* (118), and day by day she became ever happier to "meditate the divine mysteries" so that God captured her imagination and it was a pleasure to remain in his presence (120). Surin himself made use of the same method of preemptive, active imagination that he taught Jeanne des Anges. In his own autobiographical account, written partly in the third person, the Jesuit tells of incidents such as this one, when he was assailed by a devil during the night:

> the enemy came back and made its apparition in the same form as a serpent, twisting around his [Surin's] limbs and biting in order to keep him from sleeping and to give him impure thoughts. The Father then discovered a marvelous remedy in his recourse to the Holy Virgin, forming the image of the Virgin holding the Infant Jesus as he had seen in pictures. As soon as that image took form in his imagination, he felt the strength of that infernal serpent ebbing and then losing all its power [. . .] and in a little while all was peaceful and the Father fell back asleep.[63]

The following day the devil, speaking to him through the mouth of the possessed Jeanne des Anges—who "channeled" her seven demons as spokeswoman—gave a theoretical explanation for the tactic that had thwarted his assault during the night. He explained that he had attempted first to attack Surin through the simple physical senses and then through the mental representation of sensation, imagination. But Surin had already filled his mind with the image of the Virgin, leaving no space for other impressions. "Seeing," said the devil, "that I cannot reach you in your senses (*que je ne pouvais opérer en la partie sensible*), I tried to get into your imagination, and I found an obstacle."

Jeanne's daily meditations gave her increased autonomy. By occupying her imagination, like de Sales's Philothée, she pushed out the demonic and the sexual. This growing self-reliance did not sit well with Surin's superiors:

> for there was strong disapproval of [Father Surin's] approach in dealing with me, and most of all that he did not want me to view the devil as the author of my disorders, and also because [Father Surin] did not exorcise me very much. (149).

The result of the conflict between the development of Salesian inwardness and the demand for showy public exorcisms was the spectacular series of public "exits" of the devils. The most astounding of these demonic departures occurred only when Surin was about to be removed from Jeanne's case.[64] Had he and Jeanne been separated prior to her restoration to spiritual health, the approach through meditative practice would have appeared to be defeated. It was at the moment of being confronted with this danger that Jeanne, clearly won over to the cause of spiritual self-cultivation (and, undoubtedly, loyal to Surin himself), heard the voice requiring the voyage to the tomb of François de Sales (164–65). While the exorcisms in Loudun brought many travelers, Jeanne des Anges's voyage to Annecy reached people who never could have seen her if she had not arranged this mobile display—she gives the figure of twenty thousand people a day during the Parisian stage of her trip (201). Effectively, then, in the name of the inward development of a controlled imagination, Jeanne produced an exterior display that far outdid the show exorcisms that she and Surin considered obsolete. In the name of the *Introduction to the Devout Life*, and of its positive doctrine of using the mental world of sensation, Jeanne des Anges arranged one of the most graphic modern campaigns to promote the curative power of a highly developed inner life.

THREE

Picturing Ourselves in the World: Pascal's *Pensées*

It is not unusual to hear the seventeenth century described as the century of reason, and that description usefully reminds us of the powerful influence of thinkers like Bacon, Descartes, Hobbes, and of widely read textbooks such as the Port-Royal *Logic, or the Art of Thinking Well*. Yet often the Cartesian form of reason is held forth as the only significant model of seventeenth-century rationalism. As a result, the period is considered particularly prone to abstract, disembodied thought—one thinks of two successive chapters in an important book: "Descartes's Disengaged Reason" and "Locke's Punctual Self"[1]—and certain early-modern texts are either interpreted in such a way as to fit this conception of rationalism or, if the fit becomes too difficult to achieve, are omitted altogether. Blaise Pascal has long posed a problem for the monopoly of an abstract "Cartesian rationalism." On one hand he is difficult to ignore, because he is an established part of the canon and of academic programs, but on the other hand his attitude toward Cartesian rationalism is hard to square with the dominant view of "classicism." Hence, even some of the very best and most innovative accounts of seventeenth-century France simply ignore him.[2]

Seventeenth-century thought is, however, much richer than the single, Cartesian model leads us to believe. And one way to correct this view is to look at the text that simultaneously formulated the Cartesian straw-man—reduced Descartes's thought to a rough outline of the method—and proposed another model, Pascal's *Pensées*. The latter offers a view of the human condition not only illustrated by concrete examples of social interaction and cultural difference but also presenting a view of life and thought that is inseparable from such interaction and from the parameters of experience and historicity. Pascal's reductive view of Cartesian thought—and indeed of all philosophy—allowed him to emphasize his corrective post-Cartesian statement, one in which imagination plays a huge role.

FINESSE AND DIALECTICAL UNDERSTANDING

Pascal positions himself, against Descartes, by presenting as his preferred analytical and argumentative tool a way of thinking he calls the *esprit de finesse*. It is important to understand *finesse* in order to see how Pascal describes and uses imagination.

Pascal takes aim at Cartesian thinking in the fragments describing the *esprit de géométrie* and the *esprit de finesse*, two types of mind-set that have been called in English the "mathematical" and the "discerning" mind.[3] While Pascal's purpose in writing the fragments we know as the *Pensées* was, apparently, to formulate an apology for the Christian religion, much of his argumentation derives from humanist thought and particularly from Montaigne, whose thinking Pascal partially refutes and partially perpetuates. From Montaigne—and from Epictetus—Pascal takes everyday experience as a point of departure for study, rejecting the incorporeal or metaphysical foundation chosen by Descartes:

> The writing style of Epictetus, Montaigne, and Solomon de Tultie is most useful, reaches the reader best, remains in one's memory, and is most frequently quoted, because it is entirely based on thoughts that come out of the ordinary exchanges of real life.
>
> [La manière d'écrire d'Epictète, de Montaigne et de Salomon de Tultie est la plus d'usage qui s'insinue le mieux, qui demeure plus dans la mémoire et qui se fait le plus citer, parce qu'elle est toute composée de pensées nées sur les entretiens ordinaires de la vie.]

(L.745/S.618)

The *esprit géométrique* is crude and simple, yet initially difficult, because it requires thinkers to unlearn the patterns of everyday, practical action in favor of an unnatural, artificial pattern. Learning to use the principles of geometric thinking is what Pascal calls "turning the head" or "turning one's gaze" to the side: "on a peine à tourner la tête de ce côté-là" (L.512/S.670). The *esprit de géométrie* works best in solitude, ignoring the everyday discourse of life and what is "right in front of our eyes" (*devant les yeux de tout le monde*). So it is not surprising that Descartes, the exemplar of geometric thought, so repeatedly associates his way of thinking with solitude, both in the *Discourse on Method* and in the *Meditations*. One recalls the celebrated first sentence of the *Discourse* where Descartes retells the discovery of the method in his heated room in Germany:

> The start of winter made me stop in lodgings where, not finding any entertaining conversation, and fortunately not having any cares or passions that bothered me, I remained alone all day long in a heated room.[4]

Cartesian geometric thought requires, as Pascal observes, avoiding the ordinary conversations of life both as object of contemplation and as process. Descartes himself begins the fourth part of the *Discourse* by saying that he will be talking about meditations that are "so metaphysical and so unusual that they may not suit everyone's taste."[5]

In contrast the *esprit de finesse* is not difficult to learn and takes ordinary life as its object.[6] The *esprit fin* does not turn aside but instead looks at what is in open view, yet discernible only to those with the ability to detect subtle difference and shading:

> in the *esprit de finesse* the principles are in common practice and right in front of everyone's eyes. You need not look elsewhere, nor make a special effort; you only need to have good eyesight, but it must be really good. [dans l'esprit de finesse, les principes sont dans l'usage commun et devant les yeux de tout le monde. On n'a que faire de tourner la tête, ni de se faire violence; il n'est question que d'avoir bonne vue, mais il faut l'avoir bonne.]
>
> (*L.512/S.670*)

Good vision is required because the principles of *finesse* are not only delicate but also simultaneous and multiple. And this is the major difference between Pascalian and Cartesian thought, between linear and holistic (or what one could call—and has been called by Lucien Goldmann—dialectical) thought.[7]

Descartes had described a linear process in the second, third, and fourth precepts of his method. He would, he said, divide every difficulty into pieces and would start with simple objects and then gradually work his way up to compound objects. Finally, he would make inventories and general reviews of his thought to make sure that he had not omitted anything. Descartes formulates this as the geometric model, writing that his thinking is inspired by "those long chains of reasoning, each simple and easy, that geometricians are accustomed to using."[8]

These chains or sequences of simple concepts, what Pascal calls the "rough principles," cannot be processed in what we would call "real time." This is why the geometric thinker gets lost in dealing with the more resistant everyday world where the principles cannot be thus divided and sequenced (*ne se laissent pas ainsi manier*). Pascal refuses to chop problems into sequential parts not only because ordinary life does not offer itself easily in this way, but for a more substantial reason: the parts are not knowable unless they are thought in terms of the whole:

> All things being both effects and causes, influenced and influencing, mediate and immediate, and all things being linked together by a natural and imperceptible connection that ties together the most distant and most diverse things, I hold that it is impossible to know the parts without knowing the whole, nor to know the whole without knowing each part individually.
>
> [toutes choses étant causées et causantes, aidées et aidantes, médiates et immédiates et toutes s'entretenant par un lien naturel et insensible qui lie les plus éloignées et les plus différentes, je tiens impossible de connaître les parties sans connaître le tout, non plus que de connaître le tout sans connaître particulièrement les parties.]
>
> (*L.199/S.230*)

To say that Pascal argues in favor of a form of thought that works in "real time" does not only mean that the world presents itself to us in all its simultaneous complexity and therefore needs to be seen in the "snapshots" of things together all at once, but also means that for Pascal even those moments of real interaction are part of an ongoing process that can never be stopped— hence terms like "effects and causes, influenced and influencing" (*causées et causantes, aidées et aidantes*) to display an onward rush of experience.[9] Even if we recognize and understand the complexity of the present, we have to accept its contextualization by the past and future, so that the "part" is not only related to its contemporary whole but to the future wholes that it will result in. It should therefore be thought in terms of what it will cause, and only that forward-looking view can allow us to understand it in the present. While the *esprit de finesse* is not itself necessarily imaginative—*finesse* operates whenever several related propositions are grasped simultaneously rather than sequentially—it is clear that imagination always works within a complex stream of perception, one that *unites* different moments and coordinates several senses even if it does so in a way that accentuates one aspect more than another. In fact, even to speak of an imaginative construction in graduated terms of "more" and "less" (as we must) is necessarily to leave behind the geometric model of strict "yes" or "no." Together, as used by Pascal, *finesse* and imagination allow us to appreciate the subtle, yet undeniable, dialectic of the hunt, of the card game, and of worldly ambition—social phenomena that Pascal represents as simply appearing illogical to the geometrical thinker.

Finesse is linked to another idiosyncratically Pascalian term, *sentiment*, which Buford Norman has defined as signifying "nothing less than the way people form ideas about the physical (and spiritual) universe and the way they combine ideas to reach an immediate understanding of the combination without proceeding through discursive reasoning (what the Port-Royal *Logic* calls *raisonnement* and opposes directly to *sentiment*)."[10] Because *sentiment* is *always* at work, while reasoning is prone to cease (L.821/S.661), it is easy to see how the conjoined *finesse-sentiment*-imagination could prove to be readily available for everyday dealings with the world.[11]

THINKING FROM BEHIND THE HEAD

Pascal's work abounds in particular cases and familiar life: the magistrate listening to a sermon, card players, hunters, Paul Emilius, Alexander, Aristotle with his friends. This is because truth, human truth, is only discoverable in the minute details of human experience. In fact the study of particular cases cannot be carried out simply by observation but requires a grasp of both what is observed and who is observing, of both the *inside* and the *outside* at the same time. Consider how Pascal deals with the theme of diversion (*divertissement*), that is, human occupations from conversation to hunting, or from gambling to political office. On one hand, Pascal considers the behavior from the outside and thus sees its apparently bizarre and inconsistent nature. For instance, the hunter spends the day and deploys immense effort and resources to kill a hare that is tougher and smaller than a rabbit he could buy in the market. Why does he do something so counterproductive? In order to understand cases like this, on the other hand, Pascal must imagine the situation of the hunter from within, and thus identify the need for an object to conquer and the need for the process that absorbs thought. Pascal must, therefore be able to consider at the same time each of these individuals as subject and object, from within and without, and across a series of moments, never in a single isolated moment. In short, this is a task for *finesse*.

Much of this reflection is based on Montaigne. Pascal took from Montaigne the idea, developed in a sustained way in the "Apology for Raymond Sebond" and invoked briefly in many chapters of the *Essays*, that imagination is the power that defines humanity collectively as well as individually, that imagination takes its significance not only from individual uses or misuses of imagination (an approach reminiscent of much of Epictetus and Seneca) but from the imaginative foundations of political and social institutions. Pascal also takes from Montaigne's *Essays* many of his examples of the social imagination, though he sometimes (perhaps disingenuously) makes an obtuse interpretation of Montaigne in order to propose a more "correct" interpretation of the example. Pascal's description of an institutionalized imagination, which comes very close to what we would probably call today a critique of "ideology," shows how imagination acts upon and within us even though we are usually unaware of it. In fact, this lack of awareness is what makes imagination most powerful. Imagination works to give us our worldview, our sense of the plausible, our desires, our beliefs, and even our physical stance.[12] Thanks to Gérard Ferreyrolles's luminous study, *Les Reines du monde: l'imagination et la coutume chez Pascal*, the two dominant forces in everyday human life can be seen plainly in their interaction.[13] Custom, in fact, is so closely linked to imagination that the two forces are two facets of the human condition. One appears to be more concerned with action (custom) and the other with perception (imagination), but they act together, strengthening each other. What we have the habit of doing shapes what we see, and vice versa. This is neither the choice of an imaginative individual nor a pathology of her or his way of thinking. The routine of action and perception molds imagination with such force that neither reason nor will can act freely because they are never in contact with reality or nature but only with what Pascal calls the "second nature."

We dwell, then, in a world that we imagine, following the crowd that has imagined before us. This imaginary world is maintained by our bodies themselves, for Pascal well knew that the ascetic practices by which the body could discipline or program the mind were only the tip of the iceberg.[14] Not only religious and philosophical practice, but every daily social interaction in Pascal's view, uses the body to direct perception at its juncture with the body–mind bridge, the imagination:

> That's a good one! He doesn't want me to pay homage to a man dressed in brocade and followed by seven or eight lackeys. What? He will have me whipped if I don't salute him. That garment is power. And this is just like the difference between a horse in a splendid harness compared to some other. Montaigne is comical not to see the difference and to be surprised that people perceive a difference and he is comical to ask why they do this . . . .
>
> [Cela est admirable: on ne veut pas que j'honore un homme vêtu de brocatelle et suivi de sept ou 8 laquais. Et quoi! il me fera donner des étrivières si je ne le salue. Cet habit est une force. C'est bien de même qu'un cheval bien enharnaché à l'égard d'un autre. Montaigne est plaisant de ne pas voir quelle différence il y a et d'admirer qu'on y en trouve et d'en demander raison . . .]
>
> *(L. 89/S. 123)*

The habit of respect that keeps the social order in place is a physical habit that conditions the mind. One imagines, says Pascal, that a man with strong, well-armed retainers or even one simply well dressed is a particularly important man, because it is imagination's work to take raw sense-data and organize it into patterns, principally by combining what is immediately present to sight, smell, touch, and so forth, with what we can both recall and foresee. Although in this instance Montaigne is the straight man for Pascal's joke, the *Essays* not only give Pascal a stock of examples, they also provide him with the key to unlock the social imagination. So that the sight of an ermine-dressed magistrate recalls episodes of judicial power and allows one to foresee what will happen if we do not bow, right now. Costume is the source of most of Pascal's examples of how imagination dominates man in society:

> Our magistrates are familiar with this mystery. Their red robes, their ermines that they wrap themselves in like furry cats, the palaces where they render judgment, the fleur-de-lys [. . . .] having only an imaginary science they have to take these vain instruments that strike the imagination.
>
> [Nos magistrats ont bien connu ce mystère. Leurs robes rouges, leurs hermines dont ils s'emmaillotent en chaffourés, les palais où ils jugent, les fleurs de lys [. . . .] n'ayant que des sciences imaginaires il faut qu'ils prennent ces vains instruments qui frappent l'imagination . . . .]
>
> *(L. 44/S. 78)*

Imagination is a highly trainable faculty, at least in youth, that works as a bridge or transmitter in both directions: from the mind to the senses and from the senses to the mind. Thus our beliefs shape what we see, just as what we see shapes our beliefs, and imagination prevents the world from being an incoherent flood of sensation by offering a strong, though malleable, preformed set of impressions. The empty box, a reference to the lively scientific controversy over the possibility of a vacuum, gives Pascal a striking example of this imaginative shaping of perception:

> Because you have believed since childhood, some say, that a chest was empty when you didn't see anything in it, you have believed that emptiness [vacuum] was possible. This is an illusion of your senses, reinforced by usage, that science must correct. And the others say: because you were told in school that there is no emptiness [vacuum], they corrupted your common sense, that understood so clearly before that bad impression, which now must be corrected in going back to your first nature. So what created the illusion: the senses or education?

> [Parce, dit-on, que vous avez cru dès l'enfance qu'un coffre était vide, lorsque vous n'y voyiez rien, vous avez cru le vide possible. C'est une illusion de vos sens, fortifié par la coutume, qu'il faut que la science corrige. Et les autres disent, parce qu'on vous a dit dans l'école qu'il n'y a point de vide, on a corrompu votre sens commun, qui le comprenait si nettement avant cette mauvaise impression, qu'il faut corriger en recourant à votre première nature. Qui a donc trompé, Les sens ou l'instruction?]

> *(L.44/S.78)*

Since Pascal is so persuaded of the ubiquity and the power of imagination that he proclaims "imagination controls everything" (*l'imagination dispose de tout*), what is to be done? Does Pascal belong to the historic line of thinkers who propose to limit imagination or to cure mankind of its maladies, like Gianfrancesco Pico della Mirandola, whose book on imagination contains chapters with titles like "How the disorder of the imagination, and the falsity originating in the temperament of the body and the objects of the senses, can be corrected and cured"?[15] Actually, Pascal is much more favorable to the development of imaginative power (and resigned to its powerful presence) than he is to philosophic attempts to cure it.

Pascal's *esprit fin* becomes aware of the multitude of small, interdependent aspects of "real life" that make no sense unless we see them as imagination at work. Yet seeing them as imagination at work requires an exercise in imagination on the part of the discerning observer. Here, as in Descartes, we find an exercise of placing things into doubt, but rather than beginning with a single moment of total doubt, the Pascalian observer–participant installs a layer of doubt that is always at work, making us aware that we cannot access the first nature but only the second nature of imagination and its consequent emotional determinations. Being engaged in ordinary life presents the Pascalian thinker with the best opportunity for the truly crucial and never finished study: the study of the self, not as isolated subject but as social being. Yet this self needs to be constructed by thought, just as the Cartesian "I" of the Cogito needs to be constructed. Rather than construct this self in solitude through ever-increasing subtraction or abstraction until reaching a final, undoubtable residue (as when Descartes says that to doubt requires a subject, *moi qui doute*), Pascal's *esprit fin* proceeds by grasping the relationship between observable things and then inserting himself or herself into that relationship empathically or by an imaginative identification. Self-knowledge is knowledge of the *other*—this is a central concept of Pascal's thought and of several of his kindred spirits, like La Rochefoucauld. For Pascal this indirect, or mediated, or second-hand knowledge of the self comes in part, it is true, from what we could call a universalizing tendency (as in the Cartesian "I"), but of a particular modesty and in a surprising reverse form. Pascal assumes that we are basically and potentially alike, though we occupy different positions of wealth, power, religion, and nationality. This alikeness is discernible only through a minute and meticulous observation of humanity in its most everyday occupations and feelings: not the king's unique majesty and power but his boredom, his fear of dying, his generation of future projects. Therefore, the universalism of Pascal comes from the primary discovery that we are like others rather than from the presumption that they are like us. Logically, of course, an equal sign is neutral and nondirectional, but in the order of discovery the other precedes the self in Pascal's thought, and we must construct our self-knowledge from outside in.[16] Charles Taylor, one of the few nonspecialist writers to acknowledge the importance of the Pascalian (and, generally speaking, neo-Augustinian) resistance to Cartesian thought in the seventeenth century, quotes the *Pensées*' description of the *moi*, or self, as a *monstre incompréhensible*, but then short-circuits Pascal's reflections by commenting, "What alone can bring some order to this, can give some (relative) self-understanding, is grace, which transforms the terms of our inner conflicts."[17] Yet Pascal does not give up as easily as Taylor suggests or deny the possibility of relative self-knowledge to the unbeliever or the unredeemed. After all, some degree of self-knowledge is required even for the unbeliever to set forth on the quest for religious truth.

Imagination does not only allow us to think about far away unseen things or about things beyond our ordinary physical limits, but also to see what is *right in front of our eyes*. One of the problems is that *direct self-knowledge is impossible*. Hence, the unusual, but powerful, work of dialectical discernment.

The longest fragment entitled "diversion" (*divertissement*, L.136/S.168) provides an excellent example of Pascal's analysis of imagination at work, an analysis that uses *finesse* as its analytic framework. This fragment begins,

> When I have, occasionally, considered the various labors of men, and the dangers and hardships that they risk at Court, and in war where there are so many disputes, so many passionate hazardous and often wrong-headed initiatives, etc., I have often said that all the ills of men comes from one single thing: that they are incapable of staying alone in a room.
>
> [Quand je m'y suis mis quelquefois à considérer les diverses agitations des hommes, et les périls, et les peines où ils s'exposent dans la Cour, dans la guerre d'où naissent tant de querelles, de passions d'entreprises hardies et souvent mauvaises, etc., j'ai dit souvent que tout le malheur des hommes vient d'une seule chose, qui est de ne savoir demeurer seul dans une chambre.]

This opening observation is clearly reminiscent of a Stoic diagnosis of the pathology of imagination. The wise disciple of Epictetus would recognize here the unhappiness that comes from allowing *external* and merely specious goods to draw a person away from his or her purely internal moral purpose. Pascal's solitary room simply provides a metaphor for the spiritual inwardness and solitude that are the conditions of autarky. The mind experiences these external goods as *phantasiai*, as perceptions that are formed in the imagination. If Pascal's purpose were to teach a Stoic wisdom, he would no doubt continue with the advice that each of us spend as much time as possible in solitude. We know, however, that Pascal disapproved of this Stoic ambition to transcend the pain of life. In fact, at times Pascal's description of Stoic teaching makes Epictetus sound like the Christian Satan, tempting man to rival God.[18] The comment on the solitary room becomes, for Pascal, the opening of a dialectical, *finesse*-oriented set of contrasts in which what we learn is not to avoid the tribulations and trivialities of life, but rather to understand the trace of original sin that is discernible in the absurd conduct that we cannot avoid.

Pascal goes on, in this fragment, to consider the situation of the most privileged person, the king:

> being a king is to have the most beautiful station in the world, and yet, imagine you are in the king's place, along with all its satisfactions, if he is without diversions and if he is allowed to think and reflect on what he is— that languid happiness would not sustain him—he will necessarily fall into visions of what threatens him, of possible revolts, and finally of death and diseases that are unavoidable, so that if he is without what we call diversion, he is unhappy, more unhappy than the least of his subjects who is playing and amusing himself.

> [la royauté est le plus beau poste du monde et cependant, qu'on s'en imagine, accompagné de toutes les satisfactions qui peuvent le toucher, s'il est sans divertissement et qu'on le laisse considérer et faire réflexion sur ce qu'il est— cette félicité languissante ne le soutiendra point—il tombera par nécessité dans les vues qui le menacent, des révoltes qui peuvent arriver et enfin de la mort et des maladies qui sont inévitables, de sorte que, s'il est sans ce qu'on appelle divertissement, le voilà malheureux, et plus malheureux que le moindre de ses sujets qui joue et qui se divertit.]

(L.136/S.168)

Here we recognize two different uses of imagination. First, Pascal appeals to our *finesse*, our ability to learn from the ordinary experiences of life that are before our very eyes, to engage in a thought-experiment, an exercise in applied imagination. We imagine what it must be like to be a king, and in doing so we encounter a second use—an involuntary one—of imagination: the king cannot stop his imagination from working. His mind is flooded with imaginings—precisely the kind of *phantasiai* that Seneca and Epictetus write about—that torment him with views of possible or inevitable future suffering. Thus *divertissement* serves to control this kind of undisciplined (and, in Pascal's view, undisciplinable) imagination by providing an object of perception that draws the mind away from the distant future. This new object, the source of diversion, is itself constructed by imagination. In fact, all diversions are simply a positive form of imagination in an attempt to self-medicate (as we might say) for the pain of life.

Pascal has presented, at this point in the fragment, two possible cures for the misery of the human condition: the impossible inward-turning discipline of Stoic withdrawal and the desperate outward-turning evasion of diversion. He neither recommends one nor condemns the other because what *finesse* does is detect patterns in complex juxtapositions that look plausibly life-like to us. *Finesse* is the gift on which we draw when we play games that ask us "What does not fit in this picture?" We need to keep this question of fit in mind as we continue Pascal's examples of diversion, and in the case of the king we can wonder why the king, who has everything, needs diversion. Indeed, we can wonder how he can possibly find diversion, because what could attract and hold his attention more than the preoccupations of ruling?

Pascal continues by showing us that there is no stable or objective quality in things that makes them worthy of our attention. It is not reason that "can set the price of things" (*peut mettre le prix aux choses*) but imagination (L.44/S.78). So this power confers on things a value necessary to drive the king and everyone else *outwards*—in exactly the wrong direction from the point of view of the Stoic sage—toward objects that acquire their importance only from imagination. Here it is worth recalling that Pascal is still writing from within the tradition that conceived imagination as a faculty, or way of thinking, that deals with things that are present as well as things that are absent. In other words, even what is right in front of the king's or the courtier's eyes enters the mind through imagination, just as much as the memory of earlier experience or the anticipation of pleasures or sufferings yet to come. The refrain, "Cleopatra's nose," reminding us of the impact on human history of the way Cleopatra's nose was perceived (L.413/S.32), belongs to this network of allusions to the spell that imagination casts to give certain things an almost magical power. Yet Pascal is clearly already veering toward the post-seventeenth-century emphasis on imagination as a way of thinking about things that are absent. This is clear in Pascal's reminders that we are almost always, inevitably, thinking about what is absent. The king's need for diversion comes precisely from his inability to think about the present (his mind's eye brings him ceaselessly "visions of what threatens him, of possible revolts, and finally of death and diseases that are unavoidable" and his need for something to draw his attention closer to the present, for "We never keep ourselves in the present. We remember the past; we anticipate the future . . . " (L.47/S.80).

This manipulation of attention—we recall that François de Sales describes meditation as the discipline of attention—[19] shows imagination at work. The discerning observer of the king and other important people at play sees that they are using the force of imagination against imagination. Because they have so little ability to keep their mind from filling up with images of what has been, what might have been, what might be, and what inevitably will be, men invent a sort of counterpoison in the form of more trivial images that can occupy their imagination (applying a therapy already demonstrated by Montaigne in "Of the power of imagination"). Yet they must not be aware of what they are doing or this diversion will not work.

Because imagination gives value to things, the king, like other men, will assign an absurd value to something and then pursue it in an experience of diversion:

> The nobleman sincerely believes that hunting is a great and royal pleasure, but his beater is not of that opinion. They imagine that if they had obtained that certain office, they would relax then and enjoy themselves and do not grasp the insatiable nature of cupidity. They sincerely believe that they are seeking rest and yet in reality they are only seeking commotion.
>
> [Le gentilhomme croit sincèrement que la chasse est un plaisir grand et un plaisir royal, mais son piqueur n'est pas de ce sentiment-là. Ils s'imaginent que s'ils avaient obtenu cette charge, ils se reposeraient ensuite avec plaisir et ne sentent pas la nature insatiable de la cupidité. Ils croient chercher sincèrement le repos et ne cherchent en effet que l'agitation.]
>
> *(L.136/S.168)*

This passage—one of many similar ones on the unconscious flight into diversion—calls for a small observation on language. In Pascal's day, the expression *s'imaginer* (literally, either "to imagine for oneself" or "to imagine oneself") was almost universally used simply to mean "to make a mistake, to believe something erroneously." Pascal is one of the few writers who give this reflexive verb its more substantial, literal sense. Thus, the nobleman who seeks some appointment actually *imagines* the delight that will follow, though he is also simply *mistaken* in this view. If he did not have this vivid mental picture of the delight that would follow, he would not be preoccupied with his ambition and he would end up back in the terrible situation of having to face, like the king, the image "of death and diseases that are unavoidable."

The reason that those who have the *esprit fin* can understand Pascal's argument here is that they can imagine what the courtier is imagining even though they can at the very same time stand back and imagine the courtier from the outside. This simultaneity of perception, as we know, is a major characteristic of *finesse*, and it explains why neither the Stoic nor the mathematical thinker (who could, on occasion, be the same person) can understand diversion. A mathematical-minded friend of someone who is seeking diversion through gambling might very well, and very logically, save his gambler friend some time:

> Take a man who spends his life without boredom gambling a little bit every day. Give him every morning the money that he could win gambling, but on the condition that he doesn't play: you would make him miserable. One might claim that this is because he needs the pastime of the game rather than the money. Well, let him play for nothing; he would not be caught up in the game and would be bored.

> [Tel homme passe sa vie sans ennui en jouant tous les jours peu de chose. Donnez-lui tous les matins l'argent qu'il peut gagner chaque jour, à la charge qu'il ne joue point, vous le rendez malheureux. On dira peut-être que c'est qu'il recherche l'amusement du jeu et non pas le gain. Faites-le donc jouer pour rien, il se s'y échauffera pas et s'y ennuiera.]

> *(L.136/S.168)*

The step-by-step analysis of imagination as diversion breaks down, for only by imagining the gambler (or the hunter or the king) from inside and outside, at the same time, can we understand what is going on. Another way to put this Pascalian insight is that reason alone cannot comprehend the problem of diversion because the essence of this human need is not rational. It belongs entirely to the domain of imagination, and to understand it one needs to use one's imagination. There is a *caveat*, however, to this whole study of mankind in society, for the observer must always keep in mind that he or she does not transcend the situation of those observed. That is the major distinction between Pascal's *esprit fin* and the whole mass of those whom Pascal calls *philosophes*, though at times he targets specifically the Stoics for their pretensions to transcendence.[20] The whole point, in the *Pensées*, of looking around at the world of diversions and ambitions is to realize that anything, from the highest political office to casual conversation, can be a way of filling and temporarily concentrating the imagination.

Diversion, *divertissement*, is only one of many topics that Pascal approaches through *finesse* and by showing the dominant role of imagination in society. His political analysis, much of it contained in the section of the *Pensées* labeled "Vanity," into which the most authoritative editions of the text place the long fragment "Imagination" (L.44/S.78), centers on the transference of physical force into symbolic force through the unconscious work of imagination. Yet perhaps the term "symbolic" is too abstract, as we saw in the earlier example about the impact of the appearance of powerful people (L.89/S.123). Imagination is not a way of thinking that undertakes the decoding or parsing of signs or symbols into messages. That is the work of reason and such an undertaking has about it, in the Pascalian context, something of the *esprit géométrique* with its ordered, sequential attention to principles and definitions. Imagination frames sensory perception and is the inner repository of embodied, physical sensation.[21]

This difference between the immediate perception (a characteristic in which imagination as a faculty and *finesse* merge) and the slower process of reasoning explains the conflict between Pascal's description of the politics of imagination and the corresponding description in Montaigne's *Essays* that is Pascal's starting point. Pascal's Montaigne sees absurdity where Pascal sees necessity, since Pascal places his political description deliberately at the level of the "people," in other words within a vision that does not engage in an elaborate process of reasoning to conclude that it is a good idea to fear well-dressed men with many servants. The view of the "people" thus constructed by Pascal supposes that if the aristocracy has power, it must deserve that power, where Montaigne—and the whole category of thinkers Pascal calls *demi-habiles* (the half-clever people)—sees the perpetuation of unjustified privilege. Pascal does not disagree with Montaigne's analysis but considers it simply a form of reasoning in a domain that belongs to imagination.[22] If the people were to understand the historical origin of current laws they would revolt—"It is dangerous to tell the people that the laws are not just, because the people only obey them because they think that the laws are just" (L.66/S.100)—since all worldly things that are perceived immediately and without the need for reasoning belong to imagination, as physicians and government officials know, since they wear costumes to impress their poorly-founded power on the imagination (L.44/S.78).

This brief glimpse at the complex Pascalian description of society does not penetrate into the many phases and articulations of his thought, but it does give us a basis for distinguishing Pascal's view of imagination from those who would see imagination as a pathology, as something to avoid. Pascal urges his reader to leave the common working of imagination alone. Even while showing that imagination generally diverges from reason, he does not recommend that one avoid imagining and still less does he encourage his readers to educate others to redirect their imagination. Distinguishing himself repeatedly and with a variety of terms from thinkers of all stripes who *simplify* life by adopting one polar doctrine for improving human life, Pascal contents himself with using his observations about human life to point toward the Christian redemption after death. Thus, Stoics and Epicureans are rejected as are the members of the groups Pascal designates on a more ad hoc basis as *habiles* and *demi-habiles*, all of whom have a reformist tendency in one way or another. Instead, Pascal's reader ideally becomes a member of a group of initiates who are aware of social injustice, the arbitrariness of laws, the vanity of human activities across the spectrum (including politics, scholarship, hunting, and even conversation), and the undependability of sensory perception, and who yet continue to leave these institutions and activities in place. Instead of challenging the reign of imagination—"imagination controls everything"—the Pascalian initiate becomes, in a certain sense, complicit with this state of mankind's nature, that is, mankind's "second nature" as shaped by custom as it resides in imagination's way of perceiving.

One of Pascal's expressions for this stance of learning by turning outward, toward the stream of perceptions, with a critical view yet simultaneously imagining empathically how others are imagining the world, is the "thought from the back of the head" (*la pensée de derrière la tête*): "We need to have a thought from the back, and use it to judge everything, while still speaking like the people" (*Il faut avoir une pensée de derrière, et juger de tout par là, en parlant cependant comme le peuple*, L.91 /S.125), and "I will also have my thoughts from the back of the head" (*J'aurai aussi mes pensées de derrière la tête*, L.797/S.650). This thought from behind is emphatically *not* imaginative; it is a judgment that detects the irrationality of habitual imaginative thinking yet allows that thinking to continue in order to learn from it.

Imagination, for Pascal, is therefore not a faculty that is to be cultivated in an interior space, but rather a powerful, indeed irresistible mechanism that shapes the outside world, and that governs perceptions and behavior. Since our own perceptions are skewed by that mechanism, our best strategy is to stand as far back as we can and look at the behavior of others. Their imagination-driven conduct will appear to us in all its bizarreness, just as ours will appear strange to them. Grasping this complex triangulation (our reason measures their imagination, which resembles our imagination, which is invisible to our reason) we are able, quietly, *par la pensée de derrière*, to learn a lesson about a world that we dare not change.[23]

COSMIC IMAGINATION

Imagination, as presented by Aristotle and developed by the Stoics and their modern followers, gives the mind the ability to experience alternative views of the world. It is thus the type of thinking that permits what we would call the "thought experiment," which Descartes used within fairly narrow limits. This practice of speculative imagination encompasses all hypothetical thinking that involves thinking concretely (visualizing, hearing, feeling, etc.) about a thing or event that is not present to us. Thus, we could say, in this broad sense, that Montaigne's many imaginings of death are speculative: he could die as a result of a roof tile falling on his head or he could die from a bullet. However, in Pascal's work there are a small number of fragments that call for a particularly ambitious form of speculative imagining, one that goes beyond familiar situations of the kind Montaigne describes to present experiences that are, within the physical and technological limits of the seventeenth-century author and reader, impossible. These take, in the *Pensées*, a form that we could call "cosmic imagining," since the most extensive and noteworthy of these speculations guides the reader through a vision—almost a hallucination—of mankind in the universe. This use of imagination appears in one of the longest fragments in the *Pensées*, the one that bears the title "Man's disproportion" (L.199/S.230).

What is immediately striking about this fragment is that the reader (or the interlocutor of the apologetic voice within the *Pensées*) is not only asked to picture things that are far from his ordinary experience of life but from a point of view that was physically impossible for any seventeenth-century person.[24] Rather than the mundane things and events that fill Pascal's text and that he so vividly recalls for his reader, "Man's disproportion" asks us to imagine the cosmos from a standpoint that presents the earth itself as a mere point. This text begins with an unusual, though possible, perspective before explicitly invoking imagination (in the modern sense of what we can see *only* with the mind):

> Let man then contemplate the whole of nature in its high and full majesty, and let him turn his gaze away from the base objects that surround him. Let him look at that brilliant light placed like an eternal lamp to illuminate the universe, and let earth seem to him only as a dot compared to the vast circuit that this star traces, and let him be astounded at the fact that this vast circuit itself is only a fine dot when compared to the circumference embraced by the stars that spin in the firmament. But while our gaze stops there and *imagination* continues beyond, it will wear itself out conceiving forms before nature ceases to supply them. The whole visible world is only an imperceptible trace in the vast bosom of nature.

> [Que l'homme contemple donc la nature entière dans sa haute et pleine majesté, qu'il éloigne sa vue des objets bas qui l'environnent. Qu'il regarde cette éclatante lumière mise comme une lampe éternelle pour éclairer l'univers,

que la terre lui paraisse comme un point au prix du vaste tour que cet astre décrit, et qu'il s'étonne de ce que ce vaste tour lui-même n'est qu'une pointe très délicate à l'égard de celui que ces astres, qui roulent dans le firmament, embrassent. Mais si notre vue s'arrête là que l'*imagination* passe outre, elle se lassera plutôt de concevoir que la nature de fournir. Tout le monde visible n'est qu'un trait imperceptible dans l'ample sein de la nature.][25]

This celebrated and much-quoted passage has similarities to some exercises that we saw in Salesian meditation, and no doubt goes back even further into common places of the sermon tradition.[26] We recall passages from the *Introduction to the Devout Life* in which the reader is asked to imagine the night sky appearing in the daylight or the one that presents the reader herself on an elevation between paradise and hell.[27] Yet Pascal's cosmic speculation also recalls the Cartesian imaginative failure-tests in which the philosopher invites his reader to try to imagine a mountain without a valley or to imagine a kilogon.[28] These are cases in which imagination necessarily fails, because even if reason can conceive a thousand-sided figure, human imagination cannot actually picture such a thing. Here Pascal draws the energy of his argument from an imagination that is first stimulated to a gigantic effort and then frustrated by being given a task that is beyond it.

Pascal next urges the reader to a brutal reversal of direction, first by returning to his paltry self ("Let man, returning to himself . . . " (*Que l'homme étant revenu à soi*)—an instruction that implies the trance-like state of intense imaginative meditation) and then by picturing tiny things. Again the process starts with something that a contemporary of Pascal's might have seen with the newly-invented microscope, a small zoological curiosity called a *ciron*, before plunging with the speculative imagination into physically invisible spaces that can only be seen with the mind:

to show him another equally surprising prodigy, let him look among the things he knows for the most delicate ones, let a *ciron* offer him in its minute body incomparably smaller things, limbs with joints, veins in the limbs, blood in the veins, humors in this blood, globules in these humors, vapors in these globules, and analyzing further these latest elements let him exhaust his strength in these thoughts, and let us talk about this last object that he can reach. He may think that this is the extreme of what is tiny in nature.

[pour lui présenter un autre prodige aussi étonnant, qu'il recherche dans ce qu'il connaît les choses les plus délicates, qu'un ciron lui offre dans la petitesse de son corps les parties incomparablement plus petites, des jambes avec des jointures, des veines dans ses jambes, du sang dans ses veines, des humeurs dans ce sang, des gouttes dans ces humeurs, des vapeurs dans ces gouttes, que divisant encore ses dernières choses il épuise ses forces en ces conceptions et que le dernier objet où il peut arriver soit maintenant celui de notre discours. Il pensera peut-être que c'est là l'extrême petitesse de la nature.]

Once again Pascal produces a failure of imagination that somehow is only the prelude to a new round of still smaller entities that repeat cyclically the same types of articulations on ever decreasing scales. This rhetoric of humiliation begins with an affirmative Salesian exercise, passes through a Cartesian mind-experiment with a negative outcome, and then continues into an attack on physical perception that is deeply reminiscent of Montaigne:

Our senses can perceive nothing that is extreme: too much noise deafens us, too much light dazzles us, excessive distance or nearness prevents us from seeing [. . . .] We neither feel extreme heat, nor extreme cold [. . . .]

[Nos sens n'aperçoivent rien d'extrême, trop de bruit nous assourdit, trop de lumière éblouit, trop de distance et trop de proximité empêche la vue [. . . .] Nous ne sentons ni l'extrême chaud, ni l'extrême froid [. . . .]²⁹

Although this imaginative speculation on a cosmic scale—one that places humanity in the indefinite, even indefinable point between two infinities—stands out against the social scenes that are more frequent in the *Pensées*, we can see that imagination is shaped by the *esprit de finesse* in that these passages are significant only because of the interplay between paired extremes, or rather among the impossible-to-reach extremes and the middle that is always in motion because it cannot get a firm foundation in either direction: "to us extreme things are as if they did not exist and we are nothing for them; they escape us and we escape them" (*les choses extrêmes sont pour nous comme si elles n'étaient point et nous ne sommes point à leur égard; elles nous échappent ou nous à elles*). This kind of multiple and dynamic apprehension is the contrary of the *esprit de géométrie*. It unites *finesse* with imagination in that it is available to the untrained mind without special talents, it is concrete and based (at least in its starting point) on everyday things, it calls upon the senses, and it incorporates within the things perceived in the mind the position and the actual being of the perceiver. It is therefore not disembodied but on the contrary a dynamic binding-together of perceiver and object in a constant back-and-forth movement that destabilizes the perceiver in her perception of herself by eliminating the possibility of a scale or measure in the mind's representation—imagination—of any physical thing at all:

> for who would not be amazed to see that our body, which just a moment ago was imperceptible in a universe that was itself invisible in the center of the cosmos, is now a colossus, a world or rather a totality next to the nothingness that we cannot reach.
>
> [car qui n'admirera que notre corps, qui tantôt n'était pas perceptible dans l'univers imperceptible lui-même dans le sein du tout, soit à présent un colosse, un monde ou plutôt un tout à l'égard du néant où l'on ne peut arriver.]

Now this view of the human person in the universe, which depends on grasping together the infinitely large and the infinitely small, seems to be quintessentially the work of the *esprit de finesse* in that the discerning mind judges "with a single glance" and not by theorems and definitions in a step-by-step progression. What complicates this description, however, is that the *esprit de finesse* generally works on the basis of things that are perceptible in ordinary life, things that are "right in front of everyone," whereas the cosmic vision has to be constructed following the guidance of the narrator of the *Pensées*. Complicating matters still further is Pascal's statement that "thinkers with *finesse* who have only *finesse* are not capable of the patience to peer into the first principles of speculative and imaginary things that they have never seen in the world, and that are completely outside practical life" (*les fins qui ne sont que fins ne peuvent avoir la patience de descendre jusques dans les premiers principes des choses spéculatives et d'imagination qu'ils n'ont jamais vues dans le monde, et tout à fait hors d'usage*) (L.512/S.670). The cosmic vision is certainly the product of the most advanced speculative imagination, yet it is not based in any way on principles and definitions. It does not function in such a way that each step is made convincing by the evident correctness of the preceding step in a process of geometrical reasoning. In fact, the cosmic vision does not require reasoning nor can one at any point speak of "correctness." Judgment is not needed, but only the ability to create and maintain a vision in the mind, a purely imaginative capacity. What seems to make the cosmic imagination an appeal to *finesse* is that none of its steps, none of its detail, has any effect independently but only when the whole is experienced in its final, overwhelming vision.

It may seem an astounding paradox, but when the *esprit de finesse* deals with human life in a holistic way, it ends up by assuming a metaphor that seems to belong to the competing type of mind-set, the geometric spirit. This is very peculiar, because one can see, in Pascal's description of the geometric mind at work, something very mechanistic: the plodding, step-by-step, rigid, hyperspecialized character that is powerful in its limited domain but far from the real life, visualizing, big-picture thoughts of the *fin* thinker. Yet not only does Pascal adopt the metaphor of the machine to describe human thought and behavior, he does so in order to deal with the problem that is at the center of discussions of imagination since antiquity: the triangular relationship among the mind, the body, and the perceptual bridge that links them. Pascal actually promotes the idea that human beings are in some ways "machines" in order to support the pragmatic endeavors of *finesse*.

THE PASSIONATE MACHINE

One of the most enigmatic fragments in the *Pensées* is right at the beginning:

> Order.
> A letter to a friend to encourage him to seek. And he will respond: but what good will it do me to seek, nothing appears. And answer him: do not despair. And he would reply that he would be happy to find some light. But according to that religion, even if he were to believe in that manner, it would do him no good. And so he prefers not even to seek. And at that, reply to him: The Machine.
>
> [Ordre.
> Une lettre d'exhortation à un ami pour le porter à chercher. Et il répondra: mais à quoi me servira de chercher, rien ne paraît. Et lui répondre: ne désespérez pas. Et il répondrait qu'il serait heureux de trouver quelque lumière. Mais que selon cette religion même quand il croirait ainsi cela ne lui servirait de rien. Et qu'ainsi il aime autant ne point chercher. Et à cela lui répondre: La Machine.]
>
> *(L.5/S.39)*

The response "The Machine" will no doubt always have a certain mystery to it—it has probably remained etched in the memory of readers over the generations because of its haunting incompleteness. Most commentators see this expression as Pascal's code for a line of argument about habit. Certain habits prevent belief and others encourage it. A related fragment refers to "the letter to remove the obstacles which is the discourse of the Machine, to prepare the Machine, to seek through reason" (*la lettre d'ôter les obstacles qui est le discours de la Machine, de préparer la Machine, de chercher par raison*) (L.11 /S.45). Sara Melzer gives a very clear and concise explanation of the Machine's importance to Pascal's argument: "[Pascal's] narrator describes the human body as a machine, that is formed by custom [. . . .] Just as the mind is ruled by the body, so the body is governed by a mechanical structure caught up in the trap of custom" so that "Meaning and knowledge do not proceed from the nature of things; rather, they result from semiological codes created by the habit of seeing certain elements continually associated so that their association eventually comes to seem necessary and inevitable."[30] Melzer's study of how Pascal constructs a machine in language to counter the existing machine of social custom is a convincing demonstration of the breadth of applicability of the idea of the machine in Pascal's thought. Because the machine for him is so directly equated with repetition, machines can be made out of anything that supports repetition. One of Pascal's claims to the attention of historians of science is his invention of an arithmetic machine, a machine that his sister Gilberte Périer described as exporting the thought process from the human mind into inert matter.[31]

Descartes had made machines very fashionable in the mid-seventeenth century. The idea that animals were simply machines without souls and that human beings were souls located inside a mechanical body swept the intellectual milieu to which Pascal belonged. This view became the basis, at times, for an absurd cruelty. One memoir of life among the male Jansenist thinkers who lived near the convent of Port-Royal des Champs, the *solitaires*, reports:

> There wasn't a single solitary who did not talk about the idea of the automaton. No one made a fuss about beating a dog; anyone would coldly beat a dog with a stick and would make fun of the people who pitied these animals as if they felt pain. It was said that animals were time-pieces, that their crying when they were beaten was only the sound of a little spring that had been set in motion, but that all that was without feeling.
>
> [Il n'y avait guère de solitaire qui ne parlât d'automate. On ne se faisait plus une affaire de battre un chien; on lui donnait fort indifféremment des coups de bâton, et on se moquait de ceux qui plaignaient ces bêtes comme si elles eussent senti de la douleur. On disaient que c'étaient des horloges; que ces cris qu'elles faisaient quand on les frappait n'étaient que le bruit d'un petit ressort qui avait été remué, mais que tout cela était sans sentiment.][32]

This view of animals and of the human body, as the animal part of human nature, was popularized by Descartes, yet it is only the extreme and simplified outcome of the long historical development of the soul from the body, the interior from the exterior. Pascal, as both a scientist and a Jansenist believer, was doubly immersed in the great vogue of attention to the body-machine. As an original thinker, he took pieces of this idea and rearranged them in a way that blurred the sharp line between mind and body. Instead of a rigid, "geometrical" (or Cartesian) dualism between the physical and the spiritual parts of the human being, Pascal emphasized the overlapping, much less tidy, powers that reside in imagination, the way of thinking that fills itself with the representations of physical experience while still being within the mind. In short, Pascal set forth a view of the human person in which the "machine" is no longer simply the body, but a continuum or hybrid offering great latitude for self-fashioning. Pascal's "machine" is actually a way of describing both the imagination and the body insofar as we use the latter to imprint upon minds—ours and those of others—habits of perception.[33]

Many passages in the *Pensées* converge to indicate that imagination is the point at which the structure of repetition that is a machine in the conceptual sense is linked to the body as machine in the physical sense. Influenced strongly by Montaigne and Epictetus—his two favorite authors[34]—and contending with a society swept by Descartes's philosophy,[35] Pascal made the concept of the machine into a vehicle for an active approach to living one's life, and particularly to dealing with passions. This approach derives from the Stoic view of imagination and from Montaigne's attention to the body and to custom. The "discourse of the Machine" is thus an outstanding example of the embodiment of thought, the use of sense-based ideas to effect a change in belief.

A startling example of applied imagination can be found in the well-known wager argument, from the fragment "infini rien" (L.418/S.680—in his edition Sellier gives this fragment the title "the discourse of the Machine"). After leading his audience through a lengthy calculation of gain and loss applied to the wager that God exists, Pascal supposes that the nonbeliever accepts the reasonableness of the wager but claims that his nature, the way he is made, prevents him from believing. The persuasive voice then puts forth the proposal of going through the motions of religious observance as a way of removing the obstacles to belief that exist in the nonbeliever's "passions" (of course, passions are the result of imagination, that is, of our projection of desire onto objects. It changes the way we *look at* objects). The resultant religious belief is, in the strong sense of the word, an *imaginary* belief:

> It's by doing everything as if they believed, taking holy water, having Masses said, etc. Naturally even that will make you believe and will make you dumb.
>
> [C'est en faisant tout comme s'ils croyaient, en prenant de l'eau bénite, en faisant dire des messes, etc. Naturellement même cela vous fera croire et vous abêtira.]

(L.418/S.680)

This *naturellement* is not the casual "naturally" of American English (meaning that the statement goes almost without saying, that no discussion is necessary) but rather a term that assigns the action, as well as the source, of this make-believe belief to human nature. This kind of belief is distinct from the belief originating in a supernatural force, or grace. The belief due to practice becomes a "second nature" and thus a way of looking at the world that dovetails with the whole web of preformed perceptions and corresponding emotional responses.

In Pascal's view, all our dealings with the world take place within an invented world, a kind of stage set or theme park that is so familiar to us that we really believe it is reality. Within this second nature we live out our lives in an alternation of boredom and eager, frantic desire: "The Stoics say: retire into your inner self. That is where you will find rest. And that is not true" (*Les stoïques disent: rentrez au-dedans de vous-même, c'est là où vous trouverez votre repos. Et cela n'est pas vrai*) (L.407/S.26). The problem is not outside us, argue the *Pensées*, but rather in a deep-seated restlessness that cooperates with imagination to project values onto the things of the outside world. Imagination and passion together form a program of intense centrifugal desire through which we animate and distort the world around us.

Although Pascal uses the term "passion"—usually in the plural—he abandons the etymological sense that so completely permeates Descartes's mechanistic psychology. For Descartes the term "passion" simply meant the opposite of an action. Passion is an impact that the body (the machine) transmits to the soul through the pineal gland (Descartes's desperate attempt to find a bridge from the material body to the spiritual soul). Passion is thus the opposite of an *act* of the soul when it wills something.

Pascal's major challenge to the Cartesian description is to reassign responsibility to some more inner source and to reduce the role of outward stimuli. He accompanies this reassignment with striking shift of emphasis in the enumeration and identification of the passions. As Hugh Davidson says,

"Where Descartes derives more and more passions from the half-dozen that he takes as 'primitive' or primary, Pascal tends to move in just the opposite direction; he may speak of passions in the plural, but the essential thing is to see them as coming from a single source: concupiscence."[36] Davidson's important insight is so concisely stated that it is worthwhile to dwell on both of its related points.

If Pascal writes so often of passions, in the plural, it is both because the specificity of individual passions and their consequences is much less important to him than their collective role. Where Descartes spends many pages describing the physical manifestations of such passions as indignation, sadness, and hate, Pascal is concerned neither with their manifestations nor with their common roots in the six primary emotions, but with the overriding similarity of all passions in human life.

The source of the passions is no doubt, as Davidson says, concupiscence in a broad sense, but here the most important shift from Descartes to Pascal is reassigning the active role, the causal role, to the human self. The Cartesian model of passion supposes that an external object sets off a series of physical movements that reach the "gland" and move it in such a way that the soul experiences a passion. For instance, if a dog jumped at a man the movement of animal spirits would make the man's muscles move in certain ways, and at the same time the spirits would reach the gland, make it signal the soul with a certain passion: fear, anger, admiration (in the Cartesian sense), sadness, etc. The man's soul might then attempt to counter the passion with a command, a "volition," sent through the gland to make the spirits move a different set of muscles. Descartes also supposes that the passions can be trained, just as animals can be trained.

Pascal does not deny that any of this might happen, but his dominant concern is the ultimate cause of the passions and not their immediate or proximate cause. The human being, or as he usually says, *nous*, is incomplete. This lack, and our perception of this lack, drives the passions:

> We are full of things that propel us outward.
>
> Our instinct makes us feel that we need to seek our happiness outside ourselves. Our passions push us outward, even when the objects are not present to excite us. And so the philosophers vainly say: "Retire into your selves, that is where you will find your good."
>
> [Nous sommes pleins de choses qui nous jettent au-dehors.
>
> Notre instinct nous fait sentir qu'il faut chercher notre bonheur hors de nous. Nos passions nous poussent au-dehors, quand même les objets ne s'offriraient

pas pour les exciter. Les objets du dehors nous tentent d'eux-mêmes et nous appellent, quand même nous n'y pensons pas. Et ainsi les philosophes ont beau dire: "Rentrez-vous en vous-mêmes, vous y trouverez votre bien"]

(L.143/S.176)

The discrepancy between this description of the drive as a "lack" and Pascal's own expression "We are full of things that propel us outward" is not entirely accidental, since Pascal himself associates fullness and emptiness in such statements as "How the heart of man is hollow and full of filth" (*Que le coeur de l'homme est creux et plein d'ordure*) (L.139/S.171), where the hollowness may be what *attracts* the filth, so that the *hollow* is responsible for the *full*.[37]

What Pascal seems to be attacking in this passage is the Stoic ideal of autarky, the state of a soul that is entirely free of such external stimulation and able to content itself with contemplation of thoughts that are without physical cause and entirely in control of the will or moral purpose. Such an ideal seems to be both a bad idea (since it ignores the instinct) and impossible, in Pascal's view, since thought itself generates the need for passions. In his long text on the "various commotions of men" (L.136/S.168), passion is not a perception per se but a kind of operation, an act, that affects both perception and thought. Because thought itself is too painful, the will apparently shuts down thought by diverting attention outwards toward objects chosen more or less at random. The objects then become invested with a value that comes strictly from inside the self, *coeur*. The inward source of passions explains their leveling effect, one that Pascal takes pains to uncover by placing an army commission on the same level as a rabbit, as objects of passion, that is, as instruments by which the heart prevents thought from following its otherwise inevitable path toward *ennui*.

While Pascal seems to reject the passivity of the self in the passions and also reject the opposition between passion and will that is central to Descartes's mechanistic description, he retains the idea of the machine as the mechanical repository of habit, a repository that influences thought but is not a faculty itself. In the fragment on the *automaton*, Pascal declares "we are automaton as much as mind" (661 /821). He goes on to explain that proofs only convince the mind, but custom inclines the automaton, which then carries along with it the mind without any thought. To persuade someone to believe by working through the machine is therefore in keeping with the *esprit de finesse*, since *finesse* takes a holistic view of everyday life. The mind with *finesse* does not need to turn aside, to get outside the realm of customary, practical concerns, for the world of disembodied intellection. Let us look again at the fragment on acting like a believer:

> learn at least that your inability to believe comes from your passions. Because your reason leads you toward believing and nonetheless you cannot do it, work, not to convince yourself by increasing the proofs of God, but by diminishing your passions [...] learn from those, etc. who were captives like you and who wager now all their good [....] It's by doing everything as if they believed, taking holy water, having Masses said, etc. Naturally even that will make you believe and will make you dumb.
>
> [apprenez au moins que votre impuissance à croire vient de vos passions. Puisque votre raison vous y porte et que néanmoins vous ne le pouvez, travaillez donc, non pas à vous convaincre par l'augmentation des preuves de Dieu, mais par la diminution de vos passions. [...]apprenez de ceux, etc. qui ont été liés comme vous et qui parient maintenant tout leur bien [....] c'est en faisant tout comme s'ils croyaient, en prenant de l'eau bénite, en faisant dire des messes, etc. Naturellement même cela vous fera croire et vous abêtira [...]
>
> (L.418/S.680)

As many have noted the unusual verb *abêtir* (to make someone stupid, to make someone like an animal) is an apparent reference to Descartes and to his comments about how the training of passions can be achieved in both man and beast by habit.[38] These passions are stored in physical gestures and bodily postures where they reside "without thinking about it" (L.821 /S.661). When Pascal writes of the habit of seeing kings accompanied by armed men and the cumulative effect on our passion (we fear kings, even when we do not see the armed guards), he makes explicit how the body *stores* feelings, which then influence thought:

> The habit of seeing kings accompanied by guards, drummers, officers, and all the things that bend the machine toward respect and terror causes their face, when it is sometimes alone and without these accompaniments, to impress on their subjects respect and terror.
>
> [La coutume de voir les rois accompagnés de gardes, de tambours, d'officiers et de toutes les choses qui ploient la machine vers le respect et la terreur font que leur visage, quand il est quelquefois seul et sans ces accompagnements, imprime dans leurs sujets le respect et la terreur.]
>
> (L.25/S.59)

The verb "bend" here seems to have two meanings, one physical or literal and the other figurative or spiritual: both the bending of the body as a sign of respect for the king and his force and a "bending" of the heart as expressed in the Scriptural phrase, "He disposes their hearts to believe" (*Il incline leur coeur à croire*) and "*Inclina cor meum*" (L.380/S.412).

The automatic reaction of bowing before a king, with fear and respect, is actually close to thinking with *finesse*. The geometrical thinker does things slowly, needs to go back to first principles, gradually moves through all the intermediate steps, and then arrives at a useful conclusion. The thinker with *finesse* goes right to the conclusion and sees what is obvious: the king is here, bow![39] Thinkers with *finesse* are much better off in everyday life because they use a condensed and analogic way of thinking, a shortcut based on habit. On the other hand, this association of *finesse* and habit handicaps such thinkers when it comes to scientific reasoning.[40] *Finesse* converges in this example with imagination, because Pascal describes the process by which a certain visual perception of the king is imprinted on people's minds. Even when the king does not have his usual entourage, the people still "see" (imagine involuntarily) the whole royal panoply.

This involuntary use of imagination is different from the use we have seen recommended by earlier thinkers as diverse as Quintilian and François de Sales. For them, as for Montaigne, the wise person is someone who becomes adept at imagining voluntarily rather than simply undergoing the force of social conditioning. Pascal is, of course, not simply advising his readers to submit thoughtlessly to the automatic perceptions that social institutions create and perpetuate. But he is not as optimistic as Epictetus and Montaigne. Pascal does not believe that humans can imagine things—perceive things— by force of will. On the other hand, Pascal's readers acquire two things from an understanding of the convergence of *finesse* and imagination. First, they understand their own nature and desires, and thus become open to Pascal's apologetics. And, second, they acquire a tool for programming their own imaginations through their "machine"—that is, through mental and physical repetition.

Despite Pascal's disparaging remarks about imagination in society, he still belongs to the seventeenth-century culture of positive imaginative practice. He marks a shift, it is true, toward an increasingly skeptical view of the purely inward, will-directed imagination. The view of imagination as a passive faculty that will eventually prevail at the turn of the eighteenth century already has much weight in Pascal's thought. However, he sets forth an approach for people to exploit what he sees as the pragmatic value of imagination for acquiring—slowly and through physical training—the perceptions that best suit each person's individual purposes.

FOUR

The Imagination of Loss

Marie de Rabutin-Chantal, Marquise de Sévigné, is celebrated for her letters, for her excellent networking among the Parisian élite—her friends included the wealthy and doomed superintendent of finance Foucquet, the writers La Rochefoucauld, Lafayette, and Retz and many members of the Arnauld family, those controversial religious reformers—and for having a daughter whom she loved excessively. Her letters, widely admired during her lifetime, were published with the authorization of her granddaughter after the destruction of an unknown but probably substantial portion. Today they fill three large Pléiade volumes and nourish debates about her status as one of the few women to have entered the canon of French literature before the advent of modern feminism. Her work is often mined for its wealth of information about the cultural life of her day and studied for what it reveals about the conventions of epistolary exchange and about the psychology and personal identity of a woman in the Ancien Régime.

We can assemble the pieces that Sévigné and her heirs have left us to look at a different picture, the picture of someone who deliberately marshaled the powers of her imagination in accordance with certain philosophical and theological doctrines as well as in response to a life situation that was, to a degree, determined for her. It may be, in part, pure chance that her daughter lived far from Sévigné and thus provided the occasion, or the pretext, for a thousand or so remaining letters, but Sévigné herself made it explicit in her correspondence that she did not believe in chance. She embraced, however paradoxically, an Augustinian vision of the world within which the believer's relation to God appeared in meditation on a fallen, corrupt world, from which the only being (or Being) of any significance had been withdrawn. For Sévigné, then, the practice of imagination was a way of comparing the world as she saw it around her, in her present, with the world as she remembered it, anticipated it, and desired it. For Sévigné, her daughter's painful absence was the principal, but far from the only way, in which a divine plan manifested itself to her imagination.

Marie de Sévigné was widely read and aware of the major intellectual debates of her time, including philosophy. She alludes to Descartes's *Discourse on Method*, *Meditations*, and *Treatise on the Passions of the Soul*, to Malebranche's *Christian Conversations*, and to Pascal's *Pensées*. Her daughter, Marguerite de Grignan, was a Cartesian, and Sévigné often contrasts her own more eclectic position with her daughter's position. One way of reading Sévigné's correspondence is to situate her, as observer and commentator, with respect to the contemporary publications and controversies that formed her intellectual world.

But Sévigné's own philosophical character, themes, and style are more important and interesting than her role as observer and commentator. As a moralist—in the sense of a writer who is primarily concerned with the human condition—Sévigné distinguishes her reflexions from the more strictly disciplinary interests of her daughter. Characteristically, Sévigné establishes her philosophical position by denying that she has any philosophy: "The friendship that I have for you does not bring a very deep peace to a heart as lacking in philosophy as mine...".[1] For Sévigné "philosophy" has two meanings. On one hand it means the elaboration of theoretical or abstract systems—those of Descartes, Malebranche, and Sennault, for instance—and on the other it signifies a certain stance of detachment from the world and an acceptance of Providence and the inevitability of loss, suffering, and death. Sévigné's self-characterization is negative according to *both* definitions of philosophy. She rejects the systematic abstractions dear to her daughter (e.g. "Abstract things are natural for you and unsuitable for me")[2], and she also proclaims that she is incapable of the austere or serene altitude of resignation she attributes to certain others, such as her friend Corbinelli.

Yet Sévigné has a "philosophical" position that is actually quite original if we are willing to use the term in the broad and pragmatic sense that was familiar to the people of her day. In fact, a good case can be made for placing Sévigné in that tradition of thought that can be called "existential," one inspired by the humanist revival of ethics and running from Montaigne, Pascal, and other early modern writers to Bergson and Heidegger.

Sévigné's frequent denial of her own right to be called *philosophe* is based primarily on her lack of detachment, her failure or refusal to assume the attitude of impassivity she ascribes to those around her, for instance when she writes to her daughter "you are so philosophical that there is no way to rejoice with you; you anticipate what we only hope for, and you leap ahead over the possession of things we desire so that you only see the parting."[3] However, the two senses of the term, the "high" sense of systematic inquiry and the popular sense of detached wisdom, really come together in Sévigné's case to indicate her preference for reflexion on the concrete and apparently random details of everyday life, a kind of reactive commentary rather than a hypothetical construction. Her fervently-proclaimed stance of attachment in preference to philosophical detachment is explicitly a refusal of the most popular, pervasive philosophical movement of the day, the Stoicism of Justus Lipsius, of Guillaume du Vair, of Malherbe, and even, at times, of Montaigne and Pascal. Sévigné's explicit anti-Stoicism appears early in her correspondence:

> Love my moments of tenderness, love my weaknesses; as for me, I find they suit me quite well. I like them much more than the conceptions of Seneca and Epictetus.[4]

While at times Sévigné describes her attitude as a failure or an incapacity (the passage above concerns her inability to read her daughter's letters without weeping), she often makes it clear, as she does here, that she *prefers* the feelings that come from her attachments, the highs and lows, to the tranquility of Stoicism. Her weaknesses are cultivated ones, intricate ones, that are consistently staged and proclaimed across the length of her correspondence.

Because Sévigné is very aware of what she is doing and knows the alternatives to her approach, she defines herself in terms that make sense to partisans of other positions. In fact, it seems at times as if she has picked apart the two major competing systems and used some of their concepts, usually turning them inside-out, as the basis for her own. For instance, without directly stating her own position in regard to Cartesian innate ideas, Sévigné mentions the following lively discussion at her house in Brittany, Les Rochers. She writes to her daughter:

> Monsieur de Montmoron knows your philosophy, and opposes it on every point. My son defended your *father* [Descartes]; Father Damaie was on his side, and the letter also, but these three against Montmoron were scarcely enough. He said that we can only have ideas about what comes to us through our senses. My son said that we think independently of our senses: for instance, *we think that we think.* That's a general idea of what went on.[5]

In her elliptical way, Sévigné presents this philosophical discussion between Aristotelianism, represented by Montmoron with his insistence that all ideas come through the senses, and Cartesianism, represented by Father Damaie, by Charles de Sévigné, and by Corbinelli (not physically present, but represented by his letters). Descartes, here called "your father" in deference to Marguerite de Grignan's loyalty to Descartes, presented the less scholastic position that certain ideas are independent of perception of the material world. Sévigné never gives her own position, but her frequent refusal to concur with Marguerite de Grignan's avowed Cartesianism could be seen as an indication that Sévigné inclined toward ideas that come to us through the senses. Her copious and insistent information on sensory data makes it clear that Sévigné assigns importance to the senses without taking any dogmatic stand on the possibility of innate ideas. In fact, Sévigné's position may stand between the two competing views, as if to say that we could think about innate ideas but it is much more interesting to think about the things that we see around us. Yet the things around us are only interesting to the extent that we think about them. In this regard, it is quite possible that the discussion with Montmoron concerned other aspects of Cartesianism—Sévigné says that Montmoron opposes this philosophy in every respect. Yet what she retains for her letter is the senses/mind dichotomy, a point that was of interest to her, surely, because of her constant grounding of everything in the body. She wishes, she adds, that her daughter could have participated, if only by letter, to back up Charles, because his body was getting in the way of his argument in favor of the mind's autonomy from the senses. Charles "is still bothered by his physical condition, although he is sure that he is no longer in danger," Sévigné writes, and she continues on to describe her son's physical condition, made worse by intended remedies. With a dramatic flair,

Sévigné scripts a tragi-comedy in which Charles's intellectual Cartesianism is undercut by the insistence of his body. The play of thought on the body and the body's effect on thought are repeated themes in Sévigné, and they are themes that necessarily distance Sévigné herself from the Stoics, who considered their bodies foreign objects, and from Descartes, whose gesture of grounding his metaphysics in the Cogito requires him to go through very circuitous maneuvers to recover the body later and to join it to the mind.

Sévigné is less interested in the question of whether or not our ideas come *from* the senses than she is in the ideas that we have *about* the things that we sense, have sensed, could sense, or could have sensed. In short, Sévigné's thought is centered on imagination in the then-traditional acceptation of the mental representation of physical things. Sévigné's "failure" to detach herself from things is a manifestation of her decision to experience with great intensity both things as they present themselves to her consciousness and her relationship to them, both the object as imagined and the affect. These two aspects of thought, or faculties, were closely intertwined in practical ways.

THE DOUBLE SCENE

In Sévigné's correspondence with her daughter each letter becomes a chance to invite—or compel—Mme de Grignan (always addressed, with aristocratic formality, as *vous*) to picture in vivid and sometimes grotesque physical detail the most recent events in her mother's life, and at the same time for the author to exhibit her own ability to make her daughter's distant life in Provence concretely present in her mind. These two scenes—typically one in Paris or in Brittany and the other in Provence—are part of almost every letter and show that for Sévigné imagination, as sensory thought, was a precious and highly developed faculty. At the same time Sévigné takes care to ground everything she describes, and everything she pictures for herself on the basis of her daughter's letters, in her person, in her own body.

There are times when Sévigné heaps up the detail and betrays a reportorial self-consciousness, as when she describes the funeral service for chancellor Séguier[6] or when she pens the often anthologized description of a house fire in her Marais neighborhood.[7] In these cases Sévigné seems to step back to give a panoramic view, emphasizing the visual, but in others she is wrapped in the feeling, the touch of things on her skin, as here at the baths of Vichy:

> But let's talk about the charming shower. I described it to you already. I am now at the fourth shower; I will go up to eight, my sweating is so extreme that

it soaks the mattress. I think that it is every drop of water I have drunk since I have been in the world. By the time you get to bed, truly you cannot take any more: your head and your whole body are spinning, all the humors on alert, everything is pulsating. I spend an hour without opening my mouth, and meanwhile the sweating starts, and it continues for two hours.[8]

There can be few descriptions in all of the world's collected writing that convey more intensely the experience of sweating into a bed. Sévigné's effort here is to take her reader farther into the physical sensation than she probably ever wished to go, aggressively impressing on her daughter's mind a physical closeness to her mother that is all the more striking in that it could only take place in words. That is, it is unlikely that Sévigné and Grignan would be able to experience this therapeutic transpiration simultaneously and in the same place, but the letter allows Sévigné to wrap her reader up in the covers with her.

In addition to giving immense amounts of physical detail to stimulate her reader's imagination, Sévigné describes the way she represents her correspondent in her mind, following the process that has become known to many readers as the "composition of place," to use the terms of the Jesuit guide to meditation, the *Spiritual Exercises*. Sévigné writes playfully to her daughter, pretending to be unable to finish the composition because she has lost track of her daughter's comings and goings in Provence:

I believe that you are at Lambesc, my dear, but I do not see you clearly from here; there are shadows in my imagination that [conceal] you from my sight. I had made for myself the chateau of Grignan; I could see your rooms, and I would walk on your terrace; I would go to Mass in your beautiful church. But I no longer know where I am.[9]

Sévigné often plays this game, emphasizing her activity as reader and writer trying to imagine the source of the precious letters and the place where the letters written in reply will also go. Sévigné sometimes even makes the parallel with devotional meditation explicit, referring to this imaginative recreation of the daughter's travels with a technical term from spiritual exercises, the "habitual thought": "it's what devout people call an habitual thought; it's a thought one should have for God, if one did one's duty. Nothing distracts me. I am always with you. I see that carriage that continues ahead and that will never come towards me. . . ".[10]

By fortunate coincidence—if it is a coincidence—the place being imagined was and has remained a commonplace of European and American imagination: imagining Provence was a literary activity before and after Sévigné.

However, she avoids the touristic cliché by including within her image her own sorrow at her maternal separation. The writer's own displeasure seeps into the Provence spring, contaminating its stones and flowers:

> I had someone tell me the other day what spring was like for you, and where your nightingales perch to sing. I only see stones, frightful rocks, or orange trees and olive trees that are too bitter for the birds. Give me a better idea of your countryside.[11]

Most often, the mother's imagination is fixed on the mental image of her daughter, as Sévigné conjectures she must be at a specific moment. Many times this imagining concerns travels and arrivals:

> Today I am thinking of you, my dear, as being in Lyon, having arrived in the evening, pretty tired, and perhaps needing a refreshing bloodletting; you must have been bothered by the bother of the bothersome roads.[12]

The extreme aggressiveness of Sévigné's physical thinking insists not only on intimate tactile sensations but even on penetration and bleeding, as here with the "refreshing" bloodletting! At times Sévigné does not content herself with beholding a scene from which she is absent—even though she is able to control the scene by arranging it to her taste and mood—but she actually places herself within a story told by her daughter and becomes a character in that story. For instance, after a series of letters from Marguerite de Grignan about Avignon:

> I love passionately your letters from Avignon, my dear. I read and reread them. They rejoice my imagination and the silence of the woods. It seems to me that I am there in Avignon, that I am participating in your triumph, I chat and I entertain your society [. . .], and I relish your beautiful sunshine, the charming banks of your beautiful Rhône, and the sweetness of your air . . . .[13]

Here Sévigné has made herself a guest and conversational partner within her daughter's social life. At the same time she underscores the physical quality of life of Provence, and this may seem to be a matter of little importance until we consider that many of the canonical texts of seventeenth-century French literature contain no mention of the sensations of sun and fresh air.

Although at times Sévigné's written visions seem exuberant and even hyperbolic, they do not come from a writer who is unaware that imagination is a skill and an effort. Just as she describes herself as constructing an image of Provence and then seeking to place the image of Marguerite de Grignan within that sensorial framework, so Sévigné also teaches her daughter about the management of imagination as perception. In some instances, and despite her protestations of not being a Stoic, the author sounds almost like Epictetus giving a lesson on the proper use of sense impressions, *phantasiai*:

> You must think, my dear, about restoring your mind and body; and you must make up your mind, if you no longer wish to die, in your country and among the rest of us, to see things hereafter only as they are, not to increase them and magnify them in your imagination, not to think that I am ill when I am healthy, and not to go back over a past that is past [. . .][14]

Sévigné clearly does not follow this advice, for she continually juxtaposes in her mind and her letters visions of how things *are* and how things *have been* or *could be*. Yet she knows that the faculty with which we bring forth or suppress these visions can be used for ends that we determine. In this case, Sévigné pictures her daughter picturing Sévigné and the mother has decided to intervene to modify her own maternal image in Marguerite de Grignan's mind, essential saying, "Here is how I want you to imagine me."

This double scene of the mother–daughter correspondence is an interesting, vivid, important part of Sévigné's letters, but it is not the most original and distinctive aspect of her work. The double scene of writing is part of all letter exchanges and is a well-known literary convention, enjoyed primarily in epistolary novels.[15] Sévigné's originality lies more in her particular way of allying imagination of the present and imagination of the absent so that the vivid representation of sensory experience becomes the source of consciousness of absence. In this way a lively attention to the frivolous and ephemeral is charged with weighty portent and raised as a stance toward life and toward death. To see how this is so, we need to look at the way Sévigné represents the here and now, presence and the present.

KILLING TIME: IMAGINATION AND THE HOLLOWING
OF THE PRESENT

For Sévigné there are many things that give structure to time. She has an acute sense of narrative pattern with its predictability—the trajectory from birth to death—, she remembers and anticipates events of her own life and of her friends and family members, she takes note of the seasons, and she comments on the rhythm of the epistolary exchange that itself gives to each day and hour an achingly clear character. These elements come together with surprising ease and frequency in Sévigné's text, but what she expresses with the greatest intensity is the sense of the passage of the present, the ephemeral character of the moment within which she writes. She tells her daughter, for instance, "I take a kind of pleasure, in our eternal exile, to receive your letters on the ninth day, at ten o'clock in the morning. They get to Paris on Saturday; they are tossed into the mail for Brittany, and I have them on Monday morning."[16] In this way, time is visualized as the progress of a packet of letters passing through the space that separates Sévigné from Madame de Grignan. The mother can picture the absent letters elsewhere at *this* moment and then picture them arriving in Sévigné's space at *another*, absent moment. In this manner she is perpetually thinking about what is absent either in space or in time.

Imagination, we have seen, is a way of thinking that always implies a point of perception—a point of view, in the broadest sense—because it is the mental representation of something *as we would sense it*. So that the imagined flower is necessarily conceived as perceived from above, or from close up, or as it would feel if touched. As a consequence, imagination takes generalities and translates them into experiences. Time is a generality, but yesterday is an experience—it is time with a point of view. Madame de Grignan's absence and the letter exchange give Sévigné both the coordinates and the units of measure within which she experiences both time and space. The departure from Paris for Brittany appears to Sévigné in terms of the frequency with which she pictures herself receiving her daughter's letters: "I am leaving Paris for some time, with the sorrow of not getting your letters so regularly, nor those of my son . . . "[17] The quality of time itself is intertwined tightly with the arrival or the nonarrival of her daughter's letters. She pictures to herself the desired missive and then its absence once again hollows out the present in Sévigné's typical way of perceiving the physical world as a lack. "I hoped, my dear, to find some letters from you here," she writes from Époisses, "I had already been disappointed at Auxerre. Eight or nine days without hearing a word from you seems very long to me; I am a bit sad."[18]

Sévigné's extreme consciousness of passing time, and her wish to convey this feeling to her reader, prompts her to write letters that are organized with a series of time markers that build in crescendo toward the desired letter from Madame de Grignan and then death. This may seem hyperbole to modern readers; it may appear as emotional blackmail to coerce her daughter to write more often. Yet the almost frenzied progression from banal everyday experience toward the anticipation of death is an undeniable pattern in Sévigné's writing. A letter of mid-July 1675 is an example of the writer's meticulously organized representation of time.[19] Sévigné begins by saying that she is writing from the Paris house of Arnauld de Pomponne. This is the letter's *now*. This time and place of writing will be authenticated, at the end of the letter by a note in the handwriting of Mme de Vins, Pomponne's sister-in-law: "Guess where I'm writing from, my dear; it's at Monsieur de Pomponne's. You can see from the little note that Madame de Vins will put here for you." From this time and place, that the reader is invited to imagine, Sévigné makes a flashback to the procession of Sainte Geneviève that she has just seen earlier in the day and that she describes in exquisite visual detail. Then she gives some general news, in the present, about ongoing military actions, before another brief item from an earlier day ("The other day. . . ."). At that point Sévigné shifts into her forward-looking mode that builds toward death: "We are waiting for Madame de Toscan to arrive any moment now. . . " and then "I think that we will sell your desk." Finally, the intense climactic paragraph:

I expect letters from you tomorrow morning, my dear; it is my only joy and my consolation in your absence. This absence is a strange thing, my dear. You have said what you can about it, but since it is true that time is carrying us along and bringing us death, I find that it is right to weep and not to laugh as we would do if our poor life were not passing by; I meditate often on this point. But I must touch on this as lightly as I can, and call Madame de Vins so that she can say something to you.

Having reached forward to death, a death that Sévigné can feel with each passing moment—measured as the time of waiting for the desired letters—Sévigné's letter closes the circle by leaving space on the page for Madame de Vins to place her comment that certifies the time and place in which Sévigné is writing.

Here is another typical sequence, starting in apparently random and frivolous chitchat and then heading toward a comment on death: "As for my life," she writes to her cousin Bussy, "you know how it is. I spend it with five or six friends whose company I enjoy and in doing all the tasks that have to be done, and this is no small matter. But what bothers me is that while we do nothing the days pass, and our poor life is made up of these days, and we grow older, and we die."[20]

Routinely, for Sévigné, separation leads to consciousness of time passing, measured from the present moment to some moment in the past when she was with her daughter or from the present toward an expected visit. These absent moments are vividly present to Sévigné's mind and hollow out the present, which is simply a moment used either to exacerbate the sense of loss by vivid recreations of what is absent or to harvest impressions and anecdotes that can be used to devise imaginative experiences through which she can occupy her daughter's mind with things as if they were physically shared.

Sévigné's sense of her self—and the concept of the *moi* is central and explicit in the letters—is constructed of time and its passage. Sometimes the link of time and identity becomes explicit:

> I find that the days go so quickly, and the months and the years, and for me, my dear cousin, I can no longer hold them back. Time flies and carries me away in spite of myself. In vain do I try to hold on, time pulls me away, and that thought frightens me greatly. The little Grignan boy spent the winter with us. He had a fever this spring. He only went back to his regiment two weeks ago [. . . .] Only Providence knows when we will leave for Paris. No one could carry on more breathlessly than I have been doing all about *myself,* (*de tout mon moi*), as Monsieur Nicole says, but you asked for it.[21]

In a typical fashion the letter seems to jump from one subject to another, but—also typically—the thematic thread is available on inspection. Time defines the self, the *moi*, and makes Sévigné's life what it is. She is not in control of time, but rather the experience of time is the experience of involuntary passivity. Time brings the awareness that one is not an agent, or subject, but an object that is carried away, so that the most visible, directly perceptible loss—that of things and people whose appearance and disappearance give us tangible evidence of the passage of time—is amplified by the intimate feeling of a loss of one's own power. Sévigné weaves into her comment the example of her grandson, Louis-Provence de Grignan, whose own mortality is a matter of concern, whose presence, illness, and departure structure her recent time, and whose departure embodies this theme so close to her heart. She brings to this flux the idea of an overarching, but unfathomable, intent that is Providence, and then grounds these loosely assembled elements by saying that all of this is about her *moi*, following Nicole's inspiration.

Sévigné's self, her *moi*, is always split, for two reasons. First, because everything that appears in the letters as part of what is, for her, here and now, is carefully selected to be recreated mentally by her reader. This is one reason why the world, in Sévigné's writing, is so much more detailed and vivid than much of early-modern writing. It is an interesting paradox that this attention to the concrete and the sensorial (the French *sensible*) comes at the price of a necessary detachment or double-thinking in that Sévigné is never, as far as we can tell, without a consciousness of the need to *represent* what she experiences, to formulate it in her mind in order to convey the idea to another person. An especially warm day, a showy and elaborate trial, a rousing sermon, a cold and wet winter garden, an agonizing death-bed scene—all these things are perceived by Sévigné as ready to share, as being good things to describe in writing.

There is, however, a second reason for a split in Sévigné's perception of the material world around her: her daughter is not in the here and now. As a result, not only does everything appear as material to be described so that her daughter can share imaginatively in what is present to Sévigné, but it also means that things become markers or measuring devices for absence. Sévigné sees spaces with an absence in them. She writes of "the sadness of not seeing you in that bedroom where I have seen you so many times."[22] This way of looking at places works both backward, toward the past, and forward, toward anticipated visits. Sévigné writes often about preparations for her daughter's visits, and consequently shows how she looks at her home in Paris as always partly empty, waiting for the beloved occupant: "I have had your suite fixed up, and I don't want you to find anything lacking"[23] and "There is no place in this house that does not wound me in the heart. Your whole bedroom kills me; I had a folding screen set up in the middle, to block a bit the view from a window out onto that staircase from which I saw you climb up into d'Hacqueville's carriage . . .."[24]

Things and spaces are hollowed out by Mme de Grignan's absence. They are not merely symbols or metonymies of the daughter but are transformed in the mother's perception by the doubled imaginative process that first makes Sévigné juxtapose, mentally, a vision of the same place at two different moments and, second, makes her want to formulate this perception to impress it on her daughter's imagination. In some cases, Sévigné makes this hollowing out of places fully explicit:

> Every morning I am in that garden that you know. I look everywhere for you, and all the spots where I saw you make me suffer. You can clearly see, my daughter, that the slightest things that have some connection with you have made an impression on my poor brain.[25]

These passages are numerous in the letters:

> I'm going away to a place where I will think of you ceaselessly, and perhaps too tenderly. It would be difficult for me to see that place, that garden, that pathway, that little bridge, that avenue, that meadow, that mill, that little vista, that forest, without thinking of my very dear child.[26]

Here the list of things seen goes from the general idea of place, to the garden, and then to more specific components of the garden, including an allusion to a spot that may have been recognizable to the daughter but not to other readers ("that little vista"). And while Sévigné (and later, her daughter, in reading the letter) pictures each of these sights, she is doubling that mental vision with an image of her daughter. No matter how concrete the present is, for Sévigné, it is somehow distanced, overlaid, by a distracted thought of the same place at another time or of Madame de Grignan at the present time someplace else.

DEATH AND MEDITATION

"Monsieur Foucquet is dead."[27] "Monsieur de Rambures is dead."[28] "Poor Sanguin is dead."[29] "Madame de Raray is dead."[30] "The good Païen is dead."[31] "Cardinal de Retz died yesterday."[32] "Monsieur de La Rochefoucauld died last night."[33]. And several days later, "Monsieur de La Rochefoucauld is still dead."[34] Sévigné filled her letters with announcements of death. Sometimes with sober understatement, "Monsieur de Toulongeon died in Béarn;"[35] sometimes with macabre details, "Madame de Monaco, at the moment of death, had no feature nor any trace that could make one remember her. She was a skull spoiled by a dried black skin;"[36] sometimes with a caustic final gibe, "Old Madame de Sanguin died, like a heroine, taking her cadaver on a walk through her bedroom, looking at herself in the mirror to see death in its natural state."[37] Her correspondents bring her news of death in narratives that earn her detailed praise. When her daughter writes of the death of Balthazar de Lauzier in Nîmes, Sévigné writes an admiring review of the account:

> Your narrative has all the power of rhetoric; it builds suspense, it increases curiosity, and it leads to an incident that is so sad and surprising that I was all stirred up and made a little cry that frightened my son. He came to see why I had cried out; I read him that passage. He was moved, as I was, by the feelings that your story inspires, and he cried out as I had, and maybe even a little more, because he knew that good and genuine man, and we both marveled at how uncertain is the hour and the form of our death.[38]

There are abundant deaths in these letters, but is there anything special about that? There are, after all, many reports of battles, medical treatments, recently published books, impressive and moving sermons, furniture repair, debt collection, ministerial intrigue, and most of all, social visits. Do reports of death have some special significance for Sévigné?

For Sévigné it seems as if the most perfect letter is a letter that reports a death. As a correspondent, what Sévigné needs is for someone to die: "I am tired to death of the insipidness of the news. We really need some event, as you say," she writes to her daughter, "and who cares at whose expense; since this can no longer be the death of Monsieur de Turenne, *vogue la galère!*"[39] Turenne's death is done; it is all used up after a half dozen recountings. What Sévigné regrets here is not Turenne but Turenne's death; she does not want to have Turenne back, but the *event* of his decease. This regret takes the form of a triangle: the needed event, Turenne's death, and Sévigné's mortal lassitude. Turenne's death is a subset of "event"; it is an example of a satisfactory event. Sévigné is "dying" of boredom. She needs someone else to die so that she can be reanimated.

If death did not exist, we would have to invent it—such is the underlying drive to consume a life to make a letter. Five years before Sévigné's comment about the need for an event, she received a letter from her cousin Bussy founding letter writing on a similar homicidal principle:

> I have to acknowledge to you my debt: I was so bothered about not writing to you any more, when Monsieur Frémyot happened to die, that, if he had delayed, I would have sent my condolences on the death of someone still living, or I would have rejoiced with you about some imaginary inheritance. But luck killed off that judge at just the right moment. Even though he didn't leave me any legacy, as he did you, I am grateful to him at least for giving me a pretext to start writing to you again.[40]

Now Turenne's death, that was an event! Sévigné, in four letters of July and August 1675, tells the violent end of the general, cut in two by a cannonball fired by the Imperial forces at Sasbach. Pierre Dostie has studied with care Sévigné's four successive accounts that go into increasing detail, almost like an old Polaroid print or the bit-by-bit appearance of an internet image with a slow connection. These accounts have been compared to a cinematic rendering, beginning with an establishing shot (with a panorama of the French combatants) and then the forward tracking or zoom that picks Turenne out of the crowd: "Can one doubt Providence or doubt that the cannon that chose Monsieur de Turenne from a distance, from among ten men who were around him, was not loaded for him since all eternity?"[41] However, the traditional emphasis on Sévigné's writerly skill may encourage us to forget the function of death in her letters, the importance of death as a precious material (the old usage of the term *matière* for topics as in *matière de Rome* takes on a new figurative force) that the writer gives as a gift to the reader.

The first letter about Turenne's death includes another death as well. Since Sévigné composed her letters over hours or even days, she found new events during this leisurely process. The linear sequence of paragraphs reflects composition time rather than priority of value or the chronological order of the events themselves. So before Turenne's death there is the story of the poor braid maker (*un pauvre passementier*) who is set upon by some tax collectors or some people posing as tax collectors, who seize his bed and his bowl. The braid maker grabbed three of his four children and slit their throats. As he was led off to prison he claimed that all he regretted was not having killed his wife and his fourth child as well. For Sévigné the extreme violence of the story adds to its value. The braid maker's dead children bring her own child closer since both the truth and the rarity of the event have the power to render it present in imagination for her daughter: "Just think about it! It is as true as if you had seen it, and since the siege of Jerusalem no one has ever seen such fury."[42]

These deaths may appear to be random killings reported as mere filler or *faits divers*, but later in this same letter Sévigné gives a clue to the larger issues raised by the event of death. With a remarkable change of tone, she follows the braid maker's rampage with a comment about the social scene at court mentioned in a previous letter from her daughter:

> You mention the pleasures of Versailles, and in the time that people were going to Fontainebleau to bask in delights, isn't Monsieur de Turenne killed? isn't there general consternation? doesn't Monsieur the Prince speed through Germany? isn't France devastated? Instead of seeing an end to the battles and having your brother back, we don't know what is going on. That is the world in its triumph, and plenty of surprising events, since you like them.[43]

Death erupts as a "surprising event" that will please Sévigné's reader and as such not only provides narrative material with which to maintain connection with the reader–daughter but also penetrates the surface of life and destroys its order. Death thereby vivifies the writer and reader by reminding them of the more important order underlying appearances. The list of surprising events occurs between two allusions to a higher order within the stream of mortal events. The braid maker's murders are situated by reference to the destruction of the temple in Jerusalem and to the eternal order that picked that specific moment for Turenne's death and loaded the canon since the beginning of time. Death corrects the vision of a frivolous, disconnected world by realigning it on the hidden pattern of providence.

Attached to the letter to her daughter is a letter to Sévigné's son-in-law Grignan entirely about Turenne's death and its consequences. Here too the general's death is presented as foretold: "There is an almanac that I saw; it's from Milan. For the month of July, there's 'Sudden death of a great man.' And for the month of August, 'Ah! What do I see?'"[44]

One of the way death offers material for imagination is through the repercussions, the many possibilities that a death opens up in a closed society like that of the seventeenth century. In the case of a giant like Turenne, his death requires the reconfiguration of all the upper echelon of the military command. Officers have to move around, some of them risking death just by traveling, like Condé—"Because his health is poor, and because the road is long, there is everything to fear in the meanwhile."[45] At the same time, to replace one general, the king considers whether to name eight others.

Turenne's death is exemplary in thus releasing a flood of revisions and subevents, but all deaths unblock the circulation of goods and names and thus cause everyone to become in some way different. For the nobility of Sévigné's time, and, in fact, for most of the middle class, only death and the king's command can allow the redistribution of titles and material goods among the aristocracy. So for many years in advance, people would imagine life after a certain person's death, and the actual event would set these imagined futures into circulation in conversation and letters. After all, even people's names would change when someone else died. Sévigné's cousin Bussy in a letter of February 1687 gives two examples of the movement of names and goods following a death. First comes the name change of the son of Sévigné's cousin Coligny:

> The little Andelot is growing up and is still very cute. We have had him take the name Coligny at the death of the count of Coligny-Saligny. He has the marquisate, and it doesn't seem to me that that abbé, who has just taken the sword under the name of count of Coligny, blocks your grand-nephew.[46]

But Bussy also engages in a game of predicting the redistribution of royal appointments after the death of an officer, a variant on Sévigné's report of the consequences of Turenne's death:

> As soon as I learned of the death of Maréchal de Créquy, I decided that the administration of Lorraine would go to the Maréchal de Lorges. I don't know if I guessed right....[47]

Death as pleasure—the death of other people, of course—almost always involves either surprise or suspense. In the case of Créquy's death as Bussy describes it, we see the suspense of guessing what will happen in the courtly competition set off by death. Here is one passage in which Sévigné shares with her daughter some imagined consequences of an opportune death:

> Poor Sanguin is dead. He was a good and genuine man. His family is devastated. There's an opening for a *cordon bleu*. If that appointment doesn't go to his son, I would that God would give it to Monsieur de Grignan! He would be just right to maintain the distinction that that order had always had. It is the most rewarding position possible. You can't stop me from dreaming about all of that in my *solitaire*. It looks out on one side toward a plaza at the end of the promenade [. . .] It is there that I give you this new appointment. Seriously, think about it . . . .[48]

After the most concise, matter-of-fact acknowledgment of the Sanguin family—her neighbors—in mourning, Sévigné launches into a series of visions of the future. First, she has the disagreeable thought of Sanguin junior wearing the ribbon that represented membership in the king's Ordre du Saint-Esprit and having the office that belonged to the older Sanguin, that of first *Maître d'hôtel du Roi*, but quickly that first idea is replaced by the vision of her son-in-law Grignan much more worthily filling that distinguished position. Sévigné then describes the place in her garden where she plans to fantasize about this possible future, and thus invites her daughter, first, to imagine her mother imagining M. de Grignan's new dignity and, then, to join in Sévigné's imaginings.

In the representations of death that Sévigné collects and transmits in her letters and that she appreciates in the correspondence she receives, one of the highest values is *surprise*. In the poetics of tragedy, during Sévigné's lifetime, death is primarily the object of suspense; in other words, we must have some idea of what is coming and be waiting to see what form this expected event will take: the hero must be in evident danger of death and then succumb or escape. The narrative must unfold with a beginning, a middle, and an end. In Sévigné's poetics of the letter, on the contrary, the very best deaths are not the expected ones but the surprising ones, and the narrative generally intensifies the unpredictability of the outcome. She writes to her daughter, "You always tell me about deaths that surprise me. That great Simiane, he certainly suffered from kidney stones; and then he is cured! That all goes very fast."[49] This summary of her daughter's narratives concerning Simiane enfolds the suspense concerning the character's kidney stones, suspense that turns out to be a red herring that only intensifies amazement at his sudden death. Suspense is thus rejected in favor of surprise.

Sévigné bestows special praise on Grignan's already-mentioned account of the death of Balthazar de Lauzier, with its narrative with "all the power of rhetoric" and its mounting suspense.[50] We do not have Grignan's letter but we have a testimony of its effect on the reader. Sévigné and her son are *struck* by this death and by all it signifies for them (*nous admirâmes ce que c'est que l'incertitude de l'heure et de la manière de notre mort*). This death is an occasion of *admiration*, apparently in the Cartesian sense of the term. For Descartes admiration is the primary passion and it arises

> When the first encounter with some object surprises us, and when we judge that it is new or very different from what we knew previously, or from what we supposed that it should be.[51]

What Sévigné admires is not the death nor even the account of the death but the uncertainty of death's *timing*. Moreover, Sévigné shifts from Lauzier's death to a term that is both more personal and more general, "the hour... of *our* death." Descartes's account of admiration associates this primary passion with newness. And even though Sévigné and her correspondents trade announcements of death with a predictable regularity, there does seem to be something both new and renewing about death. It is the one entirely predictable event and the most surprising event because it is the intersection between time and eternity. In telling of her own experience of reading about Lauzier's death, Sévigné insists on the involuntary and physical reaction that the letter produced. A sign of admiration in the Cartesian sense, the little cry is, like death itself, surprising. The usefulness of admiration, for Descartes, is that it impresses new things in memory:

> it causes us to learn and to retain in our memory things that we did not know previously. For we only 'admire' what appears to us rare and extraordinary: and nothing can appear to us as such unless we were previously unaware of it, and also insofar as it is different from the things that we knew; for it is this difference that causes us to call something extraordinary.[52]

Now, in one sense Lauzier's death *is* entirely new and extraordinary. Thanks to the footnotes of Duchêne's Pléiade edition of Sévigné's letters, we know that Lauzier died of apoplexy as he was walking across the Saint-Esprit bridge in Nîmes to greet the Duc de Noailles.[53] But what Sévigné's little cry of surprise seems to impress on her memory is not Lauzier's death but her own, or more generally, as she puts it, *our* death. In a certain way, death and surprise are different only in quantity. For Descartes an excess of admiration takes the form of *étonnement*, which, in modern French is a synonym of surprise but in the French of Sévigné's and Descartes's time denotes a kind of paralyzing stupefaction. Death is the form of surprise that one never recovers from since one is *étonné*—i.e. thunderstruck. In imagining her daughter's reaction to the news of Turenne's death, Sévigné writes, "I still think, my daughter, about the *étonnement* and the sorrow that you will have in regard to the death of Monsieur de Turenne."[54]

Surprising deaths and the surprise that is death itself have a particular importance for Sévigné because of her religious preoccupations. This is the other side of the amusement and admiration of death. Death is the most exciting news and the most potent stimulant for letter-writers and preserves their readers from the *fadeur*, the insipid quality, of routine; death leads to exceptional beauty of language.[55] But the news of death is also a reminder of the articulation of the frivolous order of worldliness with the predetermined but unknown moment of death, and this articulation always leads to the reminder of something unknowable and hidden in death. For Roman Catholics seeking to die in the state of grace, deaths like those of Turenne and Lauzier have a particular value as examples of unforeseen and spectacular mortality. Sévigné relates as valuable and interesting news speculation about the state of Turenne's soul on that fatal day, but all agree that he is saved: "it never occurred to any devout person that he might not be in a state of grace. It is not possible to understand that evil and sin could be in his heart."[56] Turenne's nephew, the Cardinal de Bouillon, certifies that his uncle reviewed all his sins with him at Pentecost, and "he was a thousand leagues away from any mortal sin."[57] As the threshold between time and nontime, that is, eternity, death intensifies attention to time, producing an almost slow motion or microscopic accounting of the last few days and hours, particularly within the sacramental perspective that Sévigné adopts. For this reason the timing of the death in relation to Turenne's last confession and communion is crucial. Hence the details, "He wished to make his confession in the evening, and withdrawing himself, he had given orders for the evening, and was to take communion the following day, which was Sunday."[58] At one point Turenne's death seems to become almost an apologue for the importance of time and timing in the Catholic view of salvation. Shortly before leaving for the front, Turenne had expressed his intention to put some *time* between his military activity and the moment of his death.

Bussy, commenting on Sévigné's image of the canon loaded, from all eternity, for Turenne, pushes the concept to a more technical theological level:

> Nothing has been better said, or more pleasingly, or more precisely than what you say about Providence with regard to the death of Monsieur de Turenne, about seeing the canon loaded for all eternity. It is true that this was an act of heaven. God, who normally lets secondary causes do their work, sometimes wishes to act directly himself. He did so, it seems to me, on this occasion; it is He who aimed that artillery.[59]

The contrast between the surface world of second causes in which the divine acts indirectly within the apparent randomness of everyday life and the concealed hand of providence is always, in some sense, an issue in death. Taken strictly and literally, Bussy's explication turns Sévigné's account of Turenne's death into the report of a miracle. And Sévigné clearly wants to see such a direct divine intervention into human affairs in this death, as when she tells of the role of Saint-Hilaire in Turenne's last moments. This passage begins by alluding to Roman history ("it seems to me that I am reading Roman history"), and very likely is based on passages in Livy when a god or goddess is perceived incarnate on the battlefield.

> Saint-Hilaire, lieutenant general of artillery, stopped Monsieur de Turenne, who had been galloping, to show him a battery; it is as if he had said to him, 'Monsieur, pause a moment, for it is here that you are to be killed.' The cannon shot hit then, and carried away Saint-Hilaire's arm, who was pointing to the battery, and killed Monsieur de Turenne.[60]

Saint-Hilaire, an instrument of divine intervention or of quasi-intervention, since Sévigné hedges this assertion, takes on a particular significance when we consider Sévigné's insistence on sudden death as a source of *admiration* for our *own* death, a reminder of something of which we were previously ignorant, of something new and extraordinary. Saint-Hilaire is a kind of guide to death, who stops Turenne in his forward career—as both death and *étonnement* stop anyone—and points to the gun that is about to kill Turenne. The pointing arm directs Turenne *away* from himself, underscoring the necessary inattention of Turenne to his own death—we can see the death of others but not our own—and within seconds the pointing arm is itself gone and Saint-Hilaire is directing all his attention and that of his son to the dead Turenne: " 'Be quiet, my child,' he said to him; behold (showing him Monsieur de Turenne struck dead), what we must mourn eternally . . . '."[61] It is as if the invisible hand of providence had been, so to speak, disincarnated in the lieutenant general's missing hand.[62]

Beyond Nicole, Sévigné's conception of the narrative of death rejoins Augustine's account of his relation to dramatic representations of the death of Dido. In the *Confessions* Augustine writes about the powerful effect that Dido's death, in a theatrical spectacle, had on him when he was a young man and regrets that he should be so indifferent to the thought of his own death. Sévigné's attention to the death of others, her cry of surprise and her need of the *event* that is death are manifestations of her indirect autobiographical—or autothanatographical—imagination. Death is everywhere and comes as a surprise. We should keep it constantly before our eyes, following Montaigne's advice, "At every moment let us picture it in our imagination in all its aspects."[63]

FOUNDATIONS: AUGUSTINE AND NICOLE

We cannot know Sévigné's "inner life" except through her letters, and from them we can only see the person she has decided to perform for her reader—as Michèle Longino has so insightfully demonstrated in her study of Sévigné, *Performing Motherhood*.[64] The Sévigné whose spiritual and meditative life we detect in the letters does not seem to construct an inner "cabinet" in which she dwells in separation from the conversations and activities of the world around her. Despite having a grandmother who founded the Order of the Visitation for which, initially, François de Sales prepared his two books on the devout life, Sévigné seems to unite what she calls "meditation" with observation of the physical world around her, so that her imagination is replenished constantly by the ordinary incidents of the world. Sévigné does actively imagine this world, by fixing her attention on certain things and not on others, but this is neither the methodical Ignatian type of exercise nor the Salesian everyday retreat inward. Did Sévigné simply drift into her form of meditation without any guidance or did some author or friend influence her way of seeing and using the world?

We have already noted that Sévigné's emphasis on the hollowness of life in the absence of her daughter, her cultivation of spiritual and emotional restlessness, is reminiscent of the Augustine of the *Confessions*.[65] Like Augustine, Sévigné observes her own psychology in relation to the world, but she gives much, much more attention to physical detail, anecdote, contemporary history, and conversation than does the author of the *Confessions*. In her extreme attention to the appearance of the world around her and her pattern of connecting that appearance to reflexions on the passage of time, the order of Providence, and death, Sévigné is no doubt influenced by another major textual source, Pierre Nicole's *Moral Essays* (*Essais de morale*, 1669–74). Nicole was himself an Augustinian (or Jansenist), a close associate of the religious movement centered at the convent of Port-Royal des Champs. Sévigné was exceptionally enthusiastic about Nicole's *Moral Essays*, alludes to them often, and commends them to her daughter's attention.[66]

Nicole, even more than Pascal and other Jansenists, stressed God's invisibility, even to believers. Our knowledge of God comes in two ways, taught Nicole, through the Scriptures and through all events that happen in the world, except for sin.[67] The Scriptures teach the laws, in general terms, that the believer should follow, but they do not give individual believers special warnings about what is to come.[68] For knowledge of God's will in regard to the actual world of human events, we need to observe what happens. If God's will is considered "as the cause of all that happens in the world, except sin," then we should view what happens around us "discovering through faith these great truths: that God does everything; that he orders everything; that he arranges everything; and that nothing escapes his providence; that through everything that happens in the world, he exercises either his mercy or his justice."[69] This radical identification of the order of history with God's will, not only in great events, but in *every* thing that happens (other than sin), obliges the Christian—in Nicole's view—to be observant and to ponder all things. As Nicole himself writes, this doctrine completely changes the believer's view of the world: "We will no longer see innocent people oppressed, we will only see guilty people punished. The earth will no longer be for us a place of tumult and disorder; it will be a place of equity and justice."[70] Although God's will appears in all events, and while we thus are responsible to be attentive to them, we will not understand his will, for our view is too limited, and we cannot tell how any event or pattern of events corresponds to God's plans. For instance, we cannot tell if he is punishing someone or if he is showing his mercy.[71]

Sévigné was very impressed by "Of submission to the will of God." She wrote:

> we must make acts of resignation to the order and the will of God. Isn't Monsieur Nicole admirable, yet again, on that subject? I am enchanted by it; I have not seen anything like it [. . .] But even though in carrying out [acts of resignation] we are weak, it is still a pleasure to meditate with him, and to reflect on the vanity of the joy and the sadness that we get from such illusions.[72]

The "weakness" that Sévigné concedes in carrying out Nicole's program of complete indifference actually duplicates her refusal of Stoic indifference as she found it in Seneca and Epictetus, and Nicole's identification of the world order with God's will strongly resembles the Christianized Stoicism so current at the turn of the century. Sévigné separates Nicole's doctrine into two elements, meditation and act. Apparently she has no difficulty accepting the belief in an underlying providential order, since it is a pleasure to meditate with Nicole on what happens in the everyday world and to reflect on the emptiness of our emotions. Yet she claims here as elsewhere that she is not capable of emotional indifference—and, indeed, she shows little evidence of making any attempt to acquire or perform that indifference. Instead, the greater the discrepancy between the intensity of feeling and the vanity of the cause (as perceived within the providential doctrine), the more Sévigné seems to enjoy meditating on an event or object and sharing it in the most vivid terms.

Indeed, Sévigné finds in Nicole's doctrine itself the explanation of her lack of indifference, for God *wants* her to suffer. This interpretation seems, in fact, to follow logically from Nicole's assertions that God causes everything except sin (which he simply "permits"). Basing herself on Nicole's text, she writes to her daughter:

> [God] causes our will to act according to the goals that he has determined. For instance [...] he wills that I love you with extraordinary predilection and tenderness. It pleases Him to mingle your position in life, which we desired, with cruel absences to mortify us, to make us suffer; we use those absences as he has decided. We must regard all the ills in the world, all the heresies, all the ignorance, all murders, as his sovereign will from which he is able to draw the good that he wishes [...].[73]

Both events and people's emotional reactions to those events are all covered by the doctrine of providence and are, in a sense, made worthy of our attention, since they are the result of God's intention. As Nicole wrote, the belief in providence should make us see everything differently. The scale of values that a nonbeliever—or a believer who has not learned to see properly— brings to everyday life needs to be discarded, since it cannot be affirmed that there are *good* and *bad* events or even large or small events. Sévigné's feelings for her daughter are not the result—not simply the result—of some lack of philosophical discipline on her part, but rather the result of God's will that she suffer.

In another of Nicole's moral essays, "Of self-knowledge," Sévigné found more justification for an outward-turning, observation-based meditation, as opposed to one based on introspection.[74] According to Nicole, mankind has a basic awareness of its fallen, imperfect nature, but the sharp pain of this knowledge leads people to seek reassuring representations of the self in the surrounding world. These representations or "portraits," in Nicole's terms, fill each individual's imagination with a distorted idea of the self that comes from the flattering messages obtained during social interaction. The more "important" people are in the social hierarchy, the more positive the depiction of themselves that they carry in their imagination: "A thousand things excite in them the idea of their self [*moi*], and place it before their eyes with some pleasing quality such as 'great' or 'powerful' or 'respected.'"[75] Solitude, a state traditionally urged for the acquisition of wisdom through introspection, is unbearably painful, according to the *Moral Essays*, because the soothing flow of reassuring and flattering comments from other people ceases, leaving it up to the solitary individual to provide positive self-representation or to risk the emergence of the always-gnawing sense of imperfection. The *moi* described by Nicole incorporates into its self-representation all the material circumstances ("external objects") that provide a measure of success.[76] Although Nicole does not strictly speaking deny that introspection might lead to an accurate view of the self, he considers solitary introspection and the direct discovery of the self to be so extremely painful that it is, in practice, impossible.

Nicole therefore recommends searching in the *outside* world the self-knowledge that is so difficult to acquire. The key to this breakthrough lies in the realization of our dependency on the collective social imagination for our own self-knowledge: "we must consider that [man] looks at himself as much according to a certain being that he possesses in the imagination of other people as according to what he is in reality, and that he forms his own portrait on the basis of what he knows about himself by himself but also on the basis of portraits of himself that he discovers in the minds of others."[77] So all people are making "portraits" in their minds of all the people they know, but they generally will not reveal those portraits, especially to people in positions of social power. A reasonably powerful person—the kind of person who would probably read Nicole's *Moral Essays*—cannot count on hearing a frank description of himself or herself, as could someone at the very bottle of the social ladder. What, then, is to be done? Nicole proposes two strategies, both of which require great attention to the social world around us.

For most people, according to "Of self-knowledge," few things are easier than noticing the flaws in the conduct and characters of other people. We see what they do in what we might call (the term is not Nicole's) an "objective" way, because we omit from the image that we have of their appearance and their actions any explanatory and self-justifying explanation of intention. So we imagine other people very differently from the way we imagine ourselves. Nicole's first strategy for self-knowledge is to take advantage of our obsessive critical observation of others to see ourselves as we really are, without the filter of subjective excuse and self-protection. We simply need to remember that we are just like those other people whom we ridicule. We rescript our stories about them by substituting "I" for "he" or "she" and thus obtain a useful extrapolated account of ourselves. It is this strategy that provides a justification for Sévigné's extensive descriptions of the people around her.[78]

The apparently frivolous weaving together of news of fashion, food, sickness, battles, books, and jokes in the letters, along with comments on death, anguish, solitude, regret, and love, can be understood as an application of the leveling descriptive strategy that Nicole and Pascal recommend. For these Augustinian thinkers, social hierarchies—and sometimes even philosophical ones—are crucial parts of mankind's defensive vanity, the system of sin-based concupiscence by which people avoid the horror of their fallen state. "Of self-knowledge" is a good example of the leveling approach to social description since it teaches that the people with the least access to an accurate image of themselves are the rich and powerful, whose deeds and problems make up the substance of traditional history. Pascal, in the *Pensées*, turns his reader's attention toward the frivolous social world of card games, clothing, carriages, boredom, the pursuit of prestige, passing time, the sound of chalk scraping a slate, and so forth, very much the world as described—in vastly more detail—by Sévigné. Moreover, in Sévigné's writing, unlike Pascal's, the frivolous seems to be the place where God is manifested in his relationship to us. Sévigné—even though she is an accomplished rhetorician in the broad sense of the term—does not pursue a demonstration or an apology as does Pascal. Without indulging in the traditional, usually masculine, classification of women's writing as more "natural" and presumably, therefore, more "sincere" than writing by men, we can follow Sévigné in her thematics of destitution: God acts by subtraction, or, rather, God's perpetual action *appears* to us at the moment when someone or something *disappears*, and thus the scene of death and the announcement of a death is the signal to reflect and to meditate. Yet the death of persons, and especially of the great—Séguier,

Turenne, Retz—is associated with something dramatic and exciting and even sometimes an air of grandeur and majesty that may disguise the simple brutality of the event—witness the drama of Turenne's death on the battlefield or the magnificent decor of Séguier's funeral. Whereas the small reminders of the ineluctable decline of life and of all the things to which human beings attach themselves appear when we are least protected by social convention.[79] Because the frivolous, small, fragile, impermanent, things are specifically the place where human "vanity" appears—witness the genre paintings, bearing that name (the work of Lubin Baugin has, for instance, movingly figured in Alain Corneau's film, *Tous les matins du monde*)—they are the instruments for God to remind us of our emptiness, our lack of *ousia* or substance, and our state of change, becoming, and contingency. For an Augustinian Christian, the awareness of God takes the primary form of self-awareness as a lack, as the experience of not having.

François de Sales taught Philothée the way to use her imagination in order to turn her attention aside from this frivolous world and from the friendships that might be dangerous:

> if, because of your imperfect repentance, you still have some bad inclinations, obtain for your soul a mental solitude, according to the method that I have taught you above, and withdraw yourself there as often as you can, and by a thousand renewed elevations of your spirit, renounce all your inclinations [...][80]

Sévigné, like her friends the Jansenists,[81] turns her attention toward this "fallen" world, one where she does not need to develop a carefully constructed mental solitude because her sense of solitude is only too acute.[82] From the Jansenist emphasis on the significance of all that happens, because all is the result of God's will, there is nothing in the material world that is not laden with some divine intention. And it is this material world that fills Sévigné's imagination and nourishes her meditation.

FIVE

From Imagination to Significance: The Novel from Scudéry to Lafayette

A remarkable painting by Rogier van der Weyden in the National Gallery (London) shows Mary Magdalene, sitting on the floor of a room filled with people, ignoring those around her and deeply absorbed in the book that she is reading.[1] The calm delight on her face tells us that she is far away from her worldly surroundings, alone in her thoughts. This image entirely fits François de Sales's idea of the devout life within society—Mary Magdalene is surely reading a pious book—but it also suggests the power and freedom that individuals gained as printed books became widely available to the middle class and as literacy increased.[2] Whether they read in the quiet of their *cabinet*, bedroom, or garden, or in a bustling room full of people, early-modern women and men could be far away in their thoughts, hearing words and seeing sights that were imperceptible to the people around them. In this social context, the novel flourished, giving readers a fictive world that they could enjoy alone and with others. Individuals could go off by themselves to read what their friends were also reading elsewhere at the same time (the latest, hot-off-the-press, volume of d'Urfé's *Astrée* or later of Scudéry's *Artamène* and many other multivolume stories) and then they could, and did, engage in lively discussions about the characters' actions and choices as well as about the quality of the writing.

Van der Weyden's Mary Magdalene gives a memorable icon of the multifaceted and equivocal power that both reading and the cultivation of the inner life of the mind offered the people of seventeenth-century France. The carefully nurtured power of imagination that de Sales taught his readers could certainly be used to escape not only into vivid, prayerful meditations but also into equally vivid amorous and adventurous alternatives to the routine of daily life. One of the most influential and prolific writers to make use of this imaginative freedom—like her namesake in Van der Weyden's painting—and to make the use of imagination a theme of her work was Madeleine de Scudéry (1607–1701).

Clélie, a Roman Story (*Clélie, histoire romaine*), published in ten volumes from 1654 to 1661, represents Madeleine de Scudéry at her best, and at the same time marks the beginning of the end of the great multivolume novels published over many years.[3] Just a year after *Clélie* was completed, another French namesake of the Magdalene, Marie-Madeleine de Lafayette, twenty-seven years Scudéry's junior, published *Zayde, a Spanish Story* (*Zayde, histoire espagnole*), and eight years later her slim and controversial *La Princesse de Clèves*.[4] Despite resemblances that, if they occurred today, would call down on the younger writer's head the accusation of plagiarism, the two works are very different in the way they involve the reader. Scudéry's *Clélie*, explicitly didactic, includes many passages that read like a user's manual for the imagination. Its reputation survives today as the source of the "Carte de Tendre" or "Map of the Country of Love" and that is quite appropriate, because this map is a good example of Scudéry's interest in imagination as a social practice—or more precisely as the activity of a group of people who are working together to imagine the same thing. *Clélie*, the novel, and Clélie, the heroine, both exemplify and describe positive uses of imagination as faculty.

The main story of *Clélie* concerns the perpetually deferred marriage of the young Roman noblewoman Clélie and her beloved Aronce, who are about to be wed in the first chapter of the novel and are then separated by astounding incidents that carry them around ancient Italy. Through the adventures of these two central figures and within subplots and flashbacks concerning their families and the people they meet, Scudéry tells the history of Rome at the end of the monarchy (late sixth century B.C.E.). Although the story is set in antiquity, the characters devote much time to questions of importance to seventeenth-century women of the proto-feminist *précieuse* movement: how women and men relate to each other, the nature of love and friendship, the importance of marriage, the qualities that make a person agreeable in society, and so forth. Because the characters tell many stories to one another—the novel as a whole is a series of stories-within-the-story—the way people engage in storytelling becomes an important theme in its own right. Scudéry makes it clear that storytelling, as she does it, is the practice of imagining together.

THE NARRATOR TO THE READER

One way a group of people can imagine together is to accept the discipline of imagining the same thing at the same time from a shared point of view. This is what we do when we read a novel, but novels have not always been so explicitly aimed at the detailed reproduction of sensation in the mind. A comparison of Scudéry's descriptions and those contained in earlier and contemporary novels is an interesting exercise, one that reveals a generally more dense and specific descriptive style in *Clélie* (than in, for instance, *La Princesse de Clèves*). However, the relation between textual description and the active use of imagination is something that Scudéry does not leave to chance—her work is well known for its energetically (some might say, heavy-handedly) didactic quality. Throughout *Clélie* there is an internal mirror (or mise-en-abîme) of the process of telling and receiving narrative—storytelling within storytelling—, and this internal mirror emphasizes the audience's obligation to participate by *imagining*. In a certain sense it seems very obvious that the audience should do this, but in another sense it is not. The internal narrators of these stories could instead ask their listeners to *understand*, to *decipher*, to *believe*, to *learn from* their narratives. Narrators before Scudéry did not so insistently remind their audience to imagine, but often, instead, directed the listener's or reader's attention to the truth or the didactic value of their tales.[5]

Throughout the thousands of pages of *Clélie*, we read repeatedly, "Imagine for yourself, Madame..." (*Imaginez vous donc, Madame...* [I, 353]) or "imagine what Aronce's suffering was like" (again, *imaginez-vous* [I, 599]). To stress the fact that the appeal to the imagination includes visualization and other sensory representation, the narrator often guides the listener to the details. In telling the story of Lucius Junius Brutus, the internal narrator Herminius, says "in order to experience this pleasant surprise, *recall to your imagination* the way Brutus appeared to you only two days ago (*remettez vous bien dans l'imagination). See him* with that dark and unhappy expression that suggests neither kindness nor wit, and *remember* that stupid manner that he affects and that makes what he says, even when it is sensible, seem utterly meaningless" (III, 168, emphasis added). Imagination thus goes beyond the simple notion "Brutus is mentally challenged" to involve the listener (and indirectly the reader) in reconstructing an image of the precise gestures and postures and the tone of voice that Brutus affected.

The instruction to "imagine" or to "recall to your imagination" leads to the vivid imaging that we recognize from the rhetorical tradition as *enargeia*, though in *Clélie* it is usually separated from the typical rhetorical context. The narrator can guide the listener to such "enargic" representation by using the imperative (as in the previous examples) or by describing a character who is imagining. So the audience, in order to follow the narration, must also imagine—at a second degree, imagining a character imagining. For instance, Brutus is party to a conversation in which certain expressions set in motion his imaginative activity: "Brutus . . . *felt* in that instant all the hatred he had for Tarquin well up fresh in his heart. It seemed to him that his father and his brother *had just died*: he *saw* the overthrow of his house as *if it had just happened*: all Tarquin's and Tullie's crimes *filled his imagination* . . . " (IV, 636). We can recognize the vividness of the sensory reproduction (the *enargeia*) in the emphasis on the *presentness* and thus the *presence* of the actual things, persons, and events.

Appealing to the audience's visualizing capacity, Scudéry—through her internal narrators—differs markedly from her younger contemporary Lafayette. Once the listeners have been told to participate by filling their imagination they are given the details necessary to carry out this instruction. In the "Story of Artemidore" told by Zenocrate there is a long description of a palace at a place called Carisatis with many reminders to the audience members that they must participate actively in constructing the image of the place in their minds. One reason that imagination is required is that discourse fails to do the place justice ("no one can represent it adequately" IV, 796). However, Zenocrate tells his listeners,

> Imagine that as you enter you find a courtyard of an immensity in proportion to the edifice that is visible on the left as you arrive, and this symmetry is infinitely pleasing to the eye (IV, 799).

One of the most remarkable things about this description, though we might take it for granted today, is the care given to specifying the point of view and to describing all details from that specific point of view, which is mobile. The description that follows is *subjective* and the audience is invited to take the place of a moving, seeing person that is created by the words of the narrator. Therefore, there are objects on the right, on the left, above, below, and so forth. Zenocrate continues this virtual guided tour by saying,

> you must imagine for yourselves that on top of this mountain that I told you about, there is a great terrace esplanade, along which there is an allée lined with tall trees, as beautiful as any in the whole world. One reaches this allée by climbing two magnificent staircases, and between these one sees two balconies with marble balustrades; and from there one can see so many different things [...] (IV, 799).

The point of view moves with the listener who is projected, imaginatively, into the scene and moves along a certain track, reaching specific points from which new areas become visible. The cooperative and coordinated activity of representing perceptual data is sometimes referred to as *filling* the imagination of the reader. This description of a garden, like that of a house or a person, are said to "fill the imagination with agreeable things, that give pleasure and amusement" and are contrasted with "useless genealogies" (VI, 810–11).

The term "filling" (*remplir*) is more than casual. Scudéry's novel is a vehicle for her own proposals for cultural reform, and she puts a great deal of stock in modifying the way people used words. In the midst of all the main narrative movements in *Clélie* there is always time for the characters to drop everything else to engage in seminar-like discussions of emotional or (as we would say) psychological terms. Thus, the differences among various kinds of jealousy or between inconstancy and infidelity receive detailed attention from Clélie, Aronce, and their fellows.

Given the number of times that the term "imagination" appears, it is only fitting that this concept be distinguished from a potentially confusing notion that also crops up in the novel, *rêverie*—revery or daydreaming. Scudéry draws a technical distinction between *imagination* and *rêverie*. The former is, as we have seen, a mental activity that is directed by intention and consists of calling to mind specific perceptions. Revery, on the other hand, is characterized by *not* being directed and by *not* representing any object with the precision of description:

> not everyone can daydream; [...] there are many who talk about it but who don't really know what it is like to allow one's mind to wander little by little, surrendering to the heart's whimsies rather than bowing to the commands of

that overbearing reason, that wants us to think nothing except what reason itself authorizes. To daydream sweetly one must let the mind roam, and let it go where it wishes; one must be alone; one must be in the countryside; one must have in one's spirit something that is nice; one must be of a somewhat melancholic temperament; one must want to think about nothing at all, yet think about something nonetheless; or one must want to think about something, and yet think about nothing at all (VI, 890–91).

This definition, given by the character Cléodamas (owner of the garden described above), presents several notable differences between imagination and revery. The most significant are the lack of direction in revery and its lack of focus. It would be difficult to find statements in Scudéry supporting a negative approach to imagination—imagination does not succeed by failing, nor does it work by accident. Revery, on the other hand, is definable in Scudéry's world only negatively. Although it thrives in many of the same situations that fit imagination (solitude and retreat), there is no indication that it is in any way a *re*-production or even perception of an object. Its objects, in fact, are always somehow in-between: revery is the thought that slips in or slips away, thus eluding perception—perception, which hold things in its grasp. The closest revery comes to being definable in a positive way is as an alternative to reason, and in this way revery confirms the alliance between imagination and reason while setting itself apart from both. Revery is thus an opponent of imagination in Scudéry's world.

THE GARDEN OF FORKING PATHS: CLÉLIE AND THE NOVEL OF POSSIBILITIES

In reading Scudéry's novel we are called to participate by visualizing, smelling, hearing, and generally by reproducing in our minds the world as it is described by the many storytellers. Our participation is complicated, however, by the characters' hyperactive imagination. Even when they are not telling tales, they are engaged in virtuoso mental "world-building." One important sequence in *Clélie*, concerning the marriage of Tarquin the Proud and his wicked lover Tullie after they have each killed their first spouse, shows how the characters' constant imagining of new possible courses of action requires that the reader develop equivalent skills. The characters are continually producing alternative stories in their minds and sometimes in their conversations as they think ahead to what will happen or what may happen given certain conditions. Tarquin's brother and the first husband of Tullie,

Prince d'Amériole tells Tullie's sister, known simply as "the Princess," what is going to happen if each of them marries the person that her father the king, Servius Tullius, has designated for them. Amériole also presents, more briefly, the vision of an alternative future if they elope together to live in Corinth (II, 904ff). Shortly before this conversation Servius Tullius tells someone why he has planned for each of his two daughters a marriage with a man completely different from them in moral character; in each case a virtuous person will be married with an unscrupulous, overly ambitious one. Tullius provides also two "scenarios" one for the case of a marriage between the two ambitious young people and one for the case of the marriage of opposites, the one that he has commanded. And at the time of the conversation between Amériole and the Princess, Tullie and Tarquin are each (in his and her own minds) setting out the way the future may be in view of the coming marriages. So that the novel shows the characters as living only very tenuously in the here and now, since the characters invest so much of their energy in this forward-looking inventory of possibilities, not only the general situation (e.g. if Tullie marries Amériole . . .) but the consequences, what will happen subsequently and how it will *feel*.

This repeated, ever-shifting mental picture of the future is sometimes shared but is more often secret both because characters are imagining how they are perceived by others and are therefore performing a role that will produce the proper outward appearance. Because each character has individual interests that diverge from the interests of the other characters, he or she needs to picture the ramifications of all their cumulative and collective acts. This activity, sometimes called foresight, creates a story with the story.[6] Here, for instance, is an account of the thoughts of Tullie and Tarquin, the murderous daughter and son-in-law of Servius Tullius:

> This cruel man and this unholy woman had foreseen that by having the Prince and the Princess die at the same time, people would think what they did, indeed, think: but Tarquin and Tullie had also seen much more danger for themselves if they killed them separately. For if the Princess had lived longer than Prince Ameriole, she could have told her father the King what she knew about the Prince's death. Besides, Tullie did not want to poison her husband unless she was certain that Tarquin would poison his wife, for fear that if she had eliminated to Tarquin's advantage the man who could rival him for the throne, Tarquin might not complete the plan. Tarquin, for his part, could not go through with murdering his wife, unless he was sure of his brother's death, for he imagined clearly that if his brother had survived the Princess, he would have tried to avenge her . . . . (II, 973–74).[7]

This passage shows why Scudéry's novels are not easy for modern readers. It is not so much the sheer length of the work as the complex layering of the narrative that we find daunting. After all, it is difficult enough to keep track of which character is telling the story at any given moment in *Clélie*, but in addition we have to grapple with the multiple "non-stories," so to speak, that fill the characters' minds and occupy page after page of the novel. These non-stories are the characters' fictive creation of the constantly shifting potential future, which they picture for themselves in striving toward a decision about how they will act. The non-stories contain events, gestures, emotions, and words (what they or someone else would say under certain circumstances), and these internal fictions reach us in the future conditional and subjunctive mode—not the most user-friendly of verb forms in our day. And the non-stories that take place within the minds of the characters include speculation about what will be going on inside the minds of other characters under various alternative scenarios!

It is important to note that the proliferation of alternatives and mental visions is not due to women characters specifically. Scudéry's creation of the story of Tarquin and Tullie is extremely meaningful within the history of imagination in the seventeenth century because it emphatically does *not* describe imagination as a feminine faculty. Scudéry makes her position on the issue of gender and imagination very explicit in a discussion among the characters and also provides an illustration of imagination at work in a male/female couple, Tullie and Tarquin. In a complicated four-way conversation about the advantages and disadvantages of each gender, Tullie is ferociously unfavorable to women—or to women in the traditional conception of their "nature"—while her sister the Princess finds much good to say about women's lot. Eventually this discussion comes to the comparison of men and women, including their way of thinking. The "good" male character, Ameriole, takes the side of women:

—"I will have to defend your sex against you. I am convinced that ladies are capable of all the great virtues and that they have even more intelligence than men. In fact, if you observe men and women carefully in those places where their education is just about the same, as it is in rural areas, you will see that women appear much more intelligent than men. So we must conclude that Nature gave more intelligence to you women than to us men."

—"I admit that what you say is true. And in general terms we women have much imagination and much intelligence. But just the same, we have little courage . . . ." (II, 878–79).

Imagination appears here as a good mental quality, paired with wit or intelligence (*esprit*) and not specific to women even though they have at least as much of it as men. This is one of many cases in *Clélie* where imagination appears as an integral part of intelligence and is much to be desired.[8] However, shortly after Tullie participates in this conversation and specifically adds the term "imagination" to praise of women's "wit" (*esprit*), the narrative gives us reason to compare Tullie's imagination to her husband Tarquin's in such a way that it is clear that he has just as much imagination, perhaps more, and certainly an imagination that takes a different form.

Tarquin is a protean character. Before the putsch that makes them Queen and King of Rome, Tarquin manages to convince many very different people that he is like them. With religious people he is scrupulously religious, with libertines he is licentious and blasphemous, and with philosophers he is philosophical (II, 982). His ability to change his behavior corresponds apparently to an ability to imagine many different convergent conspiracies but also to foresee an equal number of contingencies and countermeasures. Under each of his hundreds of appearances is a hyperactive mind that generates hundreds or thousands of scenarios, but his absorption in this inner world of detailed plotting is revealed only by "something somber, proud, and wicked" (II, 983) always present in his eyes but unnoticed by most people. For his wife, his attention to all these branching strategies and outcomes makes Tarquin "too prudent" and even harmfully prudent (*d'une prudence si nuisible*, II, 998).

If Tarquin has an imagination that makes him aware of too many possibilities and slows down his ambitious advance toward tyranny, Tullie has no less imagination but one that leads to a different result. Instead of picturing *many* outcomes, Tullie perceives only one, but she does so with such force and vividness that all other possibilities evaporate:

> she did not have a mind that could configure itself in a hundred different ways like Tarquin. It was just the opposite: she had so completely fixed in her mind that she was above everyone around her and that everyone had obligations towards her, that she owed nothing to anyone, and that Fortune owed her victory, that she felt no need to be pleasant or to be loved. (II, 983–84).

Scudéry is describing imagination at work here, just as much as in the case of Tarquin, but it is a different kind of imaginative thinking. Tullie formed a single strong image (*elle s'estoit tellement mis dans la teste*) of her future domination over Rome and considered that no other future could possibly occur. Unlike Tarquin, whose imagination works in cooperation with those of other people to produce collaborative images of present and future through conversations in which each participant helps confirm or modify the view of present and future worlds, Tullie has a "one-track" mind that does not take into account anyone else's perception of the world, including self-perception. Although our usual use of the term "imaginative" would assign to Tarquin a greater strength of imagination, this would be to favor quantity over sheer strength and insistence. Tullie's mind imagines one single outcome to the exclusion of all others. This gives her energy and confidence in her plans. If this couple succeeds, it seems in Scudéry's narrative to be a result of the combination of these two types of imagination, for Tarquin and Tullie possess their specific imaginative ability in an extreme form, one through exceptional multiplicity and the other through exceptional force. The two are joined by a willingness to entertain in their thoughts—and hence, later, in their actions—actions and consequences from which other people would shrink. So Tullie is not contradicted by Tarquin when she declares that their success in seizing power will make all their crimes "disappear": "all imaginable crimes are wiped away, when they are followed by success" (II, 996). And the difficulty of the novel—or rather of the internal narrator of this story, Herminius, and his audience—in grasping the reality of Tarquin's and Tullie's conduct is that what they did finally in grabbing and exercising power was to take "cruelty beyond anything that imagination can conceive" (II, 1019). Clearly the imagination of these two anti-heroes is stronger than the reader's.

LOVE'S SPECTRAL BODY

The case of Tullie and Tarquin illustrates the political value of imagination. These two cruel characters out-maneuver others because they out-imagine them. Scudéry's novel, however, shows that a well-developed imagination can serve amorous purposes as well. The most spectacular achievement of a well-directed erotic imagination is to permit two people to have trysts without meeting physically. While the late twentieth century would later devise amorous encounters at a distance through "cyber" relationships, Scudéry had anticipated a form of synchronous emotional experience at a distance using letters and imagination. In this way Lucinius Junius, known as Brutus, and his beloved Lucrèce can compensate for the difficulty they have in meeting publicly:

> Since both of them were of a passionate nature, they sought to console each other by arranging trysts in their minds (*se donnant des assignations d'esprit*), so to speak. They agreed upon an hour, each day, during which they promised to think of each other. And what is remarkable is that Brutus often awaited that hour with as much impatience as if he were actually about to see Lucrèce. He found something so sweet in being certain that she was really thinking about him, just at the moment when he was thinking about her, that when he was carrying on about the delight that this kind of meeting gave him, I did not doubt that he was more madly in love than any other man (III, 529).

Herminius, who tells this story, ascribes Brutus's pleasure to the intensity of his love, but clearly this is not an adequate explanation. Many other characters in *Clélie* are described as suffering frightfully from the absence of their beloved. Brutus is not more passionately in love than others, but he does have a stronger and better-disciplined imagination. The strength of Brutus's imagination seems rather to be the source of his pleasure, for this hour of "contact" with Lucrèce draws its sweetness from his ability to imagine that she is imagining him at the same time.

Scudéry does not propose a spiritualistic description of action at a distance, as if the lover were sensing brain waves or emotional emanations sent by Lucrèce; rather, the force of Brutus's certainty of what Lucrèce is doing at that moment is contained entirely in Brutus's own mind. The unshakable conviction of this *positivement* recalls the happy results that Montaigne derived from using "magic" medallions to cure impotency, as we have seen in "Of the Power of the Imagination." Even if Lucrèce were to miss a session of these *assignations d'esprit* Brutus would still be able to carry on by himself because of his mental ability to perceive Lucrèce's imagined actions in regard to him. It is important to emphasize that what Brutus represents to himself is not a mere intention on Lucrèce's part, but rather a series of acts and embodied attitudes that are part of an "assignation." These include, presumably, withdrawal into a quiet place, certain postures and facial expressions consistent with a mind focused on something physically absent, the gestures of rereading a letter or poem sent earlier by Brutus and of writing with a stylus on tablets, and so forth. These are the things that Brutus himself is doing, and such acts occupy real time.

By having her characters set a certain time of day for these exercises of shared emotion at a distance, Scudéry underlines the resemblance between these exercises and religious meditation, which, we recall, has a set relation to the meditator's daily schedule according to the instructions of François de Sales. And like religious meditation, this amorous meditation seeks to protect itself from the corrosive influences of society, either by locating the meditative act in a specific solitary place (writing cabinet or garden) or by creating an interior mental space into which the meditator withdraws, sometimes cutting off sensory stimulus from the outside:

> You need to know that having stayed so late, I was with him at the hour he had agreed upon with Lucrèce. All of a sudden I could see that he was no longer with me, even though I was still with him. I could see, in other words, that his mind was somewhere else and not on what I was saying to him. He behaved like a man who has something on his mind and who really wants to be alone. I left him for some time in this condition.... (III, 530).

Brutus's appearance coincides perfectly with the practice of imaginative meditation, particularly in the signs of his withdrawal from the surrounding material and social world. Yet this is not simply the melancholy and uncontrolled distraction that is almost universally attributed to lovers in the seventeenth century. Instead, Brutus and Lucrèce are said to have trained themselves to contain this distraction within a schedule and thus to withdraw in accordance with their will. This voluntary "distraction" is deeper and more satisfying than random impassioned musings because it has a vividness that makes these concentrated moments almost as satisfying as the physical presence of the beloved.

The most distinctive thing about this regular imaginative practice is that its power derives from its dual nature, or at least from its fictively dual nature. Brutus's pleasure and success at withdrawing into the mental tryst comes from the amplifying power of imagining Lucrèce doing the same thing. The result is like a hall of mirrors in which there is no end to the framing of meditation within meditation. Brutus imagines Lucrèce imagining Brutus imagining Lucrèce imagining Brutus... etc. If Brutus were simply to be picturing what Lucrèce might be doing at a given time of day—talking with her friends, picking flowers, or bathing—this could certainly provide him some delight. But that delight is increased geometrically by supposing that Lucrèce is picturing what Brutus is doing at that very moment. At first it might seem that this is a deeply narcissistic type of pleasure, since the image of Brutus is framed by the image of Lucrèce, but Brutus is at the center. However, this "narcissism" is rendered dynamic by the fact that Lucrèce's imagination is what gives value to the image of Brutus. In fact, the movement back-and-forth is such that finally it becomes impossible to stop at any given character's image.

This dual amorous imagination—or fiction of duality—results in writing. The outlet of the erotic stimulation in Scudéry's novel is not physical climax nor the passionate verbal exchanges that sublimate and replace physical sex in many of the scenes of seventeenth-century novels, but rather writing, which is another form of imagination. Writing becomes interchangeable with purely interior imagining. Brutus tells his friend Herminius that during the hour scheduled for communing with Lucrèce, "he had promised to give her a full hour. And if I was not going to have the kindness to speak to him about Lucrèce, I had to refrain from speaking to him and let him muse or write" (III, 531).

Brutus's practice of uniting himself with his beloved, though absent, Lucrèce stands somewhere midway between Salesian structured meditation and Sévigné's more free-form daily mental assignations with her absent daughter. Like Sévigné, Brutus finds writing to be a conduit and relief for the intense internal excitement of his imaging. Letters are tokens, almost fetishes, used as the point of departure for his scheduled journey to the inward utopia where he and Lucrèce escape from the constraints of their actual situation.

THERAPY AND THE MAP FOR LOVE

We have seen that imagination, as a conscious practice, appears in *Clélie* to enrich the audience's participation in the narrative process, to enable political action, and to provide solace for unhappy lovers. The most important use of imagination in *Clélie*, however, is philosophical and therapeutic. Here is one passage in which Scudéry takes up the education of the imagination as a direct heir of Montaigne and the Stoic tradition. Close to the center of the novel— at the beginning of volume six of the ten volumes—there is an extremely significant discussion of death and the fear of death. Given the associations we have already seen between death and imagination in both the neo-Stoic tradition and the Christian meditation movement, Scudéry could hardly have expected her readers to overlook the seriousness and the contextual connotations of this discussion. The matter arises when one of Clélie's friends named Flavie admits that she is extremely fearful and particularly in regard to death: "For although Flavie was a very intelligent person, she had the weakness of not controlling her feelings and of suffering a host of needless fears" (VI, 674). Her friends exchange views on the matter of death—its advantages (it ends all inequality and unhappiness) and its evils (it destroys beauty and friendship). When Flavie expresses her own fear of death, her words are an echo of Montaigne. It is the omnipresence of death that disturbs her: "when I think that one can die at any moment and that one can die in a thousand different ways, I can feel my heart grow cold, and I just about lose my mind." Her friends diagnose her problem as a disorder of the imagination, for "as she has a lively imagination, she sees dangers where there are none" (VI, 676), and Flavie agrees entirely that her plight is due to an undisciplined imagination: "But after all, even though reason blames me, imagination dominates my heart, and makes me feel whatever it chooses." (VI, 679–80).

Imagination is the faculty that is indispensable for perception—the past, present, and future all pass through this faculty, which allows the mind to register the information of the senses. Flavie's problem is that her imagination is stuck, so to speak, not only in an active mode but within a limited repertory of associations. So she does not only *think* about death in the abstract, she *sees* death, as her friend Colatine remarks, where it never occurred. In other words, all her sensory perceptions are overlaid with an image of people dying and she apparently cannot separate the actual perception from the potential perception, what is coming from outside the mind from what is being generated within the mind—all of this seems equally concrete. Flavie gives a partial enumeration of the objects (or rather, sensations) that set off her fears:

> So I fear diseases of all kinds, major and minor; I fear thunder; I fear fire and water, cold and heat, evening dew and fog, and I fear that the earth might quake in Rome as it did in Sicily. (VI, 678).

Scudéry's seventeenth-century reader, and many readers today, will recognize that Flavie's disorder is an allusion to Montaigne's reflexions on the imagination of death. The statement that starts off the discussion in *Clélie* ("when I think that one can die at any moment and that one can die in a thousand different ways . . . ") strikingly resembles Montaigne's advice, in "That to philosophize is to learn to die," "Let us have nothing in our minds as often as death. At every moment let us picture it in our imagination in all its aspects." (*Essays*, 86/60). Flavie's imagination is doing exactly what Montaigne said our imagination should do, but where the *Essays* recommend this outcome as the result of deliberate development of imagination, Flavie's imagination is out of control and independent of her reason.

The discussion among Clélie's friends on the matter of how to think about death seems to be Scudéry's way of taking up one of Montaigne's central themes. *Clélie* does not contain a detailed program, as the *Essays* do, but this passage of the novel is a good illustration of how Scudéry approaches the management of imagination. First of all, Flavie's problem consists of a solitary imaginative practice (or, rather, in her case, a bad habit or even the uncontrollable result of her individual nature, as Herminius says [VI, 683]), whereas imagining in *Clélie* is generally beneficial and positive when it is shared, the result of two or more persons directing their mental perceptions in a coordinated way. Secondly, how a person uses her imagination is a subject of general interest within her circle of friends—even though imagination is still a faculty that is *within* each individual, it can be shared through conversation. Through that sharing the individual's inner perceptions may sometimes (though probably not in Flavie's case) be modified. Finally, the heroine Clélie has the last word on imagining death. She responds to Platine, who has described her own elaborate approach to the perception of death, by simply saying,

> As for myself... I am not like you, because I think about death when the occasion arises. I think about it without fear, since inevitably one day I will have to see it even closer, and I suppose that it is best that death not be entirely unknown to me. (VI, 686).

In the matter of death, then, Clélie seems to think that the aggressive imaginative practice of the early Montaigne is not fruitful, and that multiplying the perceptions of death by creating constant scenarios of dying is not a good use of imagination. Instead, she simply accepts its presence (apparently in the present) without training herself to recall or anticipate it.[9] This "wisdom" about imagination and death closes the discussion with Clélie, not surprisingly, in a position of dominance.

The *Carte de Tendre*, or Map of the Country of Love, is the only part of Scudéry's novel that still lives in the consciousness of the general public. François Cheauveau's engraving of this "map" for the first volume of *Clélie* has been reproduced in countless textbooks and websites. Yet among modern readers only a few know what role this image plays in Scudéry's novel. The *Carte de Tendre* is another therapeutic activity on the part of the heroine Clélie. She uses it to show her friends how imagination can be *directed*, how individuals can improve their ability to visualize life by following the advice of others, and, in short, how imagination can be not an isolated or marginal practice but an essential part of social life. Scudéry was, of course, far from original in proposing an allegorical map to convey psychological concepts and she was entirely of her time in believing that individuals could learn to modify the way they pictured emotional states by following the instruction of a book or of a spiritual director, yet she clearly was unusual in her day in proposing a secular education of the mind to improve social interaction. Where François de Sales saw imagination as constructing a place of solitary internal refuge for the individual in the midst of a troublesome and potentially distracting social life, Scudéry saw the opportunity for forging a *common* vision in a variety of organized groups.

The conversation that gives rise to the *Carte de Tendre* occurs in the very first part of *Clélie*, within a flashback by the secondary character, Célère, friend and companion of the hero Aronce. Célère is telling Aronce's story and giving particular attention to how the young man of (at first) unknown family origins falls in love with the fascinating Clélie. About two-thirds of the way through the volume, Célère tells about an occasion during which Clélie presided over a conversation of several people including her two suitors, Horace and Aronce, and a newly arrived gentleman from Rome, Herminius. The latter is in love with a woman in Rome but develops an intense, even passionate "friendship" with Clélie. She is surrounded by so many people who lay claim to her friendship that she must make distinctions. Not all her friends are Tender Friends (*tendres Amis*) she says. Some of them are half-friends, also known as agreeable acquaintances. Others, more "advanced" are new Friends, while there are also simply Friends. The latter include Friends from habit, solid Friends, and particular Friends. But in the highest, most select category are the tender Friends, who are so well placed in Clélie's heart that there is no higher, more advanced category.

The *Carte de Tendre*, with its spatial presentation of psychological categories, arises at this juncture in the conversation, after Clélie has enumerated the categories of friendship, when the "new friend" Herminius asks how *far* it is from New Friendship to Tendre, and Aronce seizes on the spatial metaphor to refer to the relation among the types of friendship as a "country" with a "map" known to very few (I, 392). Herminius actually does not originate the spatialized view of friendship but merely renders it a bit more concrete, a bit more pragmatic, on the basis of Clélie's use of terms like "progress" and "advanced" to indicate a hierarchy in friendships.

It is in this conversational environment or workshop that imagination becomes explicit, first in the common and even pejorative form that is current in *Clélie* as in much seventeenth-century usage, *s'imaginer*: "Maybe you imagine [*Peut-estre vous imaginez vous*], Clélie replied, that it is only a short walk from New Friendship to Tenderness; that's why, before you start out, I will promise to give you the map of this country even though Aronce believes it is uncharted" (I, 392–93). Clélie's mapping project springs up directly in response to a misconception, or rather two misconceptions—Herminius's apparent belief that it will be easy to reach Tendre and Aronce's that there is no map of that "country." These two misconceptions belong to a form of thinking called *s'imaginer*, routinely associated with error. Although the sensory implications of imagination are not spelled out in most uses of this idiomatic expression, Clélie's comment to Herminius that he imagines only a short distance between new and tender friendship may lead us to suppose that Herminius has an actual mental "picture" of the journey, rather than a purely abstract or quantitative idea that could be expressed in a numeral. Aronce's comment about the map definitely proceeds from another imaginative problem. He thinks that there is no existing (and perhaps, no possible) visualization of the relationship among items on Clélie's list. In promising a map, Clélie will on one hand correct a spatialized misconception and on the other hand provide a way to imagine something that Aronce seems to believe to be entirely outside the realm of imagination.

Surrounding the account of Clélie's initiative in promising an image of otherwise abstract relationships in question, there are narrative comments that call attention to the cooperative work of storyteller and audience. The *Carte de Tendre* episode occurs, we recall, within a flashback: Célère is telling Aronce's adventures for the Princesse des Léontines (even readers with a copy of Scudéry's novel open next to them at this moment can be forgiven for feeling dizzy in the baroque layers and twists of this ten-volume work). Célère asks the Princess to *imagine* Aronce's feelings when he receives Clélie's written response to his first, written, declaration of love. Once again, as we have seen, the many layers of audience—the internal listener, the reader, etc.—for Scudéry's narratives are expected to participate by doing more than understanding. They are expected to lend a sensory reality to what they are hearing. In this case, the Princesse des Léontines is expected to imagine

Aronce's *feelings* when he receives Clélie's note: "Imagine, Madame, that when Aronce received the note, he felt an astonishing jolt in his heart..." (I, 353). This is a particularly challenging imaginative effort on the audience's part since it requires some mental replication of a *feeling* rather than of an "objective" sensory idea such as a specific color, taste, or sound. Scudéry thus introduces to the reader the notion of extending imagination to include the embodiment of emotional states. Such an effort extends the work of imagination to include empathy within the domain of that faculty.

Yet while the person who is hearing this story about Aronce is trying to participate by sharing his emotion, Aronce and his friend (yet also rival) Horace are trying to conjecture the feelings that Clélie has for each one of them. Tellingly, these two male figures approach love in strictly *quantitative* terms. Here is a typical exchange on the subject of love. Aronce says to Horace, "'It is not, he continued, that I am less noble than you: but assuredly I have more love [for Clélie] than you do.' 'Ah, Aronce,' replied Horace, 'I object to what you are saying; for one cannot have more love than I have...'" (I, 380). The two would-be lovers of Clélie have a simple view of their own feeling of love and of Clélie's feeling for them. Within the category "love," the only difference they perceive is on a graduated scale of more and less. Aronce and Horace are not sensitive to *qualities* or types of love, and therefore there is no way out of their head-on confrontation over Clélie. A second revealing characteristic of the two males' view of love is that it is strongly extroverted. Each man is concerned with establishing the intensity of his feeling in comparison to his rival's. Neither one of them is cultivating a "thought from behind the head" (as Pascal would say) about his feelings.

Clélie's *Carte de Tendre* offers the male characters who surround the heroine an alternative vision to this quantitative and extroverted image, which is also male-centered (the men seem almost more concerned with their standing vis-à-vis the other than in respect to Clélie). With a mental map of love, Aronce and Horace will be able to think of this emotion in *qualitative* terms, in terms of the different kinds of love as well as the different degrees of love. Further, they will have an image that encourages them to dwell in their thoughts, to picture where they stand in relation to Clélie as an inner landscape, not dissimilar from the spiritual landscapes created by followers of François de Sales. Scudéry, through Clélie, offers her characters and her readers a meditative process that bridges the gap between the purely exterior world of the senses and the purely interior world of judgment. This is the mediating, and therapeutic, function of imagination.

LAFAYETTE AND THE ANTI-IMAGINATIVE NOVEL

In contrast to Scudéry, Lafayette proposes a vigorously anti-imaginative view of the novel, while at the same time acknowledging, like Pascal, that imagination plays a huge part in everyday life.[10] She repeatedly shows the dangers of imagining and does not hold forth any hope that imagination can be controlled, directed, enhanced, or used with profit. In their passive stance toward thoughts that come from their senses, Lafayette's characters seem unaware of their own role in forming images in their mind. They are therefore victims of a rush of imagery from their surroundings or from their mind and often fail to distinguish the source of that imagery. Instead of recognizing and training their imaginative faculty in a selective way, Lafayette's characters devote exceptional energy and ingenuity to the quest for *significance*.

They are concerned with significance in two meanings of the word. First, in the more technical sense, the characters are obsessed with sign-making. They perceive the world as a set of *signs* and the people in it as producers and receivers of signs. Second, in another current use of the term, the characters are deeply concerned with the importance, the practical value, of what they can learn from the world around them. While they take scant initiative to call the material world to mind in vivid form, they energetically filter what they see and hear—few other senses are mentioned in Lafayette's writing—to reach the useful information that can be gleaned.

The characters, moreover, are not alone in this preference. The narrator's neglect of physical description is a notorious characteristic of Lafayette's style. But rather than speaking of this aspect of her style in negative terms, we can frame it as a partial return to the exemplary narrative of such forebears as Marguerite de Navarre, whose narrators in the *Heptameron* (1558) call their audience's attention to the significance or moral lesson of each tale.[11]

In Lafayette's novels, the terms *imagination, imaginer,* and their variants are not defined nor used in the technical traditional sense of a special way of thinking about physical things. Yet imagination, as the thought of the physical, plays a crucial role in the plots of Lafayette's stories even when—*especially* when—the term "imagination" is not used. This nonconvergence of concept and act is startling in the context of a society in which discussions of imagination had spread far beyond the community of professed philosophers and had occupied significant passages of *Clélie*, a work that Lafayette and her social and intellectual circle knew well. Of course, Lafayette's *characters* had not read *Clélie* even if the novelist herself had, and therefore her characters need not show that they are aware of the power and danger of representations of the body in thought.

Let us consider the use of the language of imagination in *La Princesse de Clèves*.[12] We know that the verb *imaginer* appears thirty-one times, and of these it is reflexive twenty-four times. In keeping with contemporary usage, Lafayette employs the reflexive usually to indicate error, that is, an involuntary misperception of the way things are, as was the case of Herminius in the *Carte de Tendre* episode of *Clélie*.[13]

Lafayette uses the noun *imagination* only five times in *La Princesse de Clèves*, but these five instances significantly concern only the Duc de Nemours and the Princesse de Clèves, not any of the other characters. The term also appears at crucial moments of the novel, oddly located toward the beginning and the end, not in middle. The narrator writes of Nemours's imagination only once, at the time when he is thinking of his possible future as the husband of Queen Elizabeth of England. He is on the verge of an immense enterprise that would determine his whole future life and, although he is far from the English court, all his actions and thoughts are turned toward this plan:

> Meanwhile the Duke of Nemours had remained at Brussels, completely taken up with his plans for England. He was always sending and receiving messengers. His hopes grew from day to day, and at last Lignerolles told him that it was time for him to appear and finish in person what had been so well begun. He received this news with all the satisfaction that an ambitious man can feel at seeing himself raised to a throne simply through his reputation. He had gradually grown so accustomed to the contemplation of this great piece of good fortune that whereas at first he had regarded it as an impossibility, all difficulties had vanished from his imagination, and he foresaw no obstacles. (273/16).

This whole passage illustrates the power of imagination. Nemours's presence in Elizabeth's court and mind is purely imaginary, since she has never met him. Likewise, for Nemours, a possible life as husband of this queen consists of perceptions that are generated by his mind alone out of the words of his emissary Lignerolles and others. Even though the verb "to imagine" is almost invariably associated in Lafayette's work with error or impossibility, Nemours's situation here is more complex. He had imagined obstacles to achieving this desired goal, but these obstacles faded away as he got accustomed to the idea of his royal marriage. Were these obstacles merely "imaginary" in the sense of being illusions, illusions purged from his thought by progressive adaptation to the realistic assessments of Lignerolles? Or is Nemours simply continuing to make use of his imagination in the positive sense by planning ahead—for instance, in picturing his arrival in England with the "magnificent outfit" that he subsequently orders from Paris?

The shift in Nemours's life that is told only two paragraphs later conveys a contrast between what is imagined and what is real by going far beyond any of the "obstacles" that Nemours probably had in mind. He had not imagined the Princesse de Clèves and the obstacle that would arise from his own contrary passion. His imagination misled him doubly. It made him see a tempting and glorious future with Elizabeth, on one hand, and its initial representation of obstacles to that future did not include the "obstacle" that actually arises in the midst of these negotiations. Nemours was blindsided by the apparition of the Princess. He has a passive relation to his imagination and does not control it. So he is at the mercy of the appearances that enter his consciousness.

The term "imagination" does not reappear in *La Princesse de Clèves* until after the death of Mme de Chartres and the subsequent confession (*aveu*) that the Princess makes to her husband. Then the term appears four times in connection with the heroine's thoughts. First, when she is alone in the garden pavilion at Coulommiers and Nemours comes for a second time to spy on her, and then three times after the death of M. de Clèves. In none of these cases does she deliberately try to imagine anything—each of these instances exemplifies involuntary thought. Three times imagination seems to signify a form of error of perception or of judgment and the other time appears to be a temptation, something that virtue requires her to resist.[14] Lafayette, then, persists in marking imagination negatively and in associating it closely with the heroine's love for Nemours, love laden with a burden of guilt. As in the sole case of Nemours's experience of "imagination" (as expressed in its noun form), this way of thinking is stimulated by the possibility of an amorous relationship that is never fulfilled. In short, little good seems to come from "imagination" in Lafayette's terms; it is deceitful, tempting, misleading, and when it corresponds to the richness of the real it is merely dismissed. Who could have supposed that Nemours was really watching his beloved through the window of the garden pavilion? The Princess thinks "that she had been mistaken, and that the vision of Monsieur de Nemours was an effect of her imagination" (387/90), yet Nemours is actually there.

In short, it seems that Lafayette writes outside of the movement that conceives imagination as a way of thinking that should be voluntarily used and defines imagination as a way of thinking about material things, rather than simply as any form of erroneous thought. Do the physical world and sensory perception play such a small part in Lafayette's work that she does not need to take into account any of the domain of the imagination as the thought of the physical? The thought of the physical, and specifically of the human body, is in a way central to Lafayette's characters, but there is a strange elision of the physical in her work. She displays its power, a power that surpasses all others—or almost all, since the Princesse de Clèves apparently escapes from it in the end—and yet silences the physical at the same time.

Let us consider what happens in the novel two paragraphs after the statement that Nemours has ceased to imagine obstacles to his marriage with Elizabeth. He arrives in Paris to equip himself with all that he needs to present a striking figure at the English court (costuming his body to impose his desirability and importance on the imagination of Elizabeth and her subjects), and then he *sees* the Princesse de Clèves. Her power, the reader already knows, comes from the way her body is perceived—not from her intellectual gifts, not from her wealth, and especially not from her political connections. During Nemours's absence from the court, the young Mlle de Chartres—the future Princess de Clèves—had appeared: "At that moment there appeared at court a beauty to whom all eyes were turned, and we may well believe that she was a faultless beauty, since she aroused admiration where all were well accustomed to the sight of beautiful women" (259–60/7). Modern first-time readers of *La Princesse de Clèves* are often surprised by the absence of description in Lafayette's novel, and this characteristic is nowhere more striking than in the disembodied manifestation of the heroine's perfect body. How are we to imagine this heroine? And how did the other characters of the novel imagine her, that is, how did they represent to themselves the way she looked and sounded? These questions do not seem to be very important ones for Lafayette, even when she writes about something physical. The single sentence announcing the heroine's arrival at court turns away from any consideration of the embodiment of this beauty toward a scale of perfection and toward social effect. Instead of imagination, judgment is the faculty or the way of thinking stressed by Lafayette.

The paradox of Lafayette's approach to the physical world is that the physical has greater importance (has more effect) than for most other seventeenth-century writers, yet the physical is immediately translated into a set of abstractions. The narrator does not give, neither directly nor indirectly, the specific characteristics that make Mlle de Chartres beautiful, but does, with an approach typical of Lafayette's descriptions, allow the reader to learn of the impact of this beauty through another character. The closest we come to a description of the heroine is an account of the thoughts of her future husband when he sees her in a jeweler's shop:

> Monsieur de Clèves gazed at her admiringly, wondering who this beauty was whom he did not know. He perceived from her bearing and her suite that she must be a lady of high rank. She was so young that he thought she must be unmarried, but since she had not her mother with her, and the Italian, who did not know her, addressed her as 'madame,' he was in great doubt, and stared at her with continual surprise... (261/8).

We know that the appearance of Mlle de Chartres has struck the Prince de Clèves and that this vision will alter his life. However, rather than dwell on all that is implied by the concise expression "he gazed at her admiringly," rather than let us know what he saw, the narrator follows Clèves's thoughts through a procedure of translating all visual (and other) information about this unknown woman into social markers. She is wealthy and socially important, probably unmarried, and unusually modest. Lafayette so strongly encourages interpretation of gestures, costume, tone of voice, and every other physical clue as signs of some veiled message that characters and readers are all on the alert to decipher meanings rather than to dwell on their sensuous envelope. These novelistic priorities—putting significance over sensation—abundantly displayed in her earlier novel *Zayde* as well as in *La Princesse de Clèves*, set up a strange relationship between the reader and the characters. On one hand we seem to follow their thoughts with unusual clarity and even intimacy. The accepted description of Lafayette's narratives as "psychological" and as *romans d'analyse* conveys this aspect of a discourse that penetrates deeply into the mind of each important character so that we not only know what she or he is thinking and feeling but sometimes even know more about their emotions than the characters themselves do. On the other hand, Lafayette refuses to share with the reader one all-important category of thought, sensory thought, even when the narrator explicitly states that the characters are overwhelmingly preoccupied by their senses.

A few hours after the incident at the Florentine jeweler's shop, the Prince de Clèves goes to a gathering in the apartment of Madame, sister of the king. He has already been possessed by a passionate love for the unknown woman, and his love is in the first instance based on her beauty ("He was so struck by her beauty and evident modesty that from that moment he conceived for her the greatest love and esteem" [261 /9]). Speaking with Madame, he is totally absorbed by the vision he has had that afternoon—"he was so full of the wit and beauty of Mademoiselle de Chartres that he could speak of nothing else"—(262/9). He proceeds to describe this woman, only to have Madame declare that such a woman does not exist: "there was no such person as he described, and if there were, every one would have known about her." This crucial moment in the novel displays the working of the characters' imagination while denying the reader access to that imagination. The prince *describes* the unknown woman—doing for the courtiers what Lafayette refuses to do for the readers—giving them the indications needed to compose a mental image of this woman. The prince's own thought has been so overpowered by Mlle de Chartres's appearance that forms of thought other than imagination have seemingly been routed, except to the extent that a form of inventive thinking—what we could call imagination's shadow—has worked to endow the purely physical with an extra-physical aura, here called "wit" (*esprit*). So in the few hours that elapsed since he saw the woman he loves, her beauty and her gestures have expanded for him into the intangible domain of wit or intelligence, an endowment of which the narrative gives no trace within the account of the encounter at the shop.

The future Princesse de Clèves is already an *imaginary* character in two distinct senses. First, she exists within the imagination of the prince and of those to whom he describes her—she requires, therefore, the effort to imagine—and, second, she is said by Madame to be without existence except in the mind.[15] Lafayette does not use the *term* imagination in either sense in this passage—this lacuna is as striking as the omission of all physical description of the characters—yet she displays imagination at work both as the thought of the physical and the thought of the nonexistent. It seems as if Lafayette has *taken the physical and made it nonexistent*, conflating the two criteria of imaginative thinking (that it be thought of the physical and that it be able to occur in the absence of the thing thus thought).[16] This early passage of *La Princesse de Clèves* is a good example of the game that Lafayette plays with imagination: she displays it at work, shows its powerful and even crippling hold on the characters, does not designate it by name, and withholds from the reader the content of the characters' imagining.

We can only speculate about Lafayette's reason for playing this game, but it seems clear that she does not want to present imagination as being a way of thinking with a positive (helpful, constructive, edifying) use and as being within the control of the will. Rather than being, as for Montaigne in his Stoic moments, the way that thought masters the physical by anticipating and extending the work of the senses, imagination in Lafayette's novels seems rather to be the way the physical overwhelms and cripples the work of the mind. In the passage we have just considered, the prince does not choose to imagine Mlle de Chartres, but instead her appearance has so conquered him that he is immediately gripped by passion and cannot think or speak of anything else.

Yet there is at least one incident in *La Princesse de Clèves* that seems to correspond to a deliberate attempt at imagining, at a mental representation of a physical object in its absence. The Princess withdraws alone one evening to her garden pavilion in Coulommiers to contemplate a painting of the siege of Metz, where the Duc de Nemours was a prominent combatant. In leaving Paris for her country house, she had taken particular care to have these paintings brought with her baggage. Alone in her pavilion, she ties knots on an "Indian cane" that once belonged to Nemours, and she goes up to the painting with a torch to look closely at it, apparently to see Nemours's likeness. Unlike Scudéry or the many earlier writers who provide details about the experience of imagining, Lafayette's narrator remains resolutely *outside* the heroine's thoughts during this scene so that we can only infer what is going through her mind. We recognize the conditions of imaginative practice that we have seen in the tradition: voluntary solitude, intense preoccupation with a thought ("a grace and gentleness that reflected on her face the feelings that filled her heart" and "she gazed at this portrait with a rapt attention such as love alone could give" [386/89]), material objects that are related to the chosen object of meditation (in this case the painting of the siege of Metz takes the place of religious painting and the cane takes the place of the crucifix). Even the heroine's dress and unkempt hair fit the iconography of the meditative topos of penitent Magdalene.[17]

Lafayette has set up a meditative situation that follows many procedures familiar to François de Sales and has placed into that situation an erotic content resembling passages from Scudéry's novels, and then denied the reader direct access to the heroine's thoughts during this episode of imagination. The heroine herself seems to be aware of some of the functions attributed traditionally to imagination. For instance, she knows that imagination can produce sensory experience out of purely mental stimuli; that is, the mind can form sensation without an external material cause. When Nemours thrusts himself toward her, she attributes what she sees to the intensity of her thought ("an effect of her imagination,"387/90).[18] The stunningly unusual device of narrating this incident through the point of view of Nemours himself, watching the woman he loves use her imagination to make him mentally present to her when he is, unbeknownst to her, physically within reach, makes it seem as if this whole scene is generated by Nemours's imagination. If it were, this incident would be Lafayette's version of the Brutus–Lucretia practice of dual coordinated imagination (see above, p. 158). The narrator, at this point, draws the reader's attention to the lover's imagination:

> It would be impossible to describe everything that Monsieur de Nemours felt at this moment. To see, in the deep night, in the most beautiful spot in the world, the woman he adored; to see her without her seeing him, busied with things that bore reference to him and to the hidden love she felt for him—all that is something no other lover ever enjoyed or imagined. (386/90).

The structure of this sentence, built primarily of infinitives rather than inflected predicate verbs and deliberately impersonal or universal rather than specific nouns (*une personne, à lui . . . elle*) suggests a scenario rather than a real event even before the verb *imaginé* appears. As is typical of Lafayette, the verb itself appears in the negative, here hyperbolically so (*n'a jamais . . . ni . . . nul*). This incident is told as something that really happened (within the "real" of the novel world) even though, according to the text, it is so unusual that it has never even been imagined before.

It is tempting to view this incident as a triumph of Lafayette's novelistic imagination. One might see her narrative as supremely "imaginative" by virtue of her having devised an incident that surpasses what has been imagined before—or *not* imagined before. However, what most strongly characterizes this whole scene is not its sensory quality—although it is more concretely detailed than is usual in Lafayette's style (e.g. the heat, the play of light and shadow, the heroine's informal apparel)—but an intensely logical brinkmanship, the insistence on *not* providing access to the heroine's imagination and on the set of ontological and cognitive conditions that distinguish this scene from all others ("to see her without her seeing him"). In a context in which the sensory and emotional values might dominate, Lafayette's habitual thematic preoccupations drive the narrative toward the basic insoluble *metaphysical* problem of desire, the "obscure object of desire." Or, in terms familiar to twentieth-century readers, "What do men want?" Does Nemours want this privileged access to the intimacy of his beloved even at the price of refraining from contact or communication with her? Or does he prefer to show himself, his desiring self, to her even at the cost of causing her to retreat into her social facade of modesty and virtue? We recall Madame's remark to the Prince de Clèves when he tells of seeing the mysterious beauty for the first time—"there was no such person as he described"—that are oddly appropriate for Nemours.[19] The woman Nemours sees in the garden pavilion, the woman engaged in a passionate and deliberate imaginative activity, can be seen only because she believes she cannot be seen. Once Nemours thrusts himself forward into the room with the princess, she immediately ceases her imagining. In order to see her in a way that corresponds to this hitherto *un*-imagined scene, Nemours must resist any contact that would allow the heroine to know what we the narrator and readers know. In other words, in order to preserve this privileged vision, Nemours must make sure that no one in his world knows what he has seen. And if no one knows this, then the incident remains suspended in a mode of experience that is somewhere between material reality and purely mental experience.

Lafayette thus uses this incident of concentric imagining (Nemours's quasi-imaginative vision framing the princess's imagining of Nemours) to deprive Nemours's "real" experience of its reality and to conflate it with an apparently imagined erotic scene. This *de-realization* is the opposite of the practice of imagination as we have seen it in other writers, who use imagination to endow purely mental representations with the sensory qualities of the concretely real. We, along with Nemours, infer that the princess is engaged in the more traditional process of providing herself with a sensory and sensuous experience of the absent Nemours. Yet what the narrative contains and displays is rather the experience of physical presence that conceals the all-important series of thoughts that endow the immediately perceptible, concrete scene with its value. Lafayette seems to be exemplifying here the metaphysical conception of an endless spiral of desire, which transcends and empties the physical realm. Or, to draw a comparison from the doctrines of imagination in the seventeenth century, Lafayette's work corresponds to François de Sales's *Treatise on Divine Love* (1614) rather than to his *Introduction to the Devout Life* (1609). In the *Treatise*, de Sales evokes the experience of a spirituality that goes beyond imagination because it no longer needs the support of sensory representation. To compare Lafayette and de Sales on this point is not to suggest an influence of the religious author on the novelist but to emphasize the similar depreciation of the physical.[20]

What Nemours feels in the garden pavilion is the powerful excitement of the heroine's *thought*. Despite the spectacular charms of this "perfect beauty" revealed by her condition of relative undress—"it was warm, and her head and shoulders had no other covering than her loosely fastened hair"—the narrative emphasizes that Nemours is fascinated more by her thoughts. For this reason the summary of what "no other lover ever enjoyed or imagined" culminates with the pleasure of seeing the woman "completely preoccupied" (*tout occupée*) with her thoughts of him. It is for her imagined Nemours that she is in a state of disordered undress and of "rapt attention." Simply seeing the princess in a similar place and costume but sound asleep or reading would not endow the scene with the value that comes here from the unseen, the heroine's still-concealed imagination. A peak at the slightly clad princess might have sufficed for some other hero, or even for Nemours himself earlier in his pursuit of Mme de Clèves, but Lafayette has pushed him upward on this spiral of desire toward a desire for more than physical possession.

This is, for Nemours, as good as it gets, and perhaps for the Princess as well. The events of that evening, misconstrued by M. de Clèves, lead to his death, a death precipitated—perhaps—by his imagination. The heroine's husband certainly becomes more gravely ill because of what he infers from the incomplete report of a gentleman he has sent to spy on Nemours. Here, as elsewhere in her novel, Lafayette plays with a figure of speech that has been described as central to her writing, ellipsis.[21] The spy, in a certain sense, tells his master nothing. In fact those are the informant's very words: "'I have *nothing* to report,' answered the gentleman, 'from which it is possible to form an accurate judgment. It is true that Monsieur de Nemours entered the garden in the woods two nights running, and called at Coulommiers the next day with Madame de Mercoeur'" (392/93, emphasis added). This succinct report frames a void into which the Prince de Clèves can project his interpretation, although he has no apparent consciousness of the freedom that is offered to him by this void. We know that the Prince instantly reached the conclusion that Nemours had a tryst with the Princesse de Clèves, but the narrator tells us nothing about the mental process that leads to this conclusion. Was he tormented by the *image* of his wife in Nemours's arms? Or was his thought purely a judgment, an abstraction on the order of "I have been betrayed?"[22] This latter supposition, however farfetched, lies within the range of possibilities open to the reader in Lafayette's two-tiered approach to narrative imagination. On one hand, the characters really *do* imagine, that is, their thought apparently takes into account sensory consciousness. On the other hand, the reader is neither given access to the imagining of the characters —to the way their mind experiences sights, sounds, smells, touch, and taste—nor is the reader guided toward any similar mental representation of the characters and their world. What was Nemours's hair like, was it wavy or straight? Did he wear a wig while he wandered in the woods thinking of the Princess? What were the slight but powerful specifics of the heroine's appearance that made her so much more charming than other young blonde women of the court?

After the scene in the pavilion, the novel does not share with us any further instances of enjoyable imaginings on the part of the heroine. Instead, the moment of her deliberate enjoyment of amorous imagination is associated with the guilt she feels for her husband's death.[23] This pavilion scene is a culminating moment, therefore, in the practice of imagination in *La Princesse de Clèves*. Yet it is prepared by an earlier event in the same location, when Mme de Clèves avows to her husband that she is in love with another man. The two incidents are connected by more than their location and even by more than their parallel construction as intimate moments observed by the *voyeur* Nemours. The earlier case of the *aveu* is also said to be something that had never been imagined by anyone. Lafayette has, in both instances, insisted on the theme of reality as the (almost?) unimaginable.

The dominance of reality over the realm of the imagined in this instance is a clue to Lafayette's general approach to imagination, one that is far from the technique of intentional imagining that runs throughout Scudéry's *Clélie*. To the extent that imagination, in the traditional philosophical sense, en-compasses both the perception of what is present and the representation of what is past or merely potential, this way of thinking appears in Lafayette's novels in the form of a severe limitation in the characters' abilities. They all *perceive* the world vividly in the present and they are driven to passionate extremes by the impact of beauty as well as by a host of minute visual and auditory signals that they detect and on which they spend countless hours of thought. Yet the characters generally have no freedom from the flow of perceptions, which they absorb passively. They are incapable of providing for themselves the margin of liberty that comes from a mastery of imagination in its potential for an *active* and inventive control of sense perception. As a result the Princesse de Clèves, the Prince de Clèves, the Duc de Nemours and the others are tormented by a sense of the inevitable aggression of the world around them. This aggression takes two forms: the obsession with significance and abdication of alternatives.

In their perception of the physical world, the characters are driven by a quest for the adequate interpretation of what they see and hear. As a consequence, sensory reality is quickly sorted, and only those details that bear significance are retained. The treatment of blushing is a case in point.[24] When the heroine blushes on hearing a compliment paid to her by the Duc de Nemours, both the heroine's mother and Nemours immediately start decoding the blush: "Madame de Chartres saw at once why her daughter did not go to the ball [. . . .] the confusion of Madame de Clèves made him suspect that the dauphiness's conjecture was not without some foundation in fact" (287/25). Throughout the novel such verbs of perception as "to appear," "to see," "to perceive" (*paraître, voir, percevoir*) provide the signposts of a novelistic structure based on the characters' constant interpretation of the voluntary and (more often) involuntary physical details that come to their attention. And the characters are, as a consequence, dependent on the stream of perceptions—particularly on sight—as these perceptions reach their awareness (through the involuntary imagination of the present), for these perceptions are the basis of the inferences that the characters are constantly making. In their quest for significance and their reduction of the external world to a system of signs (generally in the form of clues in the form of glances, absences, clothing), Lafayette's characters do not give themselves the freedom of detachment from messages which they receive and outcomes that derive ineluctably from those messages. While they do have an interior life, that life could not be farther from the world imagined by Montaigne, by the disciples of François de Sales, or even by Scudéry's characters. This inner world is a fevered reviewing of significant moments of the outer world from which the heroine, her husband, and Nemours cannot free themselves even for a moment. In this respect, Lafayette's characters lack *imagination*, in the sense of the capacity and the will to envisage the world freely, to master the flow of images, and to create alternatives to the world as immediately perceived by the senses. In their case imagination is crushed by the pressure of immediate sensory perception, on one side, and by the almost frantic exercise of judgment, on the other.

One of the important capacities of imagination, particularly as it is taught in the Stoic tradition, is to liberate the thinker from the tyranny of time. The sage inhabits the moment of her choosing, be it the present, the future, or the past. The exercises of philosophizing to learn to die (and to support other calamities) may indeed create apathy (the freedom from suffering), but they also can permit life in the present by concentration on the world in its objective sensory reality. The painful condition of Lafayette's characters is to so invest the present with significance that it loses all savor in the rush to understand its consequences, yet they are generally unable to create an inner world that could replace the present, as can de Sales's Philothée. As if to remind us of the danger of imagination, *La Princesse de Clèves* allows us to glimpse it once at work, in the heroine's garden pavilion, where her carefully contrived fantasy turns to guilt-laden disaster.

SIX

How the Ancients Modernized Imagination

Toward the end of the seventeenth century, France was stirred by the controversy known as the Quarrel of the Ancients and the Moderns. The confrontation between the partisans of antiquity and the champions of modernity had become inevitable. For a century, the French had been boasting both of being uniquely new and of being faithful to the ancient past. It is tempting to suppose that what we consider to be "modern" in the nineteenth and twentieth centuries derives from the Moderns of the Quarrel. As Joan DeJean has shown, however, the Moderns did not win, and subsequent French culture has a decided mixed ideological ancestry.[1] The importance of imagination to nineteenth and twentieth century culture does not flow from a Modern defense of imagination as a useful faculty. Instead, the Quarrel emphasized the dangers and defects of imagination, wiping out the positive idea of imaginative practice. To say that the Quarrel "modernized" imagination is to note a delicious irony. The Ancients made imagination seem such a negative thing that when this faculty reappeared in the subsequent century it had to be reinvented on a new basis.

In the last decades of the seventeenth century, it became common in literary criticism to denounce writers as being *too* imaginative.[2] The Ancients especially made use of this accusation, pushing imagination off onto the Moderns, who, from time to time, shot back accusations about excess imagination on the part of the Greek and Roman classics, especially Homer.[3] Instead of promoting imagination as a practice, the Modern spokesmen, particularly Charles Perrault, proclaimed the value of reason, rules, and art (in the sense of artifice) in opposition to the elements central to the Ancient position: the weight of tradition, an undefinable "taste" or genius on the part of the rare, gifted writer, and fidelity to the "natural."

In this debate between Ancients and Moderns, a new cultural audience was making its presence felt, an audience largely composed of women readers and writers.[4] The Ancients mocked the proliferation of contemporary fashionable writers and their public, particularly the female public that tended largely to be on the Modern side.[5] It is not a surprise then to see that the Ancients, in hurling toward the Moderns accusations that their literature was full of imagination but lacking in "genius" or natural talent, would gradually tie imagination to the feminine in an intentionally negative sense.[6]

IMAGINATION AND THE SUBLIME

In 1674 the celebrated satirist, poet, and influential man of letters, Nicolas Boileau (1636–1711) published a collection of works that included his versified *Art poétique* and his translation of *On the Sublime*. Although the Quarrel of the Ancients and the Moderns did not break out into open conflict until 1687, during a session of the French Academy, the divergence between modernists and partisans of Greco-Latin antiquity had been growing for decades. In translating a text attributed to the third-century orator Longinus, Boileau was clearly striking a blow for the Ancients.[7] The full title of Boileau's translation is *Treatise on the sublime, or on the marvelous in discourse, translated from the Greek of Longinus.*[8] Identifying the sublime with the marvelous *in discourse*, Boileau does not associate the marvelous with imagination. From his preface we can learn much about what the sublime (and thus, the marvelous) meant to this influential critic and translator.[9] Perhaps surprisingly, Boileau's sublime does not concern events that are unusual or hard to believe. It does not concern any kind of inner vision of the real world or any alternative reality. As the subtitle of the translation indicates, the sublime is the "marvelous in discourse," and Boileau's preface holds to a narrow, even technical, view of discourse: the choice of proper words, arranged in the proper order, and used in the proper circumstances to produce a certain effect on the audience. This desired effect is not the vivid representation of sights, sounds, smells, and so forth. Instead the sublime "raises up, ravishes, carries away" (338); it is the "Extraordinary, the Surprising, and [. . .] the Marvelous in discourse." Triggered by an unexpected combination of words (*un seul tour de paroles*) or a single thought (*une seule pensée*), the sublime—without using sense perceptions—overwhelms the audience in an instant.

Boileau's view of the sublime is close to a mathematical one, a certain highly unusual proportion between discourse and meaning, between signifier and signified. In the sublime, the signifier is unexpectedly small and the signified exceptionally large. When he distinguishes between the so-called "sublime style" and the true sublime, Boileau takes great pains to give an accurately quantified view of discourse and meaning: "The sublime style always uses big words; but the Sublime can be found in a single thought, a single figure, a single turn of phrase" (338). He gives two vivid examples of this proportion of word to meaning—a proportion so abnormal that we might well consider it an effective disproportion. Immediately after distinguishing the "sublime style" from the sublime, he quotes *Genesis*: "God said 'Let there be light; and there was light'" (*Dieu dit: Que la lumière se fasse; et la lumière se fit*). Boileau also gives a quotation from Corneille's *Le Cid*, from the scene in which the father of the Roman champions, the Horaces, believes a report that his surviving son has turned and run when he finds himself alone in combat against the three Alban warriors. Horace's sister asks her father, "'What would you have had him do against three?' He replied brusquely," says Boileau, "'Let him die.'"[10] Both of these examples combine concision with understatement. Not only are there very few words but the huge significance of the content is stated without acknowledgment of its extent. There are no adjectives or adverbs to point out the transcendental force required to make light *ex nihilo* or the peculiar strength of character required of a father to wish for the death of his son. These examples show the artistic nature of the sublime as a mastery of the grammatical tools necessary to produce the stunning disproportion of sound to meaning—both examples turn on the use of the subjunctive. This apparently minor or even pedantic observation actually points to a large, political feature of Boileau's sublime (as we will see shortly), but even without considering the ideological ramifications of these examples, it is clear that they are striking *formulations*. It is hard to see how *more* could be said with *less*, or how a single vowel sound could deliver a more effective "punch line" than *fit* or *mourût* in the concluding words of the quotations. Initially, at least, Boileau's exemplification of the sublime does cling very close to a semantic, nonimaged, nonsensual, and extremely verbal effect, so that the marvelous really is *in discourse*. The treatise on the sublime was, after all, attributed to a skilled professional of public speaking, who took seriously the methodic use of language.

Yet there is more than technique at stake here. What do these two examples of the subjunctive have in common besides concision and understatement? We should not forget that both expressions are also *commands* of astounding power. The two situations from which these examples come show what a person of authority (God the Father and the father of the Horaces, respectively) can do with a single phrase. All it takes is "let there be light" for light to be. The spareness of the phrasing implicitly contrasts the verbal fluff of everyday, weak, discourse (lots of words, little action) with the verbal power of the true master (few words, immense action). And although father Horace's expression is not followed by the death of his son, Corneille's tragedy leaves no doubt that an authoritative word can lead to death. Given that both of these examples of sublime discourse are also examples of paternal discourse, we will not be surprised to see that Boileau has a highly virile and even *macho* view of the *marvelous* or sublime, a view that is amply supported by the translated treatise.

What Boileau does with the *Treatise on the sublime* is propose an action-oriented, outward, masculine, and tight-lipped aesthetic to contrast with what he perceives as the imaginative, inward-oriented, feminine, and wordy aesthetic of the moderns. Oddly enough the audience of the sublime discourse that Boileau conceives is, in a sense, feminized—if the "masculine" is considered the gender of action and domination and the "feminine" is considered the gender of submission. The audience of the sublime style does not see it coming but is swept off its feet, struck speechless (*étonné*) by the power of the speaker who, in one concise verbal gesture has somehow said it all.

Longinus's treatise as translated by Boileau remains very strongly on the "supply-side" of verbal art, the training of the speaker to have an impact on an audience by a clever control of words. Contrary to future uses of the concept of the "sublime" or of the "marvelous" to describe transcendent experience or contemplation of nature, here the emphasis is on figures of speech, word choice, and delivery or performance.[11] For Longinus the sublime presupposes a gift of speaking well without which all technique is vain. For a gifted person, however, there are five sources of the sublime: elevation of spirit, vehemence or pathos, correct use of figures of speech, choice of words and diction, and word arrangement. All of these categories show the desire to impress an audience with a strong sense of hierarchy, separating the noble from the low. Most of them *could* be treated with an attention to the imagination, but Boileau's Longinus generally avoids developing them in that direction, cutting short a discussion that seems about to start. For instance, in writing about Homer's "decline" from the *Iliad* to the *Odyssey*, Longinus says,

> You don't find there that throng of movements and passions heaped one on top of the other. There is no longer that same power, and, so to speak, that same upswelling of discourse so fitting for action, and mixed with so many naive images of things. (355).

These "naive images" could be the starting point for a consideration of how an author visualized a scene and gave specific detailed cues for the audience to recreate or "see" the scene, but Longinus does not develop this line of thought nor does Boileau in his published remarks on the treatise. The criticism of Homer does, however, put Longinus's authority behind a cause dear to Boileau, the preference for "action" over analysis. The *Odyssey* is weaker than the *Iliad* not only because it devotes less space to strictly war-related topics but also because the Trojan war is set at a distance in time and thus reflected upon by the narrator-heroes. The mediation of subjective memory and the related emotional response makes the tale of Ulysses's return less noble: "the sad incidents that happen in the Iliad are often lamented by the heroes of the Odyssey as if they were well-known misfortunes that happened long before" (354). The distinction Longinus makes here, one that we know from its later development in Romanticism as the opposition between "naive" and "sentimental" discourse, implicitly but strongly condemns the recreation of past events through the imaginative memory and its associated sharing through narration. Even though the "action" of Homer's *Iliad* is narrated, it is easier for the audience to forget the mediation of language and to be swept away by the heroic carnage.

Throughout the treatise, Longinus insists on the speaker's need to make the audience become less vigilant and lower its critical standards so that rhetorical tactics that would otherwise be recognized and even rejected will pass unobserved.[12] This is a recurrent theme of the *Treatise on the sublime*, but one of the most striking examples is also one of the rather infrequent mentions of imagination. It occurs in the chapter "Of images":

> For since in all things we pause to look at the shiny and sparkling parts, the audience's mind is easily carried away by an image that the speaker gives in the midst of reasoning; and this image, *striking the imagination, keeps the audience from examining the proofs so closely* because of the blazing light with which the image covers and surrounds the speech [. . . .] But that's enough said about the kind of Sublimity that consists of thoughts [. . .] (366–67, emphasis added).

Although Longinus concludes this chapter on images by saying that this kind of sublimity comes from "*the nobility of soul*, or from *imitation*, or from *imagination*" (367), the advice concerning imagination shows a remarkable difference from the other sources of sublime. Greatness of soul and the power of imitation are positive qualities attributed to the orator or to the great heroes or patrons of whom he speaks. Oddly, however, Longinus does not present— in any other passage—imagination as a distinct quality of the orator. Instead, as we see from the example of imagination at work in the practice of rhetoric, imagination is a quality (or perhaps a defect) that appears mostly on the side of the audience. Rather than giving advice on how the orator should develop his imagination or defining what the imagination of an orator is, Longinus only says how useful it is to strike the audience's imagination. The implication is that an orator can have too much imagination but that an audience cannot—though the audience, being passive, must simply be guided by the active oratorical force.[13] The negative and passive attributes of imagination are further established by the purpose with which this faculty is associated: a deception made possible by disrupting the power of judgment. The "image" in question is not necessarily something fabulous or innovative, but merely a sense perception in the traditional Aristotelian mode. It fixes the audience's attention on something concrete, because the audience is assumed to be sense-oriented and inferior to the speaker in mental discipline.[14]

Although Boileau's prefatory *Remarks* on Longinus are a direct expression in Boileau's own voice, when we read the translation of the *Treatise* itself we have to grapple with questions about Boileau's adoption of the Greek author's doctrine. Philip Lewis has described Boileau as appropriating Longinus's text as his own.[15] A passage that concerns imagination in rhetorical training stands out for the particular tension between the Greek's anti-monarchical stance and Boileau's own proximity to the Bourbon monarchy. Longinus describes the deforming effect of monarchy on the *imagination* of boys, limiting their future speaking ability:

> But we, he continued, who have learned from our earliest years to suffer the yoke of a legitimate domination, who have been swaddled, so to speak, in the customs and the behavior of a Monarchy, while we still have a pliable imagination that can be easily formed; in a word, we who have never tasted that flowing and fecund spring of eloquence—I mean, liberty—what happens ordinarily for us is that we become great and magnificent flatterers. (400).

The term "imagination" is rare in Boileau and even in his translation of Longinus, so it leaps out here as central to the formation of future orators. Yet there is an odd consistency, for once again "imagination" is placed in the position of receptiveness and passivity. Before they become men, while they are still in their "tender" years and can be shaped or written upon—"impressions" here is still a live metaphor (*lors que nous avions encore l'imagination tendre, et capable de toutes sortes d'impressions*), bringing to mind the shaping of clay or wax—their view of the world is constructed for them by the men in charge. Imagination is thus associated with the weak, opposed to the strong, and dissociated from will and adulthood. It is also seen as a conservative faculty insofar as it keeps the shape it is given, not as a faculty that can continue throughout life to reformulate the view of the world.

The rhetorical use of imagination in Boileau's Longinus comes into sharp focus if we compare his exploitation of the listener's imagination to the teaching of Quintilian that we saw above.[16] In Quintilian's view, the gifted public speaker will develop *his own* imagination and become an imaginative person (*euphantasiotos*). By giving himself a vivid inner vision of an event about which he is arguing, Quintilian's orator would speak with much greater fire, urgency, and conviction. Boileau endorses a different view of imagination in rhetoric, in which the cool, levelheaded writer or speaker will inflame and exploit the audience's imagination.

FÉNELON AND THE IMAGINATION OF CHILDREN

The Ancient view that imagination is prevalent among the weak, the feminine, and the childish became the basis for innovations in childhood education. Boileau's younger contemporary, François Salignac de La Mothe-Fénelon (1651–1715), was a prolific writer on religious, political, and educational topics. His novel *The Adventures of Telemachus* (*Les Aventures de Télémaque*, 1699–1717), written while he was preceptor of the Duc de Bourgogne, second son of Louis XIV, was an immediate and long-lasting publication success.[17] Part of his educational program for his young pupil, *The Adventures of Telemachus* puts into practice many of the ideas about imagination that Fénelon had presented in his treatise *On the Education of Girls* (*De l'éducation des filles*, 1687).[18]

In *On the Education of Girls*, Fénelon writes copiously about imagination and its usefulness in the education of children. Yet, at the same time, he shares the belief of his contemporaries among the Ancient camp that imagination is a childish and "feminine" way of thinking, one that can be used in a controlled way not by the person whose thoughts are at the center of this work—the child—but by the adult educator. This is a decisive shift away from the emphasis in such earlier writers as Montaigne and de Sales on the individual adult's use of his or her *own* imagination. For Fénelon, as for Boileau, imagination is not a skill that is to be taught but a weakness that is to be exploited, not an *active* way of thinking that can be directed by any alert and properly educated adult but a *passive* way of thinking that abounds in those individuals whose minds have not matured to the point at which reason replaces imagination.

His low regard for imagination might lead us to assume that Fénelon would try to exclude this type of thinking from his educational program or that he would at the very least try to minimize it. Nothing could be further from the truth: Fénelon is paradoxically one of the greatest promoters of imagination in all of the seventeenth century. He is convinced that educators have repeatedly failed because they do not center the instruction of children on sensory perception, that is, imagination.

The child, boy or girl, according to Fénelon, has a soft and impressionable brain. He means this quite literally. The child's brain receives the mark of sights, sounds, and other sensory data just as a warm piece of wax receives the imprint of a ring. Thus, Fénelon connects his educational program directly with the central Western philosophical text on imagination, Aristotle's *De Anima*, where we read that "a sense is what has the power of receiving into itself the sensible forms of things without the matter, in the way in which a piece of wax takes on the impress of a signet-ring without the iron or gold; what produces the impression is a signet of bronze or gold, but not *qua* bronze or gold."[19] For Fénelon this metaphor dovetails nicely with medical ideas about the development of the brain. The child's brain is literally a soft, warm lump on which the senses leave their mark:

> The substance of their brain is soft and grows harder every day. As for their mind, it knows nothing—everything is new to it. This softness of the brain permits everything to imprint itself there, and the surprise caused by new things draws their intense interest and makes them very curious [. . . .] The brains of children are both hot and damp, and that makes children move about continuously.[20]

From Fénelon's point of view, this sense-oriented and receptive mental nature is simply an unavoidable fact about children. In a way, of course, Fénelon is surprisingly "modern" in that he adopts the concept of developmental appropriateness long before it became a central doctrine of childhood education in the Western world. Yet in another sense Fénelon may appear to be entirely within the tradition of antiquity in that he views imagination as being simply the means by which the mind internalizes the impressions of the outside world. Although he does not bother to define "imagination," it is clear that this is an entirely sense-oriented way of thinking. In writing, he advises, "strike their imagination energetically, do not present anything to them that is not couched in terms of sensory images (*images sensibles*)" (125).

Methodically basing his approach to education—*éducation* being a term with a more inclusive meaning than its current English cognate and signifying "upbringing," or, in other words, the general formation of the child and not only scholastic or intellectual learning—on the conviction that the child is a sensory sponge, Fénelon urges the creation of an educational stage-set where the child will record and store away all that he or she sees, hears, and feels. Education must begin *immediately*, he claims, and not wait until the child is able to speak, since imagination—the stored assemblage of all impressions—is at work long before language and in view of the coming of language. Basing himself on Augustine, Fénelon describes the foundation of language in the physical:

> The child [. . .] notices the object that is signified by each word. He does this, sometimes guided by the natural movements of the speaker's body that touch or show the objects about which one is speaking, and sometimes guided by the insistent repetition of the same word to denote the same object. Indeed, the temperament of the child's brain gives the child a wonderful capacity to be imprinted with all these images. (96).

One result of this insight into the child's imagination is that Fénelon takes into account minute physical details that would be of little, or of only accidental, importance to an educator committed to a reason-centered pedagogy. Hence, it matters not simply *what* one tells or shows a child, but *how*. The tone of voice, the facial expression, the body language, the time of day, all details of the circumstances of a lesson must be calculated in view of the trace that will be left in the child's memory.[21] The educator or governess or any adult who spends time in the child's presence must therefore make a very unusual effort to pay attention to many details that are normally of little importance to an adult. In fact, the pedagogic attention that Fénelon advocates reverses the usual hierarchy by which "content" or the rational element in all communication or action is given value far above matters of style. In order to mold the child's mind—that warm, soft, and wet thing—Fénelon is obliged to devote the greatest amount of attention to imagination, the mental activity that dominates the child, even though imagination is inferior to reason.

Oddly enough, a pedagogy that is based on the culture of naturalness and the avoidance of artifice, needs to adopt a high degree of artifice, and even outright deceit, to reach its ends. Here is a typical reflection on this subject:

> At this age, when the child is praised and when she has not yet been con-tradicted, she conceives chimerical hopes, that lead to an infinite number of mistakes during the rest of life. I have seen children who believed that people were talking about them every time they heard someone talk in secret, because they noticed that this had often been the case. They supposed that every-thing about them was exceptional and admirable. Consequently, you should watch over children without showing them that you are thinking much about them. (99).

The governess needs to *conceal* from the child her constant attention in order to keep the child from considering itself the center of the world. So that in order to form the child's correct perception of the world it is necessary to deceive the child by a form of theatre. It is precisely at the moment when the governess is most attentive to the child, most concerned about the child, that she must feign nonchalance, not simply in her words—which, after all, are primarily directed toward the child's largely undeveloped reason—but especially in those outward indications that will be grasped by the child's overdeveloped imagination: tone of voice, touch, glances, etc.

Fénelon's ideas about the child's imagination influenced his most endur-ing published work, *The Adventures of Telemachus*, a novel that was conceived as a didactic book to be read by the Duc de Bourgogne and was first printed in circumstances that are still obscure in 1699.[22] This text is clearly based on Fénelon's belief that young people must be educated through their imagination and that they must be educated without realizing that the primary purpose of an activity is instruction. It presents itself simply as a novel, like so many others in the seventeenth century, that continues or fills-in gaps in well-known narratives of antiquity. Constructed to permit the easy identification of the intended reader, the young duke, second in line for the throne of France, with the hero of the novel, Telemachus, son of Ulysses, *The Adventures of Telemachus* is one of the seventeenth-century narratives that is richest in concrete detail. In the eighth book, for instance, Venus, craving vengeance against Telemachus for having overcome love, rises up to Olympus to demand Jupiter's help:

> She rises toward radiant Olympus, where the Gods were assembled around the throne of Jupiter. From this point, they see the stars that spin beneath their feet. They perceive earth's globe as a little pile of mud. The immense seas appear to them as drops of water sprinkled on this piece of mud. In their sight, the greatest kingdoms are only a little sand that covers the surface of that mud.[23]

Although Fénelon's descriptive style may not be remarkable nor especially detailed by more recent standards, this fairly typical passage from *The Adventures of Telemachus* is far more concrete in its description than the work of Lafayette or even Scudéry. It is not, however, more "realistic." On the contrary, Fénelon guides his reader through vivid sensual representations of entirely fantastic events. How the earth looks to the Olympian gods is a pure exercise in imagination, unfettered by reality even though it is governed by conventions of literary verisimilitude, based on a reading of Greek and Latin literature.

Fénelon engages a wide range of the senses: smell, sight, sound, taste. For instance, in the description of a celebratory sacrifice and feast:

> Between the city and the enemy army, they sacrificed one hundred snow-white heifers and just as many bulls of the same color, with gilded and beribboned horns. One could hear echoing in the nearby mountains the frightful moaning of the victims falling beneath the holy knife [. . . .] The sacrificers burned incense on the altars and it formed a thick cloud perfuming the countryside with its sweet fragrance. . . .

From the twenty-first century perspective, this description does not immediately draw forth the adjective "imaginative;" we can recognize here the commonplaces of ancient literature and especially a good knowledge of Homer. But our post-Romantic habit of understanding imagination as "creative" makes it difficult to see that *any* appeal to thinking with the senses is imaginative, to Fénelon's way of thinking. The fact that these descriptions simply require that the writer and the reader engage in conventional semantic association (*victime* + sound = *mugir*) does not prevent those associations from indicating "sensory" rather than purely intellective thought.

Fénelon's intended reader is an adolescent and adolescents are inclined to think with the body and about the body through *images sensibles*. In fact, Fénelon seems to have been attentive to the adolescent boy's fascination with those things that would be indecorous if they were not so thoroughly authorized by the classical tradition. For instance, not only does the blood of the victim drip from the altar but the augurs (*aruspices*) "interpreted the entrails that were still quivering" (199). The description of Telemachus's descent to the underworld includes lightening, thunder, earthquake, a terrible smell, and cold sweat bathing the hero's body (305). These sensory descriptions seem to be the price to pay for the more abstract lessons in economic policy, foreign affairs, public relations and even nutrition that fill long stretches of *The Adventures of Telemachus* and that are frequently heavily weighted toward nonsensory (nonimaginative) thinking. Mentor, for instance, teaches Idoménée, king of Salente:

> Sobriety makes the simplest food very tasty. It gives both the most vigorous health and the purest and most dependable pleasures. You should limit your meals to the best ingredients, prepared without sauces. This art of stimulating men's appetites beyond their real need is the art of a poisoner. (219).

In such passages, even when writing about physical and even corporeal matters, Fénelon moves into a nonsensory vocabulary, showing that one can write of eating, for instance, by engaging readers' imaginations or their judgment.

Yet a striking feature of Fénelon's novel, even in the midst of the most detailed physical descriptions, is that imagination appears as an explicit topic within the characters' conversations only in *negative* terms. One of the philosophically inclined characters who convey moral lessons compatible with Mentor's doctrines, Hasaël, juxtaposes the hateful and dangerous power of sexuality—as seen in the cult of Venus—with the enlightenment of the intellectual life. Those who do not seek the transcendent truth of the spirit live in a world of shadows; they are "carried away by the pleasures of the senses, and by the charm of *imagination*" (92 emphasis added). The only exception to the negative presentation of this faculty is one that replicates, within the novel, the relationship of Fénelon to his reader. That is, the teller of the story is an older, wiser person whose gift for vivid presentation allows the younger, less experienced person to be captivated and guided by the rhetorical power of the teller. Telemachus says of the Egyptian sage Termosiris that when the latter told a story, "he told things so well that you believed you *saw* them" (53, emphasis added). All the credit for this visualization is given to the narrator, not to the listener. Imagination, in this way, is simply part of the structure turned toward the reader, to permit the reader to experience the story in both sensory and intellectual ways. Yet neither Fénelon, as general narrator of *The Adventures of Telemachus*, nor Mentor as Telemachus's teacher encourages, his disciple to develop imagination as an independent skill.

This split between a highly descriptive style in Fénelon's presentation to the reader and a total absence of any *positive* instruction on the ways of thinking with the senses actually carries out a distinction that has become thoroughly familiar to modern literary criticism. For us, as we see from innumerable studies, it is *literature* and the *arts* that are imaginative. Literature does not instruct us in the ways of the imagination but uses and proceeds from imagination. We find it normal that Fénelon as a writer uses imagination, but we would probably be somewhat disconcerted at seeing imagination appear as an activity that the characters undertake, unless they are characters in a novel about writers.

In the case of *Telemachus* it is no doubt obvious that the reader and several of the characters of the novel are meant to be similar, or to have similar roles. If the young Duc de Bourgogne is the initial intended audience, then clearly he was intended to perceive Telemachus as an ideal version of himself, the heroic son of a heroic father but also a young man in need of instruction. So Telemachus, within the story, and Fénelon's pupil in the real world are both receivers of the instruction that comes largely from Mentor-Minerva's words but also from the "adventures" themselves, the experiences of Telemachus. Within the story of *Telemachus*, other characters learn as well, and some both learn and convey their learning in their words (e.g. Philoctète). If someone other than the duc de Bourgogne plays the role of reader, then the instruction conveyed by the novel is interpreted *mutatis mutandis*—even someone who is not going to be a prince can learn, first, what are the qualities of a good prince and thus the qualities that a subject can expect of a good prince, and second, what makes a state happy and prosperous.

None of these lessons explicitly concerns the training of the mind to use the way of thinking about material things that is imagination. Thus, the split between the skills to be acquired by a prince and by all those who surround him usefully in a prosperous state, on one hand, and the skills needed to write a novel such as *The Adventures of Telemachus*, on the other hand, is quite sharp. The writer needs to possess the imagination to describe the physical world—and *absent* physical world—in its sensory details, but no one else is assigned this task. The reader, doubtless, is meant to imagine the scenes described, but the narrative voice does not intervene to urge particularly vivid, concentrated, or participatory thinking along these lines. It is not hard to understand why Fénelon does not include any definite injunction to picture what is happening (as Scudéry often does). If Fénelon considers his reader to be a young person, then the author assumes that thinking about physical things, *choses sensibles*, is not only a capacity that the reader already possesses in abundance but even an inclination that is all *too* powerful.[24] Thus, the author's inclusion of detailed description is both a concession to, and an alert exploitation of, the discursive needs of the reader.

The reader, as a young and thus excessively imaginative person, is extremely limited in what he can produce, imaginatively, on his own. This is so because the child, though possessing a mind that is alert to all sensory stimulation, is *re*active rather than active in its mental activity, possessing a "wonderful capacity to be imprinted with all these images."[25] Thus, the child-reader depends on the *active* imagination of the writer to be able to represent mentally such events as a Greek sacrificial feast, Calypso's island, the descent to the underworld, and many other entirely foreign and new things. This vast array of colorful detail will, following Fénelon's educational doctrines, fix itself in the child's mind while at the same time holding the child's attention for instructional purposes. The reader's imagination is thus used and filled but not developed as an independent and active faculty.

As a consequence of this division of activity between the writer and the reader, writers of novels are required to be able to imagine actively while readers need only imagine reactively or passively. In this latter sense literature, *belles lettres*, will stimulate the reader's imagination, but only insofar as the reader is a receiver of literature. The active imagination is henceforth the property of that group of people who produce literary works, and the study of imagination becomes, increasingly, a branch of poetics. Fénelon was of his time in assigning imagination to the specialized disciplines of pedagogy, literature (as we know it), and the visual arts. Yet for Fénelon and his fellow partisans of the Ancients, to locate imagination in this way was not a recognition of something wonderful and intrinsically valuable about imagination. On the contrary, they set imaginative thinking in the "creative" arts not only below reason (as do most earlier writers who mention imagination) but in the position of a potentially dangerous concession to the needs of certain publics. The positive valuation of imagination as *creative* later occurs in conjunction with a revolution in the way of thinking about childhood and the natural world that would have horrified Fénelon if he had been able to foresee it. The hot, wet, absorbent, and sensorily oriented mind of the child would never have seemed to Rapin, Boileau, and Fénelon a valuable source of creative energy.[26] Yet the child's passivity and orientation toward the world of the senses forms the basis of the educational program of Fénelon's successor, the Genevan polymath Jean-Jacques Rousseau.

FROM IMAGINATION TO SENSIBILITY

Jean-Jacques Rousseau is today widely seen as a key figure in the development of Romanticism, and Romanticism in turn is usually described as advancing and even sacralizing the concept of the creative imagination. For instance, Allan Bloom's much discussed book *The Closing of the American Mind* attributes to Rousseau an exceptional influence and one that culminates in the rehabilitation of imagination: "After him, community, virtue, compassion, feeling, enthusiasm, the beautiful and the sublime, *and even imagination, the banished faculty, had their innings against modern philosophy and science.*"[27] Bloom is not wrong, and yet most of what Rousseau had to say about imagination is vehemently negative. In understanding just how Rousseau could have given imagination its "innings," we can recognize retrospectively just how distinct was the seventeenth-century approach to imagination. With Rousseau the will-driven, individualistic and active imagination that provided an inner retreat and gave thinkers freedom from immediate influence of the senses is replaced by a new concept, *sensibility*, that is involuntary and outward turning. In this shift, the relatively democratic belief that almost anyone can learn to direct her or his imagination is replaced by an three-tier society of the corrupt, the learner who has been saved from society, and the transcendent teacher.

In Rousseau's vast corpus of writings, one in particular descends directly from the tumultuous culture wars of the end of the seventeenth century.

Emile, or on Education (1762) specifically mentions Fénelon's *Adventures of Telemachus*.[28] Both are stories of a boy's education and also models of educational reform. Rousseau's book, much more than Fénelon's, comments extensively on imagination, and provides a guide to protecting the boy against his imagination. Rousseau was quite conscious of the traditional, scholastic, theory of imagination as a faculty that intervened between the raw stimulus of the senses and the generalizing, abstract power of judgment.[29] This background is evident in the ideal educational model for boys that he sets forth in *Emile*, where a tutor openly modeled on Rousseau has complete educational control over a wealthy but otherwise quite ordinary boy named Emile. Rousseau's text, which weaves together anecdotes of his own teaching experience, advice in the imperative about how the reader should teach a child, resounding maxims, and narrative passages concerning the adventures of a first-person teacher and the boy Emile, devotes much space to the education of the senses. As a key text in the history of what we know today as developmental psychology, *Emile* begins with the limited mental and sensory activity of the infant and counsels against premature introduction of mental tasks that are beyond the child's capacity. At the beginning of life, according to Rousseau, memory and imagination do not yet function, and the infant is entirely dominated by the senses. So the tutor works to help the child associate what he senses with the object that produces the sensation (44). As part of this learning, the child must encounter pain and learn about the relation between certain objects and the unpleasant sensations they can cause. The child must become used to pain and not overly tender or sensitive. Rousseau claims that the education of the senses is the most neglected part of traditional teaching: "The first faculties that develop and mature in us are the senses. These are the first faculties we should cultivate; they are instead the only ones we forget about, the ones we most neglect" (137). The positive training of the senses through routine is one of the first steps toward a major goal of *Emile*: reducing the activity of the child's nascent imagination. Through exercises that Rousseau describes as "purely natural and mechanical" (138) the child will learn to recognize immediately what he hears, what he sees, what he smells, and so forth. This immediate, habitual perception will forestall imaginative mental creations. Especially important for this purpose are games played at night in the dark, so that Emile will not behave like almost all ordinary people, even very smart and rationalistic ones, who are afraid when they are in the dark because their imagination causes them to create mental pictures of possible danger: "If I hear a noise, I hear thieves; if I hear nothing, I see ghosts . . ." (144).

The educator's purpose in conducting games played in the dark is to *kill imagination* with habit, for only new objects, says Rousseau, stimulate imagination (144): "For objects that we see every day, it is not imagination that operates but rather memory [. . .]." Since the child has no imagination, this training is aimed at heading off the future imaginings of the adult.

Imagination develops in adolescence about the same time as the individual matures sexually. In the state of nature, the adolescent becomes interested in sex later than he would in society, especially in the most refined societies:

Nature's instruction is late and slow; that of men is almost always premature. In the former case, the senses awaken the imagination; in the latter, the imagination awakens the senses. It gives them a precocious activity that cannot fail to weaken individuals, first of all, and then in the long term the human race itself. A comparison that is of broader application and more trustworthy than one based on climate is that puberty and a strong sexual urge always arrive earlier among civilized and educated peoples than among barbarous and ignorant ones. (251).

The challenge for the educator is to prevent or at least direct the boy's imagination away from the attractive images of sex. The best way to do this is to hold the boy close to the world of the senses. Rousseau does not fear the direct perception of sex but rather mental images that depart from reality and embellish it. Refined people, by inventing terms and practices to (partially) conceal sex while alluding to it, simply stimulate imagination. In contrast,

One needs to have lived among coarse and simple people to know how long a happy ignorance can prolong the innocence of children. It is a spectacle both touching and comical to see both sexes, protected only by the impunity of their hearts, continue into the bloom of their growth and beauty the naïve games of childhood and show by their companionship the purity of their pleasure. (252).

This openness, which remains at the level of the sense perceptions and does not activate the imagination, is in contrast to the "soiled imaginations" of refined society.

Even in a society that is not close enough to nature to permit the mingling of the two sexes in the naïve way, simple and direct language in response to the boy's question about sex will quench any drift toward imagination. In fact, the more coarse and unpleasant detail the educator gives the child, the better: "Joining to coarse words the unpleasant ideas that match them, we stifle the first flare-ups of imagination: we do not forbid him to say these words and to have these ideas; but we give him, without his realizing it, a certain aversion to remembering them" (254). In Emile's education, solitude is prized, but this ideal solitude is not the solitude of most young people and certainly not the solitude of the followers of Montaigne, of François de Sales, or of Sévigné. They would have books and would read. For Rousseau, this solitary reading and the *silence du cabinet* is terribly dangerous because it awakens and feeds the imagination. Rousseau urges educators to maintain the boy in an ideal solitude, away from corrupting influences of books—"reading is the plague of childhood" (115)—and conversation, in order to allow nature to follow its slow course of development without the harmful intervention of mental representations that outrun actual physical experience.

Yet Rousseau admits the need to bow before the inevitable onset of the pubescent imagination. It can be controlled and directed—not by the adolescent, but by the skilled teacher—with the help of a well-chosen book. Here, Rousseau seems to be taking his cue from Fénelon, but in doing so he also emphasizes for his French readers how different is the pedagogical world of *Emile* from that of the author of *The Adventures of Telemachus*. Rousseau takes a position that, like so much in his pedagogy, seems to be a radicalized version of Fénelon. Like Fénelon, he prefers that his pupil not imagine actively but simply absorb the vivid representations the teacher provides. But Rousseau goes much, much further than Fénelon in curtailing the imaginative wanderings of the male adolescent. Where Fénelon exploits the exotic world of Homeric Greece to sublimate and allegorize the adolescent's aggressive and sexual nature, preparing him for an adult life of princely duty, Rousseau chooses as Emile's only permissible reading a book that brings the child back to his childhood experience. Where *Telemachus* draws the boy's thoughts out of his self-centered childhood, Rousseau chooses as his ideal book an adventure that simply presents the child with the quintessence of childhood experiences based on physical sensation and an almost exclusive relationship to things, rather than people.

At a first reading of *Emile* it is surely hard to resist amazement and even a laugh when Rousseau reveals his choice of Emile's first book. Indeed, Rousseau builds into his announcement all the suspense of a televised awards show. His buildup begins with the ringing declaration, "I hate books" (*Je hais les livres*). Vehemently declaring his hatred of books—the world of purely mental representation, devoid of actual physical and sensory experience— Rousseau longs for some way to bring to his pupil in some concentrated form the fruit of all those patiently repeated life lessons that sediment themselves into the child's knowledge. Rousseau dares to dream of "a situation where all the natural needs of man appear in sense experience (*d'une manière sensible*) to the mind of the child" (210). This epitome of experiential, material learning would be for his pupil, as Rousseau says, "the first exercise for his imagination." Rousseau knows that he has his reader's attention and plays with his curiosity: "What is this marvelous book? Is it Aristotle? is it Pliny? is it Buffon? No; it's Robinson Crusoe" (211).

Why *Robinson Crusoe*? Rousseau explains that the value of this book is that it depicts a man completely isolated from society and depending entirely on himself for his survival. Rousseau goes even further to make it clear that the portions of Defoe's text not concerned with Robinson's experience on the island are of no importance—the novel is interesting *débarrassé de tout son fatras*, "with all the nonsense discarded" (211). Emile is not going to read this book with the attention of a literary critic. In fact, he should be so unaware of *Robinson Crusoe* as a constructed representation, as a thing made out of words and ideas, that he has an almost hallucinatory experience of identification with Defoe's character:

> I want [Emile] to get obsessed about this book so that he is always thinking about his fort, about his she-goats, about his plantings. Let him learn in detail, not in books, but from things, everything you need to know in such a situation. Let him believe that he is Robinson himself; let him see himself dressed in skins, with a big hat, a big sword, the whole grotesque outfit of this character, except for the parasol that he won't need. (211).

As an imaginative exercise, one that the child does not devise but accept from his teacher, the Robinson Crusoe experience simply doubles back on the child's earlier learning from *objets sensibles*, from the objects of the senses. Robinson Crusoe is a man who lives in the ideal solitude that Rousseau has tried to construct for his pupil. Where Rousseau as pedagogue acts as a barricade between Emile and the social world, Defoe has simply placed an ocean. The book *Robinson Crusoe* is meant as a last-ditch effort to shield Emile both from his nascent imagination (which marks a withdrawal from the world of the senses themselves in favor of a supplement or replacement for the senses) and from the awareness of human society, especially of the company of women.

The Robinson Crusoe game marks the end of the pedagogy of the *sensible* in its early, literal meaning.[30] With regret, Rousseau acknowledges that after this point, the teacher will have to bow to the inevitability of Emile's awareness of human society and thus a shift to learning based on human relationships:

> If your pupil were alone, you would have nothing to do; but everything that surrounds him inflames his imagination. The torrent of prejudices carries him along: in order to hold him back, you have to push him in the opposite direction. You must arrange for sentiment to obstruct imagination, and for reason to silence the opinion of men. The source of all passions is sensibility, and imagination determines their course. (256).

First comes the pedagogy of sense (based on the directly perceived physical world), then the pedagogy of imagination (based on the mental recreation of that physical world, with the help of Defoe's book), and now the pedagogy of "sensibility." With the concept of sensibility Rousseau introduces something that we did not find in any of the earlier French authors who wrote about imagination. The term "sensibility" itself is ancient, but it was not a central concept. For Rousseau, it is not only important but even crucial. In Rousseau's *Emile*, it is not an exaggeration to say that imagination is rejected and sensibility is put in its place, or that the term "imagination" is emptied of its traditional meaning and made into a container for this new, positive quality of sensibility. Yet this important quality of Emile's mind comes to us with little definition and with a confusing pedigree.

The child, as Rousseau points out, has no imagination but only the senses. Therefore the child is *sensible*: "We are born sensitive, and, from the moment of our birth, we are affected in various ways by the objects that surround us" (*Nous naissons sensibles, et, dès notre naissance, nous sommes affectés de diverses manières par les objets qui nous environnent*, 8) This first and oldest meaning of the term *sensible* simply acknowledges the physical senses as our sole source of knowledge of the outside world. It is certain that Rousseau approves strongly of acknowledging and developing the senses—in opposition to the mental faculty that is able to combine, modify, or distort the information that comes from the senses—and that Rousseau's ideal adolescent is so habituated to the sensory reality of his body that he finds no interest in imagining his or anyone else's body.

However the *sensibility* that Rousseau begins to promote at this point in *Emile*—at puberty, corresponding to the fourth of the five parts of the book—is not exactly the same thing as the sensibility that consisted merely of the ability to receive sensory data. In this passage, as in many later ones,

Rousseau links sensibility with sentiment, and sentiment is emphatically not, for him, a reaction to an external physical stimulus. Instead, sentiment, which Rousseau may have gotten from Pascal or some other writer in the Augustinian-Jansenist current, seems to be an inherent part of the human mind or spirit that conditions how people perceive the world and themselves in relation to the world.[31] Here is the knotty paragraph in which Rousseau juxtaposes sentiment, sensibility, and imagination:

> The first sentiment to which a carefully-raised young man is susceptible is not love, but friendship. The first act of his nascent imagination is to teach him that there are other people like himself, and the human race affects him before sex does. So this is another advantage of prolonged innocence: it is to profit from his nascent sensibility to plant in the heart of the young adolescent the first seeds of humanity: an advantage that is so precious because it is the only time of life when this attention can have a true success. (258).

Both imagination and sensibility are "nascent" (*naissante*) in the adolescent. The exact relationship is not clear, but somehow imagination, which seems to be an inevitable concomitant of adolescence, has been kept free of any sexual content so that it fills instead with nonsexual images of people. In the imagination, the encounter of these images produces a new kind of sensibility—or awareness—, not to objects (through the senses, in the ancient meaning of the term) but to people through the mental image of people as being like himself. This mental representation of other people as being like himself contrasts with Rousseau's description of the slightly less developed child raised outside socially corrupting influences, the natural child who "loves his sister the way he loves his watch, and his friend like his dog" (256).

Unlike the sensibility of the child, which simply reacts to objects, this new sensibility is joined with the mental representation of people. Moreover, unlike Montaigne deliberately making mental images of possible deaths or Sévigné picturing her daughter's home, Rousseau's adolescent does not deliberately create images of people. Instead, this "first act" of the adolescent imagination comes to the boy as a new and apparently irresistible idea that he had no intention of calling forth—*Le premier acte de son imagination naissante est de lui apprendre qu'il a des semblables. . . .* This passage is one of scores in *Emile* that present imagination primarily as an *involuntary* activity. It is most often bad—sexual images being among the worst—but it can occasionally be useful.

The choice of the term *sensibilité*, though slightly confusing after the many passages in which this quality is reserved for such physical, sensory perception as touch, sight, and hearing, is enormously important in Rousseau's recovery and reconstruction of imagination. By using this term, Rousseau stresses a kind of mental activity that will fit into the conceptual spectrum between judgment, on one side, and simple sense perception on the other. In this place, the traditional location of imagination as the bridge between sensation and judgment, Rousseau seeks to encourage an alternative to traditional imagination.

To evoke this activity, Rousseau uses language previously used for pure sensory, physical perception because sensibility—in the new meaning that the author assigns to it—is closer to sense perception than to the ancient faculty of imagination. The crucial difference between sensibility and the earlier type of imagination is that sensibility is both involuntary and outward-turning.

The adolescent does not choose to be sensible. The new social sensibility that Rousseau establishes as the ideal is no more the conscious work of the adolescent than is the child's sense of touch. The *objets sensibles* that surround the child and educate him "naturally" do so by causing various degrees and types of sensation in response to the child's instinctively curious explorations. In this way, the child's education through the senses has a remarkably but paradoxically "passive" character. The child is constantly in motion but is on the receiving end of the formative impact of the physical world. The child's body is active, but his mind is passive, impressionable, and incapable of detaching itself from the stream of sense data. Insofar as he considers the child a tender object on which the world impresses itself, Rousseau is in the same pedagogical world as Fénelon.

In addition to being involuntary on the child's part, the early education by sense objects is entirely outward-turning. This early education simply consists of exposing the child to a multitude of sensations, not at all of trying to stimulate or direct the interior faculties such as imagination and memory, for these are entirely inactive in the child. Almost all of Rousseau's energetic pedagogical pronouncements aim at removing the social buffers between the child and the environment: "let him run, let him play, let him fall down a hundred times a day, so much the better: he will learn all the sooner to pick himself up" (61). Rousseau's child will be covered with bruises, but happy in his freedom of contact with the outside world of sensation.

What happens in the child's mind is the direct result of what happens to the child's body. Awareness moves from outside to inside.

With the beginning of adolescence in part IV of *Emile*, Rousseau's choice of the term *sensible* for a stage of development that leaves behind the world of education through physical sensation thus comes to the reader of *Emile* laden with hundreds of pages of description of the child as a passive receiver of the outside world. Whenever the child seems on the verge of acquiring an alternative *inner* realm of ideas that could turn away from sensation, Rousseau's pedagogue has stepped in to force the boy's attention outward. So at this crucial and perilous moment when the adolescent may find his thoughts stimulated by reading or conversation to imagine some pleasurable—and probably sexual—activity, a new and age-appropriate version of sensibility is introduced to infuse imagination with the long-standing involuntary and outward-turning quality of Emile's earlier education.

Rousseau promotes sensibility as an alternative to what he considers to be the corrupting and traditional socially driven imagination because sensibility denies the adolescent a private mental space. The pedagogical project in *Emile* vigorously counters the development of an inner sanctuary of thought that Montaigne, de Sales, and others advocated. When Emile learns to be *sensible* to his fellow human beings, he experiences feelings that are induced in him by the sufferings of other people just as the child experiences pain when he touches a sharp blade.[32] Emile will therefore have no choice about his emotions and will not control them by creating images in his mind. Instead, his incipient adult emotional life is shaped by the experience of the world around him under the control of his teacher:

> . . . does man have the mastery to direct his affections according to such and such a relationship? No doubt, if he is a master who can direct his imagination onto one object or another, or to bend his imagination to this or that habit. Besides, *it is less a question of what control a man can have over himself than of the control that we can have over our pupil* through the choice of circumstances in which we place him. (257, emphasis added).

With a dismissive glance back toward Montaigne's neo-Stoic imagination, Rousseau turns resolutely toward the new educational strategy in which the pupil will not have the need to direct his imagination because he will be shaped *directly by external stimulus* under the control of his master. What the master will show his pupil is not human happiness but human distress, in order to form the new sensible imagination that turns outward rather than inward:

> The sight of a happy man inspires in others less love than envy; we would accuse him of usurping a right that is not his in enjoying an exclusive happiness. And our vanity (*amour-propre*) suffers and makes us feel that a happy man has no need of us. But who does not pity the unfortunate one we see suffer? Who would not want to free him from his ills if all it cost was the wish to do so? Imagination puts us in the place of the wretched man rather than in the place of the fortunate one. (259).

This sensible imagination is a moral extension of the original sense perceptions of the child. It instructs through direct contact with the outside world, rather than through a mental re-creation of the world in the mind. It forces the adolescent to submit to experience rather than to offer himself a mental alternative to experience. And it hurts.

For the teacher, the key to the adolescent Emile's proper education in sensibility is the control of the boy's environment. Although he cannot be entirely isolated from society, as the child would be in a perfect educational setting, Emile will be exposed only to the social circumstances that the teacher finds appropriate. Emile will not see happy, wealthy people but rather "the sad picture of suffering humanity" (260), for "no one becomes sensible unless his imagination is stimulated and is transported outside himself" (261). Rousseau repeatedly associates sensibility with this movement *outside* (*hors de lui*), an emphasis that directly counters the ancient association of imagination with the movement *inside* the mind, away from the physical outward senses. Just as the teacher of the younger Emile would place him in an environment where he could learn by falling down and picking himself up and then stand back while the child learned from experience, so too the adolescent's teacher simply creates the outward conditions for the desired experience: "what is there for us to do, then, except to offer the young man objects on which the expansive force of his heart can act, objects that will make it swell, that will make the heart spread itself over other beings, that always place him *outside of himself*" (262, emphasis added).

The teacher thus manages the adolescent's imagination, once puberty has made imagination an unavoidable activity: "When the critical age approaches, offer boys spectacles that hold their attention but not spectacles that excite them; trick their nascent imagination with objects that do not set their senses ablaze but instead dampen their activity" (273). This

management, which always works by providing or withholding outside stimulation rather than by proposing mental exercises of the Ignatian or Salesian
sort, requires the teacher to judge the proper quantity, as well as quality of the
stimulation. Generally speaking, unpleasant spectacles, scenes of suffering,
should be favored, but

> You must touch him and not harden him to the sight of human misery. If
> long subject to the same sights, one no longer feels their impression. Habit
> makes us accustomed to everything. What one sees too much, one no longer
> imagines, and it is only imagination that can make us feel the sufferings of
> others. (273).

This management of the adolescent's imagination in contact with actual
experience of selected episodes of social life (for example, a visit to a hospital
for syphilitics) is far superior to the indirect cultivation of imagination that
happens through books. Both historians and novelists, in Rousseau's view,
are insufficiently realistic and too full of imagination—"the novelist indulges
more in his or her own imagination" (283). In short, Rousseau aims at giving
his Emile contact with reality, not with fiction, so that reality will leave its
stamp on Emile's receptive, sensible, imagination.

In *Emile*, Rousseau makes it clear that he is not educating a brilliant individual, and he is not educating him for anything other than his probable
calling in life, that of a married aristocrat living far from the court.[33] Emile
will, therefore, not need to be "imaginative," neither in the way of Montaigne
furnishing for himself his "back room" nor in the way (not yet known to
Rousseau) of the creative, innovative thinker and artist. Yet *Emile* also conveys to us the image of Rousseau, the author and teacher. Does Rousseau
present himself as possessing the cultivated, deliberate, inward, masterly
imagination that he denies to his pupil Emile?

Rousseau was certainly aware of the tradition of the disciplined, inwardly
cultivated imagination, the imagination of a "master who can direct his imagination onto one object or another, or to bend his imagination to this or
that habit" (257). Yet Rousseau's superiority over Emile and over all others,
as Rousseau's voice in *Emile* makes clear, does not come from his imaginative power in the traditional sense but from an authority based on an
almost superhuman source of observations. Rousseau simply *sees* things that
others do not, and he has accumulated in his lifetime an experience that
permits him to declare the truth. "Men do not know childhood," he writes,
"this is the field of study to which I have applied myself the most" (2).[34]

Throughout *Emile*, as in most of Rousseau's writings, the author conveys a supreme confidence in his unique insight and what we moderns would no doubt call his originality—or even "imagination" in a thoroughly new, post-Enlightenment meaning. But for Rousseau this insight and even his ability to imagine this narrative of an educational model do not come from the inward-turning faculty that previously constituted imagination. There are passages of *Emile* that reveal more about the author as ideal teacher than about Emile as the less-than-ideal pupil, and here we find an implied doctrine of the status of imagination among mental faculties.

It is not the power of imagination but rather the power of experience that is central to the mental gifts of the master. Although Emile is an "imaginary pupil" (25) created for this book, he is based on a lifetime of observation. Experience is the key to knowledge, and the basis of all subsequent authority. Rousseau criticizes as a folly (as *extravagance*), for instance, teaching rhetoric to boys who do not have anything real to talk about (301), and his conviction that all speaking and writing must be based on lived experiences underpins his own dominance over both pupils and readers. From the outset of this book, Rousseau denies authority to the reader and affirms that the reader has never properly *observed* children: "Begin by studying your pupils better, for certainly you do not know them..." (2). Rousseau gestures, for his own authority, outward, toward the bracing world of hard knocks, where Rousseau as transcendent author has learned to be *sensible* through suffering. Here we see a vital difference between Rousseau's sensible imagination and most accounts of imagination that come before him.

Prior to Rousseau, a thinker who wanted to make use of imagination would call upon his or her previous knowledge in an effort to construct a mental picture through a series of combinations and variations. De Sales's *Philothée*, for instance, was advised to try out an image of her own death that would be pieced together from death scenes she had seen in real life and others she might have seen in engravings or bas-reliefs on church walls. In this very general sense, experience has always been part of any imaginative project. For Rousseau, however, the willed activity of imagining is generally denigrated. Novelists indulge in their own imaginations too much, for instance. The best imaginative activity—and the term "activity" may be an unfortunate choice here—occurs when a person is confronted directly with a real event, such as an instance of suffering. The impression made by this event, in combination with a deep inner and involuntary capacity called "sentiment," unleashes a transcendent feeling of unity, compassion, or selflessness.[35] The imaginative formation of the author Rousseau, the paradigm of the insightful, empathic observer, thus derives from his observation of all sorts of marginalized individuals and of material nature itself.

Nothing could be more contrary to the image of Rousseau the sensible observer than Montaigne with his "back room," his *arriereboutique*. Montaigne, like de Sales's Philothée, would simply close off his mind selectively to the outside world in order to construct an inner world of potential experience. Thus, imagination would be sealed off from the outside world; Montaigne noted that he felt closer to the world of the ancient Romans than to his own times and that *absence* made things more present to the mind.[36]

Rousseau, on the other hand, emphasizes both the present impact of an actual experience and the cumulative effect of such experiences to make a person into the authoritative writer that Rousseau himself has become. His experience is *broader* than anyone else's and, therefore, when he creates an "imaginary" pupil like Emile, his imagination is actually a treasury of hard-won experiences. When his critics decry Emile as "an imaginary and fantastic being, because he differs from those to whom they compare him" (303), Rousseau replies that he, the writer, is "informed by experience" (303). Then he delivers this ringing declaration of the basis of his insight:

> What makes me confident, and, I believe, rightly so, is that instead of being carried away by doctrinaire thinking (*esprit de système*), I rely as little as possible on reasoning and trust only observation. I do not base myself on what I have imagined, but on what I have seen. It is true that I have not confined my experiences within the walls of a single city nor to a single social group, but after having compared as many classes and nations as I have been able to see in a lifetime of observing them, I have eliminated as artificial what was specific to a single nation and not to another. . . . (305–06).

"I do not base myself on what I have imagined but on what I have seen"—here Rousseau contributes to the cult that Romanticism will eventually devote to the suffering genius, the one whose breadth of experience and whose pain has cast him out of his narrow self and given him the gift of sensibility. This will not be the considered, constructed imaginative space to which the social man or woman withdraws, following the counsels of Montaigne or de Sales, but rather the reactive sensible imagination that is unleashed by external stimulation.

Conclusion

Before imagination became the preeminent creative faculty during the Enlightenment and the Romantic era, it had a long and colorful story. We have traced one thread of that story, detailing the rise and fall of the idea of using imagination for positive personal ends. In the sixteenth century, alongside other perennial views of imagination (the prophetic, visionary view, and the view of imagination as a disorderly faculty), the notion of imagination as a faculty useful for a self-directed mental life began to take hold with new vigor. Then, as confidence waned in the adequacy of an inner, will-directed life, belief in the usefulness of imaginative practice diminished as well. Increasingly authors, from Pascal onward, stressed the importance of observing the world *outside* rather than in using elements of the perceived world to create a new world within. At first, and for many decades, this outer world was the world of society and human behavior. Later, with Rousseau, the outer world was associated increasingly with life outside of society, the world of lakes, rivers, mountains, storms, and plants—what later became known as "nature." Although imagination was still viewed as a fundamental human faculty, this faculty was again subject to the suspicion that had dominated before the Renaissance. Those who gave advice on using imagination no longer advised people to cultivate their own imaginative capacity but rather to learn to manipulate the imagination of other people. A small group of gifted rhetoricians and artists would thus stimulate and use the imagination of an audience. In this way, imagination no longer provided a private mental space but furnished an opening to receive stimulus from the outside world. This new form of imagination, linked with the term "sensibility," allowed its possessors to be influenced by music, painting, books, and by the spectacle of the natural world. This is the status of imagination at the dawn of the eighteenth century, when the Enlightenment and Romanticism seized upon this capacity and made of it something that would have appeared entirely foreign to the writers we have studied in this book.

Notes

PREFACE

i. Virginia Woolf, *To the Lighthouse*, Harvest Books (N.p.: Harcourt Brace, 1927 [reprinted 1955]), 9.

ii. Pierre Leclerc, comp., *Vies intéressantes et édifiantes des religieuses de Port-Royal et de plusieurs personnes qui leur étaient attachées* (N.p.: Aux dépens de la Compagnie, 1750–52), 46.

iii. James Engell, *The Creative Imagination* (Cambridge: Harvard University Press, 1981), 3.

iv. The tendency after the nineteenth century to use "imagination" as a quasi-synonym for "creativity" has been noted by many historians of imagination. M.H. Abrams, in his pivotal *The Mirror and the Lamp. Romantic Theory and the Critical Tradition* (New York: Oxford University Press, 1953), uses the term "creative imagination" in quotation marks in describing the great shift in the status of imagination in the eighteenth century (p. 275). Mark Johnson describes this "reduced view"—as one that "connotes artistic creativity, fantasy, scientific discovery, invention, and novelty. This is chiefly a result of nineteenth-century Romantic views of art and imagination..." (*The Body in the Mind: The Bodily Basis of Meaning, Imagination, and Reason* [Chicago: University of Chicago Press, 1987], 139). This use is well illustrated by Mark Amsler, ed., *Creativity and the Imagination: Case Studies from the Classical Age to the Twentieth Century* (Newark: University of Delaware Press, 1987). In the preface to this collection, the word imagination appears only once, in a paraphrase of the book title, but "metaphoricity" is mentioned several times.

Imagination appears to be either a synonym of "creativity" or of "metaphoricity" or an umbrella concept that holds both of these other terms. It is neither defined or problematized, and clearly its historical connection with sense perception has been left far behind, while the intent of *Creativity and the Imagination* is to show that "that metaphor, frames, scenarios, and schemata are crucial to all human cognition, not just to poetry or aesthetic play" (p. 7).

v. Glyn P. Norton, "Image and Introspective Imagination in Montaigne's *Essais*," *PMLA* 88, no. 2 (March 1973): 281–88.

vi. In the wake of the attacks of September 11, 2002, remarks such as the following were widely reported: "'The big failure we had on Sept. 11 was a failure of *imagination*, of *imagining* what they could do,' said Herbert E. Meyer, vice chairman of the CIA's National Intelligence Council in the Reagan administration" (*Daily Progress*, Charlottesville, Virginia, November 4, 2001, emphasis added).

vii. *The Book of Memory. A Study of Memory in Medieval Culture*, Cambridge Studies in Medieval Literature (Cambridge: Cambridge University Press, 1990), 1.

viii. The physicist Leopold Infeld, quoted by Carruthers, *The Book of Memory*, p. 2.

ix. René Descartes, "Discours de la Méthode," in *Oeuvres complètes*, edited by Charles Adam and Paul Tannery (Paris: Vrin, 1996), 37.

x. René Descartes, "Les méditations métaphysiques de René Descartes touchant la première philosophie," translated by the Duc de Luynes, in *Oeuvres complètes*, edited by Charles Adam and Paul Tannery (Paris: Vrin, 1996), 22.

xi. In Watson's account of one of the earliest Platonic uses of the term, Socrates explains (in *Theaetetus*) Protagoras's assertion that man is measure of all things: things are to each of us as they appear to us, as we sense it (aisthanesthai). Plato explores the misleading nature of this assertion and "introduces *phantasia* into this discussion to mark what we call the distinction between sensation and perception, because *aisthesis* is ambiguous in Greek" (Gerard Watson, *Phantasia in Classical Thought* [Galway: Galway University Press, 1988], 3).

xii. Although the last century has seen much research on the history of imagination—or more precisely, on the history of the theory of imagination—the work of Murray Wright Bundy remains indispensable for an overview of the subject (*The Theory of Imagination in Classical and Medieval Thought*, University of Illinois Studies in Language and Literature [Urbana: University of Illinois Press, 1927]).

xiii. Several of Aristotle's texts are the source of these commonplaces about imagination, particularly *De Anima*, *De Insomniis*, and *On Memory*. Watson and Bundy give detailed analysis of these texts.

xiv. Mino Bergamo, *L'Anatomia dell'anima da François de Sales a Fénelon* (Bologna: Il Mulino, 1991).

xv. Stephen Toulmin (*Cosmopolis: The Hidden Agenda of Modernity*), Hélène Merlin-Kajman (*L'absolutisme dans les lettres et la théorie des deux corps. Passions et politique*), and Perez Zagorin (*Ways of Lying. Dissimulation, Persecution, and Conformity in Early Modern Europe*), among others, have given important accounts of the separation of the private and often concealed life of individuals and groups from the public sphere in early-modern Europe.

xvi. For the secular counsels for separating the inner from the outer *persona*, see Chevalier de Méré, *Oeuvres complètes du chevalier de Méré*, edited by Charles-H. Boudhors, Les Textes français (Paris: Editions Fernand Roches, 1930), 3 vols; Nicolas Faret, *L'Honnest homme ou l'art de plaire à la cour* (Paris: Toussaint Quinet, 1636; première édition, 1630). For further comment on the relationship between concealment and civility in seventeenth-century France see John Lyons, "La rhétorique de l'honnêteté: Pascal et l'agrément," in *Ethos et Pathos. Le statut du sujet rhétorique*, edited by François Cornilliat and Richard Lockwood (Paris: Honoré Champion, 2000), 357–69.

INTRODUCTION

1. Gianfrancesco Pico della Mirandola, "On the Imagination," in *Cornell Studies in English*, edited and translated by Harry Caplan (Ithaca: Cornell University Press, 1930 [original edition: Basle, 1501]), 25; Antoine Arnauld and Pierre Nicole, *La Logique ou l'art de penser*, "Champs" Collection (Paris: Flammarion, 1970), 71.

2. Gerard Watson, *Phantasia in Classical Thought* (Galway: Galway University Press, 1988), 2. A.A. Long writes, "The term *phantasia* makes its main historical entry as a Platonic term of art with reference to Protagorean relativism. (*Theaetetus* 151 c) Plato uses *phantasia* to pick out the different "appearance" or "perception" that one and the same entity may generate in a pair of observers. It is important to keep this original sense in mind when considering subsequent uses of the term. *Phantasiai* are necessarily individual experiences, appearances *to individuals*. [....] Any post-Platonic philosopher who wished to refer to individual experience of any kind—the way things appear to the individual subject that experiences them—had *phantasia* available as the appropriate term" ("Representation and the Self in Stoicism," in *Stoic Studies* [Cambridge: Cambridge University Press, 1996], 267).

3. Watson, *Phantasia*, 3–6.

4. Watson, *Phantasia*, 8–9.

5. Malcolm Schofield, "Aristotle on the Imgination," in *Essays on Aristotle's De Anima*, edited by Martha C. Nussbaum and Amélie Oksenberg Rorty (Oxford: Oxford University Press, 1992), 249.

6. Bundy writes "It is the Platonic conception, rather than the Aristotelian, from which the great modern theories ultimately derive; yet it is the conception of Aristotle which was from the first the object of careful exposition, and which during the Middle Ages was the basis of the more prevalent tradition. The reasons for this comparative neglect of Plato's opinions are not far to seek. The directness of Aristotle's method in comparison with the subtle art of his master rendered the views of the former much easier of comprehension, while much of the suggestiveness of Plato's views has been lost through lack of sympathy with his artistic purposes" (*The Theory of Imagination in Classical and Medieval Thought*, University of Illinois

Studies in Language and Literature [Urbana: University of Illinois Press, 1927], 19).
This comment hints at the major divide separating us from the early-modern period, since Plato's views, as Bundy says, depend on an interest in certain *artistic* aims
and the early-modern imagination was not the sole domain of art. By the end of
the seventeenth century, the *Dictionnaire de l'Académie française* (1694) gave both
the narrow, or learned meaning, and the many less technical meanings of "imagination," covering the gamut from "La faculté de l'ame qui imagine" to "pensée,
conception" to "Creance, opinion" and finally to "Fantaisie erronée et bizarre." In
the nineteenth century, *La Grande Encyclopédie* contrasted the seventeenth-century
philosophical use of the term with the modern one: "La langue courante réunit
sous ce nom [imagination] deux facultés voisines, mais distinctes, l'une qui est le
pouvoir de conserver et de reproduire les images mentales des choses avec une vi-
vacité presque égale à celle des perceptions primitives, l'autre qui est le pouvoir
d'inventer et de créer en formant avec les idées déjà acquises toutes sortes de com-
binaisons nouvelles et plus ou moins originales. Les philosophes du XVIIe siècle,
Descartes, Pascal, Bossuet, Malebranche, etc., n'ont guère étudié que la première sous
les noms d'imagination, de fantaisie, quelquefois aussi de sens commun ou de sens
interne..."

7. In his commentary on *De Anima*, Aquinas explains *phantasia* in this way: "For
phantasia cannot happen without sense, but is only in things that have sense—in
animals, that is—and is concerned only with the things sense is concerned with,
namely, with things that are sensed. For things that are solely intelligible do not
fall to phantasia" (Thomas Aquinas, *The Commentary on the De Anima of Aristotle*,
translated by Robert Pasnau, Yale Library of Medieval Philosophy [New Haven:
Yale University Press, 1999], 337). Aquinas stresses the independence of imagination
(phantasia) from the senses, making imagination, properly speaking, the mental
perception of something in its absence "phantasia habet suas operationes in absentia sensibilium" (quoted in "De phantasia et imaginatione iuxta S. Thomam," by
Roberto Busa, S.J., in *Phantasia-Imaginatio*, Atti del Vo Colloquio internazionale
del Lessico intellettuale Europeo, edited by Marta Fattori and M. Bianchi[Rome:
Ateneo, 1988], 139.

8. "On the Soul," translated and edited by J.A. Smith, in *The Complete Works of
Aristotle*, edited by Jonathan Barnes, Bollingen Series (Princeton: Princeton University Press, 1984), 1, 641–92.

9. Among the most useful recent studies are Wolfson's review of the terminology
and structural description of the "internal senses" from the earliest commentators
to the high middle ages (Harry Austryn Wolfson, *Harvard Theological Review* 28,
no. 2 [April 1935] *The Internal Senses in Latin, Arabic, and Hebrew Philosophic Texts*),
the contributions by Malcolm Schofield and Dorothea Frede in *Essays on Aristotle's
De Anima*, edited by Martha C. Nussbaum and Amélie Oksenberg Rorty (Oxford:
Oxford University Press, 1992), and Gerard Watson, *Phantasia in Classical Thought*
(Galway: Galway University Press, 1988). Schofield notes that what Aristotle "fails
to do is to draw the threads of his discussion together, to provide a synoptic view of
phantasia as he interprets it" ("Aristotle on the Imgination"), 254.

10. As Mary Carruthers describes this *sensus communis*, it "is the receptor of all sense impressions (Avicenna defined it as 'the center of all the senses both from which the senses are diverted in branches and to which they return, and it is itself truly that which experiences'). It unites and compares impressions from all five external senses, but it is also the source of consciousness" (*The Book of Memory. A Study of Memory in Medieval Culture*, Cambridge Studies in Medieval Literature [Cambridge: Cambridge University Press, 1990], 52). Dorothea Frede sounds an important note of caution in the promotion of the "common sense" or "inner sense" as a faculty equivalent to imagination (*phantasia*) in Aristotles's thought: "the inner sense is not a faculty above the different senses but only their centre, where all the different perceptions converge. It may be permitted to speak of 'consciousness' here, but with the proviso that the inner sense *qua* sense contains not more than the imprints of the different sense-perceptions at any moment. Since even in the inner sense the imprints of the perceptible forms last only as long as the perception itself, what lingers on in it when I avert my eye is then already a *phantasia*, an after-image" ("The Cognitive Role of *Phantasia* in Aristotle," in *Essays on Aristotle's De Anima*, edited by Martha C. Nussbaum and Amélie Oksenberg Rorty [Oxford: Oxford University Press, 1992], 284).

11. Wolfson, *The Internal Senses in Latin, Arabic, and Hebrew Philosophic Texts*.

12. Some recent authors have preferred to translate *phantasia* as "representation" in order to avoid confusion with the strictly modern and more limited meaning of the term "imagination." In the present study we will prefer to maintain the older and broader "imagination" in its pre-modern sense. For an excellent statement of the reasons to prefer the continued use of the term "imagination" when discussing Aristotle and the Aristotelian tradition see René Lefebvre, "Faut-il traduire le vocable aristotélicien de *phantasia* par 'représentation'?" (*Revue Philosophique de Louvain* 95, no. 4 [November 1997]: 587–616).

13. The distinction between "fantasy" (or phantasy) and "imagination" was made during the Middle Ages and again in Romanticism, generally to privilege fantasy as a higher, more creative faculty and to limit imagination to the lower order of sensation. This distinction is generally not made by the ancient and the early-modern authors discussed in the present study. See however, Bundy, *The Theory of Imagination in Classical and Medieval Thought*, 177–224 and 257–80, and several of the articles in *Phantasia-Imaginatio*, Atti del Vo Colloquio internazionale del Lessico intellettuale Europeo, edited by Marta Fattori and M. Bianchi (Rome: Ateneo, 1988).

14. "On the Soul," 680, 427b16.

15. Dorothea Frede succinctly states the particular freedom of *phantasia* in Aristotle's doctrine, a freedom that can be seen as an advantage or disadvantage: "for Aristotle there is no need to assume any precise *correspondence* between a *phantasma* and that which it is a *phantasma* of [. . . .] *Phantasiai* can thus be separated from their origin, while perceptions cannot, and this means that they can give us a coherent picture of a situation that transcends the immediate perception. Imagination can give us the impression of a change of a certain time . . . ." ("The Cognitive Role of *Phantasia* in Aristotle," 285).

16. Frede, "The Cognitive Role of *Phantasia* in Aristotle," 283.

17. The energizing potential of an enlargement of the concept of imagination—and thus in part a "return" to the Aristotelian ideal—is exemplified by Giorgio Agamben's appeal in *Infancy and History: The Destruction of Experience*, "Nothing can convey the extent of the change that has taken place in the meaning of experience so much as the resulting reversal of the status of the imagination. For Antiquity, the imagination, which is now expunged from knowledge as 'unreal', was the supreme medium of knowledge. As the intermediary between the senses and the intellect, enabling, in phantasy, the union between the sensible form and the potential intellect, it occupies in ancient and medieval culture exactly the same role that our culture assigns to experience" (*Infancy and History. Essays on the Destruction of Experience*, translated by Liz Heron [London: Verso, 1993], 24). The meaning and importance of imagination in early-modern Europe can be seen in depth through the excellent studies in Fattori and Bianchi, *Phantasia-Imaginatio*. Of particular importance for the present study are "L'Imagination de Mersenne à Pascal" by Jean-Robert Armogathe, and "Malebranche, Arnauld et la controverse sur le rôle de l'imagination dans le langage" by Ulrich Ricken.

18. A.A. Long, "Representation and the Self in Stoicism," in *Stoic Studies* (Cambridge: Cambridge University Press, 1996), 267. Much of the following account of *phantasia* in Stoic thought follows Long closely.

19. Dan Flory, "Stoic Psychology, Classical Rhetoric, and Theories of Imagination in Western Philosophy," *Philosophy and Rhetoric* 29, no. 2 (1996): 147–67. Flory's persuasive argument for Stoicism's important place in the history of imagination is based primarily on the rhetorical tradition, rather than on the works of Epictetus, Marcus Aurelius, and Seneca.

20. The Stoic vocabulary concerning perception is complex, subtle, and not always consistent across the centuries of the activity of this school. Next to *phantasia* we find *phantaston, phantasma*, and *phantasticon*. Although the core meaning of *phantasia* seems to be an awareness of something perceived by the senses, the term seems to be more loosely used to indicate the faculty or activity through which this awareness occurs. Among the many studies concerning these distinctions, one that deserves more attention is J. Pigeaud's difficult to find article "Voir, imaginer, rêver, être fou: quelques remarques sur l'hallucination et l'illusion dans la philosophie stoïcienne, épicurienne, sceptique, et la médecine antique," *Littérature, Médecine, Société*, no. 5 (1983): 23–47.

21. There is considerable disagreement among scholars of ancient philosophy over the precise meaning of *phantasia* in Stoic writing, and particularly over the question of whether or not *phantasia* denotes *solely* an idea that is sensory in content. There is no disagreement that *phantasiai* are very often or most often sense impressions, but some recent writers hold that *phantasiai* extend beyond the senses to include consciousness in general or at least self-consciousness. A.A. Long, who holds this latter position, writes: "[the] canonical definition of *phantasia*: 'A representation is an affection (*pathos*) in the soul, which reveals itself and its cause.' [Aetius IV.12.I]. ... I take 'reveals itself' to signify the fact that any *phantasia* is experienced

as such, i.e. it is experienced as an awareness or perception of the object (its cause) that it reveals; 'reveals itself' is an attempt to capture the reflexive or phenomenological aspect of representations. The source of this definition proceeds to illustrate it by the example of seeing something white; but we should not be misled by this example into treating sense-perception as anything more than the paradigm case of representations. The Stoics, like Aristotle, maintain that representations can be of sensory or non-sensory objects . . .." ("Representation and the self in Stoicism," 271). In terms of the present study, and with the awareness that during the seventeenth century Descartes specifies that imagination is a way of thinking about *material* things, it is important to note the emphasis on sense perception, even in the example given by Long. Note, in regard to Aristotle, the prevailing view that *phantasmata* have sensory content (e.g. Frede, "The Cognitive Role of *Phantasia* in Aristotle," 285). At the same time, Long's extension of the concept of *phantasia* to include the thinker's awareness of himself or herself with reference to the external object in no way prevents *phantasia* from being primarily an experience of sense impressions. In what follows in this book, the terms "representations" and "sense impressions" will be used interchangeably by me, despite differences in emphasis by the authors of texts quoted, in which the term *phantasia* is translated in various ways.

22. For more on the presence of Epictetus in the Renaissance see Chapter I (below) and Léontine Zanta, *La Renaissance du stoïcisme au XVIe siècle* (Geneva: Slatkine Reprints 1975 [first published, 1914]).

23. Epictetus, *The Discourses as Reported by Arrian, The Manual, and Fragments*, compiled and edited by W.A. Oldfather, Loeb Classics (Cambridge, MA: Harvard University Press, 1985 [first edition 1928]), 1:8–9. Unless otherwise noted, all references to Epictetus are to this edition and will give the volume number followed by the page.

24. *Discourses*, book III, Chapter 8 (2:60–63).

25. A modern reader will probably be struck by the similarity between the "practice" recommended by Epictetus, and the practice of "mindfulness meditation" in which simple acknowledgment of what is the case is recommended as preferable to judgment, thoughts about causes and consequences, etc.

26. Book III, Chapter 12 (2:80–87).

27. Marcus Aurelius Antoninus, *To Himself*, translated and edited by C.R. Haines, Loeb Classical Library (Cambridge, MA: Harvard University Press, 1916), 222–23. Subsequent parenthetical references to this text will give the book, section number, and page of the Loeb edition.

28. "Exaleipson ten phantasian."

29. Pierre Hadot's indispensable studies, especially his *Exercices spirituels et philosophie antique* (Paris: Études Augustiniennes, 1987), cast a new light on Stoic self-cultivation. Hadot describes, for instance, how the philosopher—emperor Marcus Aurelius performed various intellectual exercises throughout his life, the purpose of which was "controlling one's inner discourse, in doing only that which is of benefit to the human community, and in accepting the events brought to us by the course of the Nature of the All" (31). The inner discourse was not speculative, academic, or abstract.

Quite to the contrary, Stoics needed to make important concepts present and bring them close to hand for the experience of daily life: "Dogmas, as Marcus says (VII, 2) run the risk of dying out, if one does not constantly reignite those inner images, or *phantasiai*, which make them present to us" (37). Hadot points out later that this is not "imagination": "*phantasia* ("representation," not "imagination")" (52). However, the vivid representation of dogma is one side of an intellectual practice (making the concepts present) that is completed by imagination (tracing the consequences of those concepts for the individual thinker). It is not surprising that strengthening the imagination was therefore a significant matter for Marcus Aurelius: "The *Meditations* do not just formulate the rules of life and the dogmas by which they are nourished; for it is not only reason which is exercised in them, but the imagination as well. For example, Marcus does not restrict himself to saying that life is short and that we all must soon die, by virtue of the laws of metamorphosis imposed by Nature. Instead, he brings to life before his eyes (VIII, 31) the court of Augustus [. . .]. Such imaginative exercises recur rather often in the *Meditations* [. . .]. It is by this means that Marcus attempts vigorously to place the dogma of universal metamorphosis before his eyes" (47–48). This constant mental training gave the philosopher the ability to distinguish between the present, the only time of importance, and the past and future. It thus liberated him from sadness and anxiety and strengthened the control of reason over his actions. Paradoxically, however, the exercises that liberated him from remembered and foreseen experiences required him to make them vividly present to his mind's eye.

30. The Stoics were committed to clear recognition of material reality. Gerard Verbeke illuminates their intellectual use of *phantasiai* in the philosophic quest to make phenomena expressible: "An expressible is not a universal concept; it is an object that subsists as a rational image. This representation is rational because the sensible object has been translated into language. In this way, the sensible image has been rationalized, while at the same time the Stoics could remain faithful to their empiricism" ("Ethics and Logic in Stoicism," in *Atoms, pneuma, and tranquillity*, edited by Margaret J. Osler [Cambridge: Cambridge University Press, 1991], 21).

31. "Overboard with opinion (*hypolepsin*) and thou art safe ashore. And who is there prevents thee from throwing it overboard?" (XII, 25, 334–35) and "in reality it is not the acts men do that vex us . . . but the opinions (*hypolepseis*) we form of those acts" (XI, 18, 308–09).

32. "To the jaundiced honey tastes bitter; and the victim of hydrophobia has a horror of water; and to little children their ball is a treasure? Or dost though think that error is a less potent factor than bile in the jaundiced and virus in the victim of rabies?" (VI, 57, 160–61).

33. "Thou has seen a hand cut off or a foot, or a head severed from the trunk, and lying at some distance from the rest of the body. Just so does the man treat himself, as far as he may, who wills not what befalls and severs himself from mankind or acts unsocially. Say thou hast been torn away in some sort from the unity of Nature . . . ..

Yet here comes in that exquisite provision, that thou canst return again to thy
unity...." (VIII, 34, 214–15).

34. Michèle Huguet, who credits the Stoics with the creation of the concept of
ennui, notes the Stoic insistence that only the present moment exists: "la pensée
stoïcienne posant que, 'seul le présent existe' ouvre une réflexion sur le temps qui,
faisant surgir l'intervalle, comme écart de vide, rend possible l'émergence de la notion
d'ennui comme épreuve subjective de cet écart" (*L'Ennui et ses discours* [Paris: Presses
Universitaires de France, 1984], 44).

35. Both Erasmus and Justus Lipsius edited his writings in the sixteenth centuries
and Thomas Lodge translated his essays in 1614. Montaigne's library included the
1557 Basle edition of *L. Annaei Senecae philosophi stoicorum omnium acutissmi opera
quae extant omnia*, as well as Seneca's tragedies.

36. Seneca uses Greek terms occasionally, but it is probably not an accident that
his best-known Hellenism is the title of his satirical work, the *Apocolocyntosis*. One
of Seneca's comments on translations appears in his letter (or essay) "To Serenus
on tranquillity of mind," where Seneca, commenting on the Greek term for this
tranquillity (*euthymia*), says, "I call it tranquillity. For there is no need to imitate
and reproduce words in their Greek shape; the thing itself, which is under discussion,
must be designated by some name which ought to have, not the form, but the force,
of the Greek term...." (*Moral Essays*, edited and translated by John W. Basore, Loeb
[Cambridge, MA: Harvard University Press, 1928–35],254:—213–215). In references
to Seneca's works, both the *Moral Essays*, the *Epistles*, and the *Epistulae Morales*, I
will give the volume number of the Loeb Classics, followed by the page number.
In Seneca's philosophical works, i.e. the "moral essays" as they are sometimes called,
the word "imaginatio" does not appear. The words most similar are "imaginarius"
and "imaginor" which each appear once, both in *De Constantia* the first at III,
3 and the second at VI, 7, according to Pierre Grimal's concordance, *L. Annaei
Senecae Operum Moralium Concordantia* (Paris: Presses Universitaires de France,
1965).

37. Epistle 91 in *Ad Lucilium Epistulae Morales*, edited and translated by Richard
M. Gummere, Loeb Classical Library (Cambridge, MA: Harvard University Press,
1989), 77:434–37.

38. *Ad Lucilium epistulae morales*, 77:276–291.

39. Epistle 55 (75: 370–373). The Latin is even more insistent on immediacy:
"Itaque mecum stude, mecum cena, mecum ambula. In angusto vivebamus..."

40. Epistle 56 (75: 372–375).

41. 75:372–375. Richard Gummere has translated "cogita" as "imagine": "Praeter
istos... alipilum cogita tenuem et stridulam vocem...." (75:372).

42. *Epistles*, 75: 380–381: "Tunc ergo te scito esse conpositum, cum ad te nullus
clamor pertinebit, cum te nulla vox tibi excutiet, non si blandietur, non si minabitur,
non si inani sono vana circumstrepet."

43. *Epistles*, 75:78–79.

44. *Epistles*, 75:106.

45. *Epistles*, 75:102–103. Seneca advises Lucilius to go beyond the idea of a happy life by taking concrete steps along the long path to wisdom: "Sed hoc, quod liquet, firmandum et altius cotidiana meditatione figendum est . . ."

46. Lucius Annaeus Seneca, *Moral Essays*, edited and translated by John W. Basore, (Cambridge, MA: Harvard University Press, 1928–35), 214:286. Seneca advises, in "On Anger," that his reader struggle to maintain the appearance of calm even when he is enraged, on the idea that gradually the mind will conform to the calm that is enacted by the body. Seneca tells Lucilius that if Lucilius misses some of his regular Stoic practice, he will lose ground: "It makes little difference whether you leave philosophy out altogether or study it intermittently; for it does not stay as it was when you dropped it, but, because its continuity has been broken, it goes back to the position in which it was at the beginning, like things which fly apart when they are stretched taut" (*Epistles 66–92*, edited and translated by Richard M. Gummere, Loeb [Cambridge, MA: Harvard University Press, 1996], 76:98–99).

47. "On Anger," in *Moral Essays* (214:340–41).

48. *Epistles*, 77:162–163.

49. *Epistles*, 75:70–71.

50. *Epistles*, 76: 166–167.

51. *Epistles*, : 100–101. This passage is a commentary by Seneca on some words of Epicurus.

52. "But if folly fears some evil, she is burdened by it in the very moment of awaiting it, just as if it had actually come,—already suffering in apprehension whatever she fears she may suffer. Just as in the body symptoms of latent ill-health precede the disease . . . so the feeble spirit is shaken by its ills a long time before it is overcome by them. It anticipates them, and totters before its time. But what is greater madness than to be tortured by the future . . ." (*Epistles*, 76: 100–101).

53. *Epistles*, 74:134–135.

54. "Quae res effecit, ut firmitatem animi sui quaerat, quam videlicet ad ea, quae timeri posse putabat, exercuit" (*Epistles*, 76: 430–431).

55. *Epistles*, 75: 436–437: "Hodie fieri potest, quicquid umquam potest."

56. "We should not manifest surprise at any sort of condition into which we are born, and which should be lamented by no one, simply because it is equally ordained for all. Yes, I say, equally ordained; for a man might have experienced even that which he has escaped. An equal law consists, not of that which all have experienced, but of that which is laid down for all. Be sure to prescribe for your mind this sense of equity . . ." (*Epistulae Morales*, 77: 226–227). While Seneca's goal is inner tranquility, we should not forget that this goal is reached by aggressive use of sensory depiction, something that we could forget in reading, for instance, the perfectly correct comment by which Charles Taylor compares Seneca to Descartes: "For Seneca, the soul no longer touched by accidents of forture is like the upper part of the universe, which rides serenely above the tempest-filled lower air" (*Sources of the Self. The Making of the Modern Identity* [Cambridge, MA: Harvard University Press, 1989], 152).

57. *Epistles*, 75:324–325.

58. Consider Seneca's vivid evocation of life under tyranny in his essay "On Mercy" (dedicated to Nero himself!): "even pleasures give rise to fear; men are not safe when they go to the festal board, for there the tongue even of the drunkard must guard itself with care" (*Moral Essays*, edited and translated by John W. Basore, Loeb [Cambridge, MA: Harvard University Press, 1928–35], 214:426–427).

59. *Epistles*, 75:426–429.

60. "On the Happy Life" in *Moral Essays*, 254:119.

61. Quintilian, Marcus Fabius Quintilianus, was born about 35 A.D. near what is now Tarragona in Spain. He received a salary from the emperor Vespasian to teach Latin rhetoric and wrote his *Institutio* toward the end of his life. He died after 96 A.D. Quintilian was thus a contemporary of Epictetus and was born shortly after Seneca's death in 39 A.D.

62. Memory techniques have been the subject of several important books. See especially Francis Yates, *The Art of Memory* (Chicago: Chicago University Press, 1966) and Carruthers, *The Book of Memory. A Study of Memory in Medieval Culture*.

63. Quintilian, *Institutio Oratoria*, edited and translated by H.E. Butler, Loeb Classical Library (Cambridge, MA: Harvard University Press, 1920), book II, section 15, (vol.1, 301). Further parenthetical references to the *Institutio Oratoria* will give book number, section number, volume, and page in this format (book II, 15; vol.1, 301).

64. Aristotle, "Rhetoric," translated by W. Rhys Roberts, in *The Complete Works of Aristotle*, edited by Jonathan Barnes, Bollingen Series (Princeton, NJ: Princeton University Press, 1991), 1, 2152 (section 1354a): "The modes of persuasion are the only true constituents of the art: everything else is merely accessory." Quintilian's attack on this view is given in the *Institutio Oratoria*, book II, 15; vol.1, 300–19.

65. Untrained speakers, for example, "rock their bodies to and fro, booming inarticulately as if they had a trumpet inside them and adapting their agitated movements, not to the delivery of the words, but to their pursuit" (book II, 11; vol.1, 280–81) and they speak "dashing this way and that, panting, gesticulating wildly and wagging their heads with all the frenzy of a lunatic" (book II, 12; vol.1, 286–87).

66. The defense of rhetoric as an art is a thread that runs throughout Quintilian's book, rising at times to explicit statement accompanied by the affirmation that this view goes without saying: "there is no one, I will not say so unlearned, but so devoid of ordinary sense, as to hold that building, weaving, or moulding vessels from clay are arts, and at the same time to consider that rhetoric, which, as I have already said, is the noblest and most sublime of tasks, has reached such a lofty eminence without the assistance of art (*sine arte*)" (book II, 17; vol.1, 327).

67. Don Flory interprets Quintilian's phrasing here as implying that the public was familiar with the term *phantasia* but only as a technical concept from the rhetorical tradition ("Stoic Psychology, Classical Rhetoric, and Theories of Imagination in Western Philosophy," 156–57).

68. "Has quisquis bene conceperit, is erit in adfectibus potentissimus. Hunc quidam dicunt *euphantasioton*, qui sibi res, voces, actus secundum verum optime

finget; quod nobisvolentibus facile continget." The translation is my own, since Butler's version does not make it clear that this experience of imagination is internal to the orator and not, in this case, shared with the audience.

69. Marjorie O'Rourke Boyle argues that Ignatius of Loyola's description of his own, highly developed imagination corresponds directly to Quintilian's presentation of this skill (*Loyola's Acts: The Rhetoric of the Self* [Berkeley: University of California Press, 1997], 31).

70. This technique made an impression, many centuries later, on Montaigne, who refers to this indirect effect of imagination on the audience in the chapter of his *Essais* "De la diversion" (III.4:838): "L'Orateur, dict la rethorique, en cette farce de son plaidoier s'esmouvera par le son de sa voix et par ses agitations feintes, et se lairra piper à la passion qu'il represente. Il s'imprimera un vray deuil et essentiel, par le moyen de ce battelage qu'il joüe, pour le transmettre aux juges..."

71. Book VI, 2; vol.2, 434–35. I have slightly altered Butler's translation.

72. Book X, 7; vol. 4, 140–41. I have slightly modified Butler's translation, in which *vis mentis* becomes "force of imagination."

73. Terence Cave, *The Cornucopian Text. Problems of Reading in the Late Renaissance* (Oxford: Clarendon Press, 1979), 36–9, 128–42.

74. Quintilian foresees the mobile office of today, for the trained orator will not need to find a quiet location to plan his coming speech: "even in the midst of legal proceedings our mind will find some vacant space for meditation, and will refuse to remain inactive... the concentration which this requires cannot be attained in a moment or even quickly" (book X, 6; vol. 4, 128–29).

75. The ambitions of the Romantic imagination are much more than poetic creativity, and even more than the embodiment of transcendent "truth." For an ambitious description of the social and ideological purposes of imagination in the nineteenth century see Forest Pyle, *The Ideology of Imagination* (Stanford: Stanford University Press, 1995).

76. Mary Carruthers, *The Craft of Thought. Meditation, Rhetoric, and the Making of Images, 400–1200* (Cambridge: Cambridge University Press, 1998).

CHAPTER I

1. "De l'expérience," *Les Essais*, edited by Pierre Villey, with a preface by V.-L. Saulnier (Paris: Presses Universitaires de France, 1965), 1065. Hereafter, parenthetical references will give first the page number of the French Saulnier edition, followed by the page number of Donald M. Frame's translation, *The Complete Essays of Montaigne* (Stanford: Stanford University Press, 1958), as for this passage: 1065/815. I have occasionally modified the English translation to sharpen the focus on imagination and mental processes.

2. Léon Brunschvicg, *Descartes et Pascal, lecteurs de Montaigne*, with a preface by Thiery Leterre, Agora, Les Classiques (Paris: Presses Pocket, 1995 [first edition 1942]), 74.

3. Richard Rorty, *Philosophy and the Mirror of Nature* (Princeton: Princeton University Press, 1979), 139.

4. Gilles Gaston Granger, "Epistémologie," in *Encyclopaedia Universalis*, vol. 8 (Paris, 1992), 566.

5. The word epistemology appeared in English in 1856 (according to the *OED*), and *épistémologie* appeared in French only in 1901 (*Dictionnaire historique de la langue française* [1992]). In English, "epistemology" is used more freely to indicate the philosophy of knowledge in general, while in French "épistémologie" is generally used to describe the philosophical study of scientific knowledge.

6. Eric Aaron Johnson, *Knowledge and Society: A Social Epistemology of Montaigne's Essays* (Charlottesville: Rookwood Press, 1994) and Joel Gerard Tansey, "Montaigne Questions: Skepticism, Epistemology, and Interrogative Rhetoric," *Dissertation Abstracts International* 55, no. 11 (1995): 3504A (Ann Arbor, MI: University of Michigan, 1995).

7. The *Essais* often turn with some amusement against knowledge that is packaged in tidy boxes and against their possessors. In "De l'institution des enfans," Montaigne states his wish to "former non un grammairien ou logicien, mais un gentilhomme" (I,26:169/125). In the "Apologie," he recalls that "Cicero reprend aucuns de ses amis d'avoir accoustumé de mettre à l'astrologie, au droit, à la dialectique et à la géométrie plus de temps que ne meritoyent ces arts," he concludes that "La plus part des arts ont esté ainsi méprisées par le sçavoir mesmes" (II,12:508/377).

8. Ann Hartle has recently made the strong and convincing argument for recognizing Montaigne within the philosophical tradition from which he was largely excluded, she argues, because of his preference for an experience-based and antideductive approach to thought (*Michel de Montaigne: Accidental Philosopher* [Cambridge: Cambridge University Presss, 2003]).

9. In Epictetus the terms *phantasia* (imagination, representation, sense-impression or appearance) and *dogmaton* (opinion or judgment) are closely associated because of mankind's tendency, according to Epictetus, to form improper judgments on the basis of appearance. In André Rivaudeau's translation of Epictetus's *Manual*, we find the "sentence" to which Montaigne was probably alluding here: "Ce ne sont pas les choses qui espouvantent les hommes, mais les opinions" (André de Rivaudeau, *La Traduction française du Manuel d'Épictète d'André de Rivaudeau*, edited and with a commentary by Léontine Zanta [Paris: Champion, 1914], Chapter V). By the turn of the seventeenth century, at the latest, *fantasie* had become so intertwined with *opinion* that Jean Nicot, in his *Thrésor de la langue françoise* (1606) writes of *fantasie* "Il vient de Phantasia mot Grec, id est imaginatio, Visio. Phantasiam, opinionem aliquando vertit Politianus." Nicot, whose bilingual French–Latin dictionary gives French expressions which he then translates into Latin, several times gives the pair "fantasie et opinion" as if they meant a single, inseparable concept, as in "Laisser une fantasie et opinion qu'on a en sa teste, *Opinionem remittere.*"

10. Ann Hartle, *Michel de Montaigne: Accidental Philosopher* (Cambridge: Cambridge University Press, 2003), 110. Hartle traces the relation between

Montaigne's abundant imagination and his claim to have a bad memory and argues convincing that for Montaigne a very good imagination could cause someone to accept familiar things uncritically (108–112).

11. For others, like Pomponazzi, Bruno, More, Montaigne, Charron, and Bacon, Stoic doctrine was an important influence, sometimes shaping their thought in the very effort of providing alternatives to Stoic formulations. An important recent book that shows the importance of neo-Stoicism in a surprisingly wide range of intellectual endeavor is Peter Miller, *Peiresc's Europe: Learning and Virtue in the Seventeenth Century* (New Haven: Yale University Press, 2000). See particularly Chapter 5, "History as Philosophy: Time and the Antiquarian," 130–154. Jason Saunders provides a good overview of Renaissance Stoicism in *Justus Lipsius. The Philosophy of Renaissance Stoicism* (New York: Liberal Arts Press, 1955).

12. Léontine Zanta's landmark study (first published in 1914) remains an invaluable guide (*La Renaissance du stoïcisme au XVIe siècle* [Geneva: Slatkine Reprints (1975)]). Theological differences strongly shaped the use to which Renaissance thinkers put Stoic doctrines. Catholics, for instance, emphasized the freedom of the will in Stoic ethics while Reformers, like Zwingli, found a providential doctrine similar to predestination (Zanta, 50).

13. John Calvin, *Calvin's Commentary on Seneca's De Clementia*, translated and edited by Ford Lewis Battles and André Malan Hugo, Renaissance Text Series III (Leiden: E.J. Brill, 1969); Simon Goulart translated and edited, *Les Oeuvres morales et meslées de Sénecque, traduites de latin en françois et nouvellement mises en lumière* (Paris: Jean Houzé, 1595); François de Malherbe, *Les epistres de Sénèque* (Lyons: Claude de la Rivière). I am indebted to Amy Graves, who drew my attention to Goulart's work.

14. The poet Angelo Poliziano's 1498 version, accompanied by an extensive commentary, was particularly influential (and, significantly, emphasized meditation as a Stoic technique). This was included in the edition of Poliziano's works that Montaigne owned (Pierre Villey, *Les sources et l'évolution des Essais de Montaigne* [Paris: Hachette, 1908 [reprint, New York: Burt Franklin: 1968]]). A member of Marguerite de Navarre's entourage, Antoine Du Moulin, translated the *Manual* for the first time into French in 1544. This is significant because those who surrounded Marguerite de Navarre, sister of King Francis I, were generally of the Catholic evangelical movement, sometimes suspected of being close to Protestant reformers. In 1567 a Protestant, André Rivaudeau, published an entirely new translation (see Léontine Zanta, *La Traduction française du Manuel d'Épictète d'André de Rivaudeau* [Paris: Champion, 1914]).

15. Guillaume du Vair, *Les Oeuvres de Messire Guillaume du Vair* (Paris: Sebastien Cramoisy, 1641 [reprinted Geneva: Slatkine, 1970]).

16. Villey writes with some disdain of Montaigne's "stoïcisme passager," remarking that "L'admiration va plus vite que la raison: on est stoïcien avant de s'être demandé si le stoïcisme convient à votre nature…" (*Les sources et l'évolution des Essais de Montaigne*, 60–62).

17. Hugo Friedrich, on the other hand, denies the existence of what he calls "Montaigne's much discussed 'Stoic phase.'" He adds that Montaigne's contemporaries, like Justus Lipsius, had misunderstood Montaigne when they considered him to be a Stoic (Hugo Friedrich, *Montaigne*, edited by Philippe Desan, translated by Dawn Eng [Berkeley, CA: University of California Press, 1991], 66). However, Friedrich himself bases this claim on an unduly limited conception of Stoicism: "Montaigne is fundamentally differentiated from the so-called neo-Stoics of the sixteenth and seventeenth centuries in that he makes a descriptive study of morality out of Seneca's normative moral philosophy. The line of neo-Stoicism proceeds, without touching Montaigne, from the humanistic philologists to Du Vair, Lipsius, Quevedo, Descartes, and Corneille" (66). While Stoicism always included a significant normative component, it also includes, in the case especially of Epictetus, an emphasis on psychological and particularly on perceptual issues that are far more subtle than the insistence on will and duty to which Friedrich seems to be limiting this philosophical school. As for the "phase" itself, the earlier chapters of Montaigne's book, as Dora Polachek has pointed out, are more and more being rescued from a tendency to undervalue them. ("Imagination, Idleness and Self-Discovery: Montaigne's Early Voyage Inward," in *Reconsidering the Renaissance. Papers from the Twenty-First Annual Conference*, edited by Mario Di Cesare [Binghamton: Medieval and Renaissance Texts and Studies, 1992], 257–69). Marcel Conche is surely correct to write that "Montaigne ne pouvait être ni stoïcien ni épicurien. Sa méthode de lecture et de réflexion s'y opposa. En effet le stoïcisme et l'épicurisme sont des dogmatismes..." and thus at odds with Montaigne's overall disposition (*Montaigne et la philosophie* [1987], 27).

18. The importance of Montaigne's difference from the Stoics on key points of what became, at least, neo-Stoic orthodoxy, appears in his refusal of a passionless indifference to life. See Christian Belin's comment on Montaigne's difference from Guillaume Du Vair on this point (*L'oeuvre de Pierre Charron: Littérature et théologie de Montaigne à Port-Royal* [Paris: Honoré Champion, 1995], 188). Glynn Norton puts it neatly: "Here Montaigne is at his eclectic best" (*Montaigne and the Introspective Mind* [The Hague: Mouton, 1975], 61).

19. The "poet's function is to describe, not the thing that has happened, but a kind of thing that might happen" ("Poetics," translated by I. Bywater, in *The Complete Works of Aristotle*, edited by Jonathan Barnes, Bollingen Series [Princeton: Princeton University Press, 1984], Chapter 9, 1451 b1, 2322).

20. The fact that Montaigne calls for an active, will-directed use of the imagination here seems, in itself, enough to set aside the exclusively pejorative use of this faculty by Montaigne according to Hugo Friedrich's brief comments (Friedrich, *Montaigne*, 123).

21. Terence Cave has pointed out to me the opposite danger, which is to assume that Montaigne always writes with technical literalness when he uses the word "imagination." It is certainly true that Montaigne uses the term sometimes very precisely and other times rather loosely, just as one might today use the term "dream" to mean the recollections of thoughts occurring in sleep or to mean an idea that

one does not take seriously, as in "I never dreamed that I would someday win the lottery."

22. See, among many other studies of this issue, Erwin Panofsky's seminal work *La Perspective comme forme symbolique et autres essais*, translated by Guy Ballangé (Paris: Éditions de Minuit, 1975). Robert Klein, in his indispensable article "L'imagination comme vêtement de l'âme chez Marsile Ficin et Giordano Bruno" (in *La Forme et l'intelligible. Ecrits sur la Renaissance et l'art moderne*, edited by André Chastel, [Paris: Gallimard, 1970], 65–88, originally published in 1956 in the *Revue de Métaphysique et de Morale*) writes of the struggle between universalization and particularization in the late sixteenth century.

23. Letter to Bartolommeo Scala, August 1, 1479, quoted in Zanta, *La Traduction française du Manuel d'Épictète d'André de Rivaudeau*, 15.

24. Zanta, *La Traduction française du Manuel d'Épictète d'André de Rivaudeau*, 28.

25. This commonplace is set forth strongly in the first chapter of Epictetus's *Manual*—or *Encheiridion*—("The *Encheiridion* of Epictetus," in *The Discourses as Reported by Arrian, The Manual, and Fragments*, compiled and edited by W.A. Oldfather, Loeb Classics (Cambridge, MA: Harvard University Press, 1985 [first edition 1928]), 482–83).

26. Louis Martz, *The Poetry of Meditation*, revised edition (New Haven: Yale University Press, 1962), 74–75; Imbrie Buffum, *Studies in the Baroque from Montaigne to Rotrou* (New Haven: Yale University Press, 1957), 103; and Terence C. Cave, *Devotional Poetry in France, c.1570–1613* (Cambridge: Cambridge University Press, 1969), 27–29, 32–33.

27. It should be noted that this more abstract side of this meditation on death appears in later additions to the chapter "Que philosopher c'est apprendre à mourir," additions that appeared in the 1588 text of the *Essais*. In other words, the emphasis on more vivid, sensory representations belongs, as Villey surmises in the notes to his edition, to a time when Montaigne was thirty-nine.

28. Montaigne was, from the very beginning, sensitive to objections that imagining death would not help very much. At first he simply said that this deliberate imagining simply must give some advantage: "On me dira que l'effect surmonte de si loing l'imagination qu'il n'y a si belle escrime qui ne se perde, quand on en vient là. Laissez les dire: le premediter donne sans doubte grand avantage" (I.20:90/63). The connection between *meditating* and *practice* was apparently stronger in Montaigne's time than in ours. Robert Estienne, in his *Dictionarium Latinogallicum* (1552) translates "Meditatio" as "Grand pensement, Meditation, Exercitation."

29. Montaigne's experiment with imagination in "De l'exercitation" is thus more complex than those later performed by Descartes when he writes, for instance, about chimeras. The chimera, if it existed, could be seen, heard, or smelled. The only reason that a chimera is not available to our senses is that it does not exist. Whereas in the experience of dying the problem is not simply in the object of the senses but in the conditions affecting the subject.

30. One scholar has seen Montaigne as a proponent of the position taken by the Stoic Chrysippus that time has no reality: "Montaigne semble faire sienne ici l'analyse de Chrysippe, analyse qui tend à nier la réalité du temps, puisque son actualité est insaisissable..." (Conche, *Montaigne et la philosophie*, 43). Chrysippus (ca. 279–206 BC) was the third leader of the Stoa, and none of his works is extant, except in fragments and quotations in the works of others. Joukovsky's book on Montaigne's view of time shows that his views are based primarily on Stoic ideas, with some Epicurean elements (Françoise Joukovsky, *Montaigne et le problème du temps* [Paris: Nizet, 1972], 69).

31. Joukovsky, 38.

32. Montaigne here quotes Lucretius, *De Rerum natura*, III, 915. Much of Montaigne's Epicurean thought comes from Seneca, who proclaimed his loyalty to the Stoa but frequently quotes Epicurus in his letters.

33. Joukovsky 184.

34. Epictetus clarifies the philosopher's gaze with the comparison of a festival or fair (*panegyris*): "Our position is like that of those who attend a fair. Cattle and oxen are brought there to be sold, and most men engage in buying and selling, while there are only a few who go merely to see the fair, how it is conducted, and why, and who are promoting it, and for what purpose. So it is also in this 'fair' of the world in which we live; some persons, like cattle, are interested in nothing but their fodder; for to all you that concern yourselves with property and lands and slaves and one office or another, all this is nothing but fodder! And few in number are the men who attend the fair because they are fond of the spectacle [. . . .] they have leisure for this one thing only—to study well the 'fair' of life before they leave it" (Epictetus, *The Discourses as Reported by Arrian, The Manual, and Fragments*, compiled and edited by W.A. Oldfather, Loeb Classics (Cambridge, MA: Harvard University Press, 1985 [first edition 1928]), vol. I, 304–07).

35. See Montaigne's comment on "that other sect that makes an express profession of pride" (the Stoics), 346–47/250.

36. Epictetus often stresses the learning that can be acquired from *everything*. The philosophical attitude is "the magic wand of Hermes" that converts bad and trivial external reality into good, as object of study (Epictetus, *Discourses*, II, 117–23).

37. This could be said even of the fluctuations of the soul itself, or what we would call psychological changes. In "De la vertu," Montaigne contrasts the "boutées et saillies de l'ame" with its "ordinaire" (II.29:705/533).

38. Montaigne called his Flemish contemporary Justus Lipsius (1547–1606) "le plus sçavant homme qui nous reste, d'un esprit trespoly et judicieux" (II.12:578/436). Lipsius in his study of Stoic physics, *Physiologiae Stoicorum*, showed that the Stoics taught the periodic destruction and recreation of the world as well as the permanent existence of matter. See Saunders, *Justus Lipsius. The Philosophy of Renaissance Stoicism* (184—214). Montaigne's library contained six books by Lipsius, with whom he corresponded. Although Lipsius published the *Physiologiae* after Montaigne's death, this major doctrine of period destruction and regeneration certainly was

known to Montaigne, who comments frequently in the *Essais* on the perpetual changes in the world around him.

39. "De la force de l'imagination," 97/68.

40. Although Rorty's name appears here as the foremost recent exponent of pragmatism, his essay "The Contingency of Selfhood" is close, in many ways to Montaigne's reflections on death, though Rorty does not mention Montaigne (Richard Rorty, *Contingency, Irony, and Solidarity* [Cambridge: Cambridge University Press, 1989], 23–43).

41. Just a little further in "De la force de l'imagination," Montaigne echoes the translation of *phantasia* by "impression" when he writes that Antiochus got a fever from Stratonice's beauty "trop vivement empreinte en son ame" (98). Cf. Jean-Paul Dumont's recollection of Stoic doctrine, "Zénon définissait la *phantasia* comme une empreinte dans l'âme" (*Le Scepticisme et le phénomène: essai sur la signification et les origines du pyrrhonisme* [Paris: Librairie Philosophique J. Vrin, 1985, second edition], 118).

42. For example the death of Epicurus in "De la gloire (II.16:620/469) and of Cato in "De la cruauté" (II,11:424/308–09).

43. John D. Lyons, *Exemplum. The Rhetoric of Example in Early Modern France and Italy* (Princeton NJ: Princeton University Press, 1989), 139–41.

44. The term ideology is here used in a broad sense, neither pejorative nor favorable, not as an explicit, conscious social or political doctrine but as a systematic, though partly unconscious, association of values, ideas, and material objects. Montaigne's analysis of collective imaginative practices seems to include the discovery of such systems, along the lines of "ideology" as Donald R. Kelley has described it: "it involves a distinctive and more or less coherent conglomerate of assumptions, attitudes, sentiments, values, ideals and goals accepted and perhaps acted upon by a more or less organized group of persons. It is both more and less than a philosophy: more because it includes the emotional, the subconscious and the irrational and must be linked to particular social patterns; less because it stops short of a rational and self-enclosed system of thought. At the same time it is more explicit and systematic than 'mentality' or [. . .] 'outlook'" (*The Beginning of Ideology. Consciousness and Society in the French Reformation* [Cambridge: Cambridge University Press, 1981], 4).

45. See also the example from the "religion des Bedoins" ("De la gloire" II.16:630/ 477) which inculcates the "creance tressalutaire" that in dying for his prince a Bedouin would pass into a body that is happier, more beautiful, and stronger than his first.

46. See below, in Chapter IV, how Pascal uses the concept of an ideological training of the body—mind unit.

47. Jean-Paul Dumont appreciates the "lucide profondeur" of Montaigne's reading of pyrrhonism and shows passage by passage the correspondences between the "Apologie" and texts of Sextus Empiricus (*Le Scepticisme et le phénomène: essai sur la signification et les origines du pyrrhonisme* [Paris: Librairie Philosophique J. Vrin,

1985 (second edition)], 47). Dumont also recalls the formative role of Stoicism in the formation of Sextus Empiricus's thought (117–125).

48. Montaigne also, in a rather risky challenge to the Vulgate account, attributes negatively, to mankind, the imaginative comparison of man to God, whereas the text of *Genesis* assigns to God the words "Faciamus hominem ad imaginem et similitudinem nostram, et praesit piscibus maris..." (1:26).

49. "L'homme n'est qu'un roseau, le plus faible de la nature, mais c'est un roseau pensant [....]" (Fragment 200, in Louis Lafuma's numbering, 231 in Philippe Sellier's , in Blaise Pascal, *Oeuvres complètes*, edited by Louis Lafuma, with a preface by Henri Gouhier, L'Intégrale [Paris: Le Seuil, 1963], 528).

50. This would mean, of course, that the animals were not "imagining," since they would not be forming sensory "images" of things—just as when we think of adding two numbers we do not need to picture the case of two oranges added to two more oranges but simply add the *quantities* as abstractions.

51. James Engell, *The Creative Imagination* (Cambridge: Harvard University Press, 1981).

52. In "Que le goust des biens et des maux depend en bonne partie de l'opinion que nous en avons," Montaigne recalls Pyrrho's story of the pig on a boat during a storm—the people were crazed with fright but the pig, having no imagination of what could happen, was perfectly calm (I.14:54–55/36–37).

53. Despite Montaigne's claims that he would like to resemble the simple laborers, he seems to take few steps in that direction. Indeed, the writing of the *Essais* directly contradicts the praise of a happiness in which speculative thought is banished. Instead, he enjoys *imagining* such a life, or sets forth dizzying reversals of fancy in which the learned man imagines being learned only in his imagination: "J'ay veu en mon temps cent artisans, cent laboureurs, plus sages et plus heureux que des recteurs de l'université, et lesquels j'aimerois mieux ressembler. La doctrine, ce m'est advis, tient rang entre les choses necessaires à la vie, comme la gloire, la noblesse, la dignité, ou, pour le plus, comme la beauté, la richesse et telles autres qualitez qui y servent voyrement, mais de loin, et un peu plus par fantasie que par nature" (487/359). Imagination is here again associated with *distance* ("de loin") while the laudable lack of imagination permits living in the here-and-now, without distance from experience.

54. "De mesnager sa volonté," III.10:1003/767.

55. Montaigne points out the importance of this retreat in "Que le goust des biens et des maux depend en bonne partie de l'opinion que nous en avons," where he notes, in regard to preparing ourselves for the future, "Ce qui nous fait souffrir avec tant d'impatience la douleur, c'est de n'estre pas accoustumez de prendre notre principal contentement en l'ame, de ne nous attendre point assez à elle, qui est seule et souveraine maistresse de nostre condition et conduite" (I, 14:57/39).

56. Saint François de Sales, *Oeuvres*, edited by André Ravier and Roger Devos, Pléiade (Paris: Gallimard, 1969), 96–103; Blaise Pascal, *Pensées*, fragment 91, in *Oeuvres complètes*, edited by Louis Lafuma, with a preface by Henri Gouhier, L'Intégrale

(Paris: Le Seuil, 1963); Descartes repeatedly seeks for himself the inner privacy to pursue his inquiry, for example, René Descartes, *Discours de la méthode*, in *Oeuvres complètes*, edited by Charles Adam and Paul Tannery (Paris: Vrin, 1996), 6, 30–31.

57. On this imagination of exemplary models, André Bridoux writes, "Le souci de l'imitation des vies exemplaires qui est, comme nous l'avons vu, un souci stoïcien par excellence, se retrouve chez Montaigne" (*Le Stoïcisme et son influence* [Paris: Librairie Philosophique J. Vrin, 1966], 200).

CHAPTER 2

1. Saint François de Sales, *Oeuvres*, edited by André Ravier and Roger Devos, Pléiade (Paris: Gallimard, 1969), 440. Subsequent parenthetical references will give the page number in this edition and will indicate by abbreviations whether the reference is to the *Introduction à la vie dévote* (IVD) or to the *Traité de l'amour de Dieu* (TAD). In addition to multitude of comments on the will in the *Traité de l'amour de Dieu*, there are many that explicitly mention the Council of Trent and the official requirement that Catholics believe in the freedom and the active cooperation of the individual will with the divine project, e.g. TAD 445, 452, 474, 481, 486, 495, 539.

2. In *Bishop Joseph Hall and Protestant Meditation in Seventeenth-Century England*, Frank Livingstone Huntley distinguishes Protestant from Catholic meditation according to five major characteristics: "philosophically it is Platonic, not Aristotelian; in psychology it is Augustinian, not Thomistic; its theology is Pauline-Calvinist; though starting with the individual it finally becomes more public than private, and bears a greater similarity to the sermon than to penitential prayer; and it finds a greater variety of subject matter in God's 'three books' [the book of God's creation, the Bible, and the meditator's soul]" (Medieval and Renaissance Texts and Studies [Binghamton, New York: Center for Medieval and Early Renaissance Studies, 1981], 8–9). Despite the subtlety of these differences in the actual texts of Bishop Hall—some of which are phrased with great similarity to the contemporaneous work of François de Sales—Huntley's comment on the three "books" is an apt way to put the receptive spirit of much Protestant meditation. In Hall's *Occasional Meditations*, in particular, the devout writer expresses the meditation as a simple reading of the signs inscribed by God in the physical world. These meditations are imaginative, in the Aristotelian-Thomistic sense of imagination, because they require the writer and the reader to perceive sensory experience. But they are also markedly hermeneutic in that they take things as ideographs for God's message, which the author uncovers for the reader. The physical world is simply a reminder of a lesson expressed by God to man. Later in the century the work of the eminent and prolific French Protestant writer Pierre Jurieu (1627–1713) makes a frontal attack against Salesian imagination-centered meditation. Jurieu's book, subtitled "Traité de l'amour divin"—clearly reminiscent of de Sales's very similar title—complains that "The imagination of Man is too active" (*A Plain Method of Christian Devotion: Laid*

Down in Discourses, Meditations, and Prayers fitted to the Various Occasions of A Religious Life, translated by W. Fleetwood [London: Printed for C. Harper, 1692], 107), and gives an account of imagination that clearly disqualifies it as a *mental* faculty. In Jurieu's view, imagination belongs to the body, as the senses themselves do: "by the Heart I understand the Seat of the Passions and Imagination; 'tis evident that both these faculties are corporeal. The Imagination is, for 'tis the place where those Images that come to us from the Senses meet, and offer themselves to our minds when their true Objects are away . . ." (217). Thus imagination is not an instrument that the mind uses to realize specific goals that it forms but rather a breach in the mind's defenses against the outside world. The devout Christian should "keep the Soul as it were lock'd up" (286).

3. The Bibliothèque Nationale de France has twenty-four seventeenth-century editions, and that collection is certainly not complete.

4. The distinction between the public and private spheres as a mechanism to bring about the end of the religious civil wars at the end of the sixteenth centuries has been especially well described by Stephen Toulmin in *Cosmopolis: The Hidden Agenda of Modernity* (New York: Free Press, 1990) and by Hélène Merlin-Kajman in "Corneille et la politique," Chapitre 1 in *L'absolutisme dans les lettres et la théorie des deux corps. Passions et politique*, Lumière Classique 29 (Paris: Honoré Champion, 2000).

5. Linda Timmermans, *L'accès des femmes à la culture (1598–1715): Un débat d'idées de Saint François de Sales à la Marquise de Lambert* (Paris: Honoré Champion, 1993), 406. Timmermans and others have described the intended audience of de Sales's book, which broadens the devout life beyond the cloister while focusing on the upper classes.

6. "On a voulu montrer [. . .] qu'il y avoit des choses corporelles que l'on concevoit d'une manière spirituelle & sans se les imaginer . . ." (Antoine Arnauld and Pierre Nicole, *La Logique ou l'art de penser*, "Champs" Collection [Paris: Flammarion, 1970], 52).

7. Aquinas states that *phantasia* is subject to our will: "the state of phantasia is up to us, when we want, because it is in our power to form something that appears before our eyes, so to speak—such as golden mountains or whatever we want to appear. This is plain in the case of people who remember and form for themselves images of things, which they see at will" (book III, chapter 4, 249–261, Thomas Aquinas, *The Commentary on the De Anima of Aristotle*, translated by Robert Pasnau, Yale Library of Medieval Philosophy [New Haven: Yale University Press, 1999], 325).

8. Michel de Montaigne, "De la force de l'imagination," in *Les Essais*, edited by Pierre Villey, with a preface by V.-L. Saulnier (Paris: Presses Universitaires de France, 1965), 103. François de Sales, born in 1567, was twenty-three years old when the 1595 edition of the *Essais* appeared.

9. Later in the seventeenth century, Pierre Jurieu attacked at length the whole concept of self-help and gave particular attention to the use of specific human faculties (*Traité de la Nature et de la Grace ou Du concours général de la Providence*

et du concours particulier [Utrecht: François Halsma, 1687]. For Jurieu the idea that someone can guide his will by using his understanding is nonsense first of all because the faculties are all corrupt ("Tous ceux qui ne sont pas Pélagiens avoüent que la corruption de l'homme a son siège généralement dans toutes les facultez de l'ame; elle est dans l'entendement par les faux jugemens, & par les erreurs; elle est dans la volonté par les mauvaises habitudes; elle est dans les passions par la revolte et par la rebellion" 183) and secondly because both imagination and judgment are, in human experience, overwhelmed by passion. Jurieu seldom mentions imagination—his main purpose is to show the weakness of human judgment—as if to indicate that training the imagination is of no importance since its role is simply to represent objects to judgment. Passion is so deeply rooted in the human soul ("le penchant qui est dans l'ame" 195) that our surrender to temptation is instantaneous: "On dit, les objets frappent premièrement les sens, les sens conduisent ces objets à l'entendement, l'entendement porte son jugement favorable ou contraire, et de là naît en suite la passion d'amour ou de haine; donc les passions naissent de faux jugemens. Je répons que cela ne se fait pas toujours ainsi, puisque nous avons prouvé que souvent les objets vont droit à la passion, et l'émeuvent sans permettre à l'entendement de faire ses réflexions" (194). When Jurieu finally mentions imagination, giving a classic account of its function—"le beau et le bon presentez aux yeux frappent l'imagination, les images formées dans l'imagination se présentent à l'entendement, l'entendement les contemple, en connoît les liaisons et les rapports, en suite la volonté y acquiesce et s'y porte" (225)—it is only to reject the project of training imagination and judgment to react to the sudden assaults of the senses.

10. John Calvin, *The Bondage and Liberation of the Will*, edited by A.N.S. Lane, translated by G.I. Davies (Grand Rapids, Michigan: Baker Books, 1996 [first published 1543]), 136.

11. *Ibid.*, 136.

12. Compare the English Protestant Joseph Hall, who like François de Sales, stresses the increase of the meditator's love of God: "God's school is more of affection than understanding," writes Hall (*The Arte of Divine Meditation*, 72). It is not clear, doctrinally, what effect an increase of love for God would have, though Hall writes that God "useth not to cast away His love on those of whom He is but known, not loved" (72), which seems to imply that the love of man for God *causes* God's love for that individual.

13. Protestants often used the term "meditation" to mean a nonimaginative practice of sustained study of a specific passage of Scripture, a use of the term that has historic basis in early Christianity. For an example of this form of meditation see the work of the prominent Calvinist author Théodore de Bèze, *Chrestiennes Méditations*, Textes Littéraires Français (Geneva: Droz, 1964) and Pierre Jurieu, *La Pratique de la dévotion, ou Traité de l'amour divin* (Rotterdam: A. Acher, 1700).

14. For an especially good description of Calvinist and Lutheran approaches to inward spirituality and for the distinction between faith, which comes from God's Spirit, and "belief," which is a merely "human fabrication," see Richard Strier, "The Heart Alone: Inwardness and Individualism," in *Love Known. Theology and*

Experience in George Herbert's Poetry (Chicago: University of Chicago Press, 1983), 143–73.

15. Louis Martz explains this doctrinal difference between Puritan meditation and the Catholic practice (*The Poetry of Meditation*, revised edition [New Haven: Yale University Press, 1962], 153–63).

16. Blaise Pascal, *Oeuvres complètes*, edited by Louis Lafuma, with a preface by Henri Gouhier, L'Intégrale (Paris: Le Seuil, 1963), 618.

17. A typical entry in Ignatius's diary is "Después, a la oración, acabada la misa, unas nuevas mociones interiores, sollozos y lágrimas, todo en amor de Jesú...." ("Diario Espiritual," in *Obras Completas*, edited by Ignacio Iparraguirre, Biblioteca de autores cristianos [Madrid: La Editorial Catolica, 1963], 344–45).

18. John W. O'Malley, *The First Jesuits* (Cambridge, MA: Harvard University Press, 1993), 27. O'Malley notes that "in a few important respects" Loyola's teachings resembled that of the *alumbrados*, who were, in turn, often considered simply to be Lutherans or Erasmians (28, and 28n11).

19. O'Malley, *The First Jesuits*, 28. O'Malley considers the "discernment of spirits" as being "at the very core of the *Spiritual Exercises*" (p. 41). Teresa of Avila makes the distinction between human will (and action) and God's will very pointedly toward the beginning of *Paternoster* (or *The Way of Perfection*, as it is known in English translation) when she urges her sisters to rely totally on God's will rather than on any effort: "never try to sustain yourselves by human artifices, or you will die of hunger, and rightly so. Keep your eyes fixed upon your Spouse: it is for Him to sustain you..." (*The Way of Perfection*, E. Allison Peers [Garden City: Image Books, 1964], 39).

20. The practice of religious meditation in England, influenced in part by Jesuit exercises and in part by Calvin and other Protestant leaders, is frequently more attentive to the desolation and suffering of the seeker. Debora Shuger describes the similarities in the writings of Lancelot Andrewes and Richard Hooker as placing the sense of God's presence "within a larger context that represents religious existence as suffused with doubt, fear of rejection, [and] a sense of the absence of God that verges on despair. They struggle with the apparent lack of justice in history, with the failure of faith, with the fear that God is indifferent or hostile. Hooker's sermons in particular are marked with a sense of desolation...." (*Habits of Thought in the English Renaissance. Religion, Politics, and the Dominant Culture* [Berkeley: University of California Press, 1990], 70). This schematic opposition of the imaginative and the hermeneutic (or receptive) forms of private devotion is merely meant to help highlight what seems to be characteristic of Salesian devotion, but the myriad of books of devotion from the late Middle Ages onward show a wide spectrum of ways of conceiving the inward relation to God. The indirect ancestry of François de Sales's work is certainly the *devotio moderna*, the Catholic movement that emphasized mental prayer and de-emphasized the intellectual element of religion. It has been argued that in the case of Anabaptist movements, at least, there was a relatively great continuity between Catholic *devotio moderna* and kindred devotional practices among Franciscan tertiaries and later Protestant emphasis on affective piety through

meditation (Kenneth Ronald Davis, *Anabaptism and Asceticism. A Study in Intellectual Origins* [Scottsdale, Pennsylvania: Herald Press, 1974], 246–55). A number of early sixteenth-century books of devotion in England have been described as laying the "groundwork of those famous imaginative constructions of Ignatius of Loyola" and as encouraging vivid mental perception of the savior and a strong emotional attachment to him (Helen C. White, *The Tudor Books of Private Devotion* [Madison: University of Wisconsin Press, 1951], 144). Like Loyola, Teresa of Avila had to defend herself against accusations of heterodox mysticism, specifically *alumbradismo*, and had to criticize explicitly visionary trances, though her position against these visions was equivocal (Alison Weber, *Teresa of Avila and the Rhetoric of Femininity* [Princeton: Princeton University Press, 1990], 145–46).

21. The condemnation of François de Salignac de la Mothe-Fénelon, archbishop of Cambrai, for his role in the Quietist controversy (1699), is the most visible and definitive reminder that the passive or hermeneutic form of meditation was not approved by the Church. Fénelon's specific instructions for the interior life are based on passivity and listening: "Nous sommes donc toujours inspirés, mais nous étouffons cette inspiration. Dieu ne cesse point de parler; mais le bruit des créatures au-dehors et de nos passions au-dedans, nous étourdit et nous empêche de l'entendre. Il faut faire taire toute créature, il faut se faire taire soi-même, pour écouter dans ce profond silence de toute l'âme cette voix ineffable de l'époux. Il faut prêter l'oreille; car c'est une voix douce et délicate, qui n'est entendue que de ceux qui n'entendent plus tout le reste" (François Salignac de La Mothe Fénelon, "Lettres et opuscules spirituelles," in *Oeuvres*, edited by Jacques Le Brun, La Pléiade [Paris: Gallimard], 590).

22. Late in the seventeenth century, for instance, Pierre Jurieu rejected doctrines, clearly based on or at least compatible with neo-Stoic ideas, of human self-improvement through management of perception and reason (*Traitté de la Nature et de la Grace ou Du concours général de la Providence et du concours particulier*).

23. Linda Timmermans takes too uniformly negative a view of imagination in the seventeenth century. She writes, "L'imagination, rappelons-le, était la faculté—peu appréciée, car source d'illusions–qu'avait l'âme de former des images, et non cette puissance créatrice magnifiée depuis le romantisme. Chez les femmes, cette faculté s'ébranle vite: lieu commun ancient, intégré dans toutes les théories psycho-physiologiques, des doctrines d'inpiration aristotélicienne au système cartésien, repris par Malebranche..." (*L'accès des femmes à la culture [1598–1715]: Un débat d'idées de Saint François de Sales à la Marquise de Lambert*, 622). Montaigne did not, as we have seen, give a simply negative view of imagination—though many passages of the *Essais* are critical of that faculty—and Malebranche wrote many decades later, during the twilight of imagination.

24. Ignatian meditation has been widely studied both by historians of religion and by literary scholars. Most recently, Christian Belin has given a description of Loyola's technique, "La Méthode ignatienne," in *La Conversation intérieure. La Méditation en France au XVIIe siècle* (Paris: Honoré Champion, 2002), 85–98. See also Majorie O'Rourke Boyle, *Loyola's Acts: The Rhetoric of the Self* (Berkeley: University

of California Press, 1997), Antonio T. de Nicolás, *Ignatius de Loyola: Powers of Imagining. A Philosophical Hermeneutic of Imagining Through the Collected Works of Ignatius de Loyola* (Albany: State University of New York Press, 1986), O'Malley, *The First Jesuits*, Richard Strier, "Sanctifying the Aristocracy: 'Devout Humanism' in François de Sales, John Donne, and George Herbert," *The Journal of Religion* 69 (1989): 36–58, Bradley Rubidge, "Descartes's *Meditations* and Devotional Meditations," *Journal of the History of Ideas* 51, no. 1 (January–March 1990): 27–49 as well as the classic studies of devotional poetry by Terence Cave, Louis Martz, and Lance Donaldson-Evans.

25. Ignatius of Loyola, *Ejercicios Espirituales*, in *Obras Completas*, edited by Ignacio Iparraguirre, Biblioteca de autores cristianos (Madrid: La Editorial Catolica, 1963), 196–273. See I. Iparraguirre's comments on the early text of the *Exercises*, 182–87.

26. André Rayez notes that during the exercises the retreat director would often hand out individual sheets for each specific meditation and that these sheets would often include an image (André Rayez, "Imagerie et Dévotion," in *Dictionnaire de la Spiritualité Ascétique et Mystique*, edited by M. Viller, J. Cavallera, and J. Guibert [Paris: Beauchesne, 1937–95], 1532. In *Pharetra divini amoris*, a 1539 publication cited by Rayez, Jean-Juste Landsberge, of the Charterhouse of Köln, makes the following suggestion for devout meditation: "Place une image du Coeur du Seigneur, ou des cinq Plaies ou de Jésus en sa Passion, en un endroit où tu passes souvent... En la regardant, souviens-toi de ton exil et de la captivité misérable du péché. Par des soupirs et un ardent désir élève ton coeur à Dieu... Si la dévotion intérieure t'en presse, tu pourrais baiser cette image en te persuadant que c'est le Coeur du Seigneur" (Rayez, 1533). This example shows how the public iconography of the church with its visual aids to prayer could be integrated into the private world of the devout person.

27. The first book of the *Introduction à la vie dévote* is closest to the Ignation meditations of the *Spiritual Exercises*, but de Sales's work gives the appearance of being more finished, more suitable for reading by the individual meditator. The text of the *Spiritual Exercises* is a strange mixture of various kinds of texts, appearing at times to offer a clear structure and at others to be a disorganized notebook of practical advice. It includes guided meditations for four "weeks"—though the term is used loosely to indicate phases, which can be condensed to fewer than seven days or stretched to twelve—as well as "rules," "methods of prayer," and advice on eating, drinking and choosing goals in life. Although at times the text addresses the reader in the second person as if the book were to be used independently by the meditator, at other times it is clear that the book is addressed to retreat directors who, in their turn, guide the meditators and make discretionary changes in some of the techniques and phases of the retreat. The course of the exercises, done in their entirety, would take about a month and would culminate in the important life choice that occasioned the retreat.

28. Mary Carruthers, in *The Book of Memory. A Study of Memory in Medieval Culture*, Cambridge Studies in Medieval Literature (Cambridge: Cambridge University

Press, 1990), points out the link of memory with the body in the teachings of Thomas Aquinas. "True memory" requires the body, whereas "intellectual memory" does not (58).

29. The term "residence" signifies here the act of residing, and not simply a space, but this act of residing establishes the privilege of the inside, "le coeur de votre coeur et l'esprit de votre esprit" (*IVD* 83).

30. François de Sales was familiar with at least some of the Stoic writers, and Thérèse Goyet writes of "sa culture stoïcienne" ("'Notre Mère, la Providence': La méthode salésienne lue par Bossuet," in *L'Univers salésien. Saint François de Sales hier et aujourd'hui* , edited by Hélène Bordes and Jacques Hennequin [Metz: Université de Metz, 1994], 368). For a comparison of the Stoic and Salesian conceptions of love and will, see Carole Talon-Hugon, "Affectivité stoïcienne, affectivité salésienne," in *Le Stoïcisme aux XVIe et XVIIe siècles*, edited by Jacqueline Lagrée (Caen: Presses Universitaires de Caen, 1994), 95–108.

31. For a stimulating and thorough description of the interior space as conceived by François de Sales, see Mino Bergamo, *L'Anatomia dell'anima da François de Sales a Fénelon* (Bologna: Il Mulino, 1991).

32. Terence C. Cave, *Devotional Poetry in France, c.1570–1613* (Cambridge: Cambridge University Press, 1969) and Louis Martz, *The Poetry of Meditation*, revised edition (New Haven: Yale University Press, 1962).

33. The combination of intense material realism and spiritual symbolism that is typical, in France, of Georges de La Tour (1593–1652) and, more broadly, of European painting in the wake of Caravaggio (1571–1610) is related to the spiritual renewal of the Catholic Reform after Trent and particularly to the use of imagination in devotion. One art historian has written, conveying the consensus, "Il semble que la singularité déterminante de l'art de La Tour consiste en une apparente contradiction entre son indéniable naturalisme [. . .] et un spiritualisme non moins évident" (Youri Zolotov, "Le Style de Georges de La Tour," in *Georges de La Tour ou La nuit traversée. Colloque à Vic-sur-Seille, du 9 au 11 septembre 1993*, compiled by Anne Reinbold [Metz: Editions Serpenoise, 1994], 159). In a similar vein Bruno Ferté has written, "Le caravagisme a bien été l'événement essentiel qui a dominé l'essor de la peinture au XVIIe siècle [. . .] Plus encore qu'une nouvelle manière de peindre, le caravagisme correspond à une nouvelle attitude spirituelle, issue de la Contre-Réforme" (Bruno Ferté, *Georges de La Tour*, with a preface by Pierre Rosenberg, Maîtres de l'Art [Paris: Gallimard, 1999], 15). La Tour's work links itself directly to the meditation movement by depicting people engaged in meditation, particularly the three different depictions of the penitent Magdalene.

34. Harry Austryn Wolfson, *Harvard Theological Review* 28, no. 2 (April 1935), *The Internal Senses in Latin, Arabic, and Hebrew Philosophic Texts*.

35. Bernard Beugnot, *Le discours de la retraite au XVIIe siècle* (Paris: Presses Universitaires de France, 1996). As we saw in the previous chapter, Montaigne's "De la solitude" argues that physical solitude is not, in itself, useful unless a person has already acquired the mental disposition of independence. François de Sales promotes Montaigne's idea aggressively, but the physical private space still has a role

in the devotions he recommends. On small, private rooms in the Renaissance and early-modern period see "Architectural Planning," in *The Italian Renaissance Interior* (New York: Harry N. Abrams, Inc., 1991), 283–320; Mirka Benes, *Villas and Gardens in Early-Modern Italy and France* (Cambridge: Cambridge University Press, 1992); and Orest Ranum, "The Refuges of Intimacy," in *Passions of the Renaissance*, A History of Private Life, edited by Roger Chartier, Philippe Ariès, and Georges Duby, translated by Arthur Goldhammer (Cambridge, MA: Harvard University Press, 1989), 207–63.

36. Il ne faut pas pourtant, Philothée, s'arrêter tant à ces affections générales que vous ne les convertissiez en des résolutions spéciales et particulières pour votre correction et amendement (*IVD* 88).

37. One can compare the *Introduction's* account of Catherine of Siena's reimagining of the physically present world to Stoic advice about managing the *phantasia* of the present. Epictetus says, for instance, "His son is dead. What happened? His son is dead. Nothing else? Not a thing. His ship is lost. What happened? His ship is lost" (*The Discourses as Reported by Arrian, The Manual, and Fragments*, compiled and edited by W.A. Oldfather, Loeb Classics (Cambridge, MA: Harvard University Press, 1985 [first edition 1928]), II, 60–61). Epictetus's approach is to recognize the incoming sense impressions without adding to them narratives and judgments. Catherine of Siena's approach takes Epictetus's advice and turns it around. Instead of saying "This is my father. Who is this? This is my father," she would say "This is my father. Who is this? This is Jesus." François de Sales referred to Epictetus as "le bon Epictète" and usually cites his *Manual* and *Discourses* in a translation by Jean de Saint-François Goulu published in Paris in 1609 (see A. Ravier's note in his edition of de Sales, 1828).

38. François de Sales writes often of the complex layers into which the will folds itself, posing a question of ethical evaluation in terms that resemble La Rochefoucauld's celebrated first maxim on the hidden desires that are beyond our knowing because they are shaped into "mille insensibles tours et retours" (François de La Rochefoucauld, *Réflexions ou sentences et maximes morales*, in *Moralistes du XVIIe siècle*, edited by André-Alain Morello and Jean Lafond, Bouquins [Paris: Robert Laffont, 1992], "maximes supprimées" no. 1, 179–81). In the *Introduction*, de Sales exclaims, "Ô Philothée, je ne sais si c'est un désir juste de désirer d'avoir justement ce qu'un autre possède justement..." (*IVD* 171). On the problem of willing to will see André Glucksmann, *Les Maîtres penseurs* (Paris: Grasset, 1977), 25.

39. John D. Lyons, "La Rhétorique de l'honnêteté: Pascal et l'agrément," in *Èthos et pathos. Le statut du sujet rhétorique*, edited by François Cornilliat and Richard Lockwood (Paris: Honoré Champion, 2000), 357–69.

40. Kathleen Wine, *Forgotten Virgo. Humanism and Absolutism in Honoré d'Urfé's "L'Astrée"*, Travaux Du Grand Siècle (Geneva: Droz, 2000), 17.

41. The exceptional standing of François de Sales in the French Catholic Church of his century can be measured by the fact that he was canonized only forty-four years after his death.

42. Lucien Goldmann, *Le Dieu caché. Etude sur la vision tragique dans les* Pensées *de Pascal et dans le théâtre de Racine*, Bibliothèque des Idées (Paris: Gallimard, 1959), 61 ff.

43. The present study is indebted to so many scholars of these related social and literary phenomena that it would take too much space to mention them all in a note. See the bibliographical entries for the work of Merlin-Kajman, Courtine and Haroche, Paige, Houdart, Zagorin, Bury, Seifert, Van Delft, and Taylor.

44. Nicolas Faret, *L'Honneste Homme, ou l'Art de plaire à la cour* (Paris: Presses Universitaires de France, 1925 [first published 1635]) and La Rochefoucauld, *Réflexions ou sentences et maximes morales.*

45. Modern use of the term *déchet* might lead us toward the idea of a by-product or waste product in sexual pleasure, but in de Sales's day it signified decay or decline in value, "A fall from former worth, or goodnesse; a decay, wast [*sic*], lessening, minishing, in gold, silver, wine, oyle, etc." (Randle Cotgrave, *A Dictonarie of the French and English Tongues* [London, 1611], Reprint. Columbia: University of South Carolina Press, 1950).

46. In fact, the *Introduction* discourages all forward-looking imagination, except for the edifying vision of judgment, hell, or paradise, and in certain cases, of the deathbed. Otherwise, even the hope of something legitimate, like life in the convent, is harmful: "L'ennemi nous procure souvent des grands désirs pour des objets absents et qui ne se présenteront jamais, afin de divertir notre esprit des objets présents esquels, pour petits qu'ils soient, nous pourrions faire grand profit. Nous combattons les monstres d'Afrique en imagination, et nous nous laissons tuer en effet aux menus serpents qui sont en notre chemin, à faute d'attention" (*IVD* 232).

47. This passage is the subject of an insightful and lively commentary by Milad Doueihi, "Elephantine Marriage," *MLN* 106, no. 4 (1991): 780–92.

48. Strict control of married sexual pleasure—presumably the reduction of sexual activity to the minimum and care in not noticing pleasure during intercourse—are the best preparation for Catholic widowhood: "Les lampes desquelles l'huile est aromatique jettent une plus suave odeur quand on éteint leurs flammes: ainsi les veuves desquelles l'amour a été pur en leur mariage répandent un plus grand parfum de vertu de chasteté quand leur lumière, c'est-à-dire leur mari, est éteinte par la mort" (*IVD* 246).

49. There is a fairly direct analogy between the situation of married devout people and celibate devout people in regard to the sexual imagination. Married people have to discipline their imagination of what is present (engage in sexual acts without attaching their "affection" to the pleasure, *IVD* 164) while the celibate must avoid attaching their "affection" to the purely mental images of sexuality.

50. *IVD*, part III, Chapter 23, "Des exercices de la mortification extérieure."

51. "Sainte Madeleine ayant l'espace de trente ans demeuré en la grotte que l'on voit encore en Provence, ravie tous les jours sept fois et élevée en l'air par les Anges, comme pour aller chanter les sept Heures canoniques en leur choeur..." (*TAD* 697).

52. Meditation, thus, is distinct from *study*: "Quelquefois nous pensons attentivement à quelque chose pour apprendre ses causes, ses effets, ses qualités; et cette pensée s'appelle étude, en laquelle l'esprit fait comme les hannetons qui volettent sur les fleurs et les feuilles indistinctement pour les manger et s'en nourrir" (*TAD* 612).

53. Choderlos de Laclos, *Les Liaisons dangereuses*, edited by Yves Le Hir, Classiques Garnier (Paris: Garnier, 1961), 177 (letter 81).

54. "Sade's Discourse on Method: Rudiments for a Theory of Fantasy," *MLN* 99, no. 5 (1984): 1059.

55. "Sade's Discourse on Method," 1057.

56. "True libertinage requires a break with all acts grounded in the senses" (Harari, 1061).

57. Jeanne des Anges, *Autobiographie*, edited by Gabriel Legué and Gilles De La Tourette (Montbonnot-St Martin: Jérôme Millon, 1985), 174. Subsequent parenthetical references to the text of Jeanne des Anges will be to this edition.

58. Jeanne des Anges, 188.

59. "Dans ce moment, le Père vit très manifestement se former sur ma main le nom de Jésus, au-dessus des noms de Marie et de Joseph, en beaux caractères vermeils et sanglants. Le nom de François de Sales fut ensuite formé sans que le Père s'en aperçût; quelques religieuses qui en étaient proches virent se former celui de François de Sales" (Jeanne des Anges, 191).

60. On Jeanne des Anges and the devils of Loudun see *La Possession de Loudun*, edited by Michel De Certeau (Paris: Gallimard/Julliard, 1980), and Nicholas D. Paige, *Being Interior: Autobiography and the Contradictions of Modernity in Seventeenth-Century France* (Philadelphia: University of Pennsylvania Press, 2001), 179–225.

61. Hélène Trépanier, "Les grâces extraordinaires ou les 'surnaturelles connaissances expérimentales' de Jean-Joseph Surin," in *Le Savoir au XVIIe siècle*, edited by John D. Lyons and Cara Welch, Biblio 17 (Tübingen: Gunter Narr Verlag, 2003), 151–60.

62. François de Sales was not yet beatified, that is, officially given the title of "blessed," until 1661, yet Jeanne des Anges refers to him with this adjective, "bienheureux François de Sales" (174).

63. Jean-Joseph Surin, "Triomphe de l'Amour divin sur les puissances de l'Enfer," in *Triomphe de l'Amour divin sur les puissances de l'Enfer et Science expérimentale des choses de l'autre vie*, with an afterword by Michel De Certeau (Grenoble: Jérome Millon, 1990), 37.

64. Hélène Trépanier's reading of Surin's account of the exorcism of Jeanne des Anges underscores the role of imagination (the thought of sensory perception) in his approach: "La *Science expérimentale* propose une sémiologie où le corps constitue un ensemble de signes qui doivent être interprétés selon le code chrétien. Le corps et les sensations sont le lieu où Dieu se manifeste" ("Les grâces extraordinaires ou les 'surnaturelles connaissances expérimentales' de Jean-Joseph Surin," in *Le Savoir au XVIIe siècle*, edited by John D. Lyons and Cara Welch, Biblio 17 [Tübingen: Gunter Narr Verlag, 2003], 157).

CHAPTER 3

1. Charles Taylor, *Sources of the Self. The Making of the Modern Identity* (Cambridge, MA: Harvard University Press, 1989), 143–76.

2. For instance Stephen Toulmin's *Cosmopolis* and Joan DeJean's *Ancients against Moderns* have in common the view that the late seventeenth-century is dominated by Cartesian rationality, and both authors celebrate the late-twentieth-century movement beyond this way of thinking. Strikingly, both these books, despite many differences of detail in their view of French intellectual life, omit any substantial discussion of Blaise Pascal. Toulmin does mention Pascal five times, including a footnote, usually in lists. On only one point does Toulmin give Pascal a significant portion of a single sentence, a comment on the *Lettres Provinciales*. DeJean does not even mention his name. Pascal has been so canonical a figure that his disappearance from Toulmin and DeJean's books points to a wider and largely silent shift in scholarship toward ignoring him in books dealing with the century as a whole (while Pascal studies flourish separately on their own). Erica Harth, in her *Ideology and Culture in Seventeenth-Century France* (1983), does not mention Pascal (or for that matter, Nicole or Arnauld), though in her *Cartesian Women* (1992), Pascal does figure in part of one paragraph. Although there is no lack of books about Pascal, there does seem to be a problem of integrating Pascal into a view of his century, so much so that the fragile Cartesian view is promoted only to be rejected in what could be called the "Cartesian straw-man" view of the seventeenth century, the view that Cartesianism was a uniform and dominant way of thinking.

3. Blaise Pascal, *Selections from The Thoughts*, Arthur H. Beattie (Arlington Heights, Illinois: Harlan Davidson, 1965), 17–20. Most English-language studies of Pascal simply leave *finesse* in French. On Pascal's shift from the *esprit de géométrie* to *l'esprit de finesse* in his rhetorical preferences see Nicholas Hammond, *Playing with Truth. Language and the Human Condition in Pascal's Pensées* (Oxford: Clarendon Press, 1994), 10–8. References in this chapter to the *Pensées* are taken from the edition by Philippe Sellier (Paris: Classiques Garnier, 1991) but the numbering of the fragments will include the Lafuma number as well (Pascal, *Oeuvres complètes* [Paris: L'Intégrale, Éditions du Seuil, 1963]). The Lafuma numbering will be noted as "L." and the Sellier numbering as "S.".

4. René Descartes, *Discours de la méthode*, in *Oeuvres complètes*, edited by Charles Adam and Paul Tannery (Paris: Vrin, 1996), 6, 11.

5. René Descartes, *Discours de la méthode*, in *Oeuvres complètes*, 6, 31.

6. In fact, one scholar has proposed defining *finesse* as shared opinion, and thus not only ordinary life but the ordinary discourse about life (Erec Koch, *Pascal and Rhetoric: Figural and Persuasive Language in the Scientific Treatises, the Provinciales and the Pensées* [Charlottesville: Rookwood Press, 1997], 132).

7. Lucien Goldmann, *Le Dieu caché. Etude sur la vision tragique dans les Pensées de Pascal et dans le théâtre de Racine*, Bibliothèque des idées (Paris: Gallimard, 1959).

8. René Descartes, *Discours de la méthode*, in *Oeuvres complètes*, 6, 19.

9. The contrast between the Cartesian linear approach and the Pascal *finesse* has been aptly described by Martin Warner as the difference between "progressive reasoning," on one hand, and "digressive reasoning" on the other (Martin Warner, *Philosophical Finesse. Studies in the Art of Rational Persuasion* [Oxford: Clarendon Press, 1989], 197), but digression, while giving a good sense of the inclusiveness of *finesse*, does not serve well to convey the necessary simultaneity of perception of the things related.

10. Norman continues, "Sentiment acts quickly—'il agit en un instant et toujours est prêt à agir' (L.821/S.661)—and grasps concepts immediately..." (*Portraits of Thought: Knowledge, Methods, and Styles in Pascal* [Columbus: Ohio State University Press, 1988], 15–6).

11. Despite the strong link between *finesse* and imagination, it is important to note one statement in Pascal's passages on *finesse* and *géométrie* that seems to run in a contrary direction: "Et les fins qui ne sont que fins ne peuvent avoir la patience de descendre jusques dans les premiers principes des choses spéculatives et d'imagination qu'ils n'ont jamais vues dans le monde, et tout à fait hors d'usage" (L.512/S.670). Although a certain type of imagination is here denied to those who think solely with *finesse* (and by implication attributed to the geometrical thinkers), this concerns only a particular use of imagination, one that is *not* connected with things that are actually seen (perceived by the senses) in the world but useful for dealing with abstract principles. One might hazard the guess that Pascal is referring to those who are trying to imagine geometric figures or visualize some other consequence of a scientific hypothesis. Moreover, Pascal does not say that the *esprit fin* cannot imagine these things but rather will not persevere long enough to understand the principles on which these hypothetical imaginings are based. In short, Pascal seems to be emphasizing the relation between *finesse* and the things of everyday life. Another cautionary note against the complete identification of imagination and *sentiment* comes from Martin Warner, who quotes fragment L.975/S.739 in which Pascal says that men take their imagination for their heart, and also fragment L.530/S.455: "Mais la fantaisie est semblable et contraire au sentiment; de sorte qu'on ne peut distinguer entre ces contraires..." (*Philosophical Finesse. Studies in the Art of Persuasion* [Oxford: Clarendon Press, 1989], 164).

12. Pierre Bourdieu has recently reintroduced the ancient rhetorical concept of a person's material embodiment, the *habitus*. See, for instance, his *Language and Symbolic Power*, with an introduction by John B. Thompson, translated by Gino Raymond and Matthew Adamson (Cambridge, MA: Harvard University Press, 1991).

13. Gérard Ferreyrolles, *Les Reines du monde. L'imagination et la coutume chez Pascal*, with a preface by Jean Mesnard, Lumière Classique (Paris: Honoré Champion, 1995).

14. Erec Koch has recently shown that the therapy of the mind through discipline of the body was not only of concern to followers of traditional ascetic practices in the seventeenth century. Koch argues convincingly that Descartes proposed an "ethics founded on the regulation of the body and its sensory and sensible responses" in distinction from "contemporary iterations of Stoicism and ascetic piety, ethics

grounded in the mastery of the will and self-mastery" ("Cartesian Aesth/Ethics: The Correspondence with Princess Elisabeth of Bohemia," North American Society for Seventeenth-Century French Literature [Portland State University, Portland, Oregon, 2004]).

15. Gianfrancesco Pico della Mirandola, "On the Imagination," in *Cornell Studies in English*, edited and translated by Harry Caplan (Ithaca: Cornell University Press, 1930 [original text 1501]), 56–63.

16. Nicholas Hammond points out that one positive aspect of Stoic teaching for Pascal may be the refusal, shared by the Stoics and Pascal, of "the attainment of self-knowledge" (*Playing with Truth. Language and the Human Condition in Pascal's Pensées*, 140).

17. Taylor, *Sources of the Self. The Making of the Modern Identity*, 357.

18. "Levez vos yeux vers Dieu, disent les uns; voyez celui auquel vous ressemblez, et qui vous a fait pour l'adorer. Vous pouvez vous rendre semblable à lui; la sagesse vous y égalera, si vous voulez le suivre. "Haussez la tête, hommes libres", dit Epictète" (L.430/S.683).

19. See Chapter II. François de Sales writes frequently of the discipline of attention, for example in the *Traité de l'amour de Dieu*, 616).

20. Fragments L.143–144/S.176–177.

21. There is an intriguing echo of the Pascalian comparison of the two types of mind in a passage that Antoine Houdar de La Motte wrote half a century later: "Il se trouve deux sortes de jugement dans les hommes. Les uns ne connaissent le vrai que par la discussion, les autres le sentent sans ce secours. Les premiers ne choisissent ou ne rejettent une idée qu'après l'avoir examinée de tous les sens et cette manière de juger, quoique la plus sûre, nuit presque toujours par sa lenteur à l'agrément parce qu'elle laisse refroidir l'*imagination* qui en est l'unique source. Les seconds, par des raisonnements soudains qu'ils auraient même de la peine à développer s'il fallait en rendre compte, embrassent d'une seule vue les défauts et les beautés des choses. Et c'est cette sorte de jugement qu'on appelle le goût" ("Discours sur le différent mérite des ouvrages d'esprit," in *Textes critiques. Les raisons du sentiment*, edited by Françoise Gevrey and Béatrice Guion, Sources Classiques [Paris: Honoré Champion, 2002], 439). Emphasis added.

22. This assignment of popular truth to imagination belongs to the complex dialectical process of "gradation," in which Pascal shows first that the people's opinion is correct (one should fear the powerful) before showing that their opinion is founded on faulty reasoning (the powerful do not actually merit their place in society) and then showing that despite the lack of logic to their position it is the right one to hold, outwardly at least (any attempt to modify the present order would lead to civil war, which is the worst of evils). This argumentation through reversal is set out in a series of fragments in the section "Raison des effets" (especially fragments L.87–L.104/S.121–136).

23. The indirectness that is required for understanding the self, following Pascal's dialectic, is exposited at greater length by his one-time collaborator (on the *Lettres Provinciales*) Pierre Nicole in his essay "De la connaissance de soi-même"

(in *Essais de morale*, edited by Laurent Thirouin [Paris: Presses Universitaires de France, 1999], 309–79). The importance of Nicole's essay for the development of the modern individual has recently been made clear in Erec Koch's article "Individuum: The Specular Self in Nicole's 'De la Connoissance de soi-même,'" paper presented at the conference of the North American Society for Seventeenth-Century French Literature, Arizona State University, May 2001 in *Pascal/New Trends in Port-Royal Studies*, compiled and edited by David Wetsel and David Canovas, Biblio 17 (Tübingen: Gunter Narr Verlag), 259–68.

24. I will refer to the person who is urged to undertake this imaginative effort as the "reader," simply because, whether or not the apologetic speaker in the *Pensées* is addressing an interlocutor who, in turn, makes specific objections, the reader must also follow through and participate in the imaginative exercise.

25. Emphasis added.

26. The imagination of the infinitely large and infinitely small has appropriately been linked to the meditative tradition by Hélène Michon (*L'ordre du coeur. Philosophie, théologie, et mystique dans les Pensées* de Pascal [Paris: Honoré Champion, 1996], 97–119).

27. Saint François de Sales, *Introduction à la vie dévote*, in *Oeuvres*, edited by André Ravier and Roger Devos, Pléiade (Paris: Gallimard, 1969), 61 and 63, introductory meditations 8 and 9.

28. Descartes distinguishes between imagination and intellectual conception by giving the example of geometrical figures that can be defined but cannot be imagined, e.g. the thousand-sided figure or kilogon (*Meditations* VI in *Oeuvres complètes*, edited by Charles Adam and Paul Tannery [Paris: Vrin, 1897–1910 [reprinted 1996]], 9, 57). On this subject see John D. Lyons, "Camera obscura: Image and imagination in Descartes's *Méditations*," in *Convergences. Rhetoric and Poetic in Seventeenth-Century France. Essays for Hugh M. Davidson,* edited by Mary B. McKinley and David Lee Rubin (Columbus, OH: Ohio State University Press, 1989), 179–95.

29. Cf. "Apologie de Raymond Sebond" (Michel de Montaigne, *Les Essais*, edited by Pierre Villey, with a preface by V.-L. Saulnier [Paris: Presses Universitaires de France, 1965], 587–600 and *The Complete Essays of Montaigne*, translated by Donald M. Frame [Stanford: Stanford University Press, 1958], 443–55).

30. Sara E. Melzer, *Discourses of the Fall* (Berkeley, CA: University of California Press, 1986), 59–61.

31. Gilberte Périer, "La Vie de Monsieur Pascal," in *Oeuvres complètes*, edited by Jean Mesnard (Paris: Desclée de Brouwer, 1964), 3, 607–8. On the importance of this invention in what could be called the "Pascal myth" as created by Port-Royal after his death see John D. Lyons, "The Sister and the Machine: Gilberte Périer's *Vie de Monsieur Pascal*," in *La Rochefoucauld, Mithridate, Frères et Soeurs*, edited by Claire Carlin (Tübingen: Gunter Narr, 1998), 181–90.

32. Blaise Pascal, "Entretien avec Monsieur de Sacy sur Epictète et Montaigne," in *Oeuvres complètes*, 3, 125–26.

33. Dominique Descotes writes, "La notion de Machine répond aussi au souci de surmonter l'inconstance: l'action sur l'automate et les habitudes a pour but de fixer

la pensée sur une croyance stable..." (*L'Argumentation chez Pascal* [Paris: Presses Universitaires de France, 1993], 39).

34. Nicolas Fontaine, in his *Mémoires*, reported Pascal's conversation with Le Maistre de Sacy: "M. Pascal lui [M. de Sacy] dit que ses deux livres les plus ordinaires avaient été Épictète et Montaigne, et il lui fit de grands éloges de ces deux esprits" (Blaise Pascal, "Entretien avec Monsieur de Sacy sur Epictète et Montaigne," edited by Jean Mesnard, in *Oeuvres complètes* [Paris: Desclée de Brouwer, 1964], 3, 130). Philippe Sellier points out the exceptional nature, given his circle, of Pascal's praise of Epictetus (*Pascal et Saint Augustin* [Paris: Armand Colin, 1970], 86).

35. Michel Le Guern, *Pascal et Descartes* (Paris: Nizet, 1971), 121–52.

36. Hugh M. Davidson, *Blaise Pascal* (Boston, MA: G.K. Hall, 1983), III.

37. Such an active view of the thinking faculty appears in fragment L.143/S.176, where Pascal enumerates three proximate causes of an outward movement: instinct, passions, and external objects. Instincts, as Buford Norman has observed, are for Pascal "very similar to principles but refer more to an awareness of something that remains from the past" (*Portraits of Thought: Knowledge, Methods, and Styles in Pascal*, 29). They are therefore associated in the *Pensées* with the first, lost, prelapsarian human nature and are not a passion. Their insight that we need to look outside of ourselves for happiness is therefore trustworthy, albeit obscure. Passions, in this fragment, are described as "pushing" us outward. The passions therefore seem to reside inside us and are active, not waiting for an external stimulus. Finally, the third cause, the objects that call to us without any (prior) thought of ours seem to correspond to the basic Cartesian model of objects which act on the soul through the stimulated animal spirits.

38. Actually Sellier's note (Blaise Pascal, *Pensées*, edited by Philippe Sellier, Classiques Garnier [Paris: Bordas, 1991], 471) does not mention Descartes, but the combined use of the terms "machine" and "bête" certainly leads to Article L of the first part of the *Passions de l'âme*.

39. Pascal, as we saw above, makes fun of Montaigne for asking why some-one would bow before a man with an impressive entourage. In effect, Pascal sees Montaigne's question as that of a geometric mind, one that cannot accept the obvious and wants to put everything to rigorous logical examination, at the expense of everyday practicality (L.89/S.123).

40. "Et les esprits fins au contraire, ayant ainsi *accoutumé* à juger d'une seule vue sont si étonnés quand on leur présente des propositions où ils ne comprennent rien et où pour entrer il faut passer par des définitions et des principes si stériles qu'ils n'ont point *accoutumé* de voir ainsi en détail, qu'ils s'en rebutent et s'en dégoûtent" (L.512/S.670, emphasis added).

CHAPTER 4

1. Marie de Rabutin-Chantal de Sévigné, *Correspondance*, edited by Roger Duchêne, Bibliothèque de la Pléiade (Paris: Gallimard, 1972–78), 2, 35 (8-7-75).

All subsequent references to Sévigné's text will be made to this edition and will give the volume, page, and the date of the letter in the U.S. format: month, day, year. English translations are my own.

2. 2, 966 (6-9-80). Sévigné here used the first person plural, we (*nous*), for herself, as she often does.

3. 3, 19 (9-22-80).

4. 1, 191 (3-18-71).

5. 3, 13 (9-15-80).

6. 1, 502–505 (5-6-72).

7. 1, 163–67 (2-23-71).

8. 2, 307 (6-1-76).

9. 1, 360 (10-7-71). The word in brackets has been conjectured by the editor, Roger Duchêne.

10. 1, 152 (9-2-71).

11. 1, 506 (5-13-72).

12. 2, 468 (6-18-77).

13. 3, 620 (6-19-89).

14. 2, 466 (6-16-77).

15. Epistolary novels and the genre of the letter itself have been the objects of intense and fruitful scholarly attention over the past several decades. See notably, Janet Gurkin Altman, *Epistolarity* (Columbus, OH: Ohio State University Press, 1982), François Jost, "Le Roman épistolaire et la technique narrative," in *Actes du VIIIe Congrès de l'Association Internationale de Littérature Comparée* (Stuttgart: Bieber, 1980), 297–304, *Writing the Female Voice: Essays on Epistolary Literature*, edited by Elizabeth C. Goldsmith (Boston, MA: Northeastern University Press, 1989), and *Epistolary Selves: Letters and Letter-Writers, 1600–1945*, edited by Rebecca Earle (Aldershot: Ashgate, 1999).

16. 2, 958 (6-5-80).

17. 2, 94 (9-9-75).

18. 2, 531 (8-21-77).

19. 2, 10–2 (7-19-75).

20. 2, 32 (8-6-75).

21. 3, 969 (7-12-91).

22. 2, 262 (4-8-76).

23. 2, 424 (10-16-76).

24. 1, 174 (3-3-71).

25. 2, 682 (9-22-79). Roger Duchêne's note on the conclusion of this passage refers, no doubt correctly, to the Cartesian doctrine of memory formation by the "impression" that the animal spirits make on the brain in response to stimuli. But it is worth noting that "impression" is also a term used in French for the Greek *phantasia*, or idea corresponding to a sense impression.

26. 1, 487 (4-22-72).

27. 2, 889 (4-3-80).

28. 1, 255 (5-18-71).

29. 3, 5 (9-8-80).

30. 2, 1033 (7-31-80).

31. 2, 1009 (7-14-80).

32. 2, 669 (8-25-79).

33. 2, 875 (8-17-80).

34. 2, 878 (3-20-80).

35. 2, 680 (9-18-79).

36. 2, 614 (6-24-78).

37. 3, 482 (1-24-89).

38. 3, 792–93 (1-1-90).

39. 2, 185 (12-11-75).

40. 1, 120 (4-21-70).

41. 2, 25 (7-31-75).

42. 2, 25 (7-31-75).

43. 2, 25 (7-31-75).

44. 2, 28 (7-31-75).

45. 2, 27 (7-31-75).

46. 3, 281 (2-20-87).

47. 3, 281 (2-26-87).

48. 3, 5 (9-8-80).

49. 3, 166 (12-13-84).

50. 3, 792 (1-1-90).

51. René Descartes, *Les Passions de l'âme*, in *Oeuvres complètes*, edited by Charles Adam and Paul Tannery (Paris: Vrin, 1996), 11, 373.

52. *Les Passions de l'âme*, 11, 384.

53. Marie de Rabutin-Chantal de Sévigné, *Correspondance*, edited by Roger Duchêne, Bibliothèque de la Pléiade (Paris: Gallimard, 1972–78), 3, 1529, letter 1180, note 4.

54. 2, 28 (8-2-75).

55. Sévigné writes to her daughter, "Je voudrais mettre tout ce que vous m'écrivez de M. de Turenne dans une oraison funèbre. Vraiment, votre lettre est d'une énergie et d'une beauté extraordinaires; vous étiez dans ces bouffées d'éloquence que donne l'émotion de la douleur" (2, 53 8-16-75).

56. 2, 54 (8-16-75).

57. 2, 50 (8-12-75).

58. 2, 78 (8-28-75).

59. 2, 48 (8-11-75).

60. 2, 44 (8-9-75).

61. 2, 44 (8-9-75).

62. Let us consider again the contrast between the ideal surprising deaths in Sévigné's letters and the ideal nonsurprising death in the poetics of French classical tragedy. The (absent) narrative of Lauzier's death, though of less political importance

than Turenne's, figures in Sévigné's letters as a highly successful and valuable surprise, because Lauzier died in the most unexpected, improbable way—of *apoplexy*. I emphasize the word, because this is the canonical example of the kind of death that might occur in a *bad* tragedy, or in a play that aspired to the status of tragedy but did not reach it. As d'Aubignac wrote in the 1640s in his treatise on drama, *La Pratique du théâtre* (Algiers: Jules Carbonel, 1927):

> Il est possible qu'un homme meure subitement, et cela souvent arrive; mais celuy-là seroit mocqué de tout le monde, qui pour dénouër une Piece de Theatre, feroit mourir un rival d'apoplexie, comme d'une maladie naturelle et commune, ou bien il y faudroit beaucoup de preparations ingenieuses.
>
> *(d'Aubignac, Pratique, 77)*

Far from making any attempt to "naturalize" or motivate the deaths of Turenne and Lauzier, Sévigné and we suppose Grignan, stress an almost magical quality. Sévigné's insistence on divine intervention is a replica of the *deus ex machina*, but a replica that is proposed with enthusiasm as necessary for the full appreciation of this admirable event.

63. Montaigne, "Que philosopher c'est apprendre à mourir" (*Essays*, I, 20:86/60). See Chapter I above.

64. Michèle Longino Farrell, *Performing Motherhood. The Sévigné Correspondence* (Hanover: University Press of New England, 1991).

65. Augustine is mentioned at least a score of times in Sévigné's letters, and the *Confessions* twice. Sévigné read this work in the translation of her friend, Robert Arnauld d'Andilly (Augustin, *Confessions*, translated by Robert Arnauld d'Andilly, Folio Classique (Paris: Gallimard, 1993 [first published 1649]).

66. Pierre Nicole, *Essais de morale*, edited by Laurent Thirouin (Paris: Presses Universitaires de France, 1999). I will refer to this selection of Nicole's work, which includes most of the essays that Sévigné emphasizes.

67. Pierre Nicole, "De la soumission à la volonté de Dieu," in *Essais de morale*, 67–107.

68. Nicole, "De la soumission," 101.

69. Nicole, "De la soumission," 92.

70. Nicole, "De la soumission," 93.

71. Nicole, "De la soumission," 102.

72. Sévigné, 1, 373–74 (10-28-71).

73. Sévigné, 2, 938–39 (5-21-80).

74. Pierre Nicole, "De la connaissance de soi-même," in *Essais de morale*, 309–79.

75. Nicole, "De la connaissance de soi-même," 314.

76. Nicole, "De la connaissance de soi-même," 316. On the role of material objects in Nicole's theory of the *moi* see Erec Koch, "*Individuum*: The Specular Self in Nicole's *De la Connoissance de Soi-Même*," paper presented at the conference of the North American Society for Seventeenth-Century French Literature, Arizona

State University, May 2001 in *Pascal/New Trends in Port-Royal Studies*, compiled and edited by David Wetsel and David Canovas, Biblio 17 (Tübingen: Gunter Narr Verlag), 263.

77. Nicole, "De la connaissance de soi-même," 317.

78. The second strategy proposed in "De la connaissance de soi-même" seems—though it is impossible to know from Sévigné's performance of herself—to be less applicable to the letters. This strategy consists of concealing one's own resentment of criticism in order to obtain access to the usually hidden "portraits" that other people form of us. On this subject see my article, "Self-Knowledge and the Advantages of Concealment," in *Culture and Authority in the Baroque*, edited by Massimo Ciavolella and Patrick Coleman (Toronto: University of Toronto Press, in press).

79. Sévigné describes her friend Corbinelli as more and more philosophical and "mourant tous les jours à quelque chose" (3, 242 11-24-85).

80. Saint François de Sales, *Introduction à la vie dévote*, in *Oeuvres*, 191.

81. Rather than name the supporters of Port-Royal, Sévigné refers elliptically to them as "nos amis," as, for instance, when she tells of M. de Longueville's confession "conduite par nos amis" (1, 547 7-3-72).

82. Koch notes that Nicole also emphasizes "the atomic solitude of the individual" ("*Individuum*," 263).

CHAPTER 5

1. National Gallery, London, number 001297. The Magdalene is seen close up, in the foreground of the picture, in a green dress and white wimple, probably seated on a low stool that is under her ample skirt, with her back rather uncomfortably up against a piece of furniture, while behind her we see a man's legs and behind him a window. This painting, from the mid-fifteenth century, was painted far before Scudéry's day and before the somber and solitary penitent Magdalenes of Georges de La Tour. The sight of a woman deeply absorbed in a book may have struck van der Weyden as almost miraculous in itself, but by Madeleine de Scudéry's time this must have become a fairly common sight.

2. The Protestant Reformation and the Catholic response after the Council of Trent led to great progress in literacy during the course of the seventeenth century. See *Lire et écrire: l'alphabétisation des Français de Calvin à Jules Ferry*, edited by François Furet and Jacques Ozouf (Paris: Editions de Minuit, 1977). Henri-Jean Martin writes that after the end of the Wars of Religion "the number of books grew unrelentingly" (*The French Book. Religion, Absolutism, and Readership, 1585–1715* [Baltimore: Johns Hopkins University Press, 1996], 38).

3. Madeleine de Scudéry, *Clélie, histoire romaine* (Paris: Augustin Courbé, 1654–61 [reprinted Geneva: Slatkine Reprints, 1973]). Parenthetical references in this chapter will be to this facsimile reprint of the 1654–61 Courbé edition, giving the volume and page numbers.

4. Both Scudéry's and Lafayette's novels were initially published under the names of male authors. The title page of *Clélie* attributes the work to "Monsieur de Scudéry"

(Madeleine's brother, Georges de Scudéry) and *Zayde* was initially attributed to Lafayette's friend Jean Regnauld de Segrais.

5. We could, for instance, compare Scudéry's work to the *Heptaméron* (1558), the very influential collection of stories from the previous century by Marguerite de Navarre.

6. Or really a story-within-the-story-within-the-story, since we learn of these mental pictures through narratives that are told within the novel to other characters. So that these are embedded narratives at the third degree.

7. The two murders and the web of kinship are carefully explained by Scudéry before this dense passage: Tullie, the cruel, ambitious younger daughter of King Servius Tullius, is married to Prince Amériole, the younger, virtuous Tarquin brother. The King's virtuous older daughter, known as "the Princess" is married to the older, cruel Tarquin brother. Among this foursome, each person is married to his/her moral opposite and is in love with his/her sibling's spouse (*Clélie*, II, 864–6 and 899).

8. For example, one of Tullie and Tarquin's sons, Sextus, "has a playful mind. He has a gift for eloquence; he is not even overly ambitious. He is cheerful, brilliant, and has a vivid imagination ..." (2, 1043).

9. Maryanne Cline Horowitz, "Michel de Montaigne's Stoic Insights Into Peasant Death," in *Renaissance Rereadings. Intertext and Context*, edited by Maryanne Cline Horowitz, Anne J. Cruz, and Wendy A. Furman (Urbana: University of Illinois Press, 1988), 236–52.

10. In this section I present a view that is quite different in emphasis from the stimulating description of Lafayette's work given by Rebecca Wilkin in her dissertation (*Feminizing Imagination in France, 1563–1678*, [University of Michigan, 2000]). In Chapter III, "Novel Imagination" (147–214), she argues that Lafayette "rehabilitates imagination" so that "For the first time in the history of the French novel, the imagination figures as a positive and productive entity." The apparently head-on collision of our positions, however, is not without points of agreement. We agree that in the last third of the century, when Lafayette published her novel, there was growing resistance, among male critics and philosophers, to the positive view of imagination, which, as Wilkin convincingly argues, was increasingly characterized as a faculty dominant in women (and thus "feminized"). Lafayette's view of imagination, as Wilkin also convincingly argues, was the result of Lafayette's understanding of the Jansenist worldview.

11. This comparison of Lafayette's narrators and the *Heptameron* needs to be strictly limited, however. The *Heptameron* narrators do not explicitly encourage their audience to "imagine" the world of their tales but they do include much more physical detail than does Lafayette.

12. The *Trésor de la Langue Française* database in ARTFL facilitates this overview. This discussion relates to the thirty-nine occurrences of the stem *imagin-* in the Emile Magne edition (Paris: Garnier, 1948). In referring to Lafayette's novel, I will give first the page number from the French edition of her *Romans et nouvelles*, edited by Alain Niderst (Paris: Classiques Garnier, 1990), and then the page number from *The Princess of Clèves*, translated by Thomas Sargent Perry, with introduction and notes

by John D. Lyons (New York: W.W. Norton, 1994). The English text of quotations is from this edition.

13. The first case of this use concerns the important and well-known difference between the way the heroine's mother educated her and the educational norm: "Most mothers imagine (*s'imaginent*) that it is enough never to speak of gallantry to their daughters to guard them from it forever. Madame de Chartres was of a very different opinion" (260/8). The narrator apparently takes a stand in favor of the new and exceptional approach by which the mother forewarns the future Princess against amorous relations by providing, rather than withholding, information about social experience—though it is also possible that the narrator merely conveys, in indirect free discourse, Mme de Chartres own disparaging view of other mothers. In either case *s'imaginent* attributes error, as it does much later when the Vidame de Chartres tells of the Queen's erroneous belief that he is in love with the Dauphiness: "The queen has taken it into her head (*s'est imaginée*) that it is with this princess that I am in love" (336/56), when in fact he is in love with Mme de Martigues. There are a few instances in which the reflexive verb does not indicate failure but rather the positive mental capacity to reflect reality. "Hence there were two cabals in the court such as you can imagine (*vous pouvez vous les imaginer*) . . ." says Mme de Chartres to her daughter in telling the story of Diane de Poitiers (280/21).

14. Imagination as error, 387/90, 399/98, and 410/105, and imagination as temptation, 401 /99. In three instances the object "imagined" is Nemours (387/90, 399/98, 401 /99) and in one case it is the duty (410/105) to end her relationship with Nemours.

15. Madame's denial of the prince's claim to have seen this extraordinary woman could even be read as a kind of parody of the Cartesian version of the ontological proof of the existence of God. Just as the concept of the perfect being implies existence (one of the perfections of the perfect being is to exist; otherwise it would be imperfect), so this exceptional woman must not exist, for otherwise she would necessarily be known by everyone.

16. We can consider in Madame's denial of the existence of the woman described by the prince something more significant than a momentary lack of information on Madame's part, and even something more significant than a hyperbolic build-up to the entrance of this superlative beauty. To tell the prince that there is no such woman as he was describing could be an early thematic marker of the solipsistic pathos of Lafayette's characters—does the object of desire actually correspond to a person existing in the "real" world? Does the woman described by the Prince de Clèves and desired by him actually correspond to Mlle de Chartres?

17. In François Chauveau's 1654 engraving (for Antoine Godeau's *Tableaux de la pénitence* [Paris: Augustin Courbé, 1654]), the saint, wearing a rough cloak, lies on her side in a grotto. Her hair falls loose around her waist and despite the alluring landscape that we can see behind her outside the grotto, all her attention is devoted to the crucifix standing on a rock before her. Reproduced in Bernard Beugnot, *Le Discours de la retraite au XVIIe siècle* (Paris: Presses Universitaires de France, 1996), 106.

18. In fact, the reader of the novel cannot know whether the heroine actually *did* "see" Nemours in the simple sense of the term—that is, was her perception based on visual information or, startled by the sound and plunged into her fantasy, did she conjure up the corresponding figure? The narrator entertains this doubt: "Madame de Clèves turned her head; and whether it was that her mind was full of this prince, or that his face was actually in the light, she thought that she recognized him; and without hesitation or turning toward him, she rejoined her maids" (387/90). We should remember that while Lafayette, the novelist, is probably aware of the writings of François de Sales, the heroine of *The Princess of Clèves* lives in a fiction that precedes his publications by many decades.

19. In the case of the Prince de Clèves, the "woman he described," the anonymous beauty at the jeweler's shop, is not entirely the same woman who will soon have a name and be known to the whole court. A major part of Clèves's vision of that woman is the uncertainty about her name and status.

20. A significant number of critics argue for the direct influence of de Sales on Lafayette. See Patrick Henry, "*La Princesse de Clèves* and *L'Introduction à la vie dévote*," in *French Studies in Honor of Philip A. Wadsworth*, edited by Donald W. Tappan and William A. Mould (Birmingham, Alabama: Summa Publications, 1985), 79–100 and Wolfgang Leiner, "La Princesse et le directeur de conscience. Création romanesque et prédication," *Biblio 17* no. 13 (1984): 45–68.

21. Joan DeJean, "Lafayette's Ellipses: The Privileges of Anonymity," in *An Inimitable Example: The Case for the Princesse de Clèves*, edited by Patrick Henry (Washington, D.C.: Catholic University of America Press, 1992), 39–70. DeJean shows how the heroine's silences endow gestures with significance and quotes the early critic Valincour on the result of this style, were it to become the norm: "we would soon see ourselves reduced to the language of angels, or at least we would be forced to speak to each other in signs" (DeJean 51).

22. It is worth noting that Lafayette constructs here an example that can illustrate both faulty inference and unexamined imagination. Epictetus and other Stoics repeatedly caution against the way imagination, when we do not learn to direct it, runs ahead in certain habitual patterns. The prudent model of remaining with what is given in the present moment—"His ship is lost. What happened? His ship is lost."—would have helped Clèves if he had been able to remain within the simple, inconclusive data provided by his informant.

23. See Rebecca Wilkin's comment on the Princess's statement to Nemours, after her husband's death, that her duty to the deceased Prince of Clèves may exist only in her imagination (*Feminizing Imagination in France*, 195). Here imagination is no longer controlled by the heroine, no longer associated with mental replication of the physical, and no longer a guide to any probable reality in the external world.

24. The importance of blushing as a cultural phenomenon has only recently received a good deal of critical attention. See Danielle Clarke, "The Iconography of the Blush: Marian Literature of the 1630's," in *Voicing Women: Gender and Sexuality in Early Modern Writing*, edited by Kate Chedgzoy, Melanie Hansen, and Suzanne Trill (Pittsburgh: Duquesne University Press, 1997), 111–28 and Mary Ann O'Farrell,

Telling Complexions: The Nineteenth-Century English Novel and the Blush (Durham: Duke University Press, 1997).

CHAPTER 6

1. *Ancients Against Moderns. Culture Wars and the Making of a Fin de Siècle* (Chicago: University of Chicago Press, 1997). See especially Chapter 4, "Culture or Civilization?" (124–50).

2. This tendency on the part of the Ancients can be seen throughout the best-known work of a prominent Jesuit literary scholar, René Rapin (1621–87). In his *Réflexions sur la poésie*, Rapin acknowledges imagination as one of the requirements of the writer's talent ("one must have a temperament with wit (*esprit*) and imagination, of power and gentleness . . ." (*Réflexions sur la poétique de ce temps et sur les ouvrages des poètes anciens et modernes*, edited by E.T. Dubois, reprint, 1675 [Geneva: Droz, 1970]), 14). Yet frequently Rapin writes of imagination as the direct opposite of genius or at most as a bad substitute for it: "people often mistake for genius things that are only the result of imagination" (14). This deprecatory allusion is echoed throughout the *Réflexions*.

3. Among those Moderns who did write extensively about imagination was Antoine Houdar de La Motte (1672–1731). With his *Discours sur la poésie en général et sur l'ode en particulier* (1707) and especially his *Discours sur le différent mérite des ouvrages d'esprit* (1716), Houdar became, along with his contemporary Abbé Jean-Baptiste Du Bos, one of the writers most responsible for the exclusive association of imagination with creativity and with the artistic professions that dominated Europe after the eighteenth century. Although Houdar presented imagination, especially after 1716, as an advantage of the Modern poet, he did this in a way that shows he had already assimilated and accepted most of the negative descriptions of this way of thinking that had been thrown back and forth in the previous decades. Indeed, Houdar seems at times to have gone back to the early sixteenth century (and to the neo-Platonic Pléiade rather than to the neo-Stoics) for some elements of his description of imagination: "It is true that because this art [poetry] requires much imagination and because an imaginative mind causes people most often to become poets, we do not expect poets to have good judgment, a quality that is usually not found when imagination is dominant. Indeed, the most common beauties of the poets consist of lively and detailed images, whereas they reason rarely and almost always superficially" (*Discours sur la poésie en général et sur l'ode en particulier*, 79). Houdar agrees with La Bruyère and with Fénelon that imagination is a faculty dominant in the immature (childish or feminine) mind and that the development of the imagination comes at the expense of reason—an antagonism that can easily and carelessly be taken for granted, even though the development of one faculty need not necessarily harm another. Houdar implies that imagination is *not* a form of thought that is cultivated but rather one that comes *naturally* to some people and inclines them to write poetry. Imagination is thus, in effect, a kind of "zero degree" or raw material of the artistic mind, found in the large body of those from among

whom the true or major poets will be drawn. One of the most "frequent" beauties of poetry—Houdar does not say that it is the best—consists of "lively images." Houdar has, without preamble, implicitly laid out a new definition of imagination: it is the faculty of creating images. Poets are not the only people who create images; this is what all people with imagination do. However, poets are, or should be (if they know their profession), the people who can sift through the disordered and prolific gush of images to select the ones that fit the textual occasion. Houdar presents the work of Homer as typical of faulty poetry written in the grip of *enthusiasm*, "a warmth of imagination that someone excites in himself and then surrenders himself to, a source of beauty and of errors, depending on whether one is blind or enlightened. But usually it is a name that people give to whatever is the least reasonable" (86). Houdar links imagination to the neo-Platonic idea of poetic *furor*, yet allows this state to be seen in terms of the medical doctrines that Fénelon had used to assign imagination to the mind of the adolescent. With this poetic *heat* we are not far from the warm, moist brain of Fénelon's child. Houdar's descriptions of Homer's imagination are often couched in terms of heat, flow, and excess. The ancient poet does not *choose* to produce images, but seems to produce them involuntarily, naturally. This set of concepts becomes more explicitly feminine and "natural" when Houdar criticizes poetic *fecundity*: "We should not always credit an author with fecundity. We are astonished at the great number of things and images that he uses, but often this abundance comes at the expense of selectivity. The author surrenders at random to everything his imagination offers him, he writes about what he should omit, he depicts objects from an angle that is irrelevant to the moment at hand, he exhausts what he should only allude to, he carelessly adds mediocre things to the excellent ones, the inert to the vivacious, the bizarre to the natural. With such an uncontrolled imagination it is not difficult to be abundant" (*Réflexions sur la critique*, 330). If we did not know that the principal object of Houdar's scorn was Homer, we might suppose that this critical reflection came directly from an Ancient, like Rapin. Houdar's comments set the stage for Enlightenment and Romantic creative imagination. Imagination, in Houdar's writing, becomes not only nonrational—it was always a separate faculty or type of thought from judgment—but both antirational and productive. Reason's role in dealing with imagination is one of *repression*: "judgment is required to repress or to accept, as the occasion warrants, the audacious proposals of imagination" (*Discours sur le différent mérite des ouvrages d'esprit*, 439). Imagination is placed squarely on the side of nature—in the sense of what happens without human intent or design—and reason (judgment) is on the side of artifice.

4. Joan DeJean, *Ancients Against Moderns. Culture Wars and the Making of a Fin de Siècle* (Chicago: University of Chicago Press, 1997), 66–77.

5. It is a significant index of the growing suspicion of imaginative practice in the last decades of the century that the negative comments about women's mystical experience and the dangerous role of imagination reported by Linda Timmermans are from such late-seventeenth-century authors as Fénelon and Guilloré (*L'Accès des femmes à la Culture [1598–1715]* [Paris: Honoré Champion, 1993], 622–23).

6. On this point see Rebecca Wilkin's *Feminizing Imagination in France, 1563–1678*, unpublished dissertation (University of Michigan, 2000), particularly Chapter II, "Of Monsters and Metaphors" (88–146).

7. In the build-up to the open Quarrel, conflict had erupted over the "marvelous" (*le merveilleux*), a concept in which the supernatural events of the officially true Christian tradition took precedence over the fables of Greco-Roman, pagan literature. Boileau shifts the ground for the defense of the Greco-Roman "marvelous" from the question of religious truth toward a more technical and aesthetic foundation.

8. *Traité du sublime ou du merveilleux dans le discours, traduit du grec de Longin.* Nicolas Despréaux Boileau, *Oeuvres complètes*, edited by Françoise Escal, Pléiade (Paris: Gallimard, 1966), 333–563.

9. In all that follows, we will be referring to the longer, 1683 version of the preface.

10. " 'Que vouliez-vous qu'il fîst contre trois?' il répond brusquement, 'Qu'il mourût.'" Boileau is quoting Corneille, *Le Cid*, act III, scene 6.

11. On the different, less stylistic views of the sublime there have been many significant studies in recent years. See, among others, *Du sublime*, edited by Jean-Luc Nancy (Paris: Belin, 1988); Louis Marin, *Sublime Poussin*, translated by Catherine Porter (Stanford: Stanford University Press, 1999 [published in French in 1995]); *Of the Sublime: Presence in Question*, translated and with an afterword by Jeffrey S. Librett (Albany: State University of New York Press, 1993).

12. On the slippery quality of Longinus's argument and his deception of the audience see Neil Hertz, "A Reading of Longinus," in *The End of the Line* (New York: Columbia University Press, 1985), 1–20.

13. In his lectures on aesthetics, Hegel takes a position on imagination that is reminiscent of (and indirectly inspired by) the discussions of genius and sublimity at the end of the seventeenth century (G.W.F. Hegel, "On Art," translation of *Vorlesungen über die Aesthetik*, translated by Bernard Bosanquet in *On Art, Religion, Philosophy*, with an introduction by J. Glenn Gray, Harper Torchbook [New York: Harper & Row, 1970], 22–127). This appears particularly on 68–70 where the proper "undivided unity" of artistic production is constituted by the imagination: "This genuine mode of production constitutes the activity of artistic *imagination*. It is the rational element which, qua spirit, only exists in as far as it actively extrudes itself into consciousness, but yet does not array before it what it bears within itself till it does so in sensuous form" (68). Hegel contrasts the ordinary imagination of an intelligent man with the imagination of the artist: "But the productive imagination of the *artist* is the imagination of a great mind and heart, the apprehension and creation of ideas and of shapes, and, indeed, the exhibition of the profoundest and most universal human interests in the definite sensuous mould of pictorial representation" (69). Hegel follows Boileau in this elevation of the artist or genius into a unique position, leaving behind the passive imagination of the ordinary person and linking the only really important kind of imagination with creativity. Of the ordinary imagination of the intelligent man, Hegel writes "For in his ideas, everything shapes itself into

concrete images, determinate in time and place, to which, therefore, names and other external circumstances of all kinds must not be wanting. Yet such a kind of imagination rather rests on the recollection of states that he has gone through, and of experiences that have befallen him, than is creative in its own strength. His recollection preserves and reproduces the individuality and external fashion of occurrences that had such and such results with all their external circumstances, and prevents the universal from emerging in its own shape" (69). Hegel seems to be criticizing this ordinary imagination for being passive (merely reproductive), too linked to memory (and therefore to the *past*, in opposition to Hegel's own modernist forward orientation toward the future), too contextual and sensuously exact in its detail. Clearly few people, in Hegel's view, have the other, good kind of imagination, which appears only in artists of great inherent talent (70).

14. Longinus also distinguishes in this chapter on "images" between the goal of images in poetry ("l'étonnement et la surprise") and in prose or rhetoric ("bien peindre les choses"). However, this distinction seems to vanish by the end of the chapter, which culminates in the advice to stun the audience rather than to represent things accurately.

15. Philip Lewis, *Seeing Through the Mother Goose Tales. Visual Turns in the Writings of Charles Perrault* (Stanford: Stanford University Press, 1996), 48–60.

16. Introduction, 01–31.

17. There have been hundreds of editions since 1699, perhaps even a thousand. See Jacques Le Brun's note in his Pléiade edition (François Salignac de La Mothe Fénelon, *Les Aventures de Télémaque*, in *Oeuvres*, edited by Jacques Le Brun, La Pléiade [Paris: Gallimard], 1264).

18. This work was first commissioned by the Duke and Duchess of Beauvillier, who sought the author's advice on the education of their daughters. It was first presented privately to the Beauvilliers and then revised for its publication in 1687.

19. Aristotle, "On the Soul" (II, ii, 424a), translated and edited by J.A. Smith, in *The Complete Works of Aristotle*, edited by Jonathan Barnes, Bollingen Series (Princeton: Princeton University Press, 1984), vol. 1, 674. On the use of the "wax" metaphor in early-modern discussions of imagination see Rebecca May Wilkin, *Feminizing Imagination in France, 1563–1678*, unpublished dissertation (University of Michigan, 2000), 105 ff.

20. François Salignac de La Mothe Fénelon, *De l'éducation des filles*, in *Oeuvres*, edited by Jacques Le Brun, La Pléiade (Paris: Gallimard), 1, 91–171; 98, 103.

21. *De l'éducation des filles*, 97.

22. See the lengthy account of this publication in François Salignac de La Mothe Fénelon, *Les Aventures de Télémaque*, in *Oeuvres*, edited by Jacques Le Brun, La Pléiade (Paris: Gallimard), 1243–52.

23. François Salignac de La Mothe Fénelon, *Les Aventures de Télémaque*, edited by Jacques Le Brun, Folio Classique (Paris: Gallimard, 1995), 162.

24. It is significant that even adults must work to limit the power of physical things, for Fénelon conceives the interior life as being beyond the imagination. Emmanuel Bury's study of interior spirituality in Fénelon's teachings of Christian

eloquence insists on the effort required in meditation to render the meditator attentive to the divine message that usually passes unnoticed: "Il faut faire taire toute créature, il faut se faire taire soi-même..." (*Opuscules spirituels*, cited in Emmanuel Bury, "Eloquence et spiritualité dans la pensée fénelonienne: convergences et tensions," in *Éloquence et vérité intérieure*, edited by Carole Dornier and Jürgen Siess [Paris: Champion, 2002], 109–29.

25. *De l'éducation des filles*, in *Oeuvres*, edited by Jacques Le Brun, La Pléiade (Paris: Gallimard), 96.

26. Fénelon's role in the Quietist controversy, in which he took the side of Mme Guyon against Bossuet to defend a receptive and passive interior life shows him to be very distant from a Salesian pro-imaginative and active form of meditation. See his "Lettres et opuscules spirituelles," in *Oeuvres*, edited by Jacques Le Brun, La Pléiade (Paris: Gallimard), 555–777.

27. Allan Bloom, *The Closing of the American Mind* (New York: Simon and Schuster, 1987), 299.

28. Jean-Jacques Rousseau, *Émile, ou de l'éducation*, edited by François Richard and Pierre Richard, Classiques Garnier (Paris: Garnier Frères, 1964), 525. The character Émile himself reads the *Aventures de Télémaque*, but only when he is essentially already formed. Patrick Riley has described Fénelon as "proto-Rousseauian" ("Rousseau, Fénelon, and the Quarrel Between the Ancients and the Moderns," in *The Cambridge Companion to Rousseau*, edited by Patrick Riley (Cambridge: Cambridge University Press, 2001), 88).

29. Rousseau also has roots in Stoicism. His educational doctrines are in many ways simply a different approach to reaching the Stoic goal of autarchy and of equanimity in the face of purely imagined harm. In *Emile*, the pages on happiness and imagination in book II (63–69) are permeated with Stoic ideals.

30. "Sensible," in fact, has two complementary meanings. It describes the things that are perceptible to the senses, the *objets sensibles*, and also the perceptive capacity of receiving this data through sensation. In this sense the child is an *être sensible*.

31. François and Pierre Richard, editors of the Classiques Garnier edition, provide a rich and suggestive bibliography of potential influences on Rousseau from the Augustinian tradition, including Pascal, Robert Arnauld, Pierre Lancelot, Pierre Nicole, and others (*Émile, ou de l'éducation*, edited by François Richard and Pierre Richard, Classiques Garnier [Paris: Garnier Frères, 1964], xli–xliv).

32. On Emile's sensitivity to the sufferings of other human beings, see Elaine Larochelle, *L'imagination dans l'oeuvre de Jean-Jacques Rousseau* (Villeneuve d'Ascq: Presses Universitaires du Septentrion, 1999), 31–33 and 64–68.

33. "I have assumed in my pupil neither a transcendent genius, nor a limited capacity for understanding. I have chosen him among ordinary minds (*esprits vulgaires*) to show the power of education on a man" (293).

34. At several points in *Emile* Rousseau conveys the attitude, not uncommon in his writing, that he is a necessarily misunderstood genius, one who writes not only with a resigned acceptance of the hostility and incomprehension of the reader but one who draws from that very hostility his authority to proclaim new truths.

See the telling anecdote in which a dinner companion says to him, "Don't speak, Jean-Jacques, they will not understand you" (108).

35. Many of the passages in *Emile* that develop the concept of *sentiment* are in the section in which Rousseau shifts from his own voice to that of the country priest, the "Vicaire Savoyard" (320–87). Whether or not these statements are endorsed as fully by Rousseau as the rest of *Emile*, both speakers advance a view of sentiment that places it in the Augustinian conceptual repertory as expounded by Pascal.

36. In the chapter "Of vanity" (III, 9): "Now, I have started a hundred quarrels in defense of Pompey and for the cause of Brutus. This friendship still endures between us; even present things we hold only by imagination" (*The Complete Essays of Montaigne*, translated by Donald M. Frame [Stanford: Stanford University Press, 1958], 763 and *Les Essais*, edited by Pierre Villey [Paris: Presses Universitaires de France, 1978], 996).

Bibliography

Abrams, M.H. *The Mirror and the Lamp. Romantic Theory and the Critical Tradition*. New York: Oxford University Press, 1953.

Addison, Joseph. "Essays on the Pleasures of the Imagination." In *The Works of Joseph Addison*. New York: G.P. Putnam, 1854, pp. 322–73.

Agamben, Giorgio. *Infancy and History. Essays on the Destruction of Experience*. Liz Heron (translator). London: Verso, 1993.

Agin, Shane. "Comment se font les enfants: Sex Education and the Preservation of Innocence." *MLA*, 117(4) (2002): 722–36.

Aguzzi-Barbagli, Danilo. "*Ingegno, acutezza*, and *meraviglia* in the Sixteenth Century Great Commentaries to Aristotle's *Poetics*." In Julius A. Molinaro (ed.), *Petrarch to Pirandello. Studies in Italian Literature in Honour of Beatrice Corrigan*. Toronto: University of Toronto Press, 1973, pp. 73–93.

Altman, Janet Gurkin. *Epistolarity*. Columbus: Ohio State University Press, 1982.

Amsler, Mark (ed.). *Creativity and the Imagination: Case Studies from the Classical Age to the Twentieth Century*. Newark: University of Delaware Press, 1987.

Antoninus, Marcus Aurelius. *To Himself*. C.R. Haines (translator and ed.), Loeb Classical Library, Cambridge, Massachusetts: Harvard University Press, 1916.

Antoninus, Marcus Aurelius. *Meditations*. Gregory Hays (translator and ed.). New York: Modern Library, 2002.

Aquinas, Thomas. *The Commentary on the De Anima of Aristotle*. Robert Pasnau (translator) Yale Library of Medieval Philosophy. New Haven: Yale University Press, 1999.

Aristotle. "On Memory." In Jonathan Barnes (ed.), *The Complete Works of Aristotle*. Bollingen Series, Princeton: Princeton University Press, 1984, pp. 714–20.

Aristotle. "On the Soul." In Jonathan Barnes (ed.), *The Complete Works of Aristotle*. Bollingen Series, Princeton: Princeton University Press, 1984, pp. 641–92.

Armogathe, Jean-Robert. " 'L'azione che viene dagli oggetti': luce fisica e luce spirituale." In *La Luce del vero: Caravaggio, La Tour, Rembrandt, Zurbarán*, Cinisello Balsamo: Silvana Editoriale, 2000, pp. 40–45.

Armogathe, Jean-Robert. "L' "Imagination" de Mersenne à Pascal." In Marta Fattori and M. Bianchi (eds), *Phantasia-Imaginatio*. Atti del Vo Colloquio internazionale del Lessico intellettuale Europeo. Rome: Ateneo, 1988, pp. 259–72.

Arnason, Johann P. "Reason, Imagination, Interpretation." In Gillian Robinson and John Rundell (eds), *Rethinking Imagination: Culture and Creativity*, London: Routledge, 1994, pp. 155–70.

Arnauld, Antoine, and Pierre Nicole. *La Logique ou l'art de penser*. Paris: Flammarion, 1970.

Arnauld, Antoine. *Oeuvres*. Paris: Sigismond d'Arnay, 1779 (facsimile, Bruxelles: Culture et Civilisation, 1962) pp. 25–31.

Arnauld, Antoine. "Réflexions sur l'éloquence des prédicateurs." In *Oeuvres*. Paris: Sigismond d'Arnay, 1779 (facsimile, Bruxelles: Culture et Civilisation, 1962).

Arnheim, Rudolf. *Visual Thinking*. Berkeley: University of California Press, 1969.

Augustine. *Confessions,* Robert Arnauld d'Andilly (translator). Folio Classique. Paris: Gallimard, 1993 [first published 1649].

Aulotte, Robert. *Montaigne. Apologie de Raimond Sebond*. Paris: Société d'Édition d'Enseignement Supérieur, 1979.

Bacon, Francis. *The Advancement of Learning*. Everyman's Library. London: J.M. Dent, 1605 [reprint 1978].

Banwart, Mary. *Hume's Imagination*. New York: Peter Lang, 1994.

Bardon, Françoise. "Le Thème de la Madeleine pénitente au XVIIe siècle en France." *Journal of the Warburg and Courtauld Institutes*, 31 (1968): 274–306.

Beaude, Joseph. "Le lexique de l'imagination dans l'oeuvre de Malebranche." In *Méthodes quantitatives et informatiques dans l'étude des textes*. Geneva: Slatkine, 1986, pp. 39–42.

Belin, Christian. *L'oeuvre de Pierre Charron: Littérature et théologie de Montaigne à Port-Royal*. Paris: Honoré Champion, 1995.

Belin, Christian. *La Conversation intérieure. La Méditation en France au XVIIe siècle*. Paris: Honoré Champion, 2002.

Benes, Mirka. *Villas and Gardens in Early-Modern Italy and France*. Cambridge: Cambridge University Press, 1992.

Bergamo, Mino. *L'Anatomia dell'anima da François de Sales a Fénelon*. Bologna: Il Mulino, 1991.

Bergoffen, Debra B. "Cartesian Doubt as Methodology: Reflective Imagaination and Philosophical Freedom." *Proceedings of the Catholic Philosophy Association*, 50 (1976): 186–95.

Beugnot, Bernard. *Le discours de la retraite au XVIIe siècle*. Paris: Presses Universitaires de France, 1996.

Bérulle, Pierre de. *Bérulle and the French School. Selected Writings*. Classics of Western Spirituality. Mahwah, NJ: Paulist Press, 1989.

Bèze, Théodore de. *Chrestiennes Méditations*. Textes Littéraires Français. Geneva: Droz, 1964.

Bizos, Gaston. *Fénelon éducateur*. 2nd edn, Paris: H. Lecène et H. Oudin, 1887.

Bloom, Allan. *The Closing of the American Mind*. New York: Simon and Schuster, 1987.

Bluche, François (ed.). *Dictionnaire du Grand Siècle*. Paris: Fayard, 1990.

Blum, Claude (ed.). *Montaigne: Apologie de Raimond Sebond, de la Theologia à la Théologie*. Paris: Honoré Champion, 1990.

Boileau, Nicolas Despréaux. *Oeuvres complètes*. Françoise Escal (ed.), Pléiade. Paris: Gallimard, 1966.

Bolton, Martha. "Confused and Obscure Ideas of Sense." In Amélie Oksenberg Rorty (ed.), *Essays on Descartes' Meditations*, Berkeley: University of California Press, 1986, pp. 389–403.

Bonhöffer, Adolf Friedrich. *The Ethics of the Stoic Epictetus*. William O. Stephens (translator). New York: Peter Lang, 1996 [first published 1894].

Bordes, Hélène and Jacques Hennequin (eds). *L'Univers salésien. Saint François de Sales hier et aujourd'hui*. Metz: Université de Metz, 1994. Actes du colloque international de Metz, 1992 pp. 17–9.

Bouhours, Dominique S.J. *La vie de Saint Ignace, fondateur de la compagnie de Jésus*. Paris: Varin, 1758 [first published 1679].

Bourdieu, Pierre. *Language and Symbolic Power*. Cambridge, MA: Harvard University Press, 1991.

Boutroux, Pierre. *L'Imagination et les mathématiques selon Descartes*. Paris: Félix Alcan, 1900.

Bouwsma, William J. "The Two Faces of Humanism: Stoicism and Augustinianism in Renaissance Thought." In *A Usable Past: Essays in European Cultural History*. Berkeley: University of California Press, 1990, pp. 9–73.

Boyle, Majorie O'Rourke. *Loyola's Acts: The Rhetoric of the Self*. Berkeley: University of California Press, 1997.

Brann, Eva T.H. *The World of the Imagination: Sum and Substance*. Savage, MD: Rowman and Littlefield, 1991.

Bremond, Henri. *Histoire littéraire du sentiment religieux en France depuis la fin des guerres de religion jusqu'à nos jours*. Paris: Bloud et Gay, 1916–1933.

Breton, Stanislas. *Deux mystiques de l'excès: J.-J. Surin et maître Eckhart*. Paris: Editions du Cerf, 1985.

Brett, R.L. *Fancy and Imagination*. The Critical Idiom. London: Methuen, 1969.

Brewer, John. "The Pleasures of the Imagination." In *The Pleasures of the Imagination: English Culture in the Eighteenth Century*. New York: Farrar Straus Giroux, 1997.

Bridoux, André. *Le Stoïcisme et son influence*. Paris: Libraire Philosophique J. Vrin, 1966.

Bright, Timothy. *Traité de la mélancolie.* Éliane Cuvelier (translator and ed.), Grenoble: Jérôme Millon, 1996 [first published 1586].

Brockliss, Laurence and Colin Jones. *The Medical World of Early Modern France.* Oxford: Clarendon Press, 1997.

Brody, Jules. *Boileau and Longinus.* Geneva: Droz, 1958.

Brody, Jules. *Lectures de Montaigne.* French Forum Monographs. Lexington, Kentucky: French Forum, 1982.

Brooke, Christopher. "Rousseau's Political Philosophy: Stoic and Augustinian Origins." In Patrick Riley (ed.), *The Cambridge Companion to Rousseau.* Cambridge: Cambridge University Press, 2001, pp. 94–123.

Brunschvicg, Léon. *Descartes et Pascal, lecteurs de Montaigne.* Agora Les Classiques. Paris: Presses Pocket, 1995 [first edition 1942].

Bundy, Murray Wright. *The Theory of Imagination in Classical and Medieval Thought.* University of Illinois Studies in Language and Literature. Urbana, IL: University of Illinois Press, 1927.

Burton, Robert. *The Anatomy of Melancholy.* Holbrook Jackson (ed.). New York: Vintage Books, 1641.

Bury, Emmanuel. "Eloquence et spiritualité dans la pensée fénelonienne: convergences et tensions." In Carole Dornier and Jürgen Siess (eds), *Éloquence et vérité intérieure.* Paris: Champion, 2002, pp. 109–29.

Bussy-Rabutin Roger, Comte de. *Correspondance avec le Père Rapin.* C. Rouben (ed.). Paris: Nizet, 1983.

Calvin, John. *Calvin's Commentary on Seneca's De Clementia.* Lewis Battles and André Malan Hugo (translators and eds). Renaissance Text Series III. Leiden: E.J. Brill, 1969.

Calvin, John. *The Bondage and Liberation of the Will.* A.N.S. Lane (ed.). Michigan: Baker Books, 1996 [first published 1543].

Campion, Edmund J. "Montaigne as Critic of Seneca and St. Augustine." *Classical and Modern Literature*, 2(2) (1982): 101–09.

Carabin, Denise. *Les idées stoïciennes dans la littérature morale des XVIe et des XVIIe siècles.* Paris: Champion, 2004.

Carré, Marie-Rose. *La Folle du logis dans les prisons de l'âme. Etudes sur la psychologie de l'imagination au XVIIe siècle.* Paris: Klincksieck, 1998.

Carruthers, Mary. *The Book of Memory. A Study of Memory in Medieval Culture.* Cambridge Studies in Medieval Literature. Cambridge: Cambridge University Press, 1990.

Carruthers, Mary. *The Craft of Thought. Meditation, Rhetoric, and the Making of Images.* Cambridge: Cambridge University Press, 1998, pp. 400–1200.

Casey, Edward S. *Imagining: A Phenomenological Study.* Bloomington: Indiana University Press, 1976.

Castoriadis, Cornelius. "Radical Imagination and the Social Instituting Imaginary." In Gillian Robinson and John Rundell (eds), *Rethinking Imagination: Culture and Creativity.* London: Routledge, 1994, pp. 136–54.

Cave, Terence C. *Devotional Poetry in France, c.1570–1613.* Cambridge: Cambridge University Press, 1969.

Cave, Terence C. *The Cornucopian Text. Problems of Reading in the Late Renaissance.* Oxford: Clarendon Press, 1979.

Cave, Terence C. "Au coeur de l'*Apologie*: la logique de l'antipéristase." In Iliana Zinguer (ed.), *Le Lecteur, l'auteur et l'écrivain: Montaigne 1492-1592-1992.* Paris: Honoré Champion, 1993, pp. 1–15.

Chanet, Pierre. *Traité de l'esprit de l'homme et de ses fonctions.* Paris: Veuve J. Camusat et P. Le Petit, 1649.

Charron, Pierre. *De la sagesse.* Corpus Des Oeuvres de Philosophie en Langue Française. Paris: Fayard, 1986 [first published 1604].

Chartier, Roger. *Lectures et lecteurs dans la France d'Ancien Régime.* Paris: Seuil, 1987.

Chartier, Roger and Guglielmo Cavallo (eds). *A History of Reading in the West.* Amherst: University of Massachusetts Press, 1999.

Chenu, Roselyne (ed.). *L'Imagination créatrice.* Neufchâtel: La Baconnière, 1971.

Chertablon, de. *La Manière de se bein preparer à la mort par des considerations sur la Cene, la Passion et la Mort de Jesus-Christ, avec de trés-belles Estampes Emblematiques.* Antwerp: George Gallet, 1700.

Chocheyras, Jacques (ed.). *Visages de la Madeleine dans la littérature européenne (1500–1700).* Grenoble: Université Stendhal, 1990.

Clark, Stuart. *Thinking with Demons: The Idea of Witchcraft in Early Modern Europe.* Oxford: Clarendon Press, 1997.

Clarke, Danielle. "The Iconography of the Blush: Marian Literature of the 1630's." In Kate Chedgzoy, Melanie Hansen, and Suzanne Trill (eds), *Voicing Women: Gender and Sexuality in Early Modern Writing.* Pittsburgh: Duquesne University Press, 1997, pp. 111–28.

Cocking, J.M. *Imagination: A Study in the History of Ideas.* Penelope Murray (ed.). London: Routledge, 1991.

Cognet, Louis. *De la Dévotion moderne à la spiritualité française.* Paris: Fayard, 1958.

Coleman, Francis X.J. *The Aesthetic Thought of the French Enlightenment.* Pittsburgh: University of Pittsburgh Press, 1971.

Coleman, Patrick. "Rousseau's Misanthropology." In *Rousseau's Political Imagination. Rule and Representation in the Lettre à d'Alembert.* Geneva: Droz, 1984, pp. 155–86.

Coleman, Patrick. *Rousseau's Political Imagination. Rule and Representation in the Lettre à d'Alembert.* Geneva: Droz, 1984.

Conche, Marcel. *Montaigne et la philosophie.* Villers-sur-Mer: Editions de Mégare, 1987.

Conley, Tom. "Legs de l'erreur: vers une cartographie politique." *Rue Descartes*, 25 (1999): 29–42.

Conley, Tom. "Montaigne *Moqueur*: 'Virgile' and Its Geographies of Gender." In Kathleen P. Long (ed.), *High Anxiety: Masculinity in Crisis in Early Modern France.* Kirksville, MO: Truman State University Press, 2001, pp. 93–106.

Cooey, Paula M. *Religious Imagination and the Body. A Feminist Analysis.* New York: Oxford University Press, 1994.

Cook, Patricia (ed.). *Philosophical Imagination and Cultural Memory: Appropriating Historical Traditions*. Durham: Duke University Press, 1993.

Cottrell, Robert. "Representation and the Desiring Subject in Montaigne's 'De l'expérience'." In Marcel Tetel and G. Mallary Masters (eds), *Le Parcours des Essais: Montaigne 1588–1988*. Paris: Aux Amateurs de Livres, 1989, pp. 97–110.

Cristofolini, Paolo (ed.). *Studi sul Seicento e sull'Immaginazione*. Pisa: Scuola Normale Superiore di Pisa, 1985.

Croquette, Bernard. *Pascal et Montaigne. Etude des réminiscences des Essais dans l'oeuvre de Pascal*. Histoire Des Idées et Critique Littéraire. Geneva: Droz, 1974.

Dandrey, Patrick. *La Médecine et la maladie dans le théâtre de Molière*. Klincksieck, 1998.

Daniel, Stephen H. "Descartes on Myth and Ingenuity/Ingenium." *Southern Journal of Philosophy*, 23 (2) (1985): 157–70.

Darmon, Jean-Charles. *Philosophie épicurienne et littérature au XVIIe siècle*. Paris: Presses Universitaires de France, 1998.

d'Aubignac, l'abbé [François d'Hédelin]. *La Pratique du Théâtre*. Alger: Jules Carbonel, 1927.

Dauenbauer, Bernard P. "The Place of Imagination in Descartes' *Meditations*." *Cahiers du dix-septième*, 1 (2) (1987): 37–46.

Davidson, Hugh M. *The Origins of Certainty*. Chicago: University of Chicago Press, 1979.

Davidson, Hugh M. *Blaise Pascal*. Boston: G.K. Hall, 1983.

Davis, Kenneth Ronald. *Anabaptism and Asceticism. A Study in Intellectual Origins*. Scottsdale, PA: Herald Press, 1974.

de Baïf, Jean-Antoine (translator). *Traité de l'Imagination tiré du Latin de Françoys Pic de la Mirandole*. Paris: André Wechel, 1557.

De Bernart, Luciana. "La Ragione senza immaginazione: considerazioni sulla logica ramista e i suoi ascendenti umanistici." In Paolo Cristofolini (ed.), *Studi sul Seicento e sull'Immaginazione*. Pisa: Scuola Normale Superiore di Pisa, 1985, pp. 129–51.

De Certeau, Michel (ed.). *La Possession de Loudun*. Paris: Gallimard/Julliard, 1980.

De Certeau, Michel. *La Fable mystique*. Paris: Gallimard, 1982.

DeJean, Joan. "Lafayette's Ellipses: The Privileges of Anonymity." In Patrick Henry (ed.), *An Inimitable Example: The Case for the Princesse de Clèves*. Washington, DC: Catholic University of America Press, 1992, pp. 39–70.

DeJean, Joan. *Ancients Against Moderns. Culture Wars and the Making of a Fin de Siècle*. Chicago: University of Chicago Press, 1997.

Delenda, Odile. "Sainte Marie Madeleine et l'application du décret tridentin (1563) sur les saintes images." In Eve Duperray (ed.), *Marie-Madeleine dans la mystique, les arts et les lettres*. Paris: Beauchesne, 1989.

Demonet, Marie-Luce. *À plaisir: Sémiotique et scepticisme chez Montaigne*. L'Atelier de la Renaissance. Orleans: Paradigme, 2002.

de Nicolás, Antonio T. *Ignatius de Loyola: Powers of Imagining. A Philosophical Hermeneutic of Imagining Through the Collected Works of Ignatius de Loyola.* Albany: State University of New York Press, 1986.

Descartes, René. *Oeuvres complètes.* Charles Adam and Paul Tannery (eds). Paris: Vrin, 1996.

Descombes, Vincent. *The Barometer of Modern Reason.* Odéon, NY: Oxford University Press, 1993.

Descotes, Dominique. *L'Argumentation chez Pascal.* Paris: Presses Universitaires de France, 1993.

Desmarets de Saint-Sorlin, Jean. *Les morales d'Epictète, de Socrate, de Plutarque et de Sénèque.* Château de Richelieu: Estienne Migon, 1653.

Dihle, Albrecht. *The Theory of Will in Classical Antiquity.* Berkeley: University of California Press, 1982.

Doueihi, Milad. "Elephantine Marriage." *MLN,* 106(4) (1991): 780–92.

Duhot, Jean-Joël. *Epictète et la sagesse stoïcienne.* Paris: Bayard Editions, 1996.

Dumont, Jean-Paul. *Le Scepticisme et le phénomène: essai sur la signification et les origines du pyrrhonisme.* 2nd edn, Paris: Librairie Philosophique J. Vrin, 1985.

Dumont, Pascal. "Est-il pertinent de parler d'une philosophie baroque?" *Littératures classiques* 36 (1999): 63–77.

Dumora-Mabille, Florence. "Entre clarté et illusion: l'enargeia au XVIIe siècle." *Littératures classiques,* 28 (1996): 75–94.

Du Vair, Guillaume. *Les Oeuvres de Messire Guillaume du Vair.* Paris: Sebastien Cramoisy, 1641 [reprint, Geneva: Slatkine, 1970].

Du Vair, Guillaume. *Manuel d'Epictète.* Collection "Jacques Haumont". Paris: Plon, 1954 [first published 1591].

Earle, Rebecca (ed.). *Epistolary Selves: Letters and Letter-Writers, 1600–1945.* Aldershot: Ashgate, 1999.

Engell, James. *The Creative Imagination.* Cambridge: Harvard University Press, 1981.

Engster, Dan. "The Montaignian Moment." *Journal of the History of Ideas,* 59(4) (1998): 625–50.

Epictetus. *Les Propos d'Epictète recueillis par Arrian auteur grec son disciple translatés du grec en français par Fr. I.D.S.F.* Paris: Jean de Heuqueville, 1609.

Epictetus. *La Traduction française du Manuel d'Épictète d'André de Rivaudeau.* Léontine Zanta (ed.). Paris: Champion, 1914.

Epictetus. *Manuale.* Angelo Poliziano and Giacomo Leopardi (translator). Milan: Mursia, 1971.

Epictetus. *The Discourses as Reported by Arrian, The Manual, and Fragments.* W.A. Oldfather (ed.). Loeb Classics, Cambridge, MA: Harvard University Press, 1985 [first edition 1928].

Escola, Marc. *La Bruyère: Rhétorique du discontinu.* Paris: Champion, 2001.

Evans, Robert C. *Jonson, Lipsius and the Politics of Renaissance Stoicism.* Durango, CO: Longwood Academic, 1992.

Everson, Stephen. *Aristotle on Perception.* Oxford: Clarendon Press, 1997.

Faret, Nicolas. *L'Honneste Homme, ou l'Art de plaire à la court.* Paris: Presses Universitaires de France, 1925 [first published 1635].

Farrell, Michèle Longino. *Performing Motherhood: The Sévigné Correspondence.* Hanover: University Press of New England, 1991.

Fattori, Marta and M. Bianchi (eds). *Phantasia-Imaginatio.* Atti del Vo Colloquio internazionale del Lessico intellettuale Europeo. Rome: Ateneo, 1988.

Ferreyrolles, Gérard. *Les Reines du monde. L'imagination et la coutume chez Pascal.* Lumière Classique, Paris: Honoré Champion, 1995.

Ferreyrolles, Gérard. "Compendium sur l'Imagination dans les *Pensées.*" In Pierre Ronzeaud(ed.), *L'Imagination au XVIIe siècl, Littératures Classiques,* 45, (2002): 139–54.).

Feyens, Thomas. *De viribus imaginationis.* Louvain: Elsevier, 1635 [first published 1608].

Fénelon, François Salignac de La Mothe. *Les Aventures de Télémaque.* Jacques Le Brun (ed.). Folio Classique. Paris: Gallimard, 1995.

Fénelon, François Salignac de La Mothe. "Les Aventures de Télémaque." In Jacques Le Brun (ed.), *Oeuvres.* La Pléiade, vol. 2, Paris: Gallimard, 1983, pp. 1—326.

Fénelon, François Salignac de La Mothe. "De l'éducation des filles." In Jacques Le Brun (ed.), *Oeuvres.* La Pléiade, vol. 1, Paris: Gallimard, 1983, pp. 91—171.

Ferté, Bruno. *Georges de La Tour.* Maîtres de l'Art. Paris: Gallimard, 1999.

Flory, Dan. "Stoic Psychology, Classical Rhetoric, and Theories of Imagination in Western Philosophy." *Philosophy and Rhetoric,* 29(2) (1996): 147–67.

Folghera, J.D. "The Imagination in Saint Francis de Sales." *American Ecclesiastical Review* 47 (1912): 434–46.

Fontaine, Nicolas. *Mémoires ou Histoire des solitaires de Port-Royal.* Pascale Thouvenin (ed.). Paris: Honoré Champion, 2001.

Fontenelle, Bernard le Bouvier de. "Digression sur les Anciens et les Modernes." In *Oeuvres complètes.* Corpus Des Oeuvres de Philosophie en Langue Française. Paris: Fayard, 1989, pp. 413—31.

Fothergill-Payne, Louise. "Seneca's role in popularizing Epicurus in the sixteenth century." In Margaret J. Osler (ed.), *Atoms, Pneuma, and Tranquillity.* Cambridge: Cambridge University Press, 1991, pp. 115–33.

Fóti, Véronique. "The Role of Imagination in Descartes's Thought." *Philosophie Moderne,* 4(1) (1983): 29–32.

Francis of Sales. *Oeuvres.* In André Ravier and Roger Devos (eds), Pléiade. Paris: Gallimard, 1969.

Frede, Dorothea. "The Cognitive Role of *Phantasia* in Aristotle." In Martha C. Nussbaum and Amélie Oksenberg Rorty (eds), *Essays on Aristotle's De Anima,* . Oxford: Oxford University Press, 1992, pp. 279–95.

Freeland, Cynthia. "Aristotle on the Sense of Touch." In Martha C. Nussbaum and Amélie Oksenberg Rorty (eds), *Essays on Aristotle's De Anima.* Oxford: Oxford University Press, 1992, pp. 227–48.

Freyberg, Bernard. *Imagination and Depth in Kant's Critique of Pure Reason.* New York: Peter Lang, 1994.

Fried, Michael. "On Aristotle's Conception of the Soul." In Martha C. Nussbaum and Amélie Oksenberg Rorty (eds), *Essays on Aristotle's De Anima*. Oxford: Oxford University Press, 1992, pp. 93–107.

Friedrich, Hugo. *Montaigne*. Philippe Desan (ed.). Berkeley: University of California Press, 1991.

Fumaroli, Marc. *L'âge de l'éloquence. Rhétorique et "res literaria" de la Renaissance au seuil de l'époque classique*. Geneva: Droz, 1980.

Fumaroli, Marc, Jean-Robert Armogathe, Anne-Marie Lecoq. *La Querelle des Anciens et des Modernes*. Folio Classique. Paris: Gallimard, 2001.

Funkenstein, Amos. *Theology and the Scientific Imagination from the Middle Ages to the Seventeenth Century*. Princeton: Princeton University Press, 1986.

Furet, François and Jacques Ozouf (eds). *Lire et écrire: l'alphabétisation des Français de Calvin à Jules Ferry*. Paris: Editions de Minuit, 1977.

Gambart, Adrien. *La vie symbolique du bienheureux François de Sales, esvesque et prince de Genève*. Paris: Aux frais de l'auteur pour l'usage des Religieuses de la Visitation, et à la disposition de celles du Fauxbourg Saint Jacques, 1664.

Garber, Daniel. *Descartes Embodied: Reading Cartesian Philosophy Through Cartesian Science*. Cambridge: Cambridge University Press, 2001.

Gelley, A. "The Two Julies: Conversation and Imagination in *La Nouvelle Héloïse*." *Modern Language Notes*, 92 (1977): 749–60.

Germain, F. "Imagination et vertige dans les deux infinis." *Revue des sciences humaines*, 99 (1960): 31–40.

Giraud, Yves. " 'Admirable Séjour d'Horreur et de Plaisir': Le paysage poétique de la Sainte-Baume au XVIIe Siècle." In Jean Jehasse, Claude Martin, Pierre Rétat, and Bernard Yon (eds), *Mélanges Offerts à Georges Couton*. Lyon: Presses Universitaires de Lyon, 1981, pp. 199–222.

Goldmann, Lucien. *Le Dieu caché. Etude sur la vision tragique dans les Pensées de Pascal et dans le théâtre de Racine*. Bibliothèque des Idées. Paris: Gallimard, 1959.

Goldschmidt, Victor. *Le Système stoïcien et l'idée de temps*. Paris: J. Vrin, 1977.

Goldsmith, Elizabeth C (ed.). *Writing the Female Voice: Essays on Epistolary Literature*. Boston: Northeastern University Press, 1989.

Goulart, Simon (translator and ed.). *Les Oeuvres morales et meslées de Sénecque, traduites de latin en françois et nouvellement mises en lumière*. Paris: Jean Houzé, 1595.

Grande, Nathalie. *Stratégies de romancières: de* Clélie *à* La Princesse de Clèves. Lumière Classique 20. Paris: Honoré Champion, 1999.

Granger, Gilles Gaston. "Epistémologie." In *Encyclopaedia Universalis*, vol. 8,. Paris: Encyclopaedia Universalis France, 1992, pp. 565–72.

Grimal, Pierre (ed.). *L. Annaei Senecae Operum Moralium Concordantia*. Paris: Presses Universitaires de France, 1965.

Grosperrin, Jean-Philippe. "Houdar de La Motte interprète de la tragédie cornélienne, ou la mort du *merveilleux* ." Conference presentation at Corneille après Corneille, 1684–1791. Rouen, 2002.

Guiderdoni-Bruslé, Agnès. "Images et emblèmes dans la spiritualité de Saint François de Sales." *XVIIe Siècle*, 54(214) (2002): 35–54.

Guyon, Louis. *Les Diverses leçons de Loys Guyon, Dolois, Sieur de la Nauche*. Lyons: C. Morillon, 1604.

Hadot, Pierre. *Exercices spirituels et philosophie antique*. 2nd edn, Paris: Etudes Augustiniennes, 1987.

Hadot, Pierre. *The Inner Citadel: The* Meditations *of Marcus Aurelius*. Michael Chase (translator). Cambridge, MA: Harvard University Press, 1998.

Haillant, Marguerite. *Culture et Imagination dans les oeuvres de Fénelon "ad usum Delphini"*. Paris: Les Belles Lettres, 1982–83.

Hall, Joseph. *The Art of Divine Meditation*. In Frank Livingstone Huntley (ed.), *Bishop Joseph Hall and Protestant Meditation in Seventeenth-Century England*. Medieval and Renaissance Texts and Studies. Binghamton, NY: Center for Medieval and Early Renaissance Studies, 1981.

Hall, Roland. "Some Uses of Imagination in the British Empiricists: A Preliminary Investigation of Locke, as Contrasted with Hume." In Marta Fattori and M. Bianchi (eds), *Phantasia-Imaginatio*. Atti del Vo Colloquio internazionale del Lessico intellettuale Europeo. Rome: Ateneo, 1988, pp. 367–78.

Hallyn, Fernand. *La Structure poétique du monde: Copernic, Kepler*. Paris: Le Seuil, 1987.

Hammond, Nicholas. *Playing with Truth. Language and the Human Condition in Pascal's Pensées*. Oxford: Clarendon Press, 1994.

Hankins, Thomas L. and Robert, J. Silverman. *Instruments and the Imagination*. Princeton: Princeton University Press, 1995.

Harari, Josué. "Sade's Discourse on Method: Rudiments for a Theory of Fantasy." *MLN*, 99(5) (1984): 1057–71.

Harth, Erica. *Cartesian Women: Versions and Subversions of Rational Discourse in the Old Regime*. Ithaca: Cornell University Press, 1992.

Harth, Erica. *Ideology and Culture in Seventeenth-Century France*. Ithaca: Cornell University Press, 1983.

Hartle, Ann. *Michel de Montaigne: Accidental Philosopher*. Cambridge: Cambridge University Presss, 2003.

Haskins, Susan. *Mary Magdalen: Myth and Metaphor*. New York: Harcourt Brace & Company, 1993.

Hatfield, Gary. "The Senses and the Fleshless Eye: The Meditations as Cognitive Exercises." In Amélie Oksenberg Rorty (ed.), *Essays on Descartes' "Meditations"*. Berkeley: University of California Press, 1986, pp. 45–79.

Hegel, G.W.F. "On Art." Translation of Vorlesungen über die Aesthetik. In *On Art, Religion, Philosophy*, Harper Torchbook. New York: Harper & Row, 1970, pp. 22–127.

Hennequin, Jacques. "Image et spiritualité chez saint François de Sales." *Revue d'histoire de l'Eglise de France*, 75 (1989): 151–57.

Hertz, Neil. "A Reading of Longinus." In *The End of the Line*. New York: Columbia University Press, 1985, pp. 1–20.

Horowitz, Maryanne Cline. "Michel de Montaigne's Stoic Insights into Peasant Death." In Maryanne Cline Horowitz, Anne J. Cruz, and Wendy A. Furman *Renaissance Rereadings. Intertext and Context.* Urbana: University of Illinois Press, 1988.

Houdar de La Motte, Antoine. *Textes critiques. Les raisons du sentiment.* Françoise Gevrey and Béatrice Guion (eds). Sources Classiques, Paris: Honoré Champion, 2002, pp. 133–238.

Houle, Martha M. "*Ingegno* Baroque et Jouissance dans Deux Textes de Tristan L'Hermite." In Marlies Kronegger (ed.), *Esthétique Baroque et Imagination Créatrice.* Actes d'un Colloque de Cérisy-la-Salle. Biblio 17. Tübingen: Gunter Narr Verlag, 1998, pp. 147–52.

Huet, Marie-Hélène. *Monstrous Imagination.* Cambridge, MA: Harvard University Press, 1993.

Huet, Pierre Daniel. *Traité de l'origine des romans.* 1670. Stuttgart: J.B. Metzlersche Verlagbuchhandlung, 1966 [Facsimile of original 1670 edition].

Huguet, Michèle. *L'Ennui et ses discours.* Paris: Presses Universitaires de France, 1984.

Huntley, Frank Livingstone. *Bishop Joseph Hall and Protestant Meditation in Seventeenth-Century England.* Medieval and Renaissance Texts and Studies. Binghamton, NY: Center for Medieval and Early Renaissance Studies, 1981.

Ignatius of Loyola. *The Spiritual Exercises.* Chicago: Loyola University Press, 1951.

Ignatius of Loyola. *Obras Completas.* Ignacio Iparraguirre (ed.). Biblioteca De Autores Cristianos. Madrid: La Editorial Catolica, 1963.

Iser, Wolfgang. *The Fictive and the Imaginary: Charting Literary Anthropology.* Baltimore: Johns Hopkins University Press, 1993.

Jansen, Katherine. *The Making of the Magdalen. Preaching and Popular Devotion in the Later Middle Ages.* Princeton: Princeton University Press, 2000.

Jaouën, Françoise. "Pascal et l'esprit de géométrie." In François Lagarde (ed.), *L'Esprit en France au XVIIe Siècle. Actes Du 28e Congrès Annuel de la North American Society for Seventeenth Century French Literature.* Tübingen: Gunter Narr Verlag, 1997, pp. 113–27.

Jeanne des Anges. *Autobiographie.* Gabriel Legué and Gilles De La Tourette (eds). Montbonnot-St Martin: Jérôme Millon, 1985.

Jeanneret, Michel. *Perpetual Motion: Transforming Shapes in the Renaissance from da Vinci to Montaigne.* Nidra Poller (translator). Baltimore: The Johns Hopkins University Press, 2001.

Johnson, Eric Aaron. *Knowledge and Society: A Social Epistemology of Montaigne's Essays.* Charlottesville: Rookwood Press, 1994.

Johnson, Mark. *The Body in the Mind: The Bodily Basis of Meaning, Imagination, and Reason.* Chicago: University of Chicago Press, 1987.

Jordan, Constance. "Montaigne's Pygmalion: The Living Work of Art in 'De l'affection des peres aux enfans'." *Sixteenth Century Journal,* 9(4) (1978): 5–12.

Jost, François. "Le Roman épistolaire et la technique narrative." In *Actes du VIIIe Congrès de l'Association Internationale de Littérature Comparée*. Stuttgart: Bieber, 1980, pp. 297–304 .

Joukovsky, Françoise. *Montaigne et le problème du temps*. Paris: Nizet, 1972.

Jurieu, Pierre. *Traitté de la Nature et de la Grace ou Du concours général de la Providence et du concours particulier*. Utrecht: François Halsma, 1687.

Jurieu, Pierre. *A Plain Method of Christian Devotion: Laid Down in Discourses, Meditations, and Prayers fitted to the Various Occasions of A Religious Life*. W. Fleetwood (translator). London: C. Harper, 1692.

Jurieu, Pierre. *La Pratique de la dévotion, ou Traité de l'amour divin*. Rotterdam: A. Acher, 1700.

Kapp, Volker. *Télémaque de Fénelon: la signification d'une oeuvre littéraire à la fin du siècle classique*. Tübingen: Gunter Narr Verlag, 1982.

Kearney, Richard. *The Wake of Imagination*. Minneapolis: University of Minnesota Press, 1988.

Kearney, Richard. *Poetics of Imagining*. London: HarperCollinsAcademic, 1991.

Kelley, Donald R. *The Beginning of Ideology. Consciousness and Society in the French Reformation*. Cambridge: Cambridge University Press, 1981.

Klein, Jürgen. "Genius, Ingenium, Imagination: Aesthetic Theories of Production from the Renaissance to Romanticism." In Jürgen Klein and Frederick Burwick (eds), *The Romantic Imagination. Literature and Art in England and Germany*. Amsterdam: Rodopi, 1996.

Klein, Robert. "L'imagination comme vêtement de l'âme chez Marsile Ficin et Giordano Bruno." In André Chastel and Robert Klein (eds), *La Forme et l'intelligible. Ecrits sur la Renaissance et l'art moderne*. Paris: Gallimard, 1970, pp. 65–88. [first published in 1956 in the Revue de Métaphysique et de Morale].

Knox, Dilwyn. "Disciplina: The Monastic and Clerical Origins of European Civility." In John Monfasani and Ronald Musto (eds), *Renaissance Society and Culture. Essays in Honor of Eugene F. Rice, Jr.* New York: Italica Press, 1991, pp. 107–36.

Koch, Erec. *Pascal and Rhetoric: Figural and Persuasive Language in the Scientific Treatises, the Provinciales and the Pensées*. Charlottesville: Rookwood Press, 1997.

Koch, Erec. "Individuum: The Specular Self in Nicole's De la Connoissance de Soi-Même." *Paper presented at the conference of the North American Society for Seventeenth-Century French Literature*, Arizona State University. In David Wetsel and David Canovas (eds), *Pascal/New Trends in Port-Royal Studies*, May 2001, Biblio 17. Tübingen: Gunter Narr Verlag, pp. 259–68.

Koch, Erec. "Cartesian Aesth/Ethics: The Correspondence with Princess Elisabeth of Bohemia." Conference paper. North American Society for Seventeenth-Century French Literature. Portland State University, Portland, Oregon, 2004.

Laclos, Choderlos de. *Les Liaisons dangereuses*. Yves Le Hir (ed.). Classiques Garnier. Paris: Garnier, 1961.

Lafayette, Marie-Madeleine. *Romans et Nouvelles*. Alain Niderst (ed.). Classiques Garnier. Paris: Bordas, 1990.

Lafayette, Marie-Madeleine. *The Princess of Clèves*. John D. Lyons (ed.). Norton Critical Editions, New York: W.W. Norton, 1994.

La Garanderie, Marie-Madeleine de. "La méditation philosophique sur le temps au XVIe siècle: Budé, Montaigne." In Yvonne Bellenger (ed.), *Le Temps et la durée dans la littérature au Moyen Âge et à la Renaissance*. Paris: Nizet, 1986, pp. 193–209.

Lagarde, François (ed.). *L'Esprit en France au XVIIe Siècle. Actes du 28e congrès annuel de la North American Society for Seventeenth Century French Literature*. Tübingen: Gunter Narr Verlag, 1997.

Lagrée, Jacqueline (ed.). *Le Stoïcisme aux XVIe et XVIIe siècles, Cahiers de philosophie politique et juridique*, 25, 1994.

Lagrée, Jacqueline. *Juste Lipse et la restauration du stoïcisme*. Paris: Librairie Philosophique J. Vrin, 1994.

La Mesnardière, H.J. de. *Traitté de la mélancholie, sçavoir si elle est la cause des effets que l'on remarque dans les possédées de Loudun*. La Flèche: M. Guyot et G. Laboe, 1635.

La Mesnardière, H.-J. Pilet de. *Raisonnemens de Mesnardière, Conseiller et Medecin de son Altesse Royale sur la nature des esprits qui servent aux sentimens*. Paris: J. Camusat, 1638.

Lamy, Bernard. *Nouvelles réflexions sur l'art poétique*. Paris: André Pralard, 1678.

Lamy, Bernard. "Les qualités du style dépendent de celles de l'imagination, de la mémoire et de l'esprit de ceux qui écrivent." In Ernstpeter Ruhe (ed.), *L'art de parler*. Munich: Wilhelm Fink Verlag, 1980, pp. 209–11 [first published 1675; Facsimile reprint. Paris: André Pralard, 1676].

Laplace, Marie-Agnès. "La Conversion à soi-même dans la vie religieuse." In Hélène Bordes (ed.), *L'Univers salésien. Saint François de Sales hier et aujourd'hui*. Metz: Université de Metz, 1994, pp. 321–32.

La Rochefoucauld, François de. *Réflexions ou sentences et maximes morales*. In André-Alain Morello and Jean Lafond(eds), *Moralistes du XVIIe siècle*. Paris: Robert Laffont, 1992, pp. 103–240.

Larochelle, Elaine. *L'imagination dans l'oeuvre de Jean-Jacques Rousseau*. Villeneuve d'Ascq: Presses Universitaires du Septentrion, 1999.

Leclerc, Pierre. *Vies intéressantes et édifiantes des religieuses de Port-Royal et de plusieurs personnes qui leur étaient attachées*. Amsterdam: Aux dépens de la Compagnie, 1750–1752.

Lefebvre, René. "Faut-Il Traduire le Vocable Aristotélicien de Phantasia par 'Représentation'?" *Revue Philosophique de Louvain*, 95 (4) (1997): 587–616.

Le Guern, Michel. *Pascal et Descartes*. Paris: Nizet, 1971.

Leiner, Wolfgang. "Métamorphoses Magdaléennes." In Gisèle Mathieu-Castellani (ed.), *La Métamorphose dans la poésie baroque française et anglaise*. Tübingen: Gunter Narr Verlag, 1980, pp. 45–56.

Lempen-Ricci, S. *Le sens de l'imagination*. Geneva: Georg, 1985.

Lestringant, Franck. "Montaigne et le corps en procès: 'De la force de l'imagination'." In François Lecercle and S. Perrier (eds), *La poétique des passions à la Renaissance*. Paris: Champion, 2001, pp. 91–109.

Lewis, Philip. *Seeing Through the Mother Goose Tales. Visual Turns in the Writings of Charles Perrault*. Stanford: Stanford University Press, 1996.

Long, A.A. "Representation and the Self in Stoicism." In *Stoic Studies*. Cambridge: Cambridge University Press, 1996, pp. 264–85.

Long, A.A. *Stoic Studies*. Cambridge: Cambridge University Press, 1996.

Longinus. *On the Sublime*. D.A. Russell (translator and ed.). Oxford: Clarendon Press, 1964.

Lories, Danielle. *Le sens commun et le jugement du phronimos: Aristote et les stoïciens*. Louvain-la-Neuve: Editions Peeters, 1998.

Lyons, John D. "Camera Obscura: Image and Imagination in Descartes's *Méditations*." In: Mary B. McKinley, David Lee Rubin (eds), *Convergences. Rhetoric and Poetic in Seventeenth-Century France. Essays for Hugh M. Davidson*. Columbus: Ohio State University Press, 1989, pp. 179–95.

Lyons, John D. "The Sister and the Machine: Gilberte Périer's Vie de Monsieur Pascal." In Claire Carlin (ed.), *La Rochefoucauld, Mithridate, Frères et Soeurs*. Tûbingen: Gunter Narr Verlag, 1998, pp. 181–90.

Lyons, John D. "Descartes and Modern Imagination." *Philosophy and Literature* 23 (1999): 302–12.

Lyons, John D. "La rhétorique de l'honnêteté: Pascal et l'agrément." In François Cornilliat and Richard Lockwood (eds), *Èthos et pathos. Le statut du sujet rhétorique*. Paris: Honoré Champion, 2000, pp. 357–69.

Lyons, John D. "Ethics, Imagination, and Surprise." *Montaigne Studies* 14 (2002): 95–104.

MacIntosh, J.J. "Perception and Imagination in Descartes, Boyle and Hooke." *Canadian Journal of Philosophy* XIII, 3 (1983): 327–52.

MacIntosh, J.J. "Robert Boyle on Epicurean atheism and atomism." In Margaret J. Osler (ed.), *Atoms, Pneuma, and Tranquillity*. Cambridge: Cambridge University Press, 1991, pp. 197–219.

Maclean, Ian. " 'Le païs au delà': Montaigne and philosophical speculation." In Ian McFarlane and Ian Maclean (eds), *Montaigne: Essays in memory of Richard Sayce*. Oxford: Clarendon Press, 1982.

Malebranche, Nicolas. *Oeuvres*. Geneviève Rodis-Lewis and Germain Malbreil (eds). Bibliothèque de la Pléiade. Paris: Gallimard, 1979.

Malherbe, François de. *Oeuvres*. Pléiade. Paris: Gallimard, 1971.

Malherbe, François de (translator). *Les epistres de Sénèque*. Lyons: Claude de la Rivière.

Marin, Louis. "Réflexions sur la notion de modèle chez Pascal." *Revue de Métaphysique et de Morale* (1967): 89–108.

Marshall, Donald G. "Ideas and History: The Case of 'Imagination'." *Boundary 2*, 10(3) (1982): 343–59.

Martin, Henri-Jean. *The French Book. Religion, Absolutism, and Readership, 1585–1715*. Baltimore: Johns Hopkins University Press, 1996.

Martz, Louis. *The Poetry of Meditation*. Revised edn. New Haven: Yale University Press, 1962.

Marx, J. "Le concept d'imagination au XVIIIe siècle." In R. Trousson (ed.), *Thèmes et figures du Siècle des Lumières. Mélanges offerts à R. Mortier.* Geneva: Droz, 1980.

Matheson, Peter. *The Imaginative World of the Reformation.* Edinburgh: T & T Clark, 2000.

Mathieu-Castellani, Gisèle. "Discours sur le corps, discours du corps dans le troisième livre des Essais." In Marcel Tetel and G. Mallary Masters (eds), *Le Parcours des Essais: Montaigne 1588–1988.* Paris: Aux Amateurs de Livres, 1989, pp. 125–34.

Matoré, Georges. "Imagination." In François Bluche (ed.), *Dictionnaire du Grand Siècle.* Paris: Fayard, 1990, p. 746.

Mayer, C.A. "Stoïcisme et purification du concept chez Montaigne." *Studi Francesi*, 72 (1980): 487–93.

McFarlane, Ian and Ian Maclean (eds). *Montaigne: Essays in Memory of Richard Sayce.* Oxford: Clarendon Press, 1982.

McFarlane, Ian D. "Montaigne and the Concept of the Imagination." In D.R. Haggis (ed.), *The French Renaissance and Its Heritage. Essays Presented to Alan M. Boase.* London: Methuen, 1968, pp. 117–37.

Mellinghoff-Bourgerie, Viviane. *François de Sales (1567–1622). Un homme de lettres spirituelles.* Geneva: Droz, 1999.

Melzer, Sara E. *Discourses of the Fall.* Berkeley: University of California Press, 1986.

Merlin-Kajman, Hélène. *L'absolutisme dans les lettres et la théorie des deux corps. Passions et politique.* Lumière Classique 29. Paris: Honoré Champion, 2000.

Michon, Hélène. *L'ordre du coeur. Philosophie, théologie, et mystique dans les Pensées de Pascal.* Paris: Honoré Champion, 1996.

Mignini, Filippo. *Ars imaginandi: apparenza e rappresentazione in Spinoza.* Naples: Edizioni Scientifiche Italiane, 1981.

Miller, Peter. *Peiresc's Europe: Learning and Virtue in the Seventeenth Century.* New Haven: Yale University Press, 2000.

Miquel, Pierre. *Histoire de l'imagination: introduction à l'imaginaire théologique.* Paris: Le Léopard d'or, 1994.

Moffitt, John F. " 'Ecce lucem': La fusione tra scienza e simbolismo nel chiaroscuro del XVI secolo." In *La Luce del vero: Caravaggio, La Tour, Rembrandt, Zurbarán.* Cinisello Balsamo: Silvana Editoriale, 2000, pp. 52–65.

Montaigne, Michel de. *Les Essais.* Pierre Villey (ed.). Paris: Presses Universitaires de France, 1965, pp. 97–106.

Montaigne, Michel de. *The Complete Essays of Montaigne.* Donald M. Frame (translator). Stanford: Stanford University Press, 1948.

Moreau, Pierre-François. "Calvin et le stoïcisme." In Jacqueline Lagrée (ed.), *Le Stoïcisme aux XVIe et XVIIe siècles, Cahiers de philosophie politique et juridique*, 25 (1994), 11—23.

Morlet-Chantalat, Chantal. *La Clélie de Mademoiselle de Scudéry. De l'épopée à la gazette: un discours féminin de la gloire.* Lumière Classique. Paris: Honoré Champion, 1994.

Morrissey, Robert J. *La Rêverie jusqu'à Rousseau. Recherches sur un topos littéraire.* French Forum Monographs 55. Lexington, KY: French Forum, 1984.

Munro, James S. *Mademoiselle de Scudéry and the Carte de Tendre.* Durham: University of Durham, 1986.

Newman, John W. *Disciplines of Attention: Buddhist Insight Meditation, the Ignatian Spiritual Exercises, and Classical Psychoanalysis.* Asian Thought and Culture. New York: Peter Lang, 1996.

Nicole, Pierre. *Essais de morale, contenus en divers traités sur plusieurs devoirs importants.* Paris: Guillaume Desprez, 1730.

Nicole, Pierre. *Essais de morale.* Laurent Thirouin (ed.). Paris: Presses Universitaires de France, 1999.

Nicolson, Marjorie. *The Microscope and English Imagination.* Smith College Studies in Modern Languages. Northampton: Smith College, 1935.

Norman, Buford. *Portraits of Thought: Knowledge, Methods, and Styles in Pascal.* Columbus: Ohio State University Press, 1988.

Norton, David L. *Imagination, Understanding, and the Virtue of Liberality.* Lanham, MD: Rowman and Littlefield, 1996.

Norton, Glyn. *Montaigne and the Introspective Mind.* The Hague: Mouton, 1975.

Novitz, David. *Knowledge, Fiction and Imagination.* Philadelphia: Temple University Press, 1987.

Nussbaum, Martha C. *The Therapy of Desire: Theory and Practice in Hellenistic Ethics.* Martin Classical Lectures. Princeton: Princeton University Press, 1994.

Nussbaum, Martha C. "Invisibility and Recognition: Sophocles' *Philoctetes* and Ellison's *Invisible Man.*" *Philosophy and Literature,* 23 (2) (1999): 257–83.

Nussbaum, Martha C. and Amélie Oksenberg Rorty (eds). *Essays on Aristotle's De Anima.* Oxford: Oxford University Press, 1992.

Nymann, Hieronymus. "De imaginatione oratio." In Tobias Tandler (ed.) *Dissertationes physicae-medicae.* Wittenberg: Z. Schreri, 1613.

O'Brien, John. "Reasoning with the Senses: The Humanist Imagination." *South Central Review,* 10(2) (1993): 3–20.

Oestreich, Gerhard. *Neostoicism and the Early Modern State.* Brigitta Oestreich and H.G. Koenigsberger (eds). Cambridge: Cambridge University Press, 1982.

O'Farrell, Mary Ann. *Telling Complexions: The Nineteenth-Century English Novel and the Blush.* Durham: Duke University Press, 1997.

O'Malley, John W. *The First Jesuits.* Cambridge: Harvard University Press, 1993.

Osler, Margaret J. (ed.). *Atoms, Pneuma, and Tranquillity.* Cambridge: Cambridge University Press, 1991.

Paige, Nicholas D. *Being Interior: Autobiography and the Contradictions of Modernity in Seventeenth-Century France.* Philadelphia: University of Pennsylvania Press, 2001.

Panofsky, Erwin. *La Perspective comme forme symbolique et autres essais.* Guy Ballangé (translator). Paris: Éditions de Minuit, 1975.

Papàsogli, Benedetta. *La Lettera e lo spirito: Temi e figure del Seicento francese.* Pisa: Editrice Libreria Goliardica, 1986.

Papàsogli, Benedetta. *Il "Fondo del cuore": Figure dello spazio interiore nel Seicento francese*. Pisa: Editrice Libreria Goliardica, 1991.

Pascal, Blaise. *Oeuvres complètes*. Paris: Le Seuil, 1963.

Pascal, Blaise. "Entretien avec Monsieur de Sacy sur Epictète et Montaigne." In Jean Mesnard (ed.), *Oeuvres complètes*. Paris: Desclée de Brouwer, 1964, pp. 76–157.

Pascal, Blaise. *Selections from The Thoughts*. Arthur H. Beattie. Arlington Heights, IL: Harlan Davidson, 1965.

Pascal, Blaise. *Pensées*. Philippe Sellier (ed.). Paris: Classiques Garnier, 1991.

Pavel, Thomas. *L'art de l'éloignement. Essai sur l'imagination classique*. Folio Essais. Paris: Gallimard, 1996.

Pease, Jacob Jerod. "Imagination and the Paradox of Fictional Emotions." Thesis, Master of Arts in Philosophy. Charlottesville: University of Virginia, 2004.

Perrault, Charles. *Parallèle des anciens et des modernes en ce qui regarde les arts et les sciences*. Geneva: Slatkine [Reprint 1979].

Pia, Mariagrazia. "Gravina e Vico: La Poesia sub specie temporis et imaginationis secondo la Metaphisica Mentis Spinoziana." *Bollettino del Centro di Studi Vichiani*, 26, 27 (1996–97): 55–74.

Pico della Mirandola, Gianfrancesco. "On the Imagination." In Harry Caplan (translator and ed.), *Cornell Studies in English*. Ithaca: Cornell University Press, 1930 [original text 1501].

Pico della Mirandola, Gianfrancesco. "De Imaginatione liber." In *Opera Omnia*. Hildesheim: Georg Olms Verlag, 1969, pp. 132–53 [first published by Henricus Petrus, Basle, 1557].

Pigeaud, J. "Voir, imaginer, rêver, être fou: quelques remarques sur l'hallucination et l'illusion dans la philosophie stoïcienne, épicurienne, sceptique, et la médecine antique." *Littérature, Médecine, Société*, 5 (1983): 23–47.

Pizzorusso, Arnoldo. "L'Imagination." In *Eléments d'une poétique littéraire au XVIIe siècle*. Paris: Presses Universitaires de France, 1992, pp. 21–37.

Polachek, Dora E. "Montaigne and Imagination: The Dynamics of Power and Control." In Marcel Tetel and G. Mallary Masters (eds), *Le Parcours des Essais: Montaigne 1588–1988*. Paris: Aux Amateurs de Livres, 1989, pp. 135–45.

Polachek, Dora E. "Imagination, Idleness and Self-Discovery: Montaigne's Early Voyage Inward." In Mario Di Cesare (ed.), *Reconsidering the Renaissance*. Binghamton: Medieval and Renaissance Texts and Studies, 1992, pp. 257–69.

Pyle, Forest. *The Ideology of Imagination*. Stanford: Stanford University Press, 1995.

Quintilian. *Institutio Oratoria*. H.E. Butler (translator and ed.). Loeb Classical Library. Cambridge, MA: Harvard University Press, 1920.

Radouant, René. *Guillaume Du Vair, l'homme et l'orateur, jusquà la fin des troubles de la Ligue*. Geneva: Slatkine Reprints, 1970 [first published 1907].

Ragghianti, Renzo. "Nota sull'immaginazione in Montaigne." In Paolo Cristofolini (ed.), *Studi sul Seicento e sull'Immaginazione*. Pisa: Scuola Normale Superiore di Pisa, 1985, pp. 115–27.

Ranum, Orest. "The Refuges of Intimacy." In Roger Chartier, Philippe Ariès, and Georges Duby (eds), Arthur Goldhammer (translator), *Passions of the Renaissance. A History of Private Life*. Cambridge, Massachusetts: Harvard University Press, 1989, pp. 207–63.

Rapin, René. *Réflexions sur la poétique de ce temps et sur les ouvrages des poètes anciens et modernes*. E.T. Dubois (ed.). Geneva: Droz, 1970.

Rapin, René. *Du Grand ou du sublime dans les moeurs et dans les différentes conditions des hommes. Avec quelques observations sur l'Eloquence des Bienséances*. Paris: Sébastien Mabre-Cramoisy, 1686.

Rathmann, Bernd. "L'imagination et le doute: essai sur la genèse de la pensée cartésienne." *Papers on French Seventeenth-Century Literature*, 8 (15–1) (1981): 57–73.

Rayez, André. "Imagerie et Dévotion." In M. Viller, J. Cavallera, and J. Guibert (eds), *Dictionnaire de la spiritualité ascétique et mystique*. Paris: Beauchesne, 1937–95, pp. 1530–35.

Ricken, U. "Malebranche, Arnauld et la controverse sur le rôle de l'imagination dans le langage." In Marta Fattori and M. Bianchi (eds), *Phantasia-Imaginatio*. Atti del Vo Colloquio internazionale del Lessico intellettuale Europeo. Rome: Ateneo, 1988, pp. 285–308.

Ricoeur, Paul. "Imagination in Discourse and in Action." In Gillian Robinson and John Rundell (eds), *Rethinking Imagination: Culture and Creativity*. London: Routledge, 1994, pp. 118–35.

Riley, Patrick. "Rousseau, Fénelon, and the Quarrel Between the Ancients and the Moderns." In Patrick Riley (ed.), *The Cambridge Companion to Rousseau*. Cambridge: Cambridge University Press, 2001, pp. 78–93.

Robinet, A. ""Imagination" dans les Oeuvres complètes de Malebranche." In Marta Fattori and M. Bianchi (eds), *Phantasia-Imaginatio*. Atti del Vo Colloquio internazionale del Lessico intellettuale Europeo. Rome: Ateneo, 1988, pp. 273–83.

Robinson, Gillian, and John Rundell (eds). *Rethinking Imagination: Culture and Creativity*. London: Routledge, 1994.

Rodis-Lewis, Geneviève. "La volonté chez Descartes et Malebranche." In Paolo Cristofolini (ed.), *Studi sul Seicento e sull'Immaginazione*. Pisa: Scuola Normale Superiore di Pisa, 1985, pp. 13–28.

Ronzeaud, Pierre (ed.). L'Imagination au XVIIe Siècle. *Littératures Classiques*, 45 (2002).

Rorty, Amélie Oksenberg (ed.). *Essays on Descartes' "Meditations"*. Berkeley: University of California Press, 1986.

Rorty, Amélie Oksenberg (ed.). "The Structure of Descartes' Meditations." In *Essays on Descartes' "Meditations"*. Berkeley: University of California Press, 1986, pp. 1–20.

Rorty, Amélie Oksenberg. "From Passions to Emotions and Sentiments." *Philosophy*, 57 (1982): 159–72.

Rorty, Richard. *Contingency, Irony, and Solidarity*. Cambridge: Cambridge University Press, 1989.

Rorty, Richard. *Philosophy and the Mirror of Nature*. Princeton: Princeton University Press, 1979.

Round, Nichoas G. "Alonso de Cartagena and John Calvin as interpreters of Seneca's De clementia." In Margaret J. Osler (ed.), *Atoms, Pneuma, and Tranquillity*. Cambridge: Cambridge University Press, 1991, pp. 67–88.

Rousseau, Jean-Jacques. *Les Rêveries du promeneur solitaire*. Henri Roddier (ed.). Classiques Garnier. Paris: Garnier Frères, 1960.

Rousseau, Jean-Jacques. *Émile, ou de l'éducation*. François Richard and Pierre Richard (eds). Classiques Garnier. Paris: Garnier Frères, 1964.

Roy, Jean-H. *L'imagination selon Descartes*. La Jeune Philosophie. Paris: Gallimard, 1944.

Rubidge, Bradley. "Descartes's Meditations and Devotional Meditations." *Journal of the History of Ideas*, 51 (1) (1990): 27–49.

Sambursky, Samuel. *Physics of the Stoics*. New York: Macmillan, 1959.

Sarasohn, Lisa Tunick. "Epicureanism and the Creation of a Privatist Ethic in Early Seventeenth-Century France." In Margaret J. Osler (ed.), *Atoms, Pneuma, and Tranquillity*, . Cambridge: Cambridge University Press, 1991, pp. 175–95.

Sartre, Jean-Paul. *L'imagination*. 4th edn, Paris: Presses Universitaires de France, 1956.

Saunders, Justin. *Justus Lipsius. The Philosophy of Renaissance Stoicism*. New York: Liberal Arts Press, 1955.

Scarpati, Claudio and Eraldo Bellini. *Il Vero e Il Falso Dei Poeti: Tasso, Tesauro, Pallavicino, Muratori*. Milan: Vita e Pensiero, 1990.

Schiffman, Zachary Sayre. *On the Threshold of Modernity*. Baltimore: Johns Hopkins University Press, 1991.

Schofield, Malcolm. "Aristotle on the Imagination." In Martha C. Nussbaum and Amélie Oksenberg Rorty (eds), *Essays on Aristotle's De Anima*. Oxford: Oxford University Press, 1992, pp. 249–77.

Scholar, Richard. "La force de l'imagination de Montaigne: Camus, Malebranche, Pascal." In Pierre Ronzeaud (ed.), *L'Imagination au XVIIe Siècle. Littératures classiques*, 45 (2002): 127–38.

Scudéry, Madeleine de. *Clélie, histoire romaine*. Paris: Augustin Courbé, 1654–1661 [reprint, Geneva: Slatkine Reprints, 1973].

Scudéry, Madeleine de. *Clélie, histoire romaine*. Chantal Morlet-Chantalat (ed.). Paris: Champion, 2001.

Seiffert, Lewis. *Fairy Tales, Sexuality, and Gender in France, 1600–1715*. Cambridge: Cambridge University Press, 1996.

Sellier, Philippe. *Pascal et Saint Augustin*. Paris: Armand Colin, 1970.

Seneca, Lucius A. *Seneca's Letters to Lucilius*. E. Phillips Barker (translator). Oxford: Clarendon Press, 1932.

Seneca, Lucius Annaeus. *Moral Essays*. John W. Basore. (translator and ed.). Loeb, Cambridge, MA: Harvard University Press, 1928—1935.

Seneca, Lucius Annaeus. *Ad Lucilium Epistulae Morales*. Richard M. Gummere (translator and ed.). Loeb Classical Library 77, Cambridge, MA: Harvard University Press, 1989.

Seneca, Lucius Annaeus. *Epistles 1–65*. Richard M. Gummere (translator and ed.). Loeb, Cambridge, MA: Harvard University Press, 1996.

Seneca, Lucius Annaeus. *Epistles 66–92*. Richard M. Gummere (translator and ed.). Loeb, Cambridge, MA: Harvard University Press, 1996.

Sepper, Dennis L. "Imagination, Phantasms, and the Making of Hobbesian and Cartesian Science." *The Monist*, 71 (4) (1988): 526–42.

Sepper, Dennis L. "Descartes and the Eclipse of Imagination, 1618–1630." *Journal of the History of Philosophy*, 27(3) (1989): 379–403.

Sepper, Dennis L. "Ingenium, Memory Art, and the Unity of Imaginative Knowing in the Early Descartes." In Stephen Voss (ed.), *Essays on the Philosophy and Science of René Descartes*. Oxford: Oxford University Press, 1993.

Serouet, Pierre. "Saint François de Sales." In M. Viller, J. Cavallera, and J. Guibert (eds), *Dictionnaire de la spiritualité ascétique et mystique*. Paris: Beauchesne, 1963, pp. 1057–97.

Sévigné, Marie de Rabutin-Chantal de. *Correspondance*. Roger Duchêne (ed.). Bibliothèque de la Pléiade. Paris: Gallimard, 1972–1978.

Shuger, Debora Kuller. *Habits of Thought in the English Renaissance. Religion, Politics, and the Dominant Culture*. Berkeley: University of California Press, 1990.

Sommella, Paola Placella. "Voyage réel et voyage imaginaire dans les Lettres de Madame de Sévigné." *PFSCL*, 13 (24) (1986): 189–206.

Sosso, Paula. *Jean-Jacques Rousseau: Imagination, illusions, chimères*. Paris: Honoré Champion, 1999.

Starobinski, Jean. *L'Oeil vivant*. Paris: Gallimard, 1961.

Starobinski, Jean. "Imagination." In F. Jost (ed.), *Actes du IVe colloque de l'association de littérature comparée*. The Hague: Mouton, 1966, pp. 952–63.

Starobinski, Jean. "En guise de conclusion." In Marta Fattori and M. Bianchi (eds), *Phantasia-Imaginatio*. Atti del Vo Colloquio internazionale del Lessico intellettuale Europeo. Rome: Ateneo, 1988, pp. 565–85.

Storch, R.F. "The Politics of the Imagination." *Studies in Romanticism*, 21 (3) (1982): 448–56.

Strier, Richard. "The Heart Alone: Inwardness and Individualism." In *Love Known. Theology and Experience in George Herbert's Poetry*. Chicago: University of Chicago Press, 1983, pp. 143–73.

Surin, Jean-Joseph. *Triomphe de l'Amour divin sur les puissances de l'Enfer et Science expérimentale des choses de l'autre vie*. Grenoble: Jérome Millon, 1990.

Talon-Hugon, Carole. "Affectivité stoïcienne, affectivité salésienne." In Jacqueline Lagrée (ed.), *Le Stoïcisme aux XVIe et XVIIe siècles, Cahiers de philosophie politique et juridique*, vol 25, Caen: Université de Caen, 1994, pp. 95–108.

Tansey, Joel Gerard. "Montaigne Questions: Skepticism, Epistemology, and Interrogative Rhetoric." *Dissertation Abstracts International*, 55 (11) (1995): 3504A. Ann Arbor, Michigan: University of Michigan.

Tarrête, Alexandre. "Le stoïcisme de Guillaume Du Vair, ou de l'utilité de la philosophie par gros temps." *Littératures Classiques*, 37 (1999): 57–67.

Taylor, Charles. *Sources of the Self: The Making of the Modern Identity.* Cambridge, MA: Harvard University Press, 1989.

Tedesco, Salvatore. *Alla vigilia dell'aesthetica: ingegno e immaginazione nella poetica critica dell'illuminismo tedesco.* Palermo: Centro Internazionale Studi di Estetica, 1996.

Teresa of Avila. *The Way of Perfection.* E. Allison Peers (ed.). Garden City, NY: Image Books, 1964.

Thornton, Peter. "Architectural Planning." In *The Italian Renaissance Interior.* New York: Harry N. Abrams, Inc., 1991, pp. 283–320.

Timmermans, Linda. *L'accès des femmes à la culture (1598–1715): Un débat d'idées de Saint François de Sales à la Marquise de Lambert.* Paris: Honoré Champion, 1993.

Tirinnanzi, Nicoletta. *Umbra Naturae: l'immaginazione da Ficino a Bruno.* Rome: Edizioni di Storia e Letteratura, 2000.

Toulmin, Stephen. *Cosmopolis: The Hidden Agenda of Modernity.* New York: Free Press, 1990.

Trépanier, Hélène. "Les grâces extraordinaires ou les 'surnaturelles connaissances expérimentales' de Jean-Joseph Surin." In John D. Lyons and Cara Welch (eds), *Le Savoir au XVIIe siècle.* Biblio 17. Tübingen: Gunter Narr Verlag, 2003, pp. 151–60.

Tuzet, Hélène. *Le Cosmos et l'imagination.* Paris: José Corti, 1966.

Verbeke, Gerard. "Ethics and Logic in Stoicism." In Margaret J. Osler (ed.), *Atoms, Pneuma, and Tranquillity.* Cambridge: Cambridge University Press, 1991, pp. 11–24.

Viller, M., J. Cavallera, and J. Guibert (eds). *Dictionnaire de la Spiritualité Ascétique et Mystique.* Paris: Beauchesne, 1937–1995.

Villey, Pierre. *Les sources et l'évolution des Essais de Montaigne.* Paris: Hachette, 1908 [reprint, New York: Burt Franklin, 1968].

Wallace, Karl R. *Francis Bacon on the Nature of Man. The Faculties of Man's Soul: Understanding, Reason, Imagination, Memory, Will, and Appetite.* Urbana: University of Illinois Press, 1967.

Warner, Martin. *Philosophical Finesse. Studies in the Art of Rational Persuasion.* Oxford: Clarendon Press, 1989.

Warnock, Mary. *Imagination.* Berkeley: University of California Press, 1976.

Watson, Gerard. *The Stoic Theory of Knowledge.* Belfast: Queen's University, 1966.

Watson, Gerard. *Phantasia in Classical Thought.* Galway: Galway University Press, 1988.

Weber, Alison. *Teresa of Avila and the Rhetoric of Femininity.* Princeton: Princeton University Press, 1990.

Wedin, Michael V. *Mind and Imagination in Aristotle.* New Haven: Yale University Press, 1988.

White, Alan R. *The Language of Imagination.* Oxford: Basil Blackwell, 1990.

White, Helen C. *The Tudor Books of Private Devotion.* Madison: University of Wisconsin Press, 1951.

Wicks, Jared, S.J. "Martin Luther: The Heart Clinging to the Word." In *Spiritualities of the Heart: Approaches to Personal Wholeness in Christian Tradition.* Mahwah, NJ: Paulist Press, pp. 79–96.

Wilkes, K.V. "Psuche Versus the Mind." In Martha C. Nussbaum and Amélie Oksenberg Rorty (eds), *Essays on Aristotle's De Anima.* Oxford: Oxford University Press, 1992, pp. 109–27.

Wilkin, Rebecca May. *Feminizing Imagination in France, 1563–1678.* (unpublished dissertation). University of Michigan, 2000.

Wine, Kathleen. *Forgotten Virgo. Humanism and Absolutism in Honoré d'Urfé's "L'Astrée".* Travaux Du Grand Siècle. Geneva: Droz, 2000.

Wolfson, Harry Austryn. "The Internal Senses in Latin, Arabic, and Hebrew Philosophic Texts." *Harvard Theological Review,* 28(2) (1935).

Woolf, Virginia. *To the Lighthouse.* Harvest Books. New York: Harcourt Brace, 1927 [reprinted 1955].

Wright, Wendy M. " 'This is What It is Made For': The Image of the Heart in the Spirituality of François de Sales and Jane de Chantal." In Annice Callahan (ed.), *Spiritualities of the Heart: Approaches to Personal Wholeness in Christian Tradition.* Mahwah, NJ: Paulist Press, 1990, pp. 143–58.

Wright, Wendy M. "A Wide and Fleshy Love. Images, Imagination and the Heart of God." *Studies in Spirituality,* 10 (2000): 255–74.

Wygant, Amy. "D'Aubignac, Demonologist, I: Monkeys and Monsters." *Seventeenth-Century French Studies,* 23 (2001): 151–71.

Wygant, Amy. "La Mesnardière and the Demon." In John D. Lyons and Cara Welch (eds), *Le Savoir au XVIIe siècle.* Biblio 17, Tübingen: Gunter Narr Verlag, 2003, pp. 323–34.

Xenakis, Jason. *Epictetus, Philosopher-Therapist.* The Hague: Martinus Nijhoff, 1969.

Yates, Francis. *The Art of Memory.* Chicago: Chicago University Press, 1966.

Zaiser, Rainer. "L'esprit de géométrie et l'esprit de finesse: le *Mémorial* de Pascal entre épiphanie de Dieu et création littéraire." In François Lagarde (ed.), *L'Esprit en France au XVIIe Siècle. Actes du 28e congrès annuel de la North American Society for Seventeenth Century French Literature.* Tübingen: Gunter Narr Verlag, 1997, pp. 129–36.

Zagorin, Perez. *Ways of Lying. Dissimulation, Persecution, and Conformity in Early Modern Europe.* Cambridge, MA: Harvard University Press, 1990.

Zanta, Léontine. *La Renaissance du stoïcisme au XVIe siècle.* Geneva: Slatkine Reprints, 1975 [first published 1914].

Zolotov, Youri. "Le Style de Georges de La Tour." In *Georges de La Tour ou La nuit traversée. Colloque à Vic-sur-Seille, du 9 au 11 septembre 1993,* compiled by Anne Reinbold. Metz: Editions Serpenoise, 1994, pp. 159–71.

Index